Through the Darkness

Through the Darkness

A Life in Zimbabwe

Judith Garfield Todd

ZEBRA

Published by Zebra Press
an imprint of Struik Publishers
(a division of New Holland Publishing (South Africa) (Pty) Ltd)
PO Box 1144, Cape Town, 8000
New Holland Publishing is a member of Johnnic Communications Ltd

www.zebrapress.co.za

First published 2007
Reprinted in 2007 (three times)

5 7 9 10 8 6 4

Publication © Zebra Press 2007
Text © Judith Todd 2007

PUBLISHING MANAGER: Marlene Fryer
MANAGING EDITOR: Robert Plummer
EDITOR: Marléne Burger
PROOFREADER: Ronel Richter-Herbert
COVER AND TEXT DESIGNER: Natascha Olivier
TYPESETTER: Monique van den Berg
INDEXER: Robert Plummer
PRODUCTION MANAGER: Valerie Kömmer

Set in 10.5 pt on 14.2 pt Minion

Reproduction by Hirt & Carter (Cape) (Pty) Ltd
Printed and bound by Paarl Print, Oosterland Street, Paarl, South Africa

ISBN 978 1 77022 002 7

For Cyndie Edge in Australia
my dearest sister

And in memory of fine men
Rod Donald of Aotearoa/New Zealand
Oki Ooko Ombaka of Kenya
Barry Streek of South Africa
Michael Hartnack, Basker Vashee and
Phil Whitehead of Zimbabwe

Contents

A Time to Rise

It's six, my son, and time to rise;
The sun has shot through the darkness
And the long day spreads before you like a kaross;
Start now, dear son; the journey is long.
There will be thunder and hailstorms
Although the weather appears calm
For the moment; beware of shelters
Offered you; rather brave it and be a Man.
Should you fall, rise with grace, and without
Turning to see who sees, continue on your road
Precisely as if nothing had ever happened;
For those who did not, the ditches became graves.

from 'On My Son's Sixth Birthday'
by Eddison Zvobgo (1935–2004)

Abbreviations

ANC: African National Congress

ANZ: Associated Newspapers of Zimbabwe

Aztrec: Association of Zimbabwe Traditional Ecological Conservation

CAZ: Conservative Alliance of Zimbabwe

CCJP: Catholic Commission for Justice and Peace

CID: Criminal Investigation Department

CIIR: Catholic Institute for International Relations

CIO: Central Intelligence Organisation

CSSD: Catholic Commission for Social Service and Development

Frelimo: Front for the Liberation of Mozambique

Hart: Halt All Racist Tours

ICC: International Criminal Court

Idasa: Institute for a Democratic Alternative for South Africa

IZG: Independent Zimbabwe Group

MDC: Movement for Democratic Change

MMT: Mass Media Trust

MNR: Mozambique National Resistance

NAM: Non-Aligned Movement

NCA: National Constitutional Assembly

NDP: National Democratic Party

OAU: Organisation of African Unity

Orap: Organisation of Rural Associations for Progress

PF Zapu: Patriotic Front – Zimbabwe African People's Union

PISI: Police Internal Security and Intelligence

PLO: Palestine Liberation Organisation

POSA: Public Order and Security Act

PTC: Posts and Telecommunications Corporation

Renamo: Mozambique National Resistance

SADC: Southern African Development Community

SWAPO: South West African People's Organisation

UANC: United African National Council

UDI: unilateral declaration of independence

Unesco: United Nations Educational, Scientific and Cultural Organisation

Unicef: United Nations Children's Fund

UNOHAC: United Nations Office for Humanitarian Assistance Coordination

Woza: Women of Zimbabwe Arise

ZANLA: Zimbabwe African National Liberation Army

Zanu: Zimbabwe African National Union

Zanu (PF): Zimbabwe African National Union, Patriotic Front

Zapu: Zimbabwe African People's Union

ZBC: Zimbabwe Broadcasting Corporation

ZCTU: Zimbabwe Congress of Trade Unions

Zidco: Zimbabwe Investment and Development Company

Zimcord: Zimbabwe Conference on Reconstruction and Development

Zimfep: Zimbabwe Foundation for Education with Production

Zimpapers: Zimbabwe Newspapers

Zipa: Zimbabwe People's Army

Zircon: Zimbabwe Institute of Religious Research and Conservation

ZNLWVA: Zimbabwe National Liberation War Veterans Association

ZPRA: Zimbabwe People's Revolutionary Army

ZPT: Zimbabwe Project Trust

ZTV: Zimbabwe Television

ZUM: Zimbabwe Unity Movement

Origins

M Y FATHER DELIVERED ME INTO ZIMBABWE AT IMPOVERISHED
Dadaya Mission in March 1943. A special ration of meat was provided
for the school's boarders to celebrate the event. Many years later, one of those
pupils, SG Mpofu, by that time managing director of the publishers Longman
Zimbabwe, told me that while they had been glad of the meat, they regretted
the birth of another white. Sam also said that each week during the Second
World War, my parents being the only ones at Dadaya with access to news
from a wireless, my father would report to the assembled school on the war's
progress. 'He had no idea that in our little black hearts we were cheering on
Hitler,' said Sam. 'We thought Hitler would get rid of you colonists for us.'

Grace and Garfield Todd had arrived in Southern Rhodesia as missionaries
from New Zealand in 1934, accompanied by my older sister Alycen, then two.
By 1948, my father, from the black background of Dadaya, had entered white
politics, the only kind permitted in the then British colony, and become
a member of parliament. In 1953 the country became part of a federation
of three territories: the white, colonial-governed Southern Rhodesia, and
the British protectorates of Northern Rhodesia and Nyasaland – today's
Zimbabwe, Zambia and Malawi. The government of Southern Rhodesia,
under the premiership of Sir Godfrey Huggins, moved lock, stock and barrel
to take over the government of the Federation of Rhodesia and Nyasaland,
leaving clear decks for newcomers. My father became prime minister of
Southern Rhodesia.

By 1958 he had been turfed out of government and parliament by the
white electorate for working towards a democracy that would embrace the
entire population of four million instead of just the quarter million who
were white. In an attempt to silence his increasing opposition to minority
rule, he was in 1965 restricted to his ranch for one year by the Rhodesian
Front government of Prime Minister Ian Smith. This was just before Smith's
unilateral declaration of independence (UDI) from Britain on 11 November,
which unwittingly accelerated the outbreak of civil war. The declaration
clearly demonstrated that if ever there was to be majority rule, it would
have to be fought for.

In January 1972, my father and I were arrested. The police presented us with detention orders signed by Rhodesia's Minister of Law, Order and Justice: 'The making of this Order is based on a belief that you are likely to commit or to incite the commission of acts in Rhodesia which would endanger the public safety, or disturb or interfere with the maintenance of public order.' We were respectively locked up in solitary confinement in the black male prisons of Gatooma, now Kadoma, and Marandellas, now Marondera. When news was smuggled out that I was on hunger strike, I was moved to the white female wing of Chikurubi Prison, Salisbury (now Harare), where there were medical facilities and I was force-fed until my strike was broken.

Thanks to worldwide protests, we were released from jail after five weeks and confined to my parents' house on their ranch, Hokonui. My father remained in detention until 1976.

In July 1972, I was allowed to leave my country for exile abroad. However, I remained classified as a detainee, which meant that my name could not be published in Rhodesia, and it was stipulated that if I returned home, it would be specifically to jail.

The 1979 Lancaster House conference brought an end to Rhodesia's civil war. Lord Soames was appointed governor. A new constitution that effectively revoked the illegal UDI was successfully introduced in Rhodesia's parliament on 11 December by the Minister of Justice, Chris Andersen. Parliament unanimously voted itself out of office, handing power back to the British. On the arrival of Lord Soames from London on 12 December, the country reverted to being the British Dependency of Southern Rhodesia. Britain assumed power over her reclaimed colony until majority rule elections for a new government could be held and legitimate independence conferred. One of Lord Soames's first acts was to lift detention orders. I was able to return home and did so in February 1980.

At Zimbabwe's independence in April 1980, my father was appointed a senator by the new prime minister, Robert Mugabe. My father retired from public life in 1985, but on 5 June 1986, he was knighted by Queen Elizabeth at Buckingham Palace for services to New Zealand and to Africa. In 2002, he was stripped of his Zimbabwe citizenship and his right to vote by the Mugabe regime, and that October he died in Bulawayo.

Over the years I kept notes and copies of letters that have now turned into this book. It is neither a history nor an analysis of events, but simply charts one person's impressions along Zimbabwe's roller-coaster ride from its birth on 18 April 1980.

CHAPTER 1

Hanging charges

F EBRUARY 1980 WAS A ROUGH MONTH WITH A CALM BEGINNING.
After nearly eight years in exile, I returned home from London to
Bulawayo through Johannesburg. This time the South African authorities
didn't trouble me. The last time, in July 1972, I was terrified when transiting
through Johannesburg.

First my passport was taken and then my air ticket. When I asked what
was happening, there was no reply. The official concerned, suddenly profoundly deaf, merely lowered his head. Seeing my distress, a passing air
hostess gave me a coin and I rang Benjamin Pogrund at the *Rand Daily Mail*.
He came to the airport with a photographer, and they recorded the fact
that, although the Rhodesians had allowed me to leave for Britain after
six months of detention at home, the South African authorities were now
holding my travel documents without explanation. Pogrund then found a
British Airways official, who retrieved my passport and ticket and put me
safely onto the flight for London.

The future then seemed bleak and I was full of sorrow. But, as 1980
unfolded, I was allowed to return to my beloved country, and I was full of
joy and hope.

Just after noon on Monday 4 February, Flight SA018 took off for
Bulawayo. Flying across the bordering Limpopo River, the atmosphere
pulsed with war. A vast, raw security clearing had been carved along the
South African side of the river and, as we approached Bulawayo, the pilot
announced that 'for obvious reasons' we were going to make a steep descent.
A large, excited party of French tourists screamed as we plummeted through
beautiful, mushrooming clouds and applauded as we touched down safely.

Bulawayo was smaller and lovelier than I remembered. My parents, with
whom I had a reunion glad beyond words, were waiting for me. But first I
had to clear immigration and answer those questions that always pursue me.
Do you have a criminal record? Yes. *What are the details?* Found guilty in 1964
of contravening the Law and Order (Maintenance) Act. *How?* By organising
a demonstration against the Smith regime's banning of the *Daily News*.
Now all that seemed so trivial, not worth even mentioning, but I knew that

concealing a criminal offence could one day lead to trouble, and I did not want trouble in my life ever again.

During the two-hour drive to Hokonui Ranch in the Midlands province, I could already spot changes. Women and children walking along the road were carrying food, packets of the staple maize-meal. This had been forbidden under Rhodesia's Operation Turkey, through which starvation was used as a weapon. One girl of about ten, a baby on her back, a big bag on her shoulder, a towel over her head, was humping along painfully by herself. There seemed to be no men walking. I remembered that eight or nine years earlier, when I was still free in Rhodesia, children and often adults, too, would wave as cars passed and shout greetings or something seditious like 'Zhiiii!' or 'Freedom!' Now no one was waving.

Two days later, an aircraft flew low and frighteningly across the sky. Under the exceedingly fragile ceasefire, the Rhodesian air force and army had been placed under control of the British interim governor, Lord Soames. The two guerrilla armies that had been fighting Ian Smith's Rhodesian Front regime, Robert Mugabe's Zimbabwe African National Liberation Army (ZANLA) and Joshua Nkomo's Zimbabwe People's Revolutionary Army (ZPRA) were wending their way to forty-five assembly points (APs) scattered under Commonwealth supervision throughout the country. Many guerrillas were still outside the APs, and people, for various reasons, were on edge, scared and filled with foreboding.

I assumed the roar in the skies was a flourish of Rhodesian pugnacity, but I was wrong. We learned that this had been a special salutation by the Scout flight of Squadron 656 of the British Army Air Corps, then based in Gwelo. The aircraft circled over APs Lima and Mike, each of which housed nineteen New Zealand monitors, saluting them on their national Waitangi Day, which commemorates a signed agreement between Maori chiefs and the British Crown. It seemed such a crazy thing to do in those fraught times. Did Squadron 656 think that the suspicious, jittery guerrillas would look at the sky, shrug and say 'Of course! It's Waitangi Day!'?

That same day, grenades were thrown at a house on Salisbury's Quorn Avenue, purchased by Zanu (PF), the Zimbabwe African National Union, Patriotic Front, for their leader, Robert Gabriel Mugabe. The grenades were futile, but frightening. The next attack was more serious. As Mugabe drove in a convoy from an election rally near Fort Victoria, a massive explosion detonated at the side of the road. Miraculously, he escaped injury, although two following cars were damaged.

On Thursday morning, 7 February, my father and I went to the Standard Bank in our little local town, Shabani. There we met Gijima Mpofu, who, with my father, was responsible for the construction of most of the buildings at the large, neighbouring Dadaya Secondary School. My father was withdrawing money for a payment to Gijima and also for a contribution requested by Zanu (PF) for a vehicle to be used during the election campaign. As I watched him hand over the funds to the waiting party agents outside the bank, I wondered how he, or any other rural store owner, had survived these locust years of unending demands from the 'freedom fighters' under the unblinking surveillance of the Smith regime.

Gijima interrupted my thoughts.

'Have you noticed anything different on your return?' he asked, then answered his own question. 'The people now are mostly black.'

The next morning my parents returned to Bulawayo on business. I remained behind, revelling in being home after so many years abroad. I was eating a delicious lunch of *nyama* (meat) and *sadza*, a thick porridge made from maize-meal, prepared as a homecoming treat by the cook, Gelina Masuku, when Honey barked.

'Soldiers!' said Gelina.

I went out to the front of the house. Three white men stood there, with the golden Labrador baying at them. They said they were looking for Garfield Todd, but could tell he was not at home.

'I am Detective Inspector Clark from Shabani,' said the leader. 'We'll be back tomorrow.'

I telephoned Bulawayo and told my parents. Then John Mukokwayarira, who worked on the ranch, came to see me. Many months previously, John had been detained by the Smith regime, going into prison a staunch supporter of one of the contenders in the forthcoming election, Bishop Abel Muzorewa, and coming out a staunch supporter of Comrade Robert Mugabe.

We sat under a shady tree and talked quietly. John thought we were in for trouble. The police had been to nearby Dadaya School and had taken the headmaster away. John wanted advice. Two election candidates – Simbarashe Mumbengegwi and Julia Zvobgo – had passed through the area the day before and met a small gathering of teachers from Dadaya and friends. They had gone on to stay at the Nilton Hotel in Shabani with the organising secretary for Zanu (PF) in the Midlands, Sam Chisorochengwe. John had just learned that Sam had been arrested in his room at three o'clock that morning. He asked if I thought their meeting had been illegal. I thought not, as surely there must be political activity before any elections if they are to be seen as free and fair?

My parents returned home that evening. My father, chairman of Dadaya's board of governors, had already instructed a lawyer to take action over the arrest of the headmaster, Samuel Mutomba, and had rung Peter Wilkinson, leader of the New Zealand monitoring group in Salisbury. Wilkinson promised to inform Governor Soames's staff. My father then rang the police in Shabani to find out what was going on. He was told to come in at eight o'clock the next day and they would tell him.

Shabani was a twenty-minute drive away, and at 7.30 a.m. that Saturday, my father went to the police. As the morning passed, my mother and I became very anxious. At last his car pulled up outside the house at 10.20 and we went out to greet him. He got out of the car smiling at us, but holding up his hand as if motioning something to stop. Then we became aware of the presence of a police vehicle and two other men, one black, one white, and heard my father saying that he was under arrest. My mother registered total shock, and protested that this couldn't be possible. But within seconds she was under complete control and, like the last time, in January 1972, when my father and I were arrested together in her presence, she organised tea for the prisoner and his captors.

The white man, in casual clothes, came onto the stoep and introduced himself as Carl Gibbard from the Criminal Investigation Department. While my parents packed a bag, I talked to Gibbard, trying both to conceal my anguish and to give my parents as long as possible alone together. Gibbard was pleasant and we talked for some time, looking out over the spectacular view of water, hills, Wedza Mountain, sky and clouds, and the magnificent Ngesi River winding northwards to the horizon past Dadaya.

I asked what the situation was regarding the auxiliaries, the forces supporting the internal factions of Bishop Muzorewa and the Reverend Ndabaningi Sithole. The two men had been temporary partners of Ian Smith in an attempted 'internal settlement', now superseded by the Lancaster House Agreement. Gibbard said that some of the groups had been disbanded. I heard later that in fact most of Sithole's auxiliaries had been assembled on some pretext and were then bombed from the air by the Rhodesians, but Muzorewa's auxiliaries, Pfumo ReVanhu, Spear of the People, were still very active.

Gibbard and I were joined by my parents. 'Do you realise what you are doing?' my mother asked. 'You are taking away a seventy-two-year-old man who has been working all his life for peace and justice. You are taking *him* away, and yet throughout the country these auxiliaries are making life miserable for people. Why don't you do something about *them*? Why come for *him*?'

'I know, I know, none of us likes this,' Gibbard replied. 'We are doing our best. We've got a magistrate coming in this morning, even though he's normally off playing golf on Saturdays. None of us likes this.'

Up the hill in her little cottage, my father's sister Edie was ill. Gibbard readily gave permission for my father to say goodbye to her, and the two set off together. Many foreign correspondents had come to report on these heady days of Rhodesia's return from quarantine into the world community, and I knew how to contact Martin Meredith of the London *Sunday Times*. I rushed to the telephone and rang him.

'Martin, listen. I haven't got long. My father is under arrest on a law and order charge. The police are here now.'

Quick as a flash, he got the picture and said he would inform Governor Soames.

Gibbard allowed me to accompany them to Shabani. He went ahead in the police vehicle with my father, and I followed with Gibbard's colleague. When we got to the police camp, we nudged slowly over a ridge up a short road behind the police station and into the isolated Special Branch section, a couple of rows of rooms set at right angles to each other. The surrounding fence was screened with hessian so that nothing could be seen of the SB's activities. A few black people were sitting around, and a bed, covered with a grey blanket, squatted on the stoep. I found my heart shrinking at the thought of what might happen in this place.

Gibbard went off to arrange the court hearing, and my father and I sat talking softly. By taking him out of circulation now, the Rhodesians were striking another blow against the possibility of free and fair elections. 'Can you *believe* it?' he kept asking me. No, I couldn't. Even sitting there in that SB area, it was very difficult to believe what was being done to this bright-eyed, white-haired man, sitting quietly on a wooden chair alongside a poster of Bishop Muzorewa, which beamed down benignly from the wall.

Eventually we were conducted to the cool, dignified courtroom. My father got into the dock, I sat below him and Gibbard sat behind me. A young man in a T-shirt, shorts and sandals was the Crown prosecutor. Soon the fifth person in this small drama appeared and took the magistrate's bench. He hadn't yet shaved and was in a safari suit. As he entered, T-shirt jumped up and shouted 'Silence in court!' We stood, sat, and the remand process went ahead.

The prosecutor asked that the accused, charged on two counts under the Law and Order (Maintenance) Act, be remanded in custody for two weeks. The first charge was aiding a person in commission of acts of terrorism, and the second was failure to report the presence of a terrorist. The prosecutor said that these were serious offences and it was believed that the accused might commit further offences, that he was in a position to interfere with witnesses, and that he had travel documents and might abscond.

'Mr Todd?' said the magistrate, Mr SP Finch.

My father stood, arms folded, and spoke with quiet intensity, saying that he had a long history in this country, and both here and abroad it was known that he had worked consistently and arduously for peace. Among witnesses he could call to attest to this fact were the vice-president of the United States; the prime minister and the Minister of Foreign Affairs of New Zealand; the British Foreign Secretary, Lord Carrington; the leader of the opposition in Britain and many others. As part of his pursuit of peace, he said, he had arranged to see the governor, Lord Soames, on the following Tuesday. He had asked for this appointment so that he could discuss the fact that there were still guerrillas out of bases who should be in assembly points and how they could be brought in.

He intended to point out to Lord Soames that it was unrealistic to expect all the guerrillas to come in when 16 000 auxiliaries loyal to Bishop Muzorewa were still roaming the country. He also intended to see both Mr Mugabe and Mr Nkomo to discuss all the problems that were besetting the country. He had worked as hard as he could for the success of the Lancaster House conference and had had close contact throughout with Nkomo and Mugabe, and had even seen General Peter Walls, head of the Rhodesian Army ...

The magistrate interrupted, making it quite clear that he was not interested in what my father had to say. 'My position is to discover whether the merits of the Crown case require you to be remanded,' he said. The Crown had led no evidence whatsoever, so it was difficult to spot any merits, let alone a case. My father sat down, his face drawn, his shoulders a little stooped.

'I am refusing bail,' said the magistrate. 'However, you may appeal to the High Court.'

T-shirt rose, hurriedly, said, 'Silence in court!' and the magistrate left. It was unreal. My father said to me later that the only time he'd been in this court before, as a witness, he'd had to borrow a jacket, as standards had been high. This time we were all dressed as if we were going on a picnic.

I followed my father and Gibbard to Shabani Prison. I had been through this before, watching prison gates being unlocked, my father entering, watching him through the fence, and seeing the steel doors opening and then shutting behind him, helpless to lift a finger on his behalf. That had been under Smith in January 1972. I hadn't expected it to be happening again under Lord Soames in February 1980. My father had a bag with him containing clothes, a Good News Bible and Bernard Levin's *Taking Sides*, which I had brought for him from London and which was inscribed 'With all good wishes from the author to Garfield Todd, the man who was right all along.' I hoped, but doubted, that circumstances would allow him to read.

When I returned home, I rang Robin Renwick, head of Governor Soames's office. I had first met him a few years previously, when he was appointed head of the Rhodesia Desk at Britain's Foreign and Commonwealth Office, and over time he had become the primary architect of the Lancaster House conference. He was as brisk and competent as ever, and didn't seem too worried. I wondered if anyone apart from those who had been in Shabani magistrate's court that morning realised that my father was facing hanging charges.

Robin said something about a ZANLA guerrilla having been arrested with a notebook that implicated my father and Dadaya's headmaster in some activity. I told him that nothing of this was mentioned in court. He seemed angry that the magistrate hadn't remanded my father out of custody, and said something was being done about this.

The telephone rang and rang and I was answering it yet again when I heard car doors slamming. My father walked round the corner, beaming, and took the receiver from me. I found that Gibbard was back on the stoep.

'You've brought my father back?' I asked.

'Yes,' he answered, looking as bemused as I felt.

Later I said to my mother, 'You know, I shook Gibbard's hand!' feeling shy that I had thanked the man who had taken my father away in the first place.

'You shook his hand?' she laughed. 'I *embraced* him!'

CHAPTER 2

First days in Zimbabwe

UNDER PRESSURE FROM GOVERNOR SOAMES, THE ATTORNEY-General had instructed the Shabani police to remand my father out of custody. Eventually Dadaya's headmaster was also released on remand. Bit by bit, we pieced the events together and discovered that one of the men my father had met outside the bank in Shabani was a ZANLA guerrilla who should have been in an assembly point. Instead, like many of his fellows, he had been kept out of the AP for electioneering purposes.

Their places in the APs were filled by very young men, *mujibas*, and women, *zvimbwidos*, who had willingly or otherwise acted as scouts, servants and consorts for the guerrillas. Anyone carrying a weapon and claiming to be a guerrilla was accepted into the APs, so the number of those apparently emerging from the bush to place themselves under the control of ceasefire monitors seemed to be swelling. This, in the case of ZANLA, eventually transpired to have been a mirage, and the results of the pending elections were already being constructed on the ground, leading to a decisive victory for Robert Mugabe's Zanu (PF).

The guerrilla outside the bank had kept a notebook in which he faithfully recorded all transactions, such as the donation made that morning by my father. When he was arrested, evidence of assistance received from my father and headmaster Mutomba was captured in the notebook. They both appeared again before the magistrate, Mr Finch, who stated that prosecution would proceed by way of summons. At their third and final appearance, he announced that the Attorney-General had withdrawn charges against them. But, said Mr Finch as a parting shot, that didn't mean the charges couldn't be preferred again at any time.

This was no frivolous matter. Their freedom and perhaps their lives now depended on the outcome of the elections. At that time we were fearful of the elections being tilted in favour of the Rhodesian 'internal settlement' alliance leader Bishop Muzorewa, which, we believed, would lead to a resumption and escalation of the civil war. We also believed that a Muzorewa regime would probably resurrect all charges against those accused of assisting guerrillas. The party-list elections, scheduled for Wednesday 27 February to Friday

29 February, thus became increasingly important, and my mother scoured newspapers for information on where mobile polling stations would be, and when. Eventually she rang our district commissioner to say that no mobile polling stations had been announced for the Shabani area. The DC said, 'That is because in the last election, your husband objected to the presence of *any* mobile polling station.'

He was right. During the 'internal settlement' election of April 1979, the rural electorate had been buffeted by guerrillas demanding a boycott and the Rhodesian forces backing Muzorewa, and my father had said that he didn't want any polling stations on the ranch. Now times had changed. Eventually mobile polling booths were agreed on for our area, and my father went to help ensure that the necessary logistics and atmosphere were in place for voting at the nearby railway settlement of Bannockburn.

'*Don't* take any notice of all these soldiers,' he said to people. 'Just be quiet and disciplined and vote.' He stopped one of our employees from voting, as he knew she was only fifteen, but he watched other young girls for whom he had no responsibility borrowing babies so as to appear old enough to legitimately cast a ballot. When the polling truck arrived, it was under the supervision of Mr Finch, the magistrate, who seemed furious. He stalked up to my father and asked: 'How many voters have you brought, Mr Todd?' Instead of truthfully answering 'none', my father folded his arms, considered the crowd and said, 'I estimate 1500 to 2000.'

'I agree,' said Mr Finch, 'and we haven't got *nearly* enough ballot papers. We will have to send for more.'

Counting took place on the following Sunday and Monday, and by midnight on Monday the results were known. Bishop Muzorewa's party had won three seats. Ian Smith's Rhodesian Front had won all twenty of the seats provisionally reserved for whites until 1987 in terms of the Lancaster House interim constitution. Joshua Nkomo's party, PF Zapu, the Patriotic Front Zimbabwe African People's Union, had won twenty seats, and Robert Mugabe's Zanu (PF) had collected fifty-seven, sweeping the board. Robert Mugabe was therefore asked by Lord Soames to form a government.

The police had displayed extraordinary judgement about whom they had chosen to arrest in the Shabani area prior to the elections. Among those eventually released were Sam Chisorochengwe, who became a member of the intelligence wing in the prime minister's office; Julia Zvobgo, who was elected to the new parliament representing the constituency under which both Hokonui Ranch and Dadaya fell; Richard Hove and Simbarashe

Mumbengegwi, both old boys of Dadaya who became cabinet ministers in the post-independence government.

Julia Zvobgo was the wife of Eddison, who had been my boss in 1972, when, during my exile, I was appointed as one of the overseas representatives of the African National Council, an alliance cobbled together in 1971 between Zapu and Zanu under the leadership of Bishop Muzorewa and the Reverend Canaan Banana. Its successful purpose was to stymie plans for a 'settlement' between Smith's regime and the British government, which would have led to independence without majority rule.

Richard Hove was much older than me, having been a pupil at Dadaya during my childhood. Simbarashe, a little younger than me, was one of a steady stream of Mumbengegwi brothers and sisters who had passed with distinction through Dadaya. During a year I spent in Australia in the late 1960s, he had been a student there, as had a mutual friend, Sekai Hove Holland. The three of us had sometimes gathered in Sydney to be homesick together.

My father called on Robert Mugabe to offer his congratulations. He told the new prime minister that in the past there had been a convention that former premiers could from time to time call on their successors for discussions, but that this had been shattered when, in 1965, he had tried to call on Smith, only to be refused an audience and then arrested and detained without charge or trial.

He said now and again he might want to call on the new prime minister and also, he said, joking, it would be nice to have an assurance that he wouldn't be detained again. Prime Minister Mugabe laughed, leaned towards my father and touched his hand. 'Garfield,' he said, 'we want you for the senate. We want those who dishonoured you to see you being honoured.'

During the period from the elections to the date set for the country's formal independence from Britain, midnight on 17 April 1980, an estimated 40 000 celebrants streamed in from across the world. In Salisbury, centre of activities, the fact of Zimbabwe's birth was highlighted by the almost unbelievable sight, after Rhodesia's long years of quarantine, of ninety-six heads of state or their representatives. Paper hats, posters and flags all over town flashed the bold, bright colours of the new Zimbabwe: black representing the majority of people; green the land; gold the mineral resources; white for peace; and the little Zimbabwe bird perched against a red star symbolising hope for the future.

The joyous atmosphere of change and hope was palpable in Rufaro

Stadium, venue of the independence ceremony, and strikingly illustrated by a joint choir from two leading schools, Girls' High and Prince Edward. The choir assembled solemnly in front of Prince Charles, there to lower Britain's Union Jack and to raise the new Zimbabwe flag. In the first of two verses the choir launched into a eulogy of Rhodesia. There were subdued groans from whites in the semi-VIP section of the stadium, whispers of 'how unfortunate', and a profound silence from the rest of the crowd. Then came the second verse, and the white children, in faultless Shona, soared into a eulogy of Zimbabwe, at which the tens of thousands of their black compatriots went wild with joyful acclaim.

Later that day the new prime minister hosted a huge lunch party to celebrate Zimbabwe's independence. One of those who had come from abroad to witness the birth of this brand new state was Frank Ferrari of the African-American Institute, to whom so many Zimbabweans owed so much. He took me with him to the lunch, where friends were practically falling over each other in the loud joy of reunion. One of them, Shridath Ramphal, the Commonwealth secretary-general, sent me that afternoon a lasting memento of the magic time: a copy of his latest book, inscribed: 'For Judith – on a very special day and with good wishes for the future it promises. Sonny Ramphal. Salisbury, 18 April 1980.'

There were, of course, moments of sadness and regret, remembering those who deserved to be there but were not. When Josiah Tungamirai, the ZANLA High Command's political commissar, saw me, he took me aside and walked me round the garden, mournfully relating details of Josiah Tongogara's death in Mozambique on the night of 26 December 1979. Tongogara, chief of defence in the ZANLA High Command, had introduced me to Tungamirai during the Lancaster House talks in London, where the two of them shared a house with Dzingai Mutumbuka and other Zanu (PF) delegates.

Tungamirai told me he had been so shattered by the tragedy of Tongogara's death that he believed his sanity had been saved only by the intervention of veteran Zanu (PF) leader Simon Muzenda, who arranged for Tungamirai's mother to come and stay with her son while he grieved. He told me that on the night of the fatality, he and Tongogara had been travelling with others in two vehicles from Maputo to Chimoio. Tungamirai said he was in the front vehicle. It was dark and the roads were bad. Tungamirai's car passed a military vehicle that had been carelessly abandoned, with no warning signs, at the side of the road. After that, he could no longer see the headlights of the following car in his rear-view mirror. Eventually they turned back, and, as he had feared, they found that Tongogara's car had struck the abandoned vehicle. Tongogara was sitting in the front passenger seat. Tungamirai told me that he had struggled to lift Tongogara out of the wrecked car. He said that as he was doing so, Tongagara heaved a huge sigh and died in his arms.

I didn't mention to Tungamirai that many people believed Tongogara had been murdered.

April 1980 vanished fast, but before the first May Day celebrated in Zimbabwe, Finance Minister Enos Nkala announced that the new government had abolished sales tax on sugar, tea, cooking oil and margarine, important supplements to the diet of the poorest citizens, and that thousands of prisoners were being released. The police and the army kept a low profile, vastly different to their provocative air before and during the election, and, at least on the surface, the transition from Rhodesia to Zimbabwe seemed to be going reasonably smoothly. This was despite many ZANLA guerrillas having remained outside the APs and the continued easy access to arms cached across the country, resulting in continuing crime and banditry.

There were some social hiccups, such as the brief arrest of Rex Nhongo, commander of the ZANLA forces, at a Salisbury hotel. He was accused of creating a disturbance when told he couldn't eat in the restaurant as he wasn't wearing a jacket and tie. Nathan Shamuyarira, Minister of Information and Tourism, then announced that jackets and ties should no longer be required for entrance to hotel facilities. This, in turn, led to further problems. John Callinicos and his wife Aelda, aunt of my husband Richard Acton, were then running the popular Park Lane Hotel, and wondered just how they would cope with unhappy and sometimes violent malcontents if they could no longer seek refuge in a dress code. Aelda said that while some young blacks were sometimes drunk and scruffy, they were seldom a problem, as they were generally happy and friendly. Some young whites could be a different matter, especially on Friday nights at the Park Lane, a favourite haunt of ex-troopies, where they had been known to threaten people and, in some cases, had even taken to exposing themselves.

I saw what they meant late one evening in the main lounge at the plush Meikles Hotel. Some young men in hats and skimpy clothes started sauntering around, drinking beer from bottles and loudly hectoring foreign guests. But before long these displays of trauma disappeared. On the whole, whites had been bowled over by Robert Mugabe's address to the nation on the eve of independence.

'Let us deepen our sense of belonging and engender a common interest that knows no race, colour or creed,' he'd said. 'Let us truly become Zimbabweans with a single loyalty. Long live our freedom.' Many heaved a sigh of relief – *Hasn't he changed?* – and stopped packing. The most disaffected were leaving anyway, if they could. One day my father gave a lift to a couple of young whites who didn't recognise him. They told him candidly that they had been in one of the undercover groups of the Rhodesian Defence Force and were soon leaving for South Africa with their unit and equipment intact.

From early on there were signs of a trend towards a one-party state. The Zimbabwe Broadcasting Corporation started sedulously referring to 'the prime minister, Comrade Robert Mugabe' and 'the president, Comrade Canaan Banana', and statements broadcast by the Ministry of Information announced in one breath 'the government and the party', although Mugabe had initially formed a post-war government of national unity.

Frederique Winter, mother of film star Dana Wynter, cautiously protested in one of the last of her many letters to the main national newspaper, the *Herald*: 'The use of the word Comrade by ZBC/TV is rather confusing: this appellation was introduced by the Russian communists after the 1917 revolution … To call our respected president or prime minister Comrade is rather presumptuous.'

One of the best things for me in the new Zimbabwe was being able to meet again many old friends, such as Justin Nyoka, now being groomed for a post in the Ministry of Information. In the early 1960s we were contemporaries at university, where Justin was on a scholarship from the Rhodesia Printing and Publishing Company. This was an extension of South Africa's Argus Group, which ran our newspapers and was beginning to train blacks for the future. The fact that Justin had made it to university, let alone that he also had a scholarship, made people jealous. Rumours were spread that he was a spy for the Rhodesians, and play was made on his surname, Nyoka, which means snake in English. When Peter Niesewand was deported from Rhodesia in 1973, the BBC lost a valuable stringer, as well as the London *Guardian* losing their correspondent. George Bennett at the BBC Africa Service, where I had freelanced, asked if I had any ideas on whom they could now use in Rhodesia, and I suggested Justin.

He was an assiduous reporter, which meant that he almost inevitably made enemies. Eventually he disappeared from his farm in Mashonaland, and it was rumoured that he had been abducted by ZANLA.

Justin had many friends at the BBC and elsewhere in London, and we all grieved over his disappearance, but there seemed nothing any of us could do. I suffered a recurring nightmare of Justin lying in a shallow grave with his mouth open and his little front buckteeth smeared with soil. He had simply disappeared and a profound silence had taken his place. But then one day, Edgar Tekere, a powerful Zanu leader, came from Mozambique to London and was interviewed by the BBC Africa Service. Julian Marshall escorted him out of Bush House and, really just making conversation, asked Tekere if there was any news of Justin.

'Oh yes,' said Tekere in an off-hand fashion. 'He's not responding very well to re-education in Maputo.'

Julian rang to tell me the wonderful yet appalling news. The best thing that could now be done for Justin was to impress upon Zanu in Mozambique that news was out that he was alive and in their hands. Julian found Zanu's telex number in Maputo and I sent off an urgent message in what I hoped was appropriate language – something like: 'To Comrade Justin Nyoka c/o Comrade Robert Mugabe. Masses of Zimbabwe thrilled to learn of your safe arrival in Mozambique and look forward to hearing your broadcasts soonest.'

There was, of course, no reply, but quite soon Zanu started parading Justin in an exhaustive propaganda drive. I went to listen to him addressing British members of parliament in a large committee room at Westminster about his long walk from Zimbabwe to Mozambique, telling them how absolutely all the people he and his comrades had met along the way whole-heartedly supported Zanu. Justin grinned at me across the room when he said that while he was walking the length and breadth of Rhodesia conducting his opinion poll, he'd even had a Coke at Todd's store near Shabani, but hadn't been able to speak to him.

At the end of the meeting we managed to hug each other but had no chance to talk, as he was so obviously still a captive. Two Zanu minders were within touching and hearing distance all the time. Now, post-independence, we were again able to talk freely, but I didn't dare ask about his time being re-educated in Mozambique. Someone must have told him that I never believed he did the Long Walk voluntarily, and while he still laughed in his old, hilarious fashion, his eyes were no longer amused and he wasn't at ease. Now, in these heydays of freedom, he was on television and radio on behalf of the Ministry of Information, saying that all those who made money from independence souvenirs had to pay 10 per cent of their profits to 'the ruling party, Zanu (PF)'. Unashamed extortion was beginning its move from back to centre stage.

In May 1980 I returned to London. On the flight from Bulawayo to Johannesburg I sat next to a pleasant middle-aged couple, who asked where I was from. I said I was a Zimbabwean. This term used to be a forthright and sometimes provocative statement of support for future majority rule as opposed to existing white supremacy, and even though it was now the correct way to state my nationality, I felt rather shy about using it. I was not flaunting the word, but I still expected a sign of distaste.

The reaction I got was one of puzzled hope. The woman said two of their children had been killed during the war. They were going to Pretoria to persuade their remaining son that things were okay now, and that he should come back home to – she seemed to hesitate between 'Rhodesia' and 'Zimbabwe' and settled on – 'our country'.

Those were emotional times for all involved with that lovely country. I felt bleak about leaving, yet, at the same time, I was happy to return to my work as project officer with the Zimbabwe Project Trust in London.

The Trust was formed in 1977 as an initiative of the Swiss Catholic order known as the Bethlehem Fathers, supported by the general secretary of the London-based Catholic Institute for International Relations, Mildred Nevile. The Bethlehem Fathers had for many years placed missionaries in Zimbabwe, some of whom had been deported by the Rhodesian Front regime. They had become anathema after they launched Mambo Press and founded their popular publication, *Moto* (fire). As the war in Rhodesia escalated, the Bethlehem Fathers' headquarters at Immensee, Switzerland, were flooded with appeals for help from members of their former flocks, many of whom had become refugees. The intention, therefore, was to provide support for refugees outside the country through the Zimbabwe Project. But now all those refugees were scheduled to be back home by the end of 1980.

While in Zimbabwe for the first weeks of 1980, I was, with the help of Michael Behr, the local representative of Oxfam (UK), doing some research about returning refugees, and had concluded that while some might find support in whatever social and physical structures remained of their former homes, others would not find enough.

Many were being sent, quite well nourished, from neighbouring states through transit centres, only to find that little awaited them in Zimbabwe. Some would have no axes to cut wood to build new huts, no cooking pots, no blankets and no money, and concerned agencies didn't yet seem sensitive to the fact that it helped returning refugees to be able to bring something home for their own self-esteem, let alone for the fellow victims of war they were returning to. Even a blanket or some soap would help, but this was not generally recognised by harried administrators who had too much to cope with anyway, and didn't welcome new slants on existing problems. So, for example, when a batch of refugees was sent home from Umtali – and this incident was probably multiplied by hundreds – the police apprehended twenty-four of them for stealing fruit from trees in private gardens. What else did they have to eat, I wondered? How demoralised did this make them feel? What did 'independence for Zimbabwe' mean as far as they were concerned?

Maybe, I reported back to my colleagues in London, there was still a role for the Zimbabwe Project to play.

CHAPTER 3

The Zimbabwe Project Trust

W E SET OURSELVES UP IN 1978 IN TWO TINY ATTICS AT 1 Cambridge Terrace, Regent's Park, London. There were three of us. The director, Father Dieter Scholz, and the administrative secretary, Brother Arthur Dupuis, had been members of Rhodesia's Catholic Commission for Justice and Peace (CCJP), and were instrumental in compiling and publishing reports on atrocities committed by the Smith regime. The Rhodesian authorities, by deporting Father Scholz at just the right time, inadvertently provided a fluent Shona, English and German–speaking expert on repression in Rhodesia to become the first director of the newly formed Zimbabwe Project Trust (ZPT).

Brother Arthur had witnessed the abduction by Rhodesian agents of prominent Zanu lawyer Edson Sithole and his secretary outside the Ambassador Hotel in central Salisbury and, fearing for his life, had fled the country. The ZPT also had access, now and then, to the services of Sister Janice McLaughlin of the American Maryknoll Sisters. She, too, had worked with the CCJP until being deported around the same time as Father Scholz.

The ZPT was named by Tim Sheehy of the Catholic Institute for International Relations (CIIR). He was a brother-in-law of mine through his marriage to Mary Ann, younger sister of Richard Acton, my husband since January 1974. My connection with the ZPT came through my appointment to the CIIR board the same year. Between us and under the broad umbrella provided by CIIR, we had good contacts not only with Zapu and Zanu and other groups in and from Rhodesia, but also with religious and secular funding agencies which, in some cases under the aegis of ZPT, were becoming involved with refugees from Rhodesia's war.

Initially, ZPT's role was to offer assistance to those responsible for the well-being of refugees in the Front Line States, particularly Zambia and Mozambique. We found donors, compiled project proposals and provided concrete assurances to donors that funds would be spent on strictly non-military ventures such as food production, medical facilities, education, and self-help activities in the camps like carpentry, welding, garment production and, to a very limited extent, entertainment – sports equipment, musical instruments and books.

I had long-standing and useful friendships with Zapu leaders in Zambia, such as Joshua Nkomo, Edward Ndlovu, TG Silundika, Willie Musarurwa and JZ Moyo, and when Sister Janice travelled to Mozambique on behalf of ZPT, she forged strong links with the Zanu leadership. Father Scholz also visited Zambia and Mozambique, strengthening links with the camps, churches and donors, and placing a colleague, Father Nigel Johnson, a qualified dentist, in the vast Solwezi camp for boys near the border with Zaire in north-western Zambia.

But now, in 1980, the refugees were starting to go home, and ZPT had to assess whether or not it still had a practical role to play. In the first few months after independence, we successfully presented proposals to the European Economic Community (EEC) for funding to rehabilitate some rural schools and hospitals in Zimbabwe, and for developmental work such as providing water storage tanks and irrigation equipment for intensive agriculture at Dadaya Secondary School. We founded the *ZPT News Bulletin*, compiled and edited by brilliant academic and former Rhodesian prisoner John Conradie. The publication was an instant success, coming as it did at a time when people and institutions throughout the world were hungry for news on Zimbabwe. We also continued raising funds and finding places for Zimbabweans studying abroad.

New government agencies had yet to be established, but since our name was already in the London telephone directory under *Zimbabwe*, we became a reference point for people wanting information about the newly named country, like Mrs Eve Bertram, aged sixty-eight, who rang to find out how she could claim Zimbabwean citizenship. Her husband had been a high-ranking civil servant in Rhodesia until Ian Smith accused him of being a quisling. He had resigned his position, and the Bertrams had left the country ten years previously 'because of Smith', she explained unnecessarily.

'I had to leave as well,' I said, just to be friendly. 'And wasn't it all, the war and everything, such a terrible waste?'

She burst into tears, sobbing inconsolably.

In January 1981, trustees and staff of ZPT and CIIR met in London to plan the future. The trustees were Mildred Nevile, general secretary of the CIIR, Father Josef Amstutz, head of the Bethlehem Fathers, and Guy Clutton-Brock, who was there with his wife Molly. Guy had been much involved in the development of the modern nationalist movement in Rhodesia from the late 1950s and in establishing the cooperative movement, first at St Faith's Mission near Rusape, and then at Cold Comfort Farm outside Salisbury. He had been deported from Rhodesia in 1971, and he and Molly now lived in a remote cottage, Gelli Uchaf, in North Wales, but remained closely in touch with people and events on the ground in Zimbabwe.

Others at the meeting were Father Mike Traber, first editor of *Moto* and another Rhodesian deportee, now based in London with the World Association of Christian Communicators, and Ian Linden, the CIIR expert on southern Africa who had replaced Tim when he accepted a job with the EEC in Zimbabwe. The upshot of the meeting was that, by July, when ZPT's financial year ended, we should expand into a southern African refugee agency. The main reason for this decision, so far as I could understand, was that some Catholic agencies that funded our administrative costs were concerned about possibly duplicating the work being done by the Zimbabwe Catholic Commission for Social Service and Development (CSSD), which they also funded.

Guy, Molly and I argued for the continued existence of the ZPT in its established form on the grounds that if ever we extended our services to refugees throughout southern Africa, this would be a gradual and natural development. If, however, we now deliberately changed our focus, we risked losing much of ZPT's present reputation and many of our contacts. Guy's arguments were simple and, to me, unassailable. We had been established because we were specifically concerned with Zimbabwe rather than the region in general. We should remain small and unpretentious. It was always disastrous to be dictated to by other agencies, which were, by nature, jealous and divisive. The best way to help southern Africa was to remain focused on Zimbabwe and strengthen it as much as possible.

We were overruled and had to accept the decision, although I believed those concerned had no idea how vast and dangerous was the area into which we were being propelled, where we couldn't possibly constructively assist. We were too small and the problems of southern Africa too large.

I was particularly unhappy as, at this meeting, I was appointed deputy director of whatever the project was going to be called to position me to take over running something I didn't think I would be able to believe in. Brother Arthur was leaving shortly for his home country of Canada, where, he said, his mother was dying 'so beautifully, just like a candle running out of wax'. Father Scholz was also leaving in July. His pioneering work with ZPT had greatly impressed Father Pedro Arrupe, Father General of the Society of Jesus, and he had been called to Rome to help establish the Jesuit Refugee Service. But first Dieter was going to Zimbabwe to discuss the future of our organisation with friends.

As Mildred Nevile later wrote to concerned funding agencies, during his visit, Dieter 'informed members of Government and others of plans to transform the Zimbabwe Project into a Southern Africa refugee service. Members of the new Government made it clear that they thought this would be a great mistake and instead made a formal request to the Zimbabwe Project that it should move its base to Salisbury and assist in the most urgent task of resettling former combatants. The long-standing identification of the Zimbabwe Project with the struggle for independence in Zimbabwe, its close association with both Zanu and Zapu and the fact that many of the new Government Ministers knew of the work of the Zimbabwe Project or had been helped by it, made such a request possible. The Government viewed the proposal as a logical extension of the work in which the Project had been engaged in the past, and it was, of course, a great compliment to the Zimbabwe Project that it should have been asked to undertake a task of such importance to the country.'

Events moved swiftly. With great generosity, since I would be based in Zimbabwe, my husband and stepson, Johnny, agreed that I should accept the appointment as director of the ZPT. Zimbabwe's Minister of Justice and Constitutional Affairs, Simbi Mubako, then offered Richard a chance of applying for a post in his ministry, where he eventually became a senior law officer. My parents found us just over an acre of land for Z$3 000 at 18 Masefield Avenue in Salisbury's suburb of Strathaven, where my father started building our house. On 1 June 1981, the Zimbabwe Project opened an office at Old Shell House in the centre of town and started its work with the ex-combatants of Zimbabwe. Richard's aunt and uncle, Aelda and John Callinicos, welcomed us to their house at 93 Twentydales Road, Hatfield, and we moved in for a long and delightful stay while our own house was under construction.

Life in the new Zimbabwe was full of excitement and pleasure for many. One of the highlights that June was a visit to Dadaya by the hero of the times, Prime Minister Robert Gabriel Mugabe. The following day I rang my parents to find out how it had gone. To my surprise, they had left for Bulawayo, from where my mother later telephoned. She said the visit had been a wonderful occasion. As chairman of Dadaya's governing board, my father had met Mugabe in Shabani, travelled to Dadaya with him, and introduced him to the staff and pupils at the church, the only building large enough to accommodate them all. My father, seated on the platform with the other dignitaries, had a recorder under his chair to tape Mugabe's speech.

The premier was so moved by the ecstatic reception accorded him that, initially, he could hardly speak. When it was all over, the prime minister and his party left immediately through the vestry and out a back door as directed by his security staff. My father didn't move. My mother went up to him, noticed the recorder still on the floor under his seat and said, 'We mustn't forget this.'

'What?' he asked.

'The tape recorder. You were recording the prime minister's speech.'

'The prime minister?' he said. 'Is he here? If he is here I should be with him. What is happening?'

It soon became obvious that my father had suffered a complete memory lapse. Later, on the way to the dining hall where people were gathering for a meal, Mugabe saw my parents standing alone on the road outside the church, stopped his car and got out to talk to them. My mother explained that she wasn't sure what had happened, but my father seemed to have lost his memory. She said Mugabe appeared desolate, but she persuaded him to continue with his schedule as if nothing had happened.

That night, my father woke a couple of times remembering things from the past week, but not Mugabe's visit. So they went to Bulawayo in the morning, where my father had a medical check-up. All was in order.

As my mother carefully explained the sequence of events, I realised that something bad had happened, and I expected the tape recorder to have been a bomb, until she passed that point. I wasn't really surprised by the story that unfolded. Dadaya and all it had meant had been the centre of my parents' life since 1934, and the sight of Mugabe addressing the rapturous assembly must have been a great climax of hope, fear, arduous work and prayer for my father. He had brought the school safely through the war, and now this was a blessing of peace.

That month, John Conradie flew from London to Harare. He had agreed to return to the country for which, while trying to liberate it, he had nearly lost his life. Narrowly escaping the death penalty for smuggling weapons of war into Rhodesia, he had instead served twelve years in prison. Now, as administrator of the Zimbabwe Project, he was well positioned to pursue his passion for agricultural collective cooperatives.

He joined the informal steering committee formed to guide our work in

Zimbabwe. Other members were Michael Behr of Oxfam; Sister Janice, now working from State House with Zimbabwe's first president, the Reverend Canaan Banana, in establishing an agricultural training college for ex-combatants in Marondera; Tim Sheehy, now with the EEC in Salisbury; and me. Before long, Sister Janice also brought three bright young ZANLA comrades onto the committee: Morris Mtsambiwa, a medical student, Vivian Maeresera, who was to become the district administrator in Marondera, and Michael Tingaiteyi Fungati, who would join the Bank of Credit and Commerce.

At the request of our trustees in Europe, I was exploring the possibility of adding some Zimbabwe-based people to their board. Dieter Scholz had suggested I should talk to the local Jesuit Provincial, Father Henry Wardale, who readily agreed to meet me. He was about sixty, with a soft, aristocratic English accent, innocent large blue eyes, white hair and a cherubic grin. He was pleasant but cautious and asked why I thought him a suitable candidate. People spoke highly of him, I said. We were anxious to maintain a Catholic link, and people already working in this field – such as Dieter, Nigel Johnson and Roland von Nidda – were all Jesuits. Father Wardale chuckled, held up his hand and said, 'Enough! I might get embarrassed.'

He said first he would have to sound out the Zimbabwe Catholic Bishops' Conference and consider the feelings of 150 strong-minded men, his fellow Jesuits in Zimbabwe, some of whom might not approve. We talked about Edson Sithole's abduction, still fresh in people's minds. Father Wardale said the Justice and Peace Commission had been just a day behind in tracking him and others to a farm where they believed he was being held by the Rhodesians. By the time they got there, the farm had been abandoned. Wardale indicated that he had a trunk of papers on this and related matters under his bed, and I often wondered – too late – what had happened to them.

In due course, the overseas trustees invited Father Wardale, the Anglican Bishop Peter Hatendi and my father to join them in safeguarding the work of the Zimbabwe Project. When I heard of the possible appointment of my father, I objected to Mildred Nevile, saying it wouldn't look good to have as trustee a man whose daughter was the director. She and her fellow trustees overruled my objection. In later months I was very thankful for this, as it turned out that my survival at the ZPT would depend almost entirely on him.

In September, three months after we opened our doors, I sent a report to the trustees stating that we had got off to a slow and sometimes difficult start:

It takes time to establish what we can do and we are really still at that stage. But I looked up from my desk yesterday and contrasted what I saw to what was happening on 1 June 1981, the day the Zimbabwe Project opened its office here. On that day I sat alone in a big office with two desks and one telephone extension; a typewriter and some paper and a few files I had brought from London. When I looked up from my desk yesterday I consciously compared that day to what I now saw around me.

Here was John Conradie cursing a mistake he had made with our beautiful photocopying machine. Next to him was our spirited new secretary, Lethwin Denenga, struggling to finish typing a 32-page document John has drawn up on our observations of the demobilisation process so far. There was Sr Janice McLaughlin walking in and opening the door into our second office where sits Morris Mtsambiwa, formerly Cde Sekayi of ZANLA, now studying medicine but working for us in the holidays. Morris was on the telephone to other comrades to remind them of a Zimbabwe Project meeting that night at the Park Lane Hotel.

Comrade Cornelius Tendai sits patiently in a corner waiting to tell us how we can help the new agricultural Batsirinai cooperative in Shamva and, as for me, I am desperately trying to finish a huge application to Bread for the World in West Germany for $100 000 for a Revolving Loan Fund we need to establish.

Then the door opens again and it is Pastor Martin Staebler who arrived last week from Germany to join the Zimbabwe Christian Council and, informally, to help us, and then the door opens again … and then all three of our telephone extensions are ringing.

In the last couple of weeks at least 100 people have passed through our offices including, I believe, our first visitor from the Central Intelligence Organisation, the dreaded CIO. Sr Janice tells me that since the murder last month of Joe Gqabi, the ANC representative here, the police and CIO are often in touch with her to find out about the people whose names were found in his house, one of them being Fr Nigel Johnson SJ who was in the refugee camps in Zambia last year on behalf of the Zimbabwe Project. As you know, Sr Janice is particularly close to Zanu having been the Zimbabwe Project representative to the refugee camps in Mozambique.

There are no problems about all this. I simply give it as an example of a general air of uncertainty amongst people like us about who are really friends amongst the representatives of all the millions of agencies, trade missions, visitors, etc., etc. to Zimbabwe today.

I also wrote about my meeting at the beginning of August with John Shoniwa, head of the government's newly instituted Demobilisation Directorate, which fell under the Ministry of Labour and Social Services. Shoniwa had been in the first batch of men sent to China by Zanu for military training in 1963, along with Emmerson Mnangagwa, who had become the minister responsible for state security. Shoniwa was reputed to have been jailed in more African countries than any other Zimbabwean, but his experiences had in no way dimmed his exuberance. His deputy at the directorate was Report Phelekezela Mphoko, former Zapu representative in Mozambique, where he had met and married a woman rumoured to be usefully connected to Samora Machel, president of the former Portuguese colony.

Shoniwa was friendly and frank, two qualities that came to characterise the collaboration starting that day between the already established Zimbabwe Project and the newly launched Demobilisation Directorate.

He explained the procedures decided upon by government for the demobilisation of an estimated 30 000 former ZANLA and ZPRA guerrillas, of whom 4 000 were women. All ex-combatants would first be attested into the army simply as a device to bring them into a body that could handle their demobilisation. The army would select those to be demobilised. These would be people with Grade 7 or lower, or who were otherwise handicapped. They would be given identity cards and a post office savings book, with which they could withdraw Z$185 per month for two years. One Zimbabwe dollar was then slightly harder than one British pound. These post office savings books would be a different colour to those held by other Zimbabweans. Shoniwa laughed when I asked if the different colour was meant to be a mark of honour. Quite to the contrary, he said. It was meant to act as a warning to post office officials to most carefully scrutinise the bearer and the identity card all ex-combatants would carry to guard against fraud.

A pamphlet would shortly be issued by the Ministry of Information detailing centres to be set up for distribution of the documents. The pamphlet would also state that there would be counsellors to advise on training and further education at these centres. But, said Shoniwa, this was hogwash, as there was no money for training and education. No one had thought about demobilisation in time to include it in the Zimbabwe Conference on Reconstruction and Development (Zimcord) documentation, which was used to raise and channel the very generous donor funding pouring into Zimbabwe.

Shoniwa was sceptical about the whole exercise. It had been announced that Z$43 million would be given to the Demobilisation Directorate, but this would cover only administration and the monthly payments to the demobilised. He said when he went to the Ministry of Lands, he was told that there was no land available for ex-combatants. He'd gone to his minister, Kangai, for funds for training and education and was told there were none. He said he had quite frankly told Minister Kangai that if demobilisation succeeded, Kangai would get the praise, but, if it failed, Kangai would get the blame. In two years' time, when demobilisation pay-outs came to an end, Kangai would probably still be Minister of Labour and Social Services, and, Shoniwa had asked him, what would he do then?

In later years, President Mugabe would answer that question in his own way.

CHAPTER 4

War wounded at Lido

N EAR THE CALLINICOS HOUSE IN HATFIELD LIVED A NEW
friend, Lieutenant General Lookout Masuku, head of Zapu's military
wing ZPRA, and third in command of the Zimbabwe National Army after
Rex Nhongo of ZANLA and Sandy MacLean of the former Rhodesian
Army. On the first anniversary of Zimbabwe's independence, Mugabe had
promoted Masuku and Nhongo to the highest rank in the army, saying 'it
is to you that we have entrusted the security and well-being of our people'.
He also appointed Josiah Tungamirai of ZANLA and Jevan Maseko of
ZPRA as major generals.

In September 1981, Masuku called me to Bulawayo, where more than
200 disabled men from ZPRA were eking out a miserable existence in a pit
called the Lido Hotel. Aaron Ndabambi, Zapu's welfare officer, had contacted
Oxfam for help. Michael Behr telephoned the head of the Department of
Social Services to see what the government planned to do about these
war-wounded ex-combatants. The result was an abusive letter from the
department to Ndabambi, telling him it was illegal to solicit funds.

Eddison Zvobgo, Minister of Local Government and Housing, visited
Bulawayo around this time, and the city council took him to Lido. He was
appalled by the conditions people were living in, and said: 'Get them out of
here!'

'Where should we put them?' he was asked. A few days later, Eddison
rang Masuku and said something had to be done. On the advice of a friend,
Callistus Ndlovu, former Zapu representative to the United States, Masuku
rang the Zimbabwe Project, and I arranged to meet him at his Bulawayo
home in the suburb of Killarney. This was his real home; the house in
Harare was simply a place to work from.

I was apprehensive about meeting a man with such a grand title, but
his welcome was so warm, smiling and relaxed that I instantly felt as if
we had been close friends for many years. He explained that, while the
demobilisation process was a most frightening time for many people,
the handicapped were being given only a lump sum of Z$600 each and a
cool goodbye. These were his men, he said. He couldn't allow them to be

28

abandoned, and he needed our help in constructing a reasonable future for them.

The men wanted to live together in a community, and, at the very least, they deserved that right. There was a piece of land available at Esigodini outside Bulawayo for Z\$30 000. Zapu had held a fête and raised Z\$6 000; they needed another Z\$4 000 for the deposit, and a guarantor for the balance. That's what Masuku wanted to discuss. He originally thought the men might be able to contribute something from their pay-out, but then discovered that they had each already received their Z\$600 and it was gone.

I said I didn't quite know what, but do something we certainly would. Always frightened of wrongly giving the impression that the Zimbabwe Project was a powerful agency, I stressed that we were small, limited and had just about depleted our administration funds. But, I said, I believed that our work must pre-eminently be with those who were the worst handicapped mentally, emotionally and physically. Yes, said Masuku, and the first thing was to arrange for me to meet them.

He telephoned Dr Isaac Nyathi, who had trained as an economist in the Soviet Union and was now in charge of a holding company, Nitram, which Joshua Nkomo and colleagues had established to look after ZPRA ex-combatants. Nitram was the name of their accountant, spelled backwards. About 4 000 had so far opted to join. They were each required to contribute Z\$50 a month from their Z\$185 demobilisation allowance. Nitram was in the process of acquiring properties, farms, smallholdings and businesses, such as the Castle Arms Hotel. The rationale was that what money was available should be invested wisely and the ex-combatants should be trained on the job in whatever venture was acquired. This seemed the only practical and speedy way to tackle unemployment.

Nyathi took me to see two smallholdings. One was called Nest Egg, where all the ZPRA archives were stored, as was a fleet of huge, strange-looking military trucks brought back from Zambia and parked under trees in whatever shade was available. They were all left-hand drive and looked like surprised dinosaurs. Nyathi laughed when I asked what they were being used for, and said they were being stored while their future was decided. He said it was going to be difficult to maintain them, as getting spare parts from their manufacturers in Eastern Europe would be a problem.

All the properties that Nitram was acquiring were going concerns and Nest Egg's use as a storage facility was incidental. Its purpose, as with everything else, was to make money, and Nyathi proudly showed me hundreds – if not thousands – of battery hens producing eggs for which, he said, there was a huge market. The venture was proving to be extremely profitable. It was an appalling sight, birds packed together, perched on wire netting and filling the air with the noise of a grotesque, unending lament.

The second smallholding was Woody Glen, and it took us some time to get in. The gate was heavily padlocked and Nyathi had to keep hooting until someone came with keys. The men at Woody Glen were winnowing a good crop of maize, and I asked if I could take a photo. Our donor agencies were always grateful for pictures they could use for fund-raising. Nyathi said the men were extremely edgy, as they had been under attack by elements of Zanu and didn't feel safe. He was preparing me for a refusal, but the men gave their assent, on condition that I photographed only the piles of maize and none of them. Nyathi then took me into the main farmhouse to show me the large supplies of medical equipment Zapu had brought back from Zambia. The future of the medical supplies, like that of the vehicles at Nest Egg, was still under discussion with the authorities but, he lamented, as time passed, so did the usefulness of all this precious medicine and equipment.

We returned to Masuku's house, where I met his wife Gift and Dumiso Dabengwa, ZPRA's head of intelligence and a member of Zimbabwe's High Command. Dabengwa's father George had been a farmer at the Gwatemba Native Purchase Area block near Dadaya. Gwatemba was a rare set-up in the former Rhodesia where blacks were allowed to purchase property and hold title. During school and then university vacations, I sometimes worked in the general dealer store and postal agency my father ran on the ranch and we used to handle mail for Gwatemba. One day, George Dabengwa came in while I was on duty and lingered to speak to me. Our local community held him in the highest esteem, and I was honoured by his company. But then he said he was feeling sad, as he had just heard that his son Dumiso had been arrested.

'What for?' I asked.

He looked at me in what seemed to be bewilderment. 'I thought you knew about politics,' he said gently and, without another word, quietly walked away, leaving my mind in turmoil. If the son of a man such as Dabengwa had been arrested because of the political situation, then what should people like me be doing?

That day at the Masukus, when I first met Dumiso, I didn't tell him of this exchange, but some time later I did. I said how proud his father had obviously been of him.

'Are you sure?' asked Dumiso. 'I didn't know.'

Masuku had arranged that I would go to Lido the next day with Nyathi. I mentioned that the men at Woody Glen had seemed very glum and on edge, and I wondered if my proposed visit shouldn't first be cleared with the people involved. Dumiso immediately offered to accompany us and introduce me to the men.

The next morning we set off with Sam Moyo, deputy head of Nitram, Aaron Ndabambi from the Zapu welfare department, and his colleagues Angeline Masuku and Eunice Ndlovu, both of whom I had met in Zambia two years before while visiting Zapu's Victory Camp for women and children outside Lusaka. Our escort then had been 'Bright Light', who requested that, on my return to London, I should send him a pair of jeans. I hadn't. When next I met Bright Light, the guerrilla, in Zimbabwe, he had become the civilian Darlington Zikhali, but was still pained about the non-delivery of the requested jeans.

Lido was on the way to the airport. To get there, as if to rub salt into wounds, there was a turn from the main road into a street named Smith. Although not expected, we were most formally welcomed by the commander in charge, Comrade Rice. He was a young man with a burned face and one eye. He wore a mild green uniform and had, it seemed, made for himself quite an attractive eye patch.

In Bulawayo's bright sunlight the situation didn't look as bad as it really was. There were just over 200 men at Lido, another 200 having been placed with relatives until a permanent abode was found. Groups sat around, some individuals seemingly withdrawn and alone. Only one little cluster was playing a game with bottle tops on a piece of cardboard.

There were bizarre signs throughout the former hotel. At the entrance were the warnings *Right of Admission Reserved* and *No persons under 17 allowed to enter licensed premises.* At the exit was the admonition *Don't forget the beer! LION LAGER!*

The building was crammed with beds arranged side by side, one thin mattress and a blanket on each, no sheets or pillows. Discipline was obviously good, as the place was clean and tidy. Electricity had been cut because of non-payment, which meant the men had to cook outside, and firewood was a problem. One of the men said he could no longer help with the cooking. Stirring a huge pot of sadza over the open fire one day, he had found that one of his legs was melting.

There was no hot water and no option but to go to bed when darkness fell. The men had been there for more than a year and conditions were deteriorating daily. Food was the greatest problem. Since they had all received their terminal demobilisation payment, rations from the Department of Social Welfare had stopped and they now depended on whatever could be found for them by Zapu. In the mornings they had a cup of tea without sugar and milk, and then they ate sadza twice a day, sometimes with cabbage and occasionally pork. The pork, more leftovers brought back from Zambia, came in tiny tins from Yugoslavia and was most unappetising. The men also had nothing to do. The sewerage system had been vastly overloaded, Lido was now a serious health hazard and the Bulawayo city council wanted to close it down.

After our tour of inspection, the men assembled around little concrete tables in the former beer garden. It was obviously a great joy for them to see Dabengwa, and they listened intently to what he had to say. Neither he nor Masuku had been to Lido before, and Dabengwa was shocked by what he found. He spoke with quiet dignity, his hallmark, and promised the men that their plight would be addressed. He said the government had not responded to their needs as well as had been hoped, that Zapu had not been as aware as it should have been that the men were not being properly catered for, and that everyone had just assumed, wrongly, that the Department of Social Services was looking after them.

It became clear why they wanted to continue living together as a group. Not only had they survived the horrors of war together, but their continued comradeship was vital to their well-being and any happiness that might yet come their way. Of those listening to Dabengwa, one very young man had no arms, another no legs, and yet another looked as if he had one eye, but, when he stood to ask a question, it became evident that the remaining eye was blind. They needed each other to help feed, clothe and clean themselves. Most had been bombed in Angola and Zambia and quite a number had been burned with something like napalm. Some, like Comrade Klaus, who had a jacket over his shoulders, looked all right, but when he moved, I spotted something white at the end of his left arm and realised it was a little plastic hand.

When Dabengwa introduced me, we learned that when they were bombed in Angola, a group of the men had had in their possession a copy of a book I had written in 1972, *The Right to Say No*, and so they said they felt they knew me. I was made to feel warmly welcome. I explained the background of the Zimbabwe Project and that we had been asked to assist the ex-combatants. We needed ideas from them and then would try to get the necessary funds to put their ideas into practice. I hoped that Dabengwa's Sindebele translation was more inspiring than what I actually said.

I promised that when they had land, we would provide further education and training in practical skills for those who wanted them. Dabengwa had already said that while the Zimbabwe Project would not be able to help with the purchase of land, it would help in all other ways. I was anxious to qualify the word 'all'. I knew that Dabengwa had been to see Sydney Sekeremayi, the Minister of Lands, Resettlement and Rural Development, and Emmerson Mnangagwa, the Minister of State (Security) in the prime minister's office, about demobilisation and, except for the question of land, had been referred by both to the Zimbabwe Project. The knowledge of their expectations made me feel quite faint.

Time passed, the people at Lido weighed heavily on my mind and, seeking solutions, I discussed their plight with anyone I could think of who might be able to help. One thing was certain. The Zimbabwe Project could not contemplate purchasing land for anyone. It also became clear that Zapu would not be able to raise enough money to buy the land at Esigodini. Eventually Dabengwa, Masuku and Nyathi came up with a possible solution. Nitram was in the process of acquiring a farm called Ascot outside Bulawayo for intensive cattle fattening. It was 4000 acres in extent and Nitram was prepared to offer 1000 acres to the people from Lido. The idea was put to them, and they were overjoyed.

I was asked to join Dabengwa, Sam Moyo, Angeline Masuku and five of the war-wounded to walk around Ascot, choose 1000 acres and start planning what would be needed. I hoped we could get emergency funding from the EEC to erect ablution blocks and that, between all men of good will, as it were, we could find enough tents to resettle the men as quickly as possible. And so with great enthusiasm we set off on our tour of Ascot.

The property was a piece of scrubby, sandy veld about thirty kilometres from Bulawayo. It would be fine as a cattle feedlot, but as a potential home it was heartbreaking. First we drove all over the flat semi-desert. Then we walked. As we trudged further and further, people fell silent and the sound of artificial legs clunking over the dry, hard, sandy ground seemed ever louder. Eventually we called a halt and looked at each other. There was really nothing to say, as this was all that was on offer. But before any planning could take place, adequate water would have to be found. Borehole experts would have to survey the entire property and decide where best to start drilling; that decision in itself, said Dabengwa, would determine the choice of the 1000 acres.

During the war my parents had acquired a tranquil house in Bulawayo's suburbs. It had belonged to Alan Ritson, who, in the late 1960s, emigrated from Britain seeking a place beyond the reach of the law and finding it in Ian Smith's post-UDI Rhodesia. On his flight from London, he carried as hand luggage a small suitcase illegally stuffed with sterling, with which he bought a farm, Tsomo, between Dadaya and Bulawayo. A veterinarian by profession, he became a successful cattle rancher. He was colour-blind when it came to people and lived accordingly. This, combined with his North Country accent, a limp and his unusual physique, resembling that of a carrot – broad shoulders tapering into little legs – made him highly unpopular with the Rhodesian authorities, whom he delighted in teasing.

He became a valued friend and, in 1972, when Standard Bank threatened to sell our ranch as my father had been detained and was unable to conduct normal business, Alan leapt to my mother's rescue and the ranch was saved. Eventually the strain of living in Rhodesia as the war escalated became too great and Alan started thinking of moving to Brazil. He left it too late. He was tied up one day and bayoneted to death by a group of black men who were probably from the Selous Scouts, although he had assumed they were ZANLA. My father wept when Feluso, Alan's right-hand man who had been present at the killing, told him that Alan had begged for his life, screaming that he was a friend of Garfield Todd.

My parents were the executors of Alan's estate. When they looked over his strange and lovely Bulawayo house, they decided to buy it as a haven in town, despite the pub built into a corner of the lounge, the guns decorating the walls, the soundproof games room and underwater seating in the pool. From the 1980s they started normalising the house, planning for the day they would leave the ranch and retire. They were beginning to spend an increasing amount of time in Bulawayo, as was I, with the Zimbabwe Project spreading its wings from Harare.

When I returned to their house that day and told them what a terrible place Ascot was, they were quiet and distressed and they, too, started trying to think of a solution. Within a month they had found one. They decided to donate a corner of their ranch, 3000 acres, to the men from Lido.

The news was received by the Zimbabwe Project, let alone the men, with relief and joy, and I took Sister Janice McLaughlin to have a look at the land. I had grown fond of her during her association with the Zimbabwe Project and enjoyed her company. She was a vivacious, slender and very popular woman with bright brown eyes and a startling but natural Afro hairstyle. 'Now that's the kind of nun I like,' Joe Culverwell, the Deputy Minister of Education, once said to me about her. Sister Janice had entered the Maryknoll Order in the United States in 1961 and, before joining the Justice and Peace Commission in Rhodesia, worked for a time in Kenya. Her parents from Pittsburgh had visited her there, and she told me with delight that when asked on entering the country if he had any dangerous weapons to declare, her father had replied: 'Only my daughter.'

We drove through the area slowly and Sister Janice exclaimed with pleasure. I knew the land quite well from walking over it at various times of my life, but I had forgotten how beautiful it was, bounded by the generous Ngesi River and bisected by two little streams, which, though it was now hot October, were still flowing. The area bordered the Runde communal lands and lay at the foot of Wedza Mountain, where the current Chief Wedza still lived. This had been one of the last strongholds of the insurgents during the Matabele Rebellion, when it was crushed by Baden-Powell with his Maxim gun. I told Sister Janice of his drawing of this mountain, with, in the foreground, two cooking pots and a tiny girl. The ironic caption was 'Booty from Wedza'.

In October 1981, Mugabe toured the nation, emphasising his belief in the urgent necessity of a one-party state. This attitude was not popular in all circles. I heard someone in Bulawayo laugh and say, 'Why doesn't he come here, say he wants a one-party state and see what reception he gets?' Then immediately the person became serious and said, 'But if he comes and gets a bad reception, then we won't get any land.'

Joshua Nkomo, demoted by Mugabe in January from the important portfolio of Home Affairs to that of Public Service, and then demoted again to Minister without Portfolio, had put his position on a one-party state to 40 000 supporters at Bulawayo's White City Stadium on 1 June. He said a one-party state was an ideal situation, but that it must not be introduced without the unanimous agreement of Zimbabwe's entire population. He warned against a forced or manipulated 'unity', and said the existence of many political parties, races and languages should not cloud the fact that Zimbabweans were one nation. 'There are fifty-two dialects spoken, but we are all one people,' he said.

In planning the Bulawayo leg of his trip, Mugabe had apparently requested that Nkomo accompany him. Nkomo had replied that, as prime minister,

Mugabe could tour any part of the country on his own. The intermediary had said, 'But he wants you to be with him.' Nkomo responded: 'He has been through the rest of the country without me. Why does he want me now?'

'Well,' said the intermediary, 'he likes having with him the members of parliament from the district he is visiting.'

'I see,' said Nkomo. 'But the problem is that I am not a member of parliament for Matabeleland. I am a member of parliament for the Midlands, and the prime minister has already toured the Midlands without me.'

So it was announced that Mugabe would tour Matabeleland in the company of Enos Nkala, founder member of Zanu, now Minister of Finance and a declared enemy of Joshua Nkomo.

There had already been warnings about the possible dire consequences of the increasingly acrimonious speeches made by politicians such as Nkala. At a recent commission of inquiry into violence between members of ZANLA and ZPRA, Brigadier Charles Grey of the National Army, and formerly of ZPRA, had refuted Nkala's claims that Zapu/ZPRA was tribalistic, pointing out that at least 70 per cent of its recruits during the war had been Shona-speaking. He warned of the dangers implicit in hate speeches made by politicians 'inciting one faction and infuriating the other'.

In July, for example, Nkala had told a Zanu (PF) rally in Bulawayo that the party's task 'from now on is to crush Joshua Nkomo and forget about him. I want to declare here that Joshua Nkomo and his group are in government by the grace of Zanu (PF). They contributed in their own small way and we have given them a share proportional to their contribution. If they now want more than their small share then we shall have to tell them that they will not have any share at all.'

I happened to be in Bulawayo on Saturday 24 October, the prime minister's big day in the city when he addressed rallies at both Ntabazinduna and Barbourfields. I thought God was being infinitely kind to both the prime minister and to those in Matabeleland who didn't want a one-party state. Against any reasonable prediction, it rained most of the day, so should the reception accorded to the prime minister fall short of expectations, both sides could blame the weather.

But I found an all-pervading anxiety about 5 Brigade, which was being set up by the North Koreans, and was told that the brigade had to start each day with a salute to 'MUGABE!' An acquaintance of mine just back from Libya was in poor circumstances and asked me to find out how he could join 5 Brigade. I asked someone who would know what qualifications one had to have, and was told (1) absolute loyalty to Prime Minister Mugabe; and (2) absolute loyalty to the ruling party, Zanu (PF). I asked whether the brigade was to be used in Mozambique to support Machel against the resurgent Renamo movement. He said no, it was designed to be used inside Zimbabwe. When I asked him whom the brigade was going to be used against, he looked absolutely blank and changed the subject.

In August, Prime Minister Mugabe had revealed that 106 North Koreans were in Zimbabwe to train 'a new force'. People had no clue about the secret deal that had been made with North Korea less than six months after Zimbabwe's independence. In October 1980, Mugabe had led a delegation of twenty people, including Education Minister Dzingai Mutumbuka and Mrs Joice Teurai Ropa Nhongo, Minister of Youth, Sport and Recreation, to the sixth congress of the Korean Republic's ruling Workers' Communist Party. He and President Kim Il Sung signed a treaty of friendship, cooperation and general agreement. Within that agreement lay the seeds of what was to emerge as 5 Brigade, a political killing machine answerable only to Mugabe, its communication equipment impenetrable by that of Zimbabwe's regular forces.

Before enough planning could be done on moving men from Lido to Hokonui Ranch, the press reported in December that Senator Todd had given 300 hectares of land to the government for the disabled; the government was very grateful and the Department of Social Services was working out how best the land could be used.

This seemed to have been a well-intentioned announcement by Minister Kangai, who said he hoped others would follow suit and donate land to his ministry. However, it was factually wrong on practically every point. The area was 3000 acres, not 300 hectares; the land had not been given to the government but to the Lido men themselves, who would form their own legal entity and hold the title deeds. But the report was useful in that, however hard everyone was already working on this scheme, it galvanised all concerned to work much harder and faster.

A team from Lido had inspected, fallen in love with and named the land Vukuzenzele, 'Wake up and do it yourself'. Through the good offices of Sister Janice, the impressive Paul Themba Nyathi had been enticed to the Zimbabwe Project from Kushinga-Phikelela Agricultural College, and the short-term future of Vukuzenzele was entrusted to him. An advance party of ten of Lido's most physically able men set up camp in tents and started stumping trees and clearing land by hand for a vegetable garden. Lookout Masuku visited them to lend encouragement, painting a word picture of what Vukuzenzele would come to mean, and promising the weary, raggedy little group of disabled that 'One day you will wake in the morning to the cry of a baby. Then you will know that indeed this is your home.'

Time had never raced by so fast. All of a sudden it was Christmas Eve and I was back on Hokonui Ranch, looking from the stoep of our house up the Ngesi River across Dadaya to Wedza Mountain and Vukuzenzele, thinking of this first Christmas on their new land for at least some of the men from Lido. By 6.30 the next morning, I had driven the ten kilometres to their little camp.

I found the fire going, water boiling, men wandering around sleepily and the scruffy little chicken they had been given a few weeks earlier by the local people over the fence in the Runde communal lands already turning into a beautiful cock, crowing tentatively. I handed over some pockets of oranges and made to leave, saying I would see them later. But they wouldn't let me go. On went the shirts, out came their three benches and, although everyone seemed very happy, Robert Mkize seemed transported. I knew that his wife in Bulawayo was expecting a baby, and asked if there was any news. He beamed. His son had been born and had been named Vukuzenzele.

The men offered me tea and we sat and feasted together. There was milk and sugar for the tea, and they each had two slices of white bread stuck together with jam. They presented me with four slices. Paul Themba Nyathi emerged from his tent. He had been hoping for a lie-in but had been disturbed by my car, and so he joined us, laughing and joking. He had established excellent working relationships with the men, demonstrated most visibly by the blisters on his hands. Paul told me later that the men could still not quite believe that the land was theirs. 'I've never owned land before,' one of them had said. 'Are you quite sure that it's all ours? Even the trees?'

The next day I went back at noon to take photos. The triangle of benches was reassembled. A plate of rice, potatoes and meat was presented to me. Then, wandering after the cattle that had passed by the tents came a small boy of about ten. He looked at us from behind a bush. Alexander Mkwananzi, a tall, rangy man with a huge grin, called him over. He came slowly, but politely. Alexander was wearing trousers and a long-sleeved shirt, so didn't look much damaged. He was affectionate and put his arm around the little boy's shoulders, but when there was no response, the men realised the child spoke Shona, not the Sindebele they were using. It was further discovered, when he was given two oranges, that he had a bird in his left hand. There was an anxious yell from some metres away, which he answered reassuringly, prompting the appearance of another boy, who had cloudy eyes and suppurating ears. Paul Themba Nyathi examined him and then turned to me, frowning. I knew exactly what he was thinking. Not only did we need a clinic for the men from Lido, but also for the local people. Eventually, after friendship seemed well and truly established, the men turned back to conversation. The cattle moved away. The boys appeared to leave, but, when I drove away, I noticed that they were behind another bush, staring entranced at the men.

What a wonderful December that was, with the joyous arrival very early one morning at the Callinicos home in Harare of an exuberant Lookout Masuku in full uniform. He had come to announce to John and Aelda Callinicos, my husband Richard and me the news of the birth of his son Zakheleni to his wife Gift in Bulawayo.

CHAPTER 5

Bulawayo

THE ZIMBABWE PROJECT OPENED A SECOND OFFICE ON
1 February 1982. About 3 000 people had been demobilised in Bulawayo
during January and we were pressured by ex-combatants to establish
ourselves in the city. Our doors opened exactly eight months after we had
formally started work in Harare.

We were in Room 30 on the third floor of Mimosa House, Ninth Avenue,
a fascinating building, rather like Old Shell House where we had our offices
in Harare, and filled with just as motley an array of people. A fellow tenant
on our floor was the Council for Disability; we were next door to Nitram,
and within two blocks of the offices that the Demobilisation Directorate
was in the process of setting up. We had one cut-off telephone, dramatic
tiger-skin-patterned wallpaper and no equipment of any kind. But both
Nitram and the Catholic Commission for Social Service and Development
had offered to lend us furniture.

Although we were moving swiftly, it had taken time to establish the
office in Mimosa House, so I was surprised on the night of 31 January to
receive a frantic telephone call from our administrator John Conradie,
imploring me not to go ahead with opening an office in Bulawayo. I was
upset and perplexed but tried to be gentle, knowing his painful antipathy to
Joshua Nkomo in particular and thus to Zapu, and thinking that he must
have had a sudden rush of revulsion at the thought of us moving into what
he might consider Nkomo territory.

John's aversion had been acquired or reinforced during his long years
of imprisonment in the company of Zanu's Maurice Nyagumbo, who
had become a close friend and whose book, *With the People*, he had edited.
Nyagumbo was now Minister of Mines. I said only that we were too far
advanced to consider pulling back. We had, for example, already hired Albert
Ngwenya to run the office. How could we pull the rug from under his feet
just a few hours before he was meant to start his first proper job in ages?

I wondered later if someone had informed John that the sky was about
to fall in.

Albert had entered our lives through Lido. While developments were going ahead apace at Vukuzenzele, where dormitories and ablution blocks were being erected under the guidance of Gijima Mpofu and my father, it would still take time for the bulk of the men to move from Lido to their new home. I had sought help from the CSSD regarding food, payment of water bills and general support. Father Thomas Peeters, head of CSSD in Bulawayo, was heavily involved in caring for returned refugees, such as the hundreds of children who had been under the care of Zapu in Zambia and had since been handed over to the good offices of the Catholic Church in Matabeleland. He was harassed but very positive, and he introduced me to Albert.

Albert was tall, thin and, just like his totem *ngwenya*, the crocodile, perpetually grinning. I explained that the Zimbabwe Project needed help with Lido. On the day we met, I took him to Lido to introduce him to the men. To our mutual astonishment, his arrival was met with loud acclamation. Many of the disabled had recognised him as a fellow survivor of the massacre of 351 inmates at Zapu's Freedom Camp, north of Lusaka, which had been bombed by the Rhodesians during the war.

The following day Paul Themba Nyathi came in from Vukuzenzele and met Albert. The three of us spent time together, and then we took Paul for a medical appointment in a busy part of town and waited outside the surgery for him. I was driving a beautiful little white Citroën Club, which the Zimbabwe Project had just acquired. With its French number plates still in place, it attracted a lot of attention. I was in the driver's seat and Albert was sitting behind me. Many people came up to greet him, to enquire about his well-being and ask what he was up to, reclined in the back of this smart new car.

Albert waved his hand graciously, laughing and repeating to his friends, 'New car, new chauffeur,' while he told me part of his story.

He had been an ordained priest working in a remote rural area until forced to flee to Botswana during the war. He underwent military training and became a political commissar for ZPRA. After the ceasefire he came back and went to an assembly point. As soon as he could, he returned to Bulawayo and, together with two friends, went to the Catholic cathedral to say he was ready to resume his duties. The three men were wearing the only clothing they had, camouflage uniform. Albert said the nuns and others who came out of the diocesan offices started shaking, some of them imploring the men not to take revenge on them. He was stunned, and repeated that he had returned to resume his duties and had no revenge to take. At that point,

Bulawayo's Bishop Karlen intervened, coming to greet them and inviting them to tea. There were big, wide cups, but the nun who was serving tea was shaking so badly that she couldn't pour the liquid into the cups, so they were invited to do so themselves. Then Albert's two friends left and he spoke to the bishop alone.

The bishop asked him what his military training in Zambia had consisted of.

'We were taught how to run up hills and how to run down hills,' Albert replied.

The bishop persisted, and said he knew that Albert had then been taken to Europe. What had he been taught there?

'We were taught how to run up snow and how to run down snow,' Albert said.

The bishop advised him to return to the assembly point, and said when they were ready for him to resume his calling as a priest, they would summon him. They never did, but they had given him temporary work at CSSD, which was about to come to an end.

Albert told me about the bombing of Freedom Camp. He said most of the people there were young refugees, but there was a hospital for soldiers and also some other military types like him around. A lot of the victims had been electrocuted. A major power line running across the camp was hit and fell on people, 'and afterwards,' said Albert, 'there they were, lying dead and looking perfect'.

He concluded by saying that there was nothing in the world he would like more than being able to work for the Zimbabwe Project and serve his comrades.

One week after we opened our Bulawayo office, Prime Minister Mugabe announced that arms caches had been found on Zapu properties, most notably Ascot farm and Hampton Ranch near Gweru. Within a fortnight a declaration was published in the *Government Gazette* banning Nitram under the Unlawful Organisations Act. All its assets and subsidiaries, such as Woody Glen and Nest Egg, were seized.

Troops were moved onto all properties associated with Zapu, including the Lido Hotel. Great play was made in the press of the 'discovery' of military vehicles at Nest Egg and medical supplies at Woody Glen, the inference being that these were important components in a plot to overthrow the government. The ZPRA archives were seized from Nest Egg and never recovered.

Mugabe said of Nkomo: 'The only way to deal with a snake is to strike and destroy its head,' and on 17 February he sacked Nkomo and most other Zapu members from his cabinet. On 11 March, Dumiso Dabengwa, Lieutenant General Lookout Masuku, Isaac Nyathi and others were arrested, and, like Morgan Tsvangirai, Welshman Ncube and others many years later, eventually charged with treason. Zakheleni Masuku was less than three months old and would never have the chance to know his father.

When Nitram was banned, its offices next door to ours were taken over by the Central Intelligence Organisation (CIO), and we swiftly got out of their way and moved to Southampton House. We had already borrowed Nitram furniture that the CIO didn't know about and which we kept. Under their very noses, Isaac Nyathi's secretary, Fildah Siwela, brought us their typewriter. We kept her too.

We had opened our Bulawayo office in the nick of time. With the closure of Nitram and the disruption of PF Zapu offices, there were few places for the ex-combatants to turn to for help, especially the inmates at Lido, who had depended on Nitram to provide their firewood and general services. By now a steady stream of construction material was going from Bulawayo to Hokonui Ranch, and just a couple of days after Nitram was closed down, a truck taking rafters from PG Timbers for the dormitories at Vukuzenzele picked up a full return load of firewood cut by the men for Lido. This exercise was repeated twice and saw Lido through until all the men had moved to their farm.

External agencies were becoming increasingly interested in our work, and Michael Behr's boss from Oxfam, Brian Walker, had visited Lido and requested us to provide recreational materials for the men, which we did. Oxfam was a major donor, so we couldn't demur and say this wasn't a top priority for us. The results were instantaneous and positive. Two football teams were formed, and the dozen or so people in wheelchairs spent hours absorbed in playing cards. The diversions helped them cope with the heavy army presence. The soldiers were invited to join in the card games, which they did with enthusiasm, and, unlikely as it sounded, I was assured that within the first week of occupation, Lido had the satisfaction of beating the army twice at football. Things were going well at Vukuzenzele. By the end of February they were already reaping vegetables from their garden and had built an ingenious oven in an anthill, where they baked bread. As well as sending firewood to their fellows in Bulawayo, they were now also sending vegetables and bread rolls.

On other fronts, the Zimbabwe Project's work was escalating. That month I wrote to Michael Behr to say that the Ministry of Lands and Resettlement had approached us to take over five farms on each of which approximately 200 ex-combatants would be resettled. Government would provide the land, which had already been purchased with funds from the British government, and all other costs would be borne by the Zimbabwe Project.

It was an enormous undertaking and we needed a reaction from Oxfam. The offer was the result of considerable work behind the scenes by John Conradie with Moven Mahachi, who, at independence, had been appointed Deputy Minister of Lands and Resettlement. Moven, like Didymus Mutasa, had been a product of the Cold Comfort Farm society, and it would be no exaggeration to say that Didymus, who had become the speaker of parliament, and John himself had been greatly influenced by Guy Clutton-Brock, whom they loved. I was not keen on the government's proposal, so I left this venture for John to pursue while I concentrated on other areas.

In my experience, the last thing most ex-combatants wanted was to toil on the land. Like other young men, they wanted jobs in town and an assured income each month that would lead to bright lights, cars, girls and fun. But they were seriously disadvantaged in the race for work, as most were barely educated. The closest they would get to what they wanted was by pooling their demobilisation allowances and buying businesses such as butcheries, bottle stores, restaurants and general dealerships, most of which eventually collapsed.

There were exceptions to what I had found to be a general aversion to agriculture, but they were few and far between. One was Vukuzenzele. Another was Simukai Collective Cooperative, a group of about eighty men and women who were pooling their monthly allowances and trying to buy a commercial farm near Salisbury. Meanwhile they had rented a derelict farm near the airport on which half of their members were raising chickens for sale in town. Unfortunately for them, they were all former ZPRA, and although they no longer had anything to do with Zapu or Nitram, when misfortune fell, it fell also on Simukai.

The army moved onto their land and, as it was near the airport, started digging for anti-aircraft missiles. When Andrew Nyathi, their chairman, came in despair to inform me, I told him the story of an ex-combatant accused of stealing gold, who was arrested and jailed. The gold was not recovered. He received a letter from his wife bewailing her misfortune. He wrote back, telling her not to panic. If she looked in their field she would find something that would make her happy. The following week she visited him at the prison to say something strange had happened. The police had arrived at their home with a team of convicts, who dug up the entire field but found nothing. Her husband grinned at her and said, 'So, now go and plant mealies.' But of course Andrew wasn't amused. Life for Simukai was just too grim.

Around this time I received a visit from a couple new to Zimbabwe, Paul Staal and Helene Gans, representing the Dutch agency Novib. They wanted to learn about the Zimbabwe Project's work, and I showed them a report containing a reference to Simukai that I had compiled for donors before the army invasion.

'It is difficult for me to try and explain to you the tremendous joy we feel so often in our work. But let me try, through the words of someone else. There is a little cooperative at present consisting of about 80 young people, three quarters of them women, trying to buy 3 000 acres of land near Salisbury from their demobilisation allowances. In the meanwhile they have rented a long-abandoned farm and half of them have moved into derelict buildings full of rats and bees. They have inherited the deserted labour force of about 100 men, women and children. While they don't have the money even to buy an aspirin for their headaches, they have established a school – with no equipment except the knowledge they themselves can pass on – for the children. We help where we can and they wrote a letter to us last week, which ended: *Please keep your hand with us. Long live Z-P!*'

Paul and Helene said this was just the kind of group they would like to meet, and I offered to take them to Simukai then and there. When we drove to the farm, they were appalled by the roadblocks and the rough demeanour of the hostile and suspicious soldiers. On our return to my office, where we were to discuss what might be done for Simukai, Paul said to me straight: 'You knew before we went that there would be roadblocks and soldiers, didn't you?'

'Yes,' I admitted.

'And you didn't warn us?'

'No.'

'Why not?'

'I thought you might not want to get involved.' Then I apologised, most sincerely, to both of them. 'I am so sorry. I underestimated you.'

I had indeed. They became important friends and Novib assumed an ever more vital role in the continuing work of the Zimbabwe Project.

Another new friend for Simukai and the Zimbabwe Project was Piers Nicolle, a very successful farmer from Banket. One day he walked into the office and straight up to my desk, proclaiming at the top of his voice: 'I'm a third-generation Zimbabwean. I'm a Nicolle and I know you're a Todd.'

It transpired that his uncle was Hostes Nicolle, a forthright former Secretary for Internal Affairs, who, in 1971, had electrified British diplomats planning a commission of inquiry under Lord Pearce. 'I told these British officials in very plain language that they were stark staring mad, and I forecast to them the implications of this stupid plan.'

The commission had been set up to test the reaction of the people of Rhodesia to proposals from the British government for a deal between them and the Smith regime, which, if accepted, would have seen independence conferred before the attainment of majority rule. The proposals were rejected.

Piers proved to be just as direct. He had come to tell me that he accepted that the Rhodesians had lost the war, but that he was going to stay in the country forever, even if, at the end of the day, it meant living in a hut and cooking on three stones. But he didn't want to live in a hut and cook on three stones, so he had come to find out about agricultural cooperatives, which, he understood, the government saw as the way forward. If he could, he would like to help make them successful. We introduced him to Simukai and he proved a valuable ally, immediately training three members as tractor drivers, providing seed and ploughing land without charge for the first year. From there on he correctly insisted on a semi-commercial relationship and charged Z$22 per hectare for ploughing.

Piers had greatly startled me by saying that my office used to be that of Hostes Nicolle, and that I had my desk in exactly the same place as Nicolle had his. As time passed, I wondered what the uncle would have thought of the development of his nephew. One day Piers bounced in and said he had come for my congratulations. He had become a member of Zanu (PF).

'How could they possibly have you?' I asked.

'Easy,' he replied. 'I went to their office in Banket and said I wanted to join. The lady said someone would come and see me. Two men did. I told them I wanted to become a member, but that first they must know three things that would not change. One, I am a Christian. Two, I have a big mouth and I don't know how to keep it shut. Three, whatever they do to me and even if I have to live in a hut and cook on three stones, I will never leave this country. So the leader of the two put out his hand, we shook, and he said, "Welcome to Zanu (PF), Mr Nicolle."'

The next time I saw Piers, he told me that, in line with the philosophy of his party and government, a workers' committee had been established on his farm. He was very proud to have been elected the first chairman.

It was estimated that about two thirds of those demobilised were former ZANLA, which meant, as we hardly ever came across former Rhodesians, that a third were former ZPRA. Our work roughly reflected the same ratio, so about one third of the projects we were involved in were now in trouble with the state.

One of the groups we had assisted was the New Tone Sound Band, some of whose members had spent time on death row during the war. Their leader, Abel Sithole, had been part of joint ZPRA/ANC initiatives, which had included Chris Hani and were crushed in the Wankie area. This had provided a pretext for the involvement of more South Africans on the Rhodesian side. Sithole had performed as a musician for many years as far afield as Tanzania, raising funds for southern African liberation movements. When he came out of jail at Zimbabwe's independence, he was ready to start all over again, and the Zimbabwe Project contributed to the cost of instruments for his new band.

The band performed at Bulawayo's Castle Arms, where people were being trained on the job as gardeners, waiters and everything else associated with the hotel business. This was another venture acquired by Nitram, another venture I had visited, another venture now banned and closed down by the state. Alas for Sithole and his colleagues, on the date that Nitram was proscribed, they had left their instruments overnight at the hotel, and so they were seized along with every other item in the hotel: plate, knife, fork and glass.

Some of these properties were placed by the state in the hands of a liquidator, whom I rang one day, hoping to retrieve the musical instruments. I could tell that he was a middle-aged white, but I hadn't met him and I was astonished that, when I explained what I wanted, he started shouting loudly at me over the telephone, abusing me for trying to assist people who had been 'plotting a coup'.

'Hang on, Mr Fraser,' I said. 'This is no good. I'm coming to see you.' Which I did. I found a stout and frantic gentleman with a very red face, who I feared might be on the verge of a heart attack. He agreed to talk to me, and I sat down with him. Then I feared that he might burst into tears. He was about to leave for Ascot, where the cattle were being rounded up for auction. He was terrified that this would offend the coup plotters, and that they might shoot him dead.

I was able to give him a different slant on the whole affair and he calmed down and felt better. But we never retrieved the instruments. The group had to start all over again, which they did initially as the Black Merchants, and then, eventually, nearly twenty years later, when as geriatrics they hit world fame, The Cool Crooners.

CHAPTER 6

Meeting the army commander

O N SATURDAY 12 FEBRUARY 1983, THE BULAWAYO *CHRONICLE* reported that Sydney Sekeremayi, Minister of State (Defence) in the prime minister's office, had said that 5 Brigade was going to operate in Matabeleland for a long time. The headline was 'Five Brigade Here to Stay'.

Not all readers could have comprehended the report, but rumours had been mounting about the commission of terrible deeds by armed forces in different parts of the country, particularly Matabeleland – rumours that are like ghastly nightmares from which you struggle but don't quite manage to awake. Then Henry Karlen, the Catholic Bishop of Matabeleland, telephoned my father to inform him that the state was perpetrating atrocities. People were being terrorised, starved and butchered and their property destroyed. Bishop Karlen said he had tried without success to make an appointment with the prime minister to tell him what was happening and to get him to stop it. The Catholics had been assembling evidence from their network of churches, schools and hospitals throughout the rural areas. The bishop asked if he could send a copy of these documents to my father and whether, as a senator appointed by Mugabe, he could seek an appointment for Karlen and others with the prime minister.

My father said he would do whatever he could. Karlen would courier the material to me and I would hold it for my father, who was due in Harare shortly.

The documents were delivered to my office on Thursday 17 February. I rang my father to report their arrival and he gave me permission to look at them, which I immediately did. Then I wished I hadn't. The events chronicled were far, far worse than I could ever have imagined. It seemed that state armed forces – whether only 5 Brigade or others too – had gone berserk in an orgy of violence against defenceless civilians. I felt so horrified, sick and faint that I longed to go straight home to bed. But I had an appointment early that evening with a representative of an overseas agency that could benefit the Zimbabwe Project. I couldn't cancel.

We met at the Quill Club, a haunt of journalists and others who relished informed gossip, in the Ambassador Hotel near parliament. We had an adequate if short conversation and then I excused myself. As I was leaving, someone hailed me. I turned and there was Justin Nyoka, now government's Director of Information, waving at me and calling, 'Judy! Come and say hello!' He was with two other men, one of whom I didn't know. When I joined them, he was introduced to me as Brigadier Agrippah Mutambara, head of the Zimbabwe National Army Staff College. The other was Lieutenant General Rex Nhongo, the army commander.

I shook hands with them, sat down and we exchanged courtesies. Justin bought me a bitterly cold Castle lager. Bishop Karlen's documents started burning in my handbag. I knew I would never have an opportunity like this again, and steeled myself to speak to Nhongo.

I suppose Bishop Karlen had thought that perhaps Mugabe did not know what was going on. Perhaps I thought that Nhongo didn't know either. I said how wonderful it was that we were having this chance meeting, as I had information about army activities in Matabeleland that he might be unaware of.

The noise around us was increasing as more people came into the club, and I could tell he was straining to hear me. I persevered and said it appeared as if the armed forces were out of control; that atrocities were being committed and that mass graves were being filled with the corpses of helpless citizens. Then I fell silent with terror. I had been noticing huge trickles of sweat pouring down Justin's temples. He was mopping his face and saying, 'Judy, keep quiet! Judy, keep quiet!' But Brigadier Mutambara intervened and said, 'No, let her speak. She may know things we don't. Let us hear what she has to say.'

Nhongo was stuttering, whether in horror or anger, I couldn't tell. I learned later that the stutter was a normal part of his speech. People passing our table kept trying to greet him, and he waved them all away. He asked me for specific localities. I said I would find out for him. He said he was going to Matabeleland by helicopter the next day, and would send a car for me so that I could go with him and show him the mass graves. I said unfortunately I couldn't, as I had only heard about them and not seen them myself. But, I said, thinking of Bishop Karlen, I might be able to find someone else to accompany him. Certainly I would try to compile information for him about what appeared to be happening. I gave Nhongo my telephone number and said that if he really wanted someone to guide him, he should let me know as soon as possible and I would try to help. Then I said goodnight and slipped away.

Early the next morning, I telephoned Bishop Karlen and told him of my meeting with the army commander. I asked permission to copy all his documents for Nhongo. He was quiet and obviously troubled, but eventually said yes, as others, including my father, of course, had, or were about to, receive copies.

At about 9.30 I received a call from our reception area a floor below my office to say that someone from the army was waiting for me in a car down-stairs. I scribbled a note to Sister Janice McLaughlin, saying something like: *The Army Commander, Lt Gen Nhongo, has sent a car for me.* I put it in a sealed envelope and gave it to Morris Mtsambiwa in an adjacent office. I said calmly, without further explanation, that I was going out, and he must deliver the note if I wasn't back before our offices closed that afternoon.

On the street I found a very smart-looking Brigadier Mutambara in khaki uniform waiting for me. He opened the passenger door at the front of the olive-green army car, I climbed in and we drove away – to where or what my mind refused to consider. I greeted the brigadier and started talking, trying to act as if everything was normal. I said I had just been on the telephone to Bishop Karlen and had told him of my meeting with Nhongo and himself the previous evening. I said Bishop Karlen was the one who had compiled the information I had talked about, and that he had given me permission to copy all the documents for the army commander.

Mutambara seemed preoccupied. He was driving in the direction of Chikurubi Prison, and started talking about himself and the fact that he was divorcing his wife, who had been unfaithful to him, and preparing to marry someone else. He stopped at a bottle store, went in and bought a couple of bottles of beer and orange juice and then proceeded to a house, which, I think, was in the Chikurubi complex. A servant let us in, not looking at us. The brigadier led me into a bedroom, opened a bottle of beer for each of us, unstrapped his firearm in its holster, laid it on the bedside table next to my head, and proceeded. I did not resist. Before long the subjugation was over, he dropped me back at our offices and, in the words of Eddison Zvobgo, I tried to continue on my road precisely as if nothing had ever happened.

> *Should you fall, rise with grace, and without*
> *Turning to see who sees, continue on your road*
> *Precisely as if nothing had ever happened;*
> *For those who did not, the ditches became graves.*

I collected the unopened letter I had left with Morris and destroyed it. Then I made copies of Bishop Karlen's documents and drafted a covering letter to accompany them to Lieutenant General Nhongo, and now, also, to Brigadier Mutambara. After the weekend I contacted Mutambara, who had given me a card with his number. We met at the reception desk of the Ambassador Hotel. I handed over an envelope for Nhongo and one for Mutambara himself, each containing a complete set of Bishop Karlen's horrifying documents on death and destruction, my letter to Nhongo and a copy of it for the brigadier. Dated Monday 21 February, it read:

Lieutenant General Nhongo
Army Commander
Zimbabwe

Dear General

It was a privilege to talk to you and your friends at the Quill Club last Thursday evening, and to hear your views. My own strong feelings were based in part on evidence which I was not then authorised to pass on to you.

I now enclose a copy of a letter and reports compiled for the Prime Minister. I believe that Cdes Sekeremayi, Muzenda, Mnangagwa and perhaps others have also been given these copies. Bishop Karlen has given me permission now to give them to you. You can see for yourself the terrible suffering which they portray, if even half of these limited reports are accurate.

It seems to me that if, in the hunt for dissidents, we inflict such enormous damage on people who are Zimbabweans, and who are poor, weak, hungry and defenceless, all we will achieve is the creation of more dissidents forever. I believe that this policy can only harm Zimbabwe. I also believe that when Zimbabweans throughout the country learn what is happening, they will lose confidence in our Government and in our National Army.

When I hear of such damage to our people I find it very difficult to sleep at night, or to work during the day. But while I am not in the position to provide these tormented peasants with food, with comfort and with safety, at least I can pass on to you what news I have of them. I am sure that you are able to help provide the food and protection, and that the army can be redirected to healing and construction.

One of the things that frightens me most is to be told of the 'disappearance' of so many young men from the affected areas – people who have never been proved to be dissidents but who probably played a brave role in the struggle for Zimbabwe – their Zimbabwe as well as ours. Surely the way to 'deal' with dissidents is to establish first why they are dissidents, then to think of remedies? In other words, surely a political solution – perhaps then backed up by the military – is required rather than an intransigent military one which, in my humble opinion, cannot be a solution but which can breed only more violence, bitterness and grief.

Thank you for your attention.

Yours sincerely,
Judith Acton

There was no further reaction from either Nhongo or Mutambara. On the same Friday that I was collected by Mutambara, I unburdened myself to Professor Noel Galen, a retired American psychiatrist and dear friend who taught psychiatry at the University of Zimbabwe's medical school, but to absolutely no one else. Noel helped me a lot.

'Holy smoke!' he kept saying, his eyes widening with horror as the account proceeded. 'Holy SMOKE!' As the days passed, I also counted myself lucky to be alive.

Noel Galen and his wife Doris, who taught law at the university, had fallen in love with Zimbabwe and were endlessly fascinated with and increasingly appalled by unfolding events. One of Noel's students was the cabinet minister Dr Herbert Ushewokunze, whom he used to address in the American way, without the H. 'Erb', he called the minister.

I had first heard of Ushewokunze when he was a Zanu delegate at the Lancaster House conference and had assembled his many children in London. The Zimbabwe Project had been approached to provide maintenance for them. At the time, I sought information from one of the senior delegates, TG Silundika.

'Who is this man, Ushewokunze?' I asked. 'What is he like?'

Silundika considered the question carefully, and replied, 'He's a brilliant ...' and then searched for the right word. 'He's a brilliant delinquent!'

In Zimbabwe's first cabinet, Dr Ushewokunze of Zanu (PF) was appointed Minister of Health, and Tarcisius Malan George Silundika of PF Zapu was appointed Minister of Roads and Road Traffic, Posts and Telecommunications.

By the beginning of 1983, the Zimbabwe Project was receiving funding from fifteen organisations in ten different countries, including Britain,

Australia, West Germany, Canada and Switzerland. We had already assisted more than fifty cooperatives comprising some 2 000 people in the fields of agriculture, carpentry, manufacturing, retailing and entertainment throughout the country. Another seventeen cooperatives with a similar number of members were next in line for funding.

Our Harare staff had increased to ten, our Bulawayo staff to six and Morris Mtsambiwa, abandoning his medical studies, had become deputy director. We had launched a zesty little newspaper for the cooperatives, which Morris had named *Vanguard*. John Conradie had left Zimbabwe and returned to Britain in October 1982, from where he continued to produce the scholarly *Zimbabwe Project News Bulletin*, which was enthusiastically received by donor agencies, academics and policy-makers. He had trained a young Zimbabwean, Joel Vito, to replace him as administrator.

We were about to launch a massive scheme with the Canadian group Cuso for education and technical training in the cooperatives, but, in the meanwhile, were offering courses lasting three or six months in carpentry, welding, building, sewing, knitting and administrative skills for groups of thirty people at a time in both Harare and Bulawayo.

A lot of our work was being pursued in conjunction with the relevant ministries, such as Community Development and Women's Affairs. A substantial countrywide literacy campaign had been spearheaded by the training of ex-combatants as teachers or animators by Kathy Bond-Stewart and, eventually, Talent Nyathi, wife of Andrew Nyathi from Simukai.

In collaboration with the Demobilisation Directorate and the Ministry of Economic Planning and Development, we had helped set up a committee of five 'experts', including Paul Themba Nyathi, whose work at Vukuzenzele was complete, to vet proposals for business initiatives from ex-combatants. This programme was funded by the EEC and allowed ex-combatants involved in an approved venture to be paid the total of their monthly allowances in advance, for use as seed capital.

With the assistance of Oxfam, America, we were operating a credit facility with the Bank of Credit and Commerce for approved cooperatives. Negotiations were also under way with the Ford Foundation and Standard Bank for further credit facilities. Unfortunately, one of John Conradie's important initiatives had fallen by the wayside. He had proposed setting up a Comrades' Development Bank, into which all the demobilisation funds made available by the state would be paid. He believed that such a large fund would attract further massive investment from which the ex-combatants would benefit. His thinking was very much along the lines of what had been envisaged by Nitram but aborted by the state. However, officials concerned at the Ministry of Economic Planning and Development did not share John's unlimited vision, so the comrades' development bank never took wing.

CHAPTER 7

Joshua Nkomo flees Zimbabwe

O N THE BRIGHT TUESDAY MORNING OF 8 MARCH 1983, I FLEW to Bulawayo from Harare with Joseph Lelyveld of the *New York Times*. He wanted to see something of our work. Lelyveld, who would later become the same newspaper's foreign editor and then editor in chief, was based in Johannesburg, where he wrote his book *Move Your Shadow: South Africa Black and White*, a clinical account of the horrors of apartheid.

The shadow in question was that of a black caddy employed by a white golfer. *Susa lo-mtunzi gawena*. Move your shadow. *Hayikona shukumisa lo saka*. Don't rattle the bag.

Albert Ngwenya fetched us at the airport and drove us to town, where, quite by chance, we saw Makhatini Guduza standing on a corner, frantically waving us down. We stopped, and Guduza, trembling like a leaf and grey with exhaustion, fear or both, said he would meet us at our nearby office a few minutes later.

Guduza was one of Joshua Nkomo's closest aides. Born near Plumtree in 1927, he had worked in Johannesburg from 1944 to 1964, becoming a chef for the Chamber of Mines. He married Poppy Lotter from Soweto and joined South Africa's African National Congress in 1950, delighting in knowing such luminaries as Walter Sisulu, Alfred Nzo, Thomas Nkobi, Dr James Moroka, Chief Albert Luthuli and Bram Fischer. He was also quietly proud of having participated in the crucially important build-up to the Congress of the People at Kliptown in Soweto, as well as in the congress itself, where the Freedom Charter was adopted on 26 June 1955. Some time after that, he was arrested on a pass offence and defended in court by the attorney Nelson Mandela.

In January 1964, Guduza returned home for a short visit, but, on a tip-off from South Africa, was detained by the Rhodesians at Gonakudzingwa (Where the banished ones sleep). There he met Nkomo and became a loyal lieutenant.

I excused myself from Lelyveld and Ngwenya and saw Guduza privately. He told me of terrible events. The previous Saturday evening, police had sealed off Bulawayo's high-density townships in one of which, Pelandaba,

Nkomo had built his home. Dr Herbert Ushewokunze, TG Silundika's 'brilliant delinquent', was now Minister of Home Affairs, in charge of the police. Within the police cordon, soldiers of 5 Brigade had searched for Nkomo, but had been unable to find him, as he was staying elsewhere. Nkomo was well aware that his life was in grave danger after verbal threats of violence from Prime Minister Mugabe: 'Zapu and its leader, Dr Joshua Nkomo, are like a cobra in the house. The only way to deal effectively with a snake is to strike and destroy its head.'

Shortly after eight that night, Nkomo received a message that his driver and two others had been shot dead in cold blood at his house. The killers then rampaged through his home, destroying all they could, smashing the windscreens of three cars with their rifle butts and slashing the upholstery. Nkomo's wife MaFuyana was with him and implored him to flee Zimbabwe. He had done so on Sunday night.

It had been past midnight when Guduza, with five other men in two vehicles, escorted Nkomo from Bulawayo to Plumtree and then a further ten kilometres south along the Empandeni road to an unguarded section of the Botswana border. They walked across the dry bed of the Ramakwabane River, and then the enormous Nkomo had to climb two fences on the Botswana side, his companions desperately helping to push him over. At 6.20 that Monday morning he had safely stepped onto the soil of Botswana.

Guduza knew that once it was discovered that Nkomo had gone, the authorities would be hunting for Guduza himself. He had returned to Bulawayo to hide his wife Poppy and family, and now it was Tuesday and he had to make a dash for it. I emptied my pockets and gave him all the money I had on me, which wasn't much, and he walked out of our lives. I was careful not to use even one cent of Zimbabwe Project money.

After Guduza left, Lelyveld asked me to go and have a cup of coffee with him. 'I can see that something terrible has happened,' he said. 'I think you should tell me about it.'

'I can't,' I replied, my mind filled with Guduza, who had yet to hide his family and get to Botswana. 'Something too awful for Zimbabwe has happened and I haven't the right to tell anyone yet.'

Lelyveld was quiet and thoughtful, and then he said, 'I think for your own sake you should tell me. I give you my word that whatever it is, I will not report it until the story has been broken by someone else.'

'Joshua Nkomo has fled Zimbabwe,' I said. 'Yesterday he crossed the border to Botswana.'

Joseph Lelyveld kept his word.

While the work of the Zimbabwe Project appeared to be going well and was attracting a great deal of favourable comment both at home and abroad, my life behind the scenes was increasingly fraught. People were suffering dreadfully, and some seemed to believe I could help more than I actually could. In July 1982, six young tourists had been abducted on the Victoria Falls–Bulawayo road. Two were American, and their fathers came to Harare. The American ambassador Robert Keeley and his wife Louise had become dear friends of my family. They invited me to dinner to meet the tourists' fathers, who were desperately seeking ideas about how to find their boys. They had hired a British firm, Control Risk, to assist in the hunt. Hundreds of people were fleeing Zimbabwe for Botswana, and it was thought that among these refugees, many of them ex-ZPRA combatants, some might have information. Control Risk wanted to consult Nkomo, and I provided a letter of introduction for them to carry to him. As far as I knew, he was still in Botswana.

I had last seen Nkomo at his Pelandaba home a few days before he fled. When I telephoned to make an appointment, he told me to get into a taxi outside any hotel in Bulawayo and instruct the driver to take me to him. 'They all know my house.' When his bodyguards allowed me into his home, it was like walking into a nightmare. There were about fifty supplicants in the huge lounge, many of them evidently bruised and with broken bones, some in bloodied bandages. Nkomo was on the telephone trying to raise help and money for them all. 'Even just ten dollars,' I heard him saying to someone he was calling.

Now it was my turn to ask for help from him:

This is to introduce a representative of the kidnapped boys. His name is Simon Adams-Dale.

I saw Cde Guduza in Bulawayo last Tuesday. He told me he had heard that someone called Cde Farai, now in Botswana, had said that the boys were dead. This may be so. However, letters have been received in response to the advertisements (promising rewards for information) indicating the opposite ... 'they are now in a healthy condition' ... 'they can speak a little of Ndebele' ...

It seems to me that there may possibly be accurate information about the kidnapped boys amongst all the people who have had to flee to Botswana. As you are now there, I am positive that you could instruct someone trusted who could get this information if it exists. You will remember our telephone call when one of the parents – Mr Bill Ellis – telephoned you while he was with me, and then you asked to speak to me. I know, and have told the suffering parents, that you would do anything for them.

I think you know me well enough not to accuse me of being interested only in the kidnapped tourists. I am trying to do everything I can for everyone, but especially for those now most at risk – the young men who gave birth to Zimbabwe. I know what is happening to them and I am trying to help. I know too, and have seen you in the most difficult of circumstances, trying and trying to help all the poor and wretched who have always come to you. I am therefore certain that if you are in Botswana for even only five minutes after you receive this letter from me, you will be able and willing to do what you can for the poor and praying parents of the kidnapped.

On the afternoon of 11 March, when I wrote the letter, Michael Behr unexpectedly called on me at my office in Harare. His Oxfam offices were downstairs in the same building, Old Shell House. Michael was a large man, about my age, with a deep voice that often sounded amused, blue bespectacled eyes, rather shaggy blond hair and a moustache. He had been of great help in establishing the Zimbabwe Project, both in London and in Zimbabwe. I was usually glad to see him, but not this time.

When he left I was so distressed, shocked, almost winded, that I made notes of what he had said. He spoke about a meeting that had been held at 4 p.m. on Thursday 24 February by our informal steering committee: Paul Themba Nyathi; Sister Janice, who now worked for the Zimbabwe Foundation for Education with Production (Zimfep); Tim Sheehy, EEC; Mike Tingaiteyi Fungati, Bank of Credit and Commerce; Michael and me. We also had a visitor, John Saxby of the Canadian agency Cuso, who was reporting on developments in our joint education programme for cooperatives. I had excused myself at 5.20 p.m., before the meeting finished.

Michael now said that I had resisted his attempt to discuss the prevailing political and security situation at the meeting. I certainly had, as I believed the subject too dangerous to allude to within our offices. I was intent on quietly keeping our work going.

It had been known for some time, he continued, that there were allegations that the Zimbabwe Project favoured Zapu. This we had never discussed as a group, but the perception had led to the project being accused of political bias – a serious allegation, whether true or not. He said there was a feeling within cooperatives, especially around Harare, that I favoured Simukai, because the members were former ZPRA; that I was 'tragically upset' by present events; that my heart lay in a certain geographical part of the world. He spoke in a rush, as if he wanted to get something off his chest without interruption. When he paused, I remained silent. Then the bombshell dropped.

Michael said that it was now known that I had offered to give evidence for the defence in the trial of Dumiso Dabengwa, Lookout Masuku, Isaac Nyathi and others who were charged with enlisting the help of foreign powers and plotting to overthrow the government by violent means. The fact that I was going to testify on their behalf in the treason trial was a serious matter that I should have referred to the steering committee, Michael said.

I was overwhelmed by his words. It was quite true that I had been approached by Bryant Elliot of Scanlen & Holderness a few days earlier with a request to be a defence witness. Elliot was looking after the Zapu defendants in that trial (just as in later years he would look after Morgan Tsvangirai and others of the Movement for Democratic Change when it was their turn to face trumped-up treason charges). But I wondered how Michael could possibly know about this, since the names of witnesses had not yet been published.

The defence wanted me to tell how I had tramped around Nest Egg, Woody Glen and Ascot with Dabengwa and others, planning how we would resettle people on Ascot and call engineers to test for water and sink boreholes – unlikely activities for men caching arms and planning a coup.

I had agreed to give evidence, but had not yet told my parents or my husband, a senior law officer in the Ministry of Justice. I was putting it off for as long as possible, knowing how anxious they would be for me. But I hadn't hesitated in agreeing.

The accused faced the death penalty if found guilty, with incalculable consequences not only for their friends and families, but also for the country.

I quite often saw Gift Masuku and her son Zakheleni, and had recently seen Dabengwa's wife Zodwa and their small daughter Nombulelo after they had been allowed a rare contact visit to Dumiso. When they returned from Chikurubi Prison, Nombulelo, then about four, had defiantly said of her father: 'He hugged me and he says that he loves me!' and had then burst into tears. I knew how they all suffered.

I told Michael that I had been asked to testify rather than offering to do so. It had been explained to me that either the prosecution or the defence could request the presence of anyone, who, if he or she declined, could then be subpoenaed.

Michael said it would have been better had I waited to be subpoenaed. He concluded by saying that he had been speaking to me on behalf of the steering committee, and he assured me that there was nothing personal in what he had said.

CHAPTER 8

Signs and signals

WITH THE ASSISTANCE OF GIJIMA MPOFU, MY PARENTS HAD designed and supervised the building of a spacious and comfortable house, including their own apartment, at 18 Masefield Avenue in Harare. Central to the open-plan dining and living room was a golden pine table with elegant, unusual markings rippling through the grain. It came from the Shabani asbestos mines, where my father ran an eating house in Maglas Township. One day, sitting at this table, he had noticed a gleam under a scratch, and had stripped what appeared to be a coal-black table, around which thousands of miners had eaten in their time. A piece of wood of such beauty emerged that he acquired it for our new home.

On Wednesday 16 March 1983, two days before my fortieth birthday, the Zimbabwe Project trustees assembled at this table. We now had a patron, the Reverend Canaan Banana, President of Zimbabwe, and a prestigious board of six trustees. Locally, they were the Anglican bishop, Peter Hatendi, Father Henry Wardale and my father. The overseas trustees were Guy Clutton-Brock, Father Josef Amstutz of the Bethlehem Fathers, and Mildred Nevile of the Catholic Institute for International Relations.

Tim Lobstein, CIIR representative in Zimbabwe, had told me that Mildred was about to visit Harare. It was time, I thought, to formalise a management committee for the Zimbabwe Project, as our work was beginning to cover so vast a field. Candidates included Michael Behr and Sister Janice McLaughlin. I had asked Tim to telex Mildred requesting her to spare time for a trustees' meeting. Mildred had agreed and the date had been set.

As the senior and original trustee, Mildred chaired the meeting. She was a warm-hearted, gracious person in her fifties, well liked and esteemed, and we were glad of her presence. But her first action was to physically sweep aside all the reports on our work that I had tabled.

'First,' she said, 'we must deal with the accusations against Judy.'

Everyone present was shocked and quiet. Her colour high and her eyes downcast, Mildred proceeded to list a series of accusations against me. Later that week, she minuted and circulated them under the heading 'Report of discussions in Harare on the future of the Zimbabwe Project

11–19 March 1983'. She had arrived in Harare on Friday 11 March, the same day that Michael Behr had confronted me. Mildred wrote:

> When I arrived in Harare accusations were made to me that the ZP was seen as a Zapu support group; that a disproportionate amount of money went to ex-ZPRA cooperatives; that the director had too high a profile and that her political relationships were reflecting badly on the project.
>
> Here I am repeating some of the very harsh things that have been said to me: that Judy's name on the list of defence witnesses to be called in the Dabengwa trial was an indication 'that she is not on our side'; the question was asked 'does she support the dissidents or doesn't she?' and 'what is the level of Judy's commitment to Zapu?' ZP is now considered a subversive organisation and some of the groups (projects) supported by the ZP will be under close surveillance.
>
> I am not very experienced in message taking of this kind and thought that it would be adequate to talk in terms of broadening the management and control of the ZP so that it was not seen as Judy's project (which it is now) and to bring someone else onto the staff as a senior appointment who was acceptable to government. In addition I wanted to ensure that more staff participation was structured into the running of the project and that a management committee was established which would be responsible for all major decisions and for the day to day overseeing of the Zimbabwe Project.

Mildred proposed that a 'cooperative leadership structure should be established', with me as the coordinator, someone else as the administrator, Paul Themba Nyathi as education officer, Morris Mtsambiwa as project officer and Albert Ngwenya as regional officer. They would be responsible to a management committee consisting of Michael Behr, Sister Janice, Michael Tingaiteyi Fungati, Vivian Maeresera (district administrator), and three government nominees from the ministries of Labour and Social Welfare, Lands and Resettlement, and Education.

> The following day I saw the director of the Zimbabwe Project and discussed the proposals with her. After some initial hesitation she agreed that she could more or less accept these proposals and would discuss their implementation with the trustees/steering committee. I hoped that the safeguards embodied in these recommendations would reassure government and that the project would be able to move forward with renewed backing and support.
>
> I am sorry to have to tell you that my judgment was completely

wrong. Perhaps the messages which I was getting were not explicit enough. More likely I am not familiar enough with the Zimbabwe 'scene' to understand what to another person would have been clear from the beginning, namely that we must ask Judy to leave and find another person to be in charge of the project.

After speaking to Judy I had a scheduled appointment with the Minister of Education, Dzingai Mutumbuka. He was someone who had related to the ZP from the beginning. I discussed our proposals with him knowing that he was already to some extent informed about the possibility of appointing an additional senior staff person who would be completely acceptable to government. To my surprise he said he thought this insufficient. We arranged to speak further on the same matter the same evening. He also told me that ZP was a very contentious issue and that it had been discussed twice in cabinet meetings. He feared for the future of the project but believed it to be doing excellent work. He does not want it to close down.

When we met later that evening he was quite unequivocal. He said that the director must leave. Unless Judy leaves, he said, the project would be closed down within the next three months.

I thought it likely that the minister had had further consultations on the matter between my morning and my evening conversations.

You will know that I have thought this over endlessly, but it is clear to me that we have no alternative in this matter. If we want the Zimbabwe Project to continue we must replace Judy.

As I write this I am waiting to see Judy and tell her of our decision later this morning. Unfortunately I leave for London tonight and having delayed my departure already for 24 hours cannot delay further. This leaves the three Zimbabwean trustees, who legally can form a quorum, with the painful and difficult task of either accepting Judy's resignation or dismissing her.

On her return to London, Mildred wrote to her fellow trustees Guy Clutton-Brock and Father Amstutz:

I am enclosing a report on discussions on the future of the ZP. I wrote this report on the morning of March 19 before leaving Harare that evening. After writing it I went to see Judy to convey to her that she will have to cease to be director of the ZP. Most unfortunately, this matter now rests in the hands of the three Zimbabwean trustees. One of them is Judy's father and the third, Father Wardale, is out of touch with the situation and we could not get hold of him to join in the discussions last week in Harare. Nevertheless, I am hoping very much that they will be able to pursue this most unfortunate affair and bring it to a conclusion, as otherwise I fear the project will be closed down.

I am afraid this will come as a shock to you. When I spoke to Judy on Saturday she said she wished to reserve her position and would be talking to the trustees about it when they meet on Monday, March 28. But I am absolutely convinced that the government is not going to change its mind on this one, and that matters have gone too far. Meanwhile the project is doing remarkably good work and is probably the most effective agency in the country at the present time.

I was thankful that Mildred had been reticent about our final meeting and had said only that I wished to reserve my position. We had sat at my golden table and Mildred had said: 'My dear, I am very sorry, but you will have to go.' I had broken down, rushed to the bathroom and wept with the taps fully turned on so that no one could hear a sound of my grief.

In our family, we had come to recognise that it's often not the person directly in the line of fire that suffers most, but those around them. When my father and I were first arrested and jailed in 1972, we knew it would be my mother and sister Cyndie who would be the most anxious and distressed. And so it was in 1983 as well.

For the first time ever, my mother said she wouldn't mind leaving the country. My father once more waded into battle, sending letters to Minister Kumbirai Kangai, under whom the Demobilisation Directorate and non-governmental organisations such as the Zimbabwe Project fell. He also wrote to Deputy Prime Minister Simon Muzenda, whom Mildred had said was one of those concerned about the Zimbabwe Project. Most importantly, he wrote to Mugabe on 20 March:

> Miss Mildred Nevile, a London-based trustee of the ZP, has just visited Harare and has informed the local trustees, Bishop Hatendi, Father Wardale and me, that Cabinet has discussed the affairs of the Zimbabwe Project and has ruled that the Director, Mrs Judith Acton (my daughter) should be dismissed because she is 'Zapu-orientated'. Miss Nevile reports that if we do not dismiss the director the project will be closed down by Government.
>
> We, the local trustees, have heard only from Miss Nevile so we are now seeking an urgent meeting with the Deputy Prime Minister and/or the Minister of Labour and Social Services whose portfolio is directly concerned with the work of the project.

I have checked the broad interests of the Zimbabwe Project in relation to former ZANLA and ZPRA comrades – which division is a matter which should not concern us – and I find that approximately two thirds of the projects are in 'Mashonaland' and one third in 'Matabeleland'. Also, with one major exception, the funds distributed by the ZP are given in similar proportion.

The exception which puts things out of proportion is Vukuzenzele in the Midlands. When my wife and I heard of the plight of war-wounded men who for two years had lived in terrible conditions in a disused hotel near Bulawayo we offered to donate land worth $26 000 – not to ex-ZPRA people but to war-wounded men in great need. This action was publicised and attracted such interest and sympathy that large sums of designated money flowed in.

Only one year after we made the donation a complex of buildings has been completed and the men are producing and selling vegetables, chickens and pigs. Besides this a splendid clinic has just been completed and war medics under the supervision of the local Government Medical Officer (GMO) are treating patients. The GMO estimates that they will serve the needs of 10 000 people in the Runde Communal Area which starts just half a mile from the centre.

Miss Nevile also spoke of the fact that Mrs Acton has been asked to give evidence, and has agreed to do so, in the trial of Dabengwa and Masuku. She says that this action is held to show that Mrs Acton is an enemy of the State! Surely anyone who has significant knowledge is duty-bound to give it in evidence if called upon to do so by either the prosecution or the defence?

I would accept, though reluctantly, a request from government to replace the present director, for political reasons, with a person of Zanu (PF) affiliation but I would be deeply shocked were Mrs Acton forced to leave entirely and so deprive the Zimbabwe Project of her expertise in management and her close and fruitful relationship with donors.

If the trustees agreed to dismiss Mrs Acton from all association with the Zimbabwe Project, should that really be the intention of government, I hold they would have betrayed the work of the project with serious consequences to many ex-combatants of both armies. They would have failed to protect the interests of the donors who obviously place full confidence in Mrs Acton.

There was no reply from the prime minister, but Muzenda wrote to say he was surprised to hear from my father regarding the Zimbabwe Project, as he had no links with it and had not met Miss Nevile during her visit. He hoped that any problems would be cleared up by Kangai, the minister concerned.

Father Amstutz wrote to me to say how sorry he was about any difficulties. He was so out of touch with the situation, he said, that he felt he couldn't be of any use, but would gladly stand down and give his place to anyone we thought would be of benefit. Guy Clutton-Brock didn't wait for the time a letter would take to reach Zimbabwe, but telephoned my father instead and dictated eight points for the trustees:

- He had received a set of papers relating to Mrs Judith Acton and the Zimbabwe Project from Miss Mildred Nevile.
- He found nothing in them to warrant criticism of Mrs Acton in her position as director of the project, let alone her dismissal.
- He judged the problem to be one of success that had caused jealousy on the part of representatives of other non-governmental organisations and some civil servants.
- The trustees should protect the Zimbabwe Project and ensure that its successful work continued.
- The trustees should ensure that the staff was adequately involved in the work of the project and if there was valid criticism on this score, steps should be taken to improve cooperation.
- He thought it wise to invite government participation on a management committee, but as observers only.
- The private life of officials, including membership of clubs, religion and political sympathies, was their own concern and should not be allowed to intrude on the affairs of the project.
- He expected Miss Nevile to phone him and would communicate his views to her in the terms stated.

Then Bishop Hatendi wrote to Mildred, inviting her 'to return to Zimbabwe as quickly as possible to explain to us the source of the allegations made' against both the project and me. In accordance with her instructions, he wrote, the trustees in Zimbabwe had been to see Kangai on 29 March. The allegations made in Mildred's report had been 'news to him', said the bishop. In addition, Kangai had read to them a copy of Muzenda's response to my father's letter. Since both men were members of the cabinet, which, according to Mildred's report, had discussed the Zimbabwe Project twice, their disclaimers had created confusion among the trustees, staff and 'all concerned' with the Zimbabwe Project. The bishop concluded: 'Will you please come over as soon as possible and clear the air?'

Meanwhile, he said, the trustees had agreed that all projects would continue as if nothing had happened; the steering committee would be suspended and a management committee would be appointed at the forthcoming meeting of trustees, which was scheduled to coincide with Mildred's visit.

Bishop Hatendi's letter was copied to all concerned, including members of the suspended steering committee. It elicited a response from Sister Janice, which she addressed to my father.

> I think we know each other well enough for me to be able to write to you frankly. I was surprised and disappointed by the decisions taken at the recent meeting of the local trustees of the Zimbabwe Project as expressed in a letter to Mildred. As far as I can see, the trustees have only aggravated the problem rather than solving it.
>
> It seems totally unnecessary to call Mildred back to answer questions that can be answered by senior members of the Zimbabwe Project staff and members of the former steering committee. It also seems most unreasonable to suspend the steering committee without first meeting with us to hear what we have to say. Because Mildred and the former steering committee tried to bring out into the open issues which have been simmering underground and which could threaten the future of the Zimbabwe Project, the trustees appear to view us as the cause of the problem.
>
> I believe that this is a time when all of us who care about Judy and the project should unite and pull together so that the invaluable work begun can continue. I would be happy to meet with you and/or the other trustees to answer any questions about the problems facing the project as I see them. I'm sure the other three members of the former steering committee would also welcome such a meeting – preferably with Judy in attendance so that there will be no cause for misunderstandings to arise.

This letter was copied to Mildred, who was not able to return to Zimbabwe as soon as requested, but who wrote again to the trustees on 10 May:

> It is clear from various letters and telexes which I have received that the trustees in Zimbabwe have adopted the position of writing off the criticisms about the project which were made to me by government ministers as being without foundation. In view of the response which

you got from Minister Kangai, this is entirely comprehensible to me. Indeed, you must be searching for an explanation of what seems a totally inexplicable attack by me on Judy as director of the project. I have even heard it said by friends of Judy in London that 'Mildred has got her knife into her'. This is not true.

What I said to trustees when I was in Harare in March was an accurate repetition of what had been said to me, though I confess that I toned down the remarks somewhat.

There can be no long-term resolution of this present unease in the project until the trustees are quite clear that I was speaking the truth. This is not to say that I have any idea of the consequences which might arise from our ignoring information received from government. But I insist that trustees must accept that I was repeating statements made to me.

I must say that when I received Senator Todd's letter dated March 20 to the Prime Minister, I thought the Prime Minister had been put on the spot. They certainly will not confront the Zimbabwe Project openly; indeed why should they? The terms in which Senator Todd's letter was addressed certainly made it harder for government to come to reach a satisfactory arrangement through private negotiation. My fear when I read the letter was that government might move against the project in other ways. But, it may be that these fears are unfounded. I still do not know.

The tone of the reports which I have received since my visit indicate that the trustees in Zimbabwe are now firmly in support of the status quo in the project and that is where the matter rests. I understand that this should be so, as you have had no evidence since my visit which leads you to think differently. Nevertheless, I also cannot believe that trustees in Zimbabwe are unaware of how things are done in delicate matters of this kind. The impression I get is that you have chosen to ignore the signs and signals which I made quite clear to you, preferring to find other explanations of what lay behind my actions.

It later became apparent that the former steering committee had never been more active, and that Bishop Hatendi in particular was a focus of their attention and was becoming fatigued. In response to Mildred's letter and some telephone calls from her, the bishop wrote to her on 20 May: 'In spite of the confusion in my mind, I am going along with the other two trustees for the sake of the Zimbabwe Project. I am, however, beginning to doubt the wisdom of my continuing to serve the Zimbabwe Project as a trustee because a confused trustee is useless. The situation is made worse by your statements: "They certainly will not confront the Zimbabwe Project openly" and "My fear when I read the letter was that government might move against the project in other ways." If the matter is a political one, I am apolitical in order to serve members of all parties. This is how I was able to minister to all returnees in 1980 without partiality.'

My father was passing through London and was scheduled to see Mildred. Bishop Hatendi concluded his letter by saying: 'I hope your meeting with Senator Todd will help me understand what is happening behind the scenes. I anxiously look forward to his report on the meeting.'

A week later, Bishop Hatendi and Father Wardale attended a meeting in the office of the Minister of Justice, Simbi Mubako, which he chaired. Also present were Michael Behr, Sister Janice, Michael Tingaiteyi Fungati and Mrs B Chanetsa, deputy secretary in the ministry, who took the following minutes:

> The minister informed them that there was concern that the Zimbabwe Project was being identified with Zapu and ZPRA and he gave three instances of allegations which they might wish to confirm or deny, viz:
> a) that the Zimbabwe Project supplied funds for Nitram;
> b) that the director had been listed without being subpoenaed to be a witness for the defence in the recent Dabengwa/Masuku case;
> c) that foreign newsmen got some of their anti-government propaganda reports about alleged atrocities in Matabeleland from Zimbabwe Project office.
>
> The minister said these charges worried supporters of the Zimbabwe Project and thought that the trustees should appreciate that they damage the image of the project with government and its supporters. The minister also stated that he and, he believed, other ministers had expressed these worries to Miss Mildred Nevile when she was last in Zimbabwe and that in as much as they touched on security no government would be expected to ignore such allegations. As the members had sought the minister's advice about the matter, the minister told them he was reluctant to give them advice that would involve personalities. He however warned them that
> a) the project must be seen to be a non-partisan body;
> b) the project must be organised in such a way that it was not connected with a political party, particularly with Zapu, as that could tarnish not only the image but the work of the organisation as a whole;

c) the project must be particularly careful so that it was not connected
with the forces that are working against government.

The minister finally explained to the members how Zapu became connected with the project. He informed them that initially, the project was
more connected with Zanu and then it was felt that Zapu combatants
should also receive assistance. He went on to say that Zapu was then
invited as well as Judy as it was realised that she had a lot of contacts.
It was however pointed out to them that at that stage, Zanu and Zapu
were very close. The minister reminded them that as the two political
parties have now split and that Nkomo was no longer in government,
the project members must be aware of this fact and be careful in their
operations. The meeting ended with the members expressing their
sincere appreciation to the minister for his willingness to see them and
more particularly for the very frank discussion they had with him.

It was many years before, by chance, I saw a copy of these minutes. Only
then could I see how cleverly managed had been this attempt to influence
Wardale and Hatendi in the absence of my father. I also noted that, despite
seeing regular reports of our expenditure, no one from the former steering
committee had pointed out that not one cent from the Zimbabwe Project
had ever gone to Nitram.

At the time I heard – I suppose from Hatendi or Wardale – that a meeting
had taken place and, when I next saw Mubako at a diplomatic reception, I
went and greeted him. We had known each other since our respective exiles
had coincided for a time in London. Along with people such as Ignatius
Chigwendere, also of Zanu, and Francis Nehwati of Zapu, Mubako had
indeed been involved in the formation of the Zimbabwe Project. The
connection with each other in this case and with CIIR was their membership
of the Catholic Church, which also provided their link to the historically
important Catholic Acton family.

Mubako had suggested that my husband Richard apply for a job in his
ministry to facilitate my return to Zimbabwe as director of the project. He
had also employed Mary Ann, Richard's younger sister and Tim Sheehy's
wife, as his secretary. I thought this was not because he was interested in titles
or nepotism, but because he was in search of excellence in the performance
of work. This was also probably why, the last time he and I had actually
talked to each other, it was over a meal at the Park Lane Hotel. The quality
of food and service at their Khaya Nyama Steak House was renowned under
the management of John Callinicos and his wife Aelda, Richard's aunt on

his father Lord Acton's side. There was also the spiciness of knowledge in the air at the Park Lane, as John and Aelda were intensely political, revelled in good relationships with practically everyone from any party and always had the latest hot gossip.

That meal had been on the eve of independence in 1980, and we were all euphoric. Simbi had a built-in asset in diplomatic relations, as he seemed to laugh most of the time, although I thought this was a nervous mannerism. But during this meal he really was laughing, and I was touched when he said he had managed to get seating for his parents at the independence celebrations in Rufaro Stadium. 'At last they have realised that it was worth their while investing in me,' he said.

When I went up to Simbi at the reception, he was, as always, friendly. I said I gathered he had been speaking about me to various people regarding the Zimbabwe Project. He apologised for anything I might have heard 'second hand', and invited me to see him in his office, which I did. Mary Ann brought us tea, and we settled in for an hour of amicable conversation, which I later précised for our trustees.

> I informed [Minister Mubako] that the Zimbabwe Project had never given even a single cent to Nitram. I wondered where he was getting this kind of negative and false information from. He said he was surprised and pleased that we had not given money to Nitram, but did not tell me his source of information.
>
> Regarding giving evidence for Dabengwa and Co I said that as he knew, I had always been interested in justice and that as a citizen of Zimbabwe I felt that I would be obliged to give evidence in any court in the land, whether called upon to do so by either the prosecution or the defence.
>
> He said there had been no objection from what he called 'my colleagues' to any of the other defence witnesses, but that it was not acceptable that I should give evidence because of what he called my past record of service to Zimbabwe and my important political standing. I really can't comment on these observations of his, and anyway the whole matter is now closed.
>
> Finally, I refuted his allegations that the overseas press were getting anti-government propaganda reports from the offices of the Zimbabwe Project. I said that during my years overseas my main target was always the press, to try and get what was then the other side of events in Rhodesia reported. I had made friends with journalists in many countries and, on the whole, I thought I had done a good job. Now these journalists

visiting Zimbabwe would, as friends, naturally get in touch with me, and a great deal of attention had been paid to the work of the Zimbabwe Project which resulted in the most favourable of publicity overseas for Zimbabwe itself. I assured him that the overseas press had never received any information from the Zimbabwe Project on matters that did not concern the work of the Zimbabwe Project.

One result that I regretted of this whole bad time was that I did not give evidence for Dabengwa, Masuku and the others at their treason trial. After Mildred had presented all the allegations against me, I had gone to see their lawyer, Bryant Elliot, and told him what was happening. If the Zimbabwe Project was closed down, it would deprive a lot of people in difficult circumstances of their last shreds of succour.

Elliot went to Chikurubi and discussed the problem with the accused. It was agreed that they would give the evidence I would have presented, and only if it were challenged would I be called to testify. The evidence was not challenged, I was not called and, on the last Wednesday of April 1983, Dabengwa, Masuku and Nyathi, along with Masala Sibanda, Nicholas Nkomo and Tshaka Moyo, were acquitted on all charges by Mr Justice Hillary Squires. The judge described Dabengwa as 'the most impressive witness any of us have seen in court for a long time' and said his actions were the antithesis of anyone 'scheming to overthrow the government'.

The Minister of Home Affairs, Dr Herbert Ushewokunze, expressed fury. 'Let it be stated that the acquittal of Dabengwa and others proves once more that the judiciary we inherited from Smith is not in tune with the present government.'

The men were immediately re-detained outside the court – and then they disappeared. Their lawyers were denied access to them. No one knew where they were and their families were panic-stricken.

Bryant Elliot went back to court two days later, and Mr Justice Sandura ordered the Commissioner of Police and the Minister of State (Security) to tell their legal representatives 'forthwith' where the men were being held and to grant them access.

The state stubbornly maintained its silence until the following Thursday, when Emmerson Mnangagwa, the minister in question, announced that they were being held at the notorious detention centre of Goromonzi and could be visited by their lawyers. Eventually they were moved back to Chikurubi Maximum Security Prison. Declared innocent by the courts, the state had nonetheless decided to treat them as guilty.

Three months later, Mugabe said the men were still being detained because the government had more information on them than did the courts. They had been arrested in March 1982. The survivors were eventually released in December 1986.

Scapegoat

WHILE THE WORK OF THE ZIMBABWE PROJECT PROCEEDED amazingly smoothly in the circumstances, members of the former steering committee were still tirelessly working for their reinstatement and my displacement.

Rumours whirled around, a painful one being the allegation that John Conradie had left the Zimbabwe Project because of me. It was Mildred who told me this. I wrote to John and said how sorry I was. He had given me totally different reasons for leaving not only the project, but Zimbabwe itself, and therefore the project as well. After receiving my letter, he took it to Mildred and asked, 'Did I ever say I left the Zimbabwe Project because of Judy?' Mildred said no, John himself had not told her that. Someone else had.

In a letter written to me at the end of March 1983, John reaffirmed his passionate belief in collective cooperatives.

> My decision to return to England was as you know equally the result of personal factors and of a determination to adhere in fact rather than in lip service to the principle of localisation/devolution i.e. that if you/one as an aid/voluntary agency worker have a competent replacement one should step aside else it seems to me the basic principle of development is betrayed.
>
> I think it would be difficult to deny that I had an equal part in the foundation of the work we are doing, the establishment of the structures, the determination of its trajectory. I have and will (? always – if it continues) a deep more than paternal interest in it. Which enables me to intervene here and say that what remains is for me to appeal to you to allow yourself to be guided in this crisis NOT by grand politics, principles, allegiances to those shadowy and shabby things that parties in my opinion are always condemned to be. Whatever you do, may I ask you rather to refer for your allegiance to the people in the co-ops in the project itself, to hold THEIR interests uppermost in your mind.
>
> As I have said (God knows enough times, to blithe disbelief) the movement has many enemies. Their opposition, even one might say their

undying enmity is class-inspired because I believe the co-ops represent an increasingly real alternative (and therefore obstacle) to the emergence of a class of black capitalist large-scale agrarian entrepreneurs. That is the real issue. The partisan issue is merely a smokescreen albeit an extremely useful one for the enemy's real intention.

Well, that will have to be it, a personal appeal to you to abandon all personal inclination and cleave to our 'constituency' and its interests as the determinant in your decisions in the difficult weeks ahead …

I believe you may see all I have said is an attempt to keep the work going, the real, small, painstaking work which outlives the grandest clash of party, principle so-called and politics and which outshines in reality again if not in media terms the weight of dozens of martyrdoms … Take *care* of yourself. Love, John

Morris Mtsambiwa, the deputy director, had entered the fray with a strong letter to trustees in May protesting the suspension of the former steering committee.

'Did the Trustees put into consideration the work that the members of the Steering Committee as individuals are doing to save the skin of the Zimbabwe Project? These allegations have come forward to members of the Steering Committee even from the CIO and some members of the Steering Committee had done all they could to save the face of the Zimbabwe Project. Why is Mildred Nevile being called back whereas some members of the Steering Committee are available anytime to answer any questions to the Trustees?'

At the end of June, Morris was offered a position in the local Oxfam office by Michael Behr, which he accepted. His departure was, for me, a relief. At the end of July, I received a friendly note from the Minister of Labour and Social Services, Kumbirai Kangai, to whom I had copied the latest report to trustees on our work. This was also a relief.

'Thank you very much for your letter. It was a very informative report to the Trustees. Contrary to what you expected, I read through the document and found it quite useful. I hope that the Project can fulfil its objectives. That will be a great asset to our country.'

I had been doing a lot of public relations work with the ministries with which we had dealings and, on receipt of this note from Kangai, I thought we could all now perhaps relax a little.

But then, on 1 August, Michael popped up from his office again. By now I was anxious to find offices elsewhere to get away from his presence in Old

Shell House, and soon we bought a house in the Avenues near the Park Lane Hotel, which turned out to be an excellent move in every way. Meanwhile, here he was, this time to inform me that, as the local representative, he would be recommending that Oxfam cease all support of the Zimbabwe Project.

I asked why. He replied that it was because my relations with government were bad. I felt sick, but kept silent. He said it was no use me continuing to sit at my desk as if nothing untoward was happening. He would be telling Oxfam that he felt no further support should be given while I remained director of the Zimbabwe Project. However, the local office might still be able to help with small grants, and, if such assistance were required, I could apply through Morris Mtsambiwa from the beginning of September.

This was not a time for us to contemplate the withdrawal of support from such an important agency as Oxfam. The end of the demobilisation programme was in sight. In November the first thirty people would stop receiving their allowances. By December, this number would rise to 1500, and, by the end of 1984, to 25000. This was against the background of something like 96000 school leavers entering the job market at the end of the year, when it was estimated that only 6000 new jobs would be available. Quite apart from traditional funding, Oxfam was also to have been our European partner in presenting a further large application to the EEC for their support of our work.

I wrote a letter to Michael, copied to Anne Lloyd-Williams at Oxfam, saying: 'I feel sure that you will agree that it is only fair that the Zimbabwe Project be given an opportunity to make its own representations to your head office on this matter. Accordingly, I would be grateful if you would set down in writing the precise reasons that underlie your recommendation. I shall be writing to Anne Lloyd-Williams regarding the EEC application, and I shall of course copy the letter to you.'

Michael responded in a letter also copied to Anne Lloyd-Williams that he couldn't set down the precise reasons in writing, that it was an internal Oxfam matter, and that when action had been decided upon, he and Oxfam would contact the Zimbabwe Project. He regretted that I had written to Anne, as 'when a "recipient" organisation feels the need to appeal to our Head Office and go over the head of the Field Representative then this places the Head Office in a very difficult position. It is my experience that if an attempt is made to drive a wedge between the Field and Head Office, whatever the rights and wrongs of the situation, then almost always and naturally so Oxfam closes ranks.'

Many years later, I had sight of Michael's four-page report of 5 August 1983 to head office, in which he said:

There can be no doubt whatsoever that ZP has played and should continue to play a vital part in the whole area of resettlement, cooperative building, demobilisation, organising training programmes, etc. There are many reports from ZP in Oxford to confirm this and the £100 000 plus that Oxfam has donated to ZP over the last two years has been well and usefully spent. Many cooperatives have been assisted, training courses in basic skills have and are still being organised. However, in certain areas it is clear that ZP has not been able to avoid getting into a situation where its non-party political credibility has been widely questioned, staff morale has fallen with John Conradie leaving, the Deputy Director resigning and the Steering Committee being suspended by the Trustees.

ZP has a history. It has tremendous support in Government circles, the members of the Steering Committee, etc., etc. But gradually it became clear that Judith had very clear ideas on how she wanted to run it and this has gradually alienated people like John Conradie and other friends of ZP. In a small place like Harare this becomes known and this is how powerful Government people up to the Prime Minister gained the impression that ZP was rapidly changing from what it had been and that these changes included, rightly or wrongly, a political bias. All this was brought to a head when Mildred Nevile visited earlier this year.

Michael also wrote: 'For further reference I would suggest that "Minutes of a meeting held in the office of the Minister of Justice on May 27 1983 to discuss matters in connection with the Zimbabwe Project", a copy of which I sent to Oxford early in June, will give useful extra information.'

At the end of September, Bishop Hatendi received a telephone call at his house from Minister Kangai, who asked him to convene a meeting of the Zimbabwe Project trustees as soon as possible for the sole purpose of dismissing me as director, as he had been given information that I was a security risk. My father drove up from the ranch to see the distressed bishop, as well as Father Wardale, who was now based at Makumbi Mission outside Harare. He brought back for me a little note in exquisite handwriting.

Dear Judy

I am most upset at your Dad's news. My deepest sympathy for this 'decision'. I can only say that I feel most deeply for this further painful injustice.

Needless to say I am right behind you (whatever that means).

I think I can understand your feelings. You will need all your reserves of toughness.

In haste and with every blessing.

Yours sincerely

Henry.

In his report to head office, Michael had written that after Mildred's departure from Harare, 'the other Trustees, dominated by Garfield Todd, were in a difficult position. Mildred had acted on information that the other Trustees did not have and when they went to see Government Ministers the same information given to Mildred was not given to them. It is difficult to see how Garfield Todd would be given information about his daughter. I'm amazed that he has not stood down on this given his close personal involvement.'

Of course, this further blow from Kangai caused my parents great distress, which, in a chance meeting, my father confided to Minister Nathan Shamuyarira. He said my father should see the prime minister, as, according to him, only Mugabe could stop whatever was happening concerning me. So once again, my father took up his pen.

Dear Prime Minister,

I am sorry to ask you to take personal note of a matter which, for my family, has caused much distress: the accusations that my daughter Judith Acton is a security risk and is, therefore, working against the State.

Fr Wardale and I recently met with Cde Kangai who had previously phoned Bishop Hatendi and had asked him to dismiss Judith from her post as Director of the Zimbabwe Project. He told us that this was a security matter and he was unable to give us details, though both Father Wardale and I protested that it was impossible for us to fulfil our responsibilities to the former combatants, to the donors, to the staff and to our wider responsibility to Zimbabwe as a whole if we had to make decisions without knowing the facts.

Since our meeting with Cde Kangai I have tried to see him again, but he was away. When I could not meet him yesterday I went to Cde Mnangagwa, Minister of State (Security). Cde Mnangagwa assured me that there is no security problem with Mrs Acton: that the only time there had been discussion about the Todd family re a security matter was in 1981 when we donated part of our ranch to the Vukuzenzele

War-Disabled Cooperative. The wisdom of this action was debated at the time and was accepted.

As I was leaving Cde Mnangagwa suggested I call on the Minister of Home Affairs in case there was something of which he was unaware. I did this, and Cde Ushewokunze said that the only question of security which had come to his attention was in December 1982. A journalist had told him that he had got a certain story from Mrs Acton. After consideration he had torn up the report, as it was an unsubstantiated allegation.

Our family is close-knit. Mrs Todd is a member of the Mass Media Trust. Richard Acton, a Senior Legal Officer in the Ministry of Legal & Parliamentary Affairs left for London last night to consult with Louis Blom-Cooper QC on the Bickle case on enemy property of which we have been reading in the *Herald*. Judith Acton has in her own way fought and suffered for the liberation of Zimbabwe and is personally responsible for raising literally millions of dollars in foreign currency which come into Zimbabwe as a by-product of the work of the Zimbabwe Project. The fourth is me, a Senator. We are all working for Zimbabwe and the allegation that one member of our family is a security risk hits us all very sorely – and, of course, it is an absurd allegation.

I would be grateful if I could meet you at your convenience. I wish to clear my family of a slur which hurts us all and which damages our ability to concentrate single-mindedly on serving Zimbabwe.

Eventually, Mugabe did agree to see my father, and after their meeting my father wrote a synopsis, headed: **CONFIDENTIAL TO THE FAMILY.**

After some difficulty I at last was given an interview with the Prime Minister on Wednesday, November 16th 1983 at 10.30 a.m. When I went into the office I felt that he was not at ease and, after greetings, he asked me rather abruptly what I wanted to say. As he had had fairly detailed letters from me, both at the beginning of the whole matter and then in October I presumed he had some idea of what was on my mind.

I said that I had come to speak about my family. There was my wife who was a member of the Mass Media Trust, Judith who was Director of the Zimbabwe Project, Richard who was a senior law officer and me, a Senator. I hoped that he did not regret having made me a Senator?

Mugabe (rather abruptly), '*And why should I regret that?*'

'Well, I am sure that you do not agree with some of the things I say?'

'*Well, within the framework of a democracy there is room for criticism if it is constructive.*'

'Richard Acton, who is concerned with three major cases in the Courts at present, considers that it is an outrageous situation where he can be trusted with so much highly confidential security information while at the same time his wife is alleged to be considered a security risk.'

'*Let me say that I knew nothing about any problems with the Zimbabwe Project until I received your letters.*'

'I went to see Cde Emmerson Mnangagwa to enquire from him about the security aspect. He was quite definite in his denial that there was any security angle to the Zimbabwe Project or to Judith, but as I was leaving he suggested I should see Herbert "in case he knows something that I'm not aware of". So I went to see Cde Ushewokunze, Minister of Home Affairs, and his reaction was the same. There was no security problem. At that point I thought of leaving the matter but I had spoken to Minister Shamuyarira and he strongly recommended that I should take the matter to you.'

'*But why come to me?*'

'I considered that if you indicated that my family was acceptable then we could forget the allegations some people are making.'

Mugabe laughed and then asked, '*But who are you concerned about?*'

'I haven't come to criticise others or to try to hurt anyone. I am concerned only to clear my family and let us get on with our work.'

'*But*' ... and he looked down at my letters which he had spread out in front of him ... '*you say that Kangai says that this is a security matter, that he said Lady Acton was a security risk?*' [For some reason Mugabe always referred to me as Lady Acton, the title still held by my mother-in-law.]

'Yes, Minister Kangai said that it was a security matter and that Judith had to go. However he changed his mind and said no one had suggested she should be dismissed, but that she could not continue as Director. When we asked for information as to why, Kangai repeated that it was a security matter and that he was therefore precluded from giving any information at all.'

The Prime Minister then said, very clearly: '*Well, at no point has this matter been a security problem. Sister Janice McLaughlin came to me with various criticisms. Why did you dismiss her?*'

'I don't think you can say we dismissed her for she was not an employee of the ZP. But we, the Trustees, decided to suspend the steering committee of which she was a member because the situation had become unworkable. I was myself present when Michael Behr, a member of the steering committee, said in a meeting of the whole staff that Judith should go. The Trustees agreed the matter had gone too far.'

'But Janice says that the ZP is a one man–one woman show; that funds were not distributed even-handedly. I think it should be the need of the person which decides an issue.'

I agreed, and said this was the criterion used.

'But I am told that assistance is given in some areas that are suspect.'

'Well, I went to see Cde Mubako who had had criticisms that Judith had been prepared to give evidence for Dabengwa ...'

'Oh, I never suggested that Mubako should take action on this matter. But it was not just Janice who had criticisms. There were others also. It was held that Lady Acton had Zapu allegiances. Of course that is no crime. I have Zapu members in my Government. But in the light of the criticisms I had heard I asked Kangai to look into the matter. Maybe he overreacted.'

In this way we talked the matter out and it was time to go. A different atmosphere now prevailed and I hesitated and asked if he had a few more minutes to spare. He said yes and I brought up the matter of hunger in Mberengwa and the dangerous shortage of food in the whole area.

'But you said that if we distributed maize in the rural areas all would be well.'

'Yes, but deliveries of maize have been stopped.'

'Why has such a thing happened?'

'I do not know but I'm told this has been done while the situation is assessed.'

'But could they not have assessed the situation without stopping deliveries? I wonder who could have given such an order?'

At the time my father did not realise the significance of this conversation, which led to an immediate inquiry into the shortage of maize in many areas of the country. This in turn led to the unveiling of what became known as the Paweni scandal, a massive scam through which funds intended for the purchase of maize were diverted to pay for criminal overcharging for transporting that maize. When the money ran out, so did food for the people. This we all learned later.

In the meanwhile my father's infinite courage in going to Mugabe brought blessed relief from attack for me, my family and the Zimbabwe Project. I continued as director of the Zimbabwe Project Trust for another five years, until 1988, when I was able to hand over everything in good order to my successor, our deputy director Paul Themba Nyathi.

There remained, for me, one recollection that puzzled me just as much as did everything else about the Michael Behr of that time. On the evening of 21 March 1983, I called to bid farewell to Nick Worrall, a journalist who was being deported from Zimbabwe as he had been reporting on atrocities by 5 Brigade uncovered in Matabeleland. Minister Shamuyarira had withdrawn his accreditation as a stringer for Britain's *Guardian*, declaring him 'an undesirable person and an enemy of the people of Zimbabwe'. I had known Nick's father John, also a journalist, who had been deported in the same manner from the same country when it was called Rhodesia.

While we were sitting outside having a drink, the telephone rang. Nick excused himself to answer it, and later came back, excitedly telling his partner Christabel Gurney: 'The NGOs have delivered their report on atrocities in Matabeleland to the prime minister.'

'Holy smoke!' I said, borrowing the phrase from Noel Galen. 'I had better get out of here. That wasn't me on the telephone, but I'm the one who is being accused of giving reports like this to the press. Who was that ringing you?'

'Michael Behr of Oxfam,' said Nick.

So far as I can remember, I encountered Michael only once after my father's conversation with Mugabe, and that was on page 185 of Peter Stiff's book *Cry Zimbabwe*, which was published in 2000. It gave me my first understanding as to what Michael had been up to in that horrible year of 1983. He and those involved with him had simply been using me as a decoy, a red herring, a distraction.

Mildred's table of accusations against me was headed 'Report of discussions in Harare on the future of the Zimbabwe Project 11–19 March 1983'. It finally became apparent that discussions on the future of the Zimbabwe Project were quite incidental to the real purpose of her visit to Zimbabwe and were, in fact, just a smokescreen used by CIIR and Oxfam. Their real work at the time lay in compiling, with others, a secret report for Prime Minister Mugabe, which was delivered to his office on 21 March, two days after Mildred had fired me and left Harare.

In writing about Nick Worrall, Peter Stiff detailed how foreign journalists at the time were having difficulties getting stories published about the atrocities they discovered were being committed by 5 Brigade in Matabeleland. Stiff wrote:

The NGOs and the genocide

Immediately after the failure of his two journalist colleagues to assist in spreading the word about what was happening in Matabeleland, Nick Worrall contacted several non-governmental organisations who had field operations there. With their field staff deployed it was impossible they could have remained ignorant of what was happening. He urged them to go public. Mike Behr, Oxfam's man in Harare, refused to get involved or to pass on any information. Oxfam was running a programme in Matabeleland and it did not want to take the chance of it being prejudiced.

'If you don't help in stopping the massacres,' Nick told him irritably, 'there won't be anybody left to benefit from your bloody programme.'

Shortly afterwards, apparently finding courage in numbers, a deputation from nine international agencies, including Oxfam, sought an interview with Prime Minister Mugabe and his security minister. They pointed out that terrible things were happening in Matabeleland, that 5 Brigade was torturing and murdering people, that hundreds of innocents had been killed and that many more had been injured or forced to flee their homes.

A reliable source said Prime Minister Mugabe dismissively told them to produce concrete evidence. The NGO Nine jointly compiled a thick report detailing atrocities committed by 5 Brigade and handed it in to the Prime Minister's office on 21 March 1983. Sources close to the NGOs said the report contained detailed accounts of deaths, injuries and mutilations obtained from medical personnel and agency staff in Matabeleland. It was supported by photographs. The report's aim, according to Nick Worrall's sources, was to halt the actions of the troops and to prevent repetitions in the future. The aid organisations, despite the volumes of first-hand evidence they had gathered over the previous six weeks, declined to release it to the press or to make press statements.

And they never did.

Among the nine agencies involved in compiling and presenting the report were Oxfam (UK) and CIIR, the representatives of which, at precisely the same time, had apparently been agonising with their friends in Zimbabwe's government about the fact that the director of the Zimbabwe Project was a security threat and must be removed.

I realised, when the account I read started sinking in so many years later, that I had simply been a scapegoat, used, abused, almost overcome, but because of the faithfulness of our trustees, my father, Father Henry Wardale, Bishop Peter Hatendi and Guy Clutton-Brock, I had managed to survive.

The policies of quiet diplomacy regarding Robert Mugabe's Zanu (PF) regime started long before Thabo Mbeki's rise to power in South Africa.

CHAPTER 10

Darkening clouds

W HILE LIFE EASED FOR ME IN 1984, IT DIDN'T FOR OTHERS.
One day, Peter Baka Nyoni, husband of Sithembiso, founder and
director of the Organisation of Rural Associations for Progress (Orap),
called with sad news from his wife's vast Ndebele family. As a result I
wrote to Emmerson Mnangagwa, Minister of State (Security), in early
December with an appeal on behalf of Christopher Ndebele, headmaster
of St Joseph's Primary School in Silobela, who was being held by the CIO
in Kwe Kwe.

I was fortunate to know Mnangagwa slightly. He had attended one of
the satellite primary schools that radiated from Dadaya Mission through
areas of the communal lands, then called native reserves. His family, like
many others, including that of Lookout Masuku's wife Gift, had moved to
Northern Rhodesia, now Zambia, in the 1950s or 1960s. I met him during
the 1979 Lancaster House conference through our mutual friend Lombe
Chibesakunda, then Zambia's high commissioner based in London. At the
time, Mnangagwa was Robert Mugabe's personal assistant. Lombe played a
significant role at the conference, during which she also became my sister.
My father, who was attending the conference as one of Joshua Nkomo's
informal advisers, had met Lombe and asked her about her family. He
discovered that she was an orphan – quite a mature orphan, but an orphan
nonetheless – so he took pity on her and adopted her.

After Zimbabwe's independence, Lombe visited us from Zambia, and
Mnangagwa took her to see Mugabe. The prime minister asked how she
had travelled from Lusaka, and she said by car. He said that must have been
a long journey. No, Lombe replied, it's about the same distance from Lusaka
to Harare by road as it is from Harare to Shabani.

'How do you know that?' he asked.

'Well,' she said, 'my father lives near Shabani and he's coming here to see
me. He says it will take him about five hours.'

'Your father lives near Shabani?'

'Yes,' said Lombe, 'and he's bringing my mother to meet me. It's so exciting.
I've never met my mother before.'

'You've never met your mother?' said the prime minister. 'That is very strange. Who is your father?'

'Garfield Todd,' said Lombe.

At that point, Mnangagwa rescued the prime minister and explained the situation. Mugabe sat back and laughed when he heard that my father had adopted Lombe.

'A lot of *very strange things* happened during the Lancaster House conference,' he said.

My letter to Mnangagwa was personal. I said that Connie, daughter of Christopher Ndebele, was soon getting married, and that members of her family – some of whom had been friends since I was a child – had asked me to bring the matter to his attention in the hope that Ndebele could be released by the CIO before the wedding.

I told him how the headmaster had been attacked and left unconscious by a group of Zanu (PF) youth militia at a bus stop in the August school holidays. The youths then proceeded to his home and set it alight. Ndebele regained consciousness and made his way to the police camp at Silobela, where he was kept in custody for his own protection while receiving treatment at nearby Loreto Hospital. Eventually he landed up with the CIO. His wife, who worked for the Ministry of Community Development in Silobela, had been searching for him and, after three months, with the help of Advocate Kennedy Sibanda, she found him in the hands of the CIO and took him his pills for high blood pressure. She was shocked by his condition. I told Mnangagwa it had been discovered that Ndebele's nephew, Jabulani Viki Ncube, was being held in the same place. He, an ex-combatant and now a medical assistant, had been working at a clinic in Gokwe when, like so many former ZPRA, he disappeared.

'Connie Ndebele,' my letter concluded, 'is marrying an ex-combatant, April Nkomo, a Captain in the Zimbabwe National Army. She is nearly full-term pregnant, now suffers from hypertension and would dearly love the presence of her father and, of course, her cousin Jabulani at her wedding. I feel confident that you might be able to help. I know how sad it is to get married when your father is in detention. That is what happened to me in January 1974 when my father couldn't attend my wedding in Rome as he was detained by the Smith regime in Rhodesia.'

The CIO informed Mnangagwa that Ndebele had been handed over to the police to be prosecuted for assisting dissidents. His family knew nothing about this, but had now established that he had been tortured by the CIO.

So, on the way home to Hokonui Ranch for Christmas, I stopped in Kwe Kwe, where the CIO had offices on the second floor of the central Chrome Building.

It was a Sunday afternoon and there was no one on duty, but I persuaded the security guard to let me in and to guide me up to the CIO offices. I left a pocket of oranges and a note saying how surprised I was that Ndebele was still being held by the CIO despite what they had told their minister, and that I would be grateful if they could ensure the oranges safely reached Ndebele with best wishes for Christmas. The point of all this was not to be provocative, but simply to let the authorities know that someone else was aware of the existence of their victim and that I was in touch with their minister. Also, the contents of a pocket of oranges can reach from one prisoner to several.

In March 1985, I received a letter from Christopher Ndebele: 'Thank you so much for the oranges. They got me in Kwe Kwe. You don't know what effect they made on all the prisoners. The very realisation that there are people who care was very relieving. It healed our physical and moral wounds. I was freed on 4/1/85.'

Connie did marry her April, and eventually took over the running of Orap from her relative and colleague Sithembiso Nyoni. In the meanwhile, while Sithembiso was still director, Orap successfully invited Home Affairs Minister Enos Nkala to be their patron. The reason given privately for this was that if Nkala declared more curfews, the work of Orap might be spared and they might still be able to deliver food to starving people. It was an interesting attempt to resist evil by accommodating it. The consequences of this became clear many years later.

Sithembiso, on her way to becoming an apple of President Mugabe's eye, stood for Zanu (PF) in the 2005 parliamentary elections and was decisively defeated in Bulawayo by the candidate for the Movement for Democratic Change (MDC), lawyer David Coltart, by 12120 votes to 3777. President Mugabe once again ignored the mandate of the electorate and appointed Sithembiso a non-constituency member of parliament, enabling him to make her Minister of Small and Medium Enterprise Development. As minister she tried but failed in 2005 to give a positive slant to Operation Murambatsvina, 'clear out the human excrement', to the appalled Mrs Anna Tibaijuka, United Nations Special Envoy, sent to Zimbabwe to measure the extent of the calamity under which 700 000 people had had their dwellings and businesses deliberately demolished by their own government. These were people believed to have voted for the MDC in the recent elections.

Connie later had to flee not only from Zimbabwe, but specifically from Sithembiso. Sithembiso's attempt to resist evil by accommodating it had simply led to eventually being overwhelmed by it.

I sometimes regretted an occasion in 1960, when I had failed to greet Robert Mugabe. I was in my last year at Queen Elizabeth secondary school and, wearing our distinctive jacaranda-blue uniform with white polka dots, about to enter the central post office when I saw Mugabe leaving, tripping fast down the stairs, looking alone and driven. In the two seconds it took to pass I contemplated greeting him, but didn't. I have sometimes thought that *he* would have remembered if I had greeted him, but instead, *I* have always remembered that I didn't. It seems a small thing not to have done, but for me it didn't turn out that way. I sometimes wondered whether I didn't greet him for fear of offending surrounding whites, or because I didn't want to be presumptuous, or because I was wearing my school uniform and didn't want to compound the minor trouble I was in at school.

As head girl of our boarding hostel, Beavan, I supervised fire drills. A bell would clang after lights-out, the prefect of each dormitory would assemble the boarders in lines, or crocodiles, outside the hostel, and I would get the overall tally and report to the matron. The latest fire drill had been unusual. I was the only one told beforehand that, when the bell was rung, we had to form the crocodiles inside the building's courtyard, not outside, and then I would get further instructions to relay to the other prefects. These turned out to be that, once counted, the boarders had to be taken back upstairs, where all windows had to be shut and doors barricaded with furniture, and then they had to sit in the middle of the floor surrounded by beds until the all-clear. We did this, at first bemused. But, once we were sitting on the floor and started to speculate, some of the girls became almost hysterical, shrilling fearfully about what blacks might do if they managed to get into the dormitories.

The next morning, with the backing of my fellow prefects, one of whom was Sally, daughter of the Clutton-Brocks, I went to the matron and said that that had obviously not been a fire drill, but a riot drill. The effect on some of the girls had been very bad, and we would not be putting them through that again. For my insubordination I was demoted from being head girl, but we didn't have any more fire/riot drills. But perhaps this incident had inhibited me further from doing anything out of the ordinary while wearing a school uniform, like greeting Robert Mugabe.

Nonetheless, I had learned a lasting lesson then, and so, at the beginning of 1985, when I saw Joshua Nkomo at Bulawayo airport, I suffered not one minute's hesitation and went straight up to him. He had returned home from exile in August 1983 to pre-empt moves to expel him from parliament. The grinding into the dust of his party Zapu and its structures was still in fast motion, and his life and those associated with him were at risk. So, at least in public, people shied away from him, and this Friday morning of 4 January was no exception.

Nkomo was sitting in the middle of the departure lounge surrounded by empty space with an old and tremulous man, who was bewailing something. I went up, apologised for interrupting, but said I just wanted to say hello. He paid me the compliment of not only lifting his head and smiling, but of lumbering to his feet. We talked for a minute and then I moved away. I went to sit just behind him, and found myself full of futile fury about the fact that people were staring at me and that I was shaking all over. More last-minute arrivals were crowding in and, seeing him, moving away. Nkomo had had a recent, rather rough haircut, and he looked very tired. There were two young men within saving distance of him, probably personal bodyguards, and, a few yards further away, two hostile and intent young men within destructive range, probably CIO. One other woman went up to Nkomo after me. He rose, smiled and greeted her, she curtsied, and then he turned back to the tale of woe. No more VIP lounge for him; no more obsequious public; no one wanting to say, 'Do you remember when we …?'

That night I crossed Masefield Avenue in Harare to see my neighbours Noel and Alex Genau. Before long, Alex started weeping, because January and February were the anniversaries of their grandson's birth in 1979, and then, when he was sixteen days old and on his mother's lap in a vehicle, being blown up by a landmine. The baby survived, but their daughter didn't. The parents of their son-in-law John had been killed just a few weeks earlier. Alex and Noel told me that, like them, John said he would never forget, but that he refused to allow himself to be destroyed by useless bitterness and anger. And, like them, he intended to stay in Zimbabwe and make the best of the rest of his life. Noel used to work for Rhodesia Railways and spent some time at Bannockburn, a railway centre surrounded by Hokonui Ranch. He told me often, always grinning with fun, how he and his white comrades had rejoiced when my father and I were arrested in 1972, and how strange but nice it was now to be friends.

My mother used to say that you could hear the beautiful English of Father Jerome O'Hea, her contemporary and head of Kutama Mission, through the perfect diction of his former pupils, such as Robert Mugabe and the linguist and diplomat Professor George Kahari. Her own pupils from Dadaya were also regarded as having excellent English, so she was slightly taken aback, although amused, by a conversation at a reception when Deputy Prime Minister Simon Vengai Muzenda said to her regarding Reginald Stephen Garfield Todd, 'Tell me honestly, do you call your husband Reginald or Stephen or Garfield?' Eddison Zvobgo, who happened to be listening, answered.

'She calls him Gaar,' he said, with a perfect New Zealand accent. 'Gaar! Gaar! All over Dadaya Mission you could hear her calling Gaar! Gaar!'

Muzenda held my parents in the highest esteem. In the 1960s, my father provided a lawyer when Muzenda was in political trouble. His dislike of me stemmed from a reception held by the Zimbabwe Project at London's Westminster Cathedral in 1978, to introduce representatives of the liberation movements to representatives of donor agencies. PF Zapu was represented by Edward Ndlovu, and Zanu (PF) by Muzenda. There were snacks for the guests, soft drinks and wine. I offered Muzenda a drink, and he said he wanted whisky. Sorry, I replied, it's not available.

'The bottle stores are still open,' he said, and locked eyes with me. I was silent, considering what to do. Then, thankfully, before either of us could say another word, Brian McKeon of the Irish Catholic agency Trocaire opened his briefcase and, with a flourish, produced a bottle of whisky.

In 1985, the Zimbabwe Project started assisting in the training of ex-combatants as prison warders. Eddison Zvobgo, by then Minister of Justice, Legal and Parliamentary Affairs, under which portfolio prisons fell, rang one morning to put a proposal to us. He said that, since independence, so many had left the prison service, fearing retribution for the past. After a real tussle with Treasury, he had managed to get permission to recruit and employ 100 more warders. But there was a catch. Each recruit had to go through six months of training, which had not been budgeted for. If, he said, we could raise the necessary Z$100 000 required for training, he would in turn enlist the 100 from the ranks of the ex-combatants. By now donor agencies had become accustomed to unusual requests from the Zimbabwe Project, but it was hard to think of someone who could relate the magic word 'development' to the training of prison warders. I told Zvobgo we would do our best, and before long the German agency Bread for the World once again came to our assistance.

Since Zvobgo had taken over the Justice portfolio, he had become very fond of my husband, who had been doing brilliant work for the ministry. But things in Zimbabwe inevitably became too much for Richard to bear. I didn't know until later that he had been required to work on cases against some of our friends, like Dabengwa and Masuku, but when they had been found innocent and then immediately re-detained, he found this gross injustice intolerable. Also, Richard was missing his extended family overseas. On Sunday 26 May 1985, Richard left Zimbabwe to attend the funeral of a dear cousin, Percy Paley, in Ireland. He never returned.

I remained grateful to him, especially on two important counts. He did not confront me with having to make a choice between him and Zimbabwe, and he also lifted a heavy burden from my shoulders. During the course of the treason trial, legal representation threatened to come to a halt because of a shortage of funds. I went to my father, he increased his bank overdraft, and I borrowed the necessary funds from him. Richard knew of this and he repaid that debt for me.

Zvobgo was sad about Richard's departure, but glad about the way the training of ex-combatants for the prison service was progressing. The very day Richard was attending Percy Paley's burial in Ireland, I was being taken to Chikurubi Prison by the prisons director Chigwida, to meet the recruits we were funding. When we arrived, the recruits assembled, there was a salute, and then we had tea together. At the table with Chigwida and me were the chief training officer and the only three women on the course. I asked one why she had joined. She said because it was such a challenge, and she was enjoying every day so far. They also repeated to me the 'golden rule', which Chigwida said was instilled during training. This was that just *being* in prison is punishment for prisoners, and that their *treatment* in prison should not be punitive.

Chigwida then took me to Harare Central Prison to see the impressive workshops being run for prisoners in a variety of skills, including book-binding, car repairs, manufacturing uniforms for the services and making crests for them from scrap metal, and sewing robes for judges and even soft sheets for newborn babies at Parirenyatwa Hospital. Chigwida took me on a tour of one of the prison farms near Chikurubi where they produced vegetables, chickens, pork, beef and crops, and lamented the fact that proceeds went straight back to the Treasury. He longed for a scheme under which income would be retained by his ministry and ploughed into improvements throughout the prison service.

Twenty years later, Mugabe had succeeded in bringing these institutions under the supervision of CIO/army factotums. Professionalism and golden rules were out the window and prisons throughout the country had collapsed into a hungry nightmare of disease and despair. The thought of sheets for Parirenyatwa Hospital seemed absurd, let alone soft sheets for babies.

We were now heading for Zimbabwe's first single-member, constituency-based elections of 1 and 2 July 1985. It was the first election to be run and supervised in every respect by Zimbabweans, with Tobaiwa Mudede cutting his teeth as registrar general. Seven parties contested the eighty black seats, and one party, one group and several independents contested the twenty seats reserved for whites until 1987 under the Lancaster House constitution. The two major parties each contesting all eighty common-roll constituencies were Mugabe's Zanu (PF) and Nkomo's PF Zapu, the initials 'PF' recalling a faint memory of the years 1976 to 1980 when the two parties worked together as the Patriotic Front.

Nkomo was conducting as vigorous an election campaign as was possible under the state of emergency that had remained in force since being declared by Ian Smith in 1965. Bishop Muzorewa's United African National Council (UANC) fielded fifty-five candidates. In 1982, Muzorewa had been arrested by security forces on suspicion of 'subversive activities' and held for nine months, eventually being released without charge. Now it was the turn of the Reverend Ndabaningi Sithole to be in exile overseas. Despite his absence, his party, Zanu-Sithole, managed to field thirty-one candidates.

Elias Rusike, managing director of Zimbabwe Newspapers, pledged free and fair reporting, but implored political leaders not to make personal attacks on each other. As if in direct response, Mugabe launched the Zanu (PF) election campaign in Plumtree with a virulent attack on Joshua Nkomo and PF Zapu, and told would-be voters that the only candidate from the area whom government would be prepared to work with in future would be Dr Callistus Ndlovu, who was standing for Zanu (PF). Ndlovu had resigned from PF Zapu two years previously and been rewarded with a cabinet appointment. Now he was standing against his cousin, PF Zapu's Dr Isaac Nyathi, who had been released from detention in Chikurubi Prison ten months previously on grounds of ill-health, leaving Dabengwa, Masuku and others still inside.

Mugabe also announced that the Zanu (PF) candidate for Beitbridge, against PF Zapu's Kembo Mohadi, was to be John Mbedzi. At the time, Mbedzi was out on bail for contravening the Law and Order (Maintenance) Act, kidnapping, illegal use of a firearm and conspiring to pervert the course of justice. By selecting him, Mugabe was declaring the ground rules for the election.

Eventually Zanu (PF) won sixty-four seats, PF Zapu fifteen and, despite the depredations of 5 Brigade's Gukurahundi, collected every seat in Matabeleland. Zanu-Sithole managed to win Chipinge, and UANC failed to win anything. Bishop Muzorewa once more fled the country.

The one white contesting party was Ian Smith's Conservative Alliance of Zimbabwe (CAZ), formed just before the election from remnants of the former Rhodesian Front. The Independent Zimbabwe Group (IZG) was a loose collection of individuals, including some members of parliament who had left the Rhodesian Front since independence and who didn't want to be seen as an opposition party as such. They wooed the white electorate on the grounds that, while they didn't differ from CAZ on specific policy issues, they could, unlike CAZ, accept the reality of majority rule, and that a strategy of cooperation with government was appropriate where possible. Seven whites ran as independents, including Chris Andersen, who had been appointed Minister of State for the Public Service. Despite Prime Minister Mugabe stating during the campaign that after the election he would conduct a clean-up 'so that we remain only with whites who want to work with government', CAZ won fifteen of the twenty seats. The IZG won four, and Chris Andersen won his constituency.

After these elections I received a letter from Mohamed Kellou, who had been Algeria's first ambassador to Zimbabwe, asking for more details. We had become close friends and he had helped soothe our way through Zimbabwe's first heartbreaks by relating his own experiences of the grim inevitability of, as he put it, the 'children of revolution eating one another'. Now, his diplomatic career over, he was practising law in Algeria and France, but remained deeply interested in Zimbabwe. I replied:

Yes, Chris Andersen is the only non-Zanu (PF) member of the Cabinet. By the time of the elections he had broken away first from the Rhodesian Front and then from the IZG, was thus acceptable to the Prime Minister and stood successfully as an Independent. Yes, you unerringly put your finger on our Prime Minister's major – as he sees it – problem by saying that you wanted to know about what you call his 'successful but non-sufficient victory' to achieve his goal of a one-party state. He was *furious* that CAZ won 15 seats and therefore can deprive him of the 70 seats he needs in Parliament to change the Constitution and implement a one-party state.

Let me tell you about a friend of mine, Dr Isaac Nyathi. He is an economist trained in the Soviet Union, and was Zapu representative to Scandinavia, then joint Chairman with Dr Bernard Chidzero, now our Minister of Finance, on joint Patriotic Front/Unesco surveys of the future of Zimbabwe. Nyathi ran Nitram, a company set up to promote the welfare of ZPRA ex-combatants and was arrested with Dabengwa and company, charged with treason, found innocent, detained, released about 10 months ago, and couldn't get work since. He had the courage to stand in these elections against Dr Callistus Ndlovu who left PF Zapu to join Zanu (PF) maybe two years ago, and was almost immediately appointed a Minister as a reward by our Prime Minister.

Nyathi and Ndlovu stood against each other in our 'free and fair' election in Bulalima-Mangwe constituency which centres on Plumtree, near the Botswana border. They are cousins. Callistus got 923 votes and Isaac got 31334. Callistus has now been appointed again as a Senator by Mugabe and is a Minister – with less than one thousand votes?

The Prime Minister Robert Mugabe now gives the impression that he is Zimbabwe and anyone who voted against his party voted against Zimbabwe. He has his own six seats to appoint to the senate. One of them was held by Denis Norman, former Minister of Agriculture. He has been sacked. Mugabe gives him praise for the wonderful work he did 'but … as the farmers voted for CAZ' he is punishing them for this by casting off Denis Norman …

So, you ask, how can the Prime Minister achieve the one-party state without his seventy votes in Parliament? He will do it through terror. This was unleashed through the Harare high-density suburbs and other parts of the country just as soon as the election results were announced. He made a speech, broadcast in Shona, '*Goborai zvigutswa!*', stating that loyal people should stump their fields and tear the weeds from their gardens. So hundreds of men and women went on the rampage, burning, looting and attacking whom they thought were members of 'minority parties'. People were killed. One man, a UANC Bishop Muzorewa supporter, who was so terribly beaten, managed to crawl into the shell of his destroyed house, got paraffin, poured it over his body, set himself alight. Dead, at last, as ordered by Mugabe. Now all these people from the high-density suburbs are being required to buy Zanu (PF) membership cards just as were all the people from the rural areas devastated earlier by 5 Brigade.

After the elections the Prime Minister announced that all those who were not Zanu (PF) in the civil service would be 'rooted out' and in my own work it has become clear that even integrated groups of ex-combatants are suffering raids to 'root out' former members of ZPRA. One group from a cooperative in Harare was yesterday called in by CIO for questioning. Quite deliberately, I think, they were taken through a room where they saw two of their comrades had been beaten to a groaning pulp. I got another message this morning about three others ... But you multiply these messages from all over and, all I can do, Mohamed, is answer your question about 'the non-sufficient victory' through Lancaster House. Mugabe's eventual victory will now be achieved through terror.

I feel I personally will be safe for a little time. All I want to achieve now is what I can, in my work, but I want to give my parents peace too. In the meantime life is getting a bit more agonising. While I type this letter to you probably one of my friends is naked, hands and feet tied behind his back, a bag drenched with water over his head. What can I do for him?

One day our Prime Minister himself may be a victim in need of help but at present he is the one steering us toward unmitigated disaster. He has appointed Enos Nkala as Minister of Home Affairs. Nkala loathes Joshua Nkomo. This puts Nkala in charge of the police and the dreaded PISI – Police Internal Security and Intelligence – which was created under his predecessor Ushewokunze. Simbi Mubako, who held the post of Home Affairs, was switched with Nkala – Mubako is now Minister of National Supplies. I shouldn't think Mubako is very happy. Apart from that there haven't been many significant Cabinet changes, except for the dismissal of Senator Norman.

The Prime Minister has said that he is not against the Ndebele. He says that only Dr Nkomo and Zapu are the enemies. Nkomo has had all his guns removed, and his bodyguards arrested. At the opening of Parliament he went up to the Prime Minister to shake hands. The PM didn't rise from his seat. Then Nkomo greeted everyone else. I think he is trying to be reconciliatory as is, I think, Smith's party, the CAZ. It's just such a pity that Smith is still around himself.

Nkomo was reported in the *Sunday Mail* of July 7 1985 as saying that the election results have been a tragedy and indicate that Zanu (PF) rule over the past 5 years has divided the country into tribal and racial groupings with, as things stand now, the Coloureds and Indians finding it difficult to fit in anywhere.

'I hope,' he said, 'it is not a forerunner of things to happen in Namibia and South Africa when they attain independence. It is a tragedy to allow tribal states.'

He said there had been serious manipulation of the voting figures, but even so, Mugabe's Zanu (PF) didn't get one seat in Matabeleland and Nkomo was asked why. He replied forthrightly that the killings and torture perpetrated in the region had made people react by voting against the party which perpetrated these evils.

I am fortunate to be bound in work which is, or should be, totally demanding. I enclose a news clipping which will give you an idea of what the Zimbabwe Project is doing. We never really intended to be so presumptuous as to try and reconcile members of the three former armies (two liberation and one Rhodesian) but we don't discriminate in our training schemes and our work has been important in helping comrades from ZANLA, Zanu (PF) and ZPRA, PF Zapu, to get to know each other and work together. The co-op mentioned in this clip, Pfungwa Imwe, represents the ex-combatants taking a giant step forward themselves by having former ZANLA, ZPRA and Rhodesian in their organisation, but that was their triumph, not ours although it's true that we managed to help.

August 1985 began with a writers' reception at Harare's Jameson Hotel. Among those present was Dambudzo Marechera. In London, before Zimbabwe's independence, a mutual acquaintance, Dewar, of the Scotch family, had arranged an unforgettable Sunday lunch-time rendezvous at our local Elizabeth Street pub for me and Marechera to meet for the first time. It was a lovely sunny day, and we had a little table on the pavement.

Dambudzo arrived late and, as the pub was due to close in about twenty minutes at two o'clock, he ordered three pints of lager and three double Scotches, all for himself. Our table was laden. Luckily Dewar was paying. Marechera caused a real stir when he walked in. He was wearing the briefest possible white shorts and vest, all the better to show off his ebony arms and legs festooned with white bandages, tied like ribbons in jaunty bows. Some time during the past week, he explained, he had been involved in an altercation at the Africa Centre and, in a rage, had lashed his body against a plate-glass window. Now he was in a happy, funny and affectionate mood, and announced that he was going home with me. I told him he certainly wasn't, knowing how horrified Richard would be if I arrived with this particular famous writer in tow. But every time I tried to leave, Marechera followed. Eventually, Dewar literally kept him pinioned while I took off and quickly disappeared around many corners.

At the Harare reception, Marechera was subdued, and Willie Musarurwa was the central figure. The previous evening, Musarurwa had been sacked as editor of our largest circulation newspaper, the *Sunday Mail*, and news of his dismissal was just starting to spread. I was late and hurried in past a cluster of people. A hand reached out, took my arm, and I said, 'Oh, hello, Willie. Congratulations!'

'There you are,' he said to the funereal-looking people surrounding him, among them George Kahari. 'That's the word you've all been searching for: Congratulations!'

Justin Nyoka then walked in, and I said we'd heard a rumour that he had been offered Willie's job.

'Yes,' Justin said, 'but I told them I couldn't possibly accept it.'

As Permanent Secretary at the Information Ministry, Justin was the guest speaker, but we couldn't hear a word. The microphone was faulty and he didn't have a hope of raising his voice above the roar of the cocktail crowd in the packed room. But we did hear quite a lot of yowling. Apparently a group of women seated in front of him, fresh from the Nairobi Conference on Women, were reacting to some remarks he had made which they deemed to be sexist. He must have been astonished.

The next day Sharlottie Msipa rang to say that her husband Cephas had been picked up that afternoon. Msipa, like his old friends and contemporaries Willie Musarurwa and George Kahari, had been PF Zapu, but in fact had joined Zanu (PF), as required for survival, and he was held for only a few hours.

The following week, PF Zapu members of parliament Sydney Malunga, Welshman Mabhena and Stephen Nkomo were arrested. The travel documents of Joshua Nkomo and his wife were seized. At the same time, Report Phelekezela Mphoko, deputy head of the Demobilisation Directorate, was picked up. This was kept very quiet, as was the news of Msipa's brief spell with CIO. They themselves almost certainly would have wanted no publicity at all. Report's detention was serious, as he was a senior civil servant holding a delicate position. I began to thank our lucky stars that the Zimbabwe Project had started going through its troubles as early as March 1983 or, these two years later, we might also have found ourselves in the sizzling fat.

I was leading a very odd life after the elections. On the one hand, friends were disappearing into the maw of the state. On the other, I was still associating with functionaries as if life in Zimbabwe were normal. At one small party I attended that August, the Minister of Education, Dzingai Mutumbuka, was guest of honour. His deputy Joe Culverwell was also present. Dzingai always referred to Joe, behind his back, of course, as JC Superstar. The subject of dissidents came up, and I asked why they always assumed these so-called dissidents were PF Zapu. They could be *agents provocateurs*, maybe from South Africa. Dzingai asked how I could question that there were dissidents when I myself knew someone like Guduza. I said of course I knew Guduza and would welcome a chance to talk to Dzingai about him. But someone changed the subject at that point, though not before Joe had said I needed re-education.

Since I had last seen Makhatini Guduza in March 1983, when he was hiding his family and about to flee Bulawayo, he had escaped to Dukwe refugee camp in Botswana, to which so many fled over the years, first from Smith and then Mugabe. Later I heard that he was approached at Dukwe by Super Zapu, whoever they were, and asked to become their leader. He refused, there was a fight, and he had to make a dash from Dukwe to Francistown.

Earlier in 1985 I had received a letter from Guduza. He gave an address in Francistown and asked me for Z$6 000 to help him start a small business. I was too scared even to reply. Only a few months previously I had told Stephen Nkomo, member of parliament and brother to Joshua, that I had heard Guduza was feeling old, poor, lonely, rejected and let down by Nkomo. Stephen said they couldn't help him, as they had heard 'disturbing' things about him. Now Stephen was locked up somewhere. It was quite obvious that the government of Zimbabwe had come to regard everyone who was not a card-carrying Zanu (PF) supporter of Robert Mugabe as a dissident.

Shortly after the writers' reception, I had lunch with Justin Nyoka and Ignatius Chigwendere. I told them how glad I was that my mother had retired from the Mass Media Trust before Shamuyarira sacked Musarurwa as editor of the *Sunday Mail*, and Justin told us the story of how he had been offered Willie's job.

He had received a letter from Shamuyarira saying that he and Prime Minister Mugabe had decided it was now time for a 'true and trusted cadre' to take over as editor of the newspaper, and Justin was the obvious candidate. Justin wrote back immediately, starting off by reaffirming his loyalty to everything and everyone possible – the party, the secretary-general, the minister, reams of titles – and then declining the offer on the grounds that to move from his position as Permanent Secretary for Information to a mere editorship would be a demotion he didn't think he deserved. He placed his reply on Shamuyarira's desk and delivered a copy for the prime minister. Since then, Justin and Shamuyarira had acted towards one another as if no offer had ever been made. But, said Justin, 'I want to come to the office each morning thinking, now how can I serve the nation today? Not, now how should I answer that bastard's letter?'

Ignatius and I laughed at the concept of Justin ever starting any morning by thinking 'now how can I serve the nation today?', and then the three of us laughed together at a report the *Herald* had carried from parliament:

> Pregnant schoolgirls are expelled as a deterrent because schools cannot be allowed to become maternity wards, the Minister of Education Dr Dzingai Mutumbuka told the Assembly yesterday. 'Boys who are found to have been responsible for such pregnancies are also expelled ... Teachers are charged with crimen injuria, apart from losing their jobs.' But, he said, the Ministry had no control over sugar daddies or businessmen.
>
> Mr John Landau (IZG, Avondale) objected to the association of businessmen with schoolgirl pregnancies. 'Being a businessman,' he said, 'I think I have to set the record straight. One is given the impression that businessmen are sexual perverts and this is unfair. A worker could make a girl pregnant just as easily.'

On the whole there wasn't much to laugh about. Report Phelekezela Mphoko's wife brought me a letter he had managed to smuggle from wherever he was being held that made reference to me. It was carefully protective, mentioning only 'that lady', and telling her she should contact me for help in getting him a lawyer. What made my throat ache were all the things in the letter she obviously didn't think would be of interest to me. He wrote how much he loved her and that she shouldn't despair. She should bring him a clean shirt every three days. She should remember that they had not been pleased with their little son's school report and encourage him to read at night instead of watching TV. Finally, he said she should think of the future of their children, and that she must knit as much as possible on her knitting machine.

There was a batch of ten hangings. The new Minister of Home Affairs, Enos Nkala, promised that the honourable members of parliament he had locked up would have a long rest. I heard that all of Joshua Nkomo's children were safely out of the country, but that he and his wife MaFuyana were having an increasingly miserable time. The symbol that PF Zapu had used for the elections was a bull, and a slogan now being chanted across the country by Zanu (PF) was *pasi ne Buru rengozi* – down with the bull of evil spirits. Minister Maurice Nyagumbo and others conducted mock funerals of bulls at which they were presented with coffins containing effigies of Nkomo.

Moto magazine had a bold and vivid cover for its latest issue, which succinctly summed up the travails of Zimbabwe. Captioned 'Aftermath of the Election', it showed a pair of hands shaking a champagne bottle, which was exploding in blood all over everything. Even the *Moto* title was splattered with blood.

CHAPTER 11

Hiding prisoners

ONE HECTIC MORNING IN AUGUST 1985, WHILE I WAS ATTENDING to a group of supplicants and knowing there was another lot still to come, a tall, thin, elegant man came and stood outside my office door and looked at me. When the first group left, he walked in. By now I was on the telephone.

'Would you mind if I sat down?' he asked in a nondescript voice.

'Not really,' I said, 'but I have a couple of urgent calls to make.'

'That's quite all right,' he said, making himself at home.

Before I finished dialling, he asked, 'Do you mind if I smoke?'

'Not at all,' I said.

While speaking on the phone, I looked at him. His face was in profile, and he was smoking and chewing the spent match at the same time. He looked very interesting, but, I thought to myself, my word – this man has problems.

Eventually he introduced himself as a member of a cooperative at Beitbridge that had long been trying to get assistance. They had sunk their demobilisation money into a supermarket and exhausted their funds before the building was completed. They applied for Z$10 000, and we hard-heartedly said no. If we gave them money to complete the building, what on earth would they use for stock? It all seemed like an open drain.

I got out their file and explained why we couldn't help, although we were sorry that they had lost their money. He said Standard Bank in Beitbridge had agreed to advance money for stock if the group completed their building. He could get a letter to this effect for the Zimbabwe Project. This changed the picture. He explained the members of his cooperative had asked him to come and see me, as he was now quite often in Harare. 'You see,' he said, long after making his request, 'I'm now one of the new boys in parliament.'

'What?' I asked. 'Are you the member of parliament for Beitbridge?'

'Yes,' he said, and put out his hand. 'Kembo Mohadi.'

He hadn't seen all the letters on file, as some had been written after his detention following the murder, 'by dissidents', of the local Zanu (PF) Senator Ndlovu. He had been one of the group against whom magistrates in both

Gwanda and Beitbridge had rejected charges on account of the torture they had undergone. Mohadi told me he hoped to be back in Harare within a fortnight. I asked why, as parliament had risen for two months. He said there was a lot of suffering in Beitbridge and he wanted to see the Minister of Home Affairs, Senator Nkala, on behalf of his constituents.

I was constantly amazed by the sheer, naked courage of those who seemed most under threat. I accompanied Mohadi to the lift, and he mentioned that he might be in a bit of trouble when he returned to Bulawayo. Could I recommend a lawyer there? I said he should talk to the people in our Bulawayo office. I learned later that he never had the chance to do so. When he reached his Bulawayo base en route to Beitbridge, he found an order to report to the police. To make sure he obeyed, a relative had been picked up and taken to Bulawayo Central police station and would be released when Mohadi turned himself in, which he did.

Little did I guess that it would be under Mohadi's hapless watch as Minister of Home Affairs some twenty years later that I was to lose my passport, my citizenship of Zimbabwe, and thus the substance of my life. He was still Minister of Home Affairs after the 2005 elections, when the police, in concert with other state forces, unleashed murderous attacks on civilians and destroyed the homes and properties of the informal business sector in settlements throughout the country. This was Operation Murambatsvina – 'clear out the human excrement'. Under Mohadi the police continued the open, flagrantly illegal use of the hostage system I had first learned about from Mohadi himself when he was its victim. Mohadi had personally learned grim lessons about the cost of opposing the wishes and designs of Robert Gabriel Mugabe in any way. He had learned the lessons by heart.

The ex-combatants who came in after Mohadi that morning had been warned off many times, as they were happy-go-lucky, hated working and owed us lots of money. They never lived up to their promises, and I had asked them to get lost, but here they were again, because three of their members had been 'picked'.

Usually when they came in, their clothes were clean, however tattered, but that day their two representatives were in a state of visible terror, and I had learned how terror can stink. They were former ZPRA and were asking for Z$200 to shift themselves and their belongings from Harare to Bulawayo. I said they should come back the next day so that I could consult my colleagues.

After they left, saying they would hide somewhere overnight, I had a soothing time with Eduardo Castro, a young former ZANLA operative, who had studied land surveying in Cuba and returned to utter despair, as no one could give him an official translation of his academic documents, without which he couldn't get a job. We had helped with this, and eventually also got him employed by the surveyor general. He was and looked miserable when he first found us. Now he looked fit, sported a Castro-style beard and had promised us every assistance when he was off duty.

Harare's annual agricultural fair was on, and we had invested Z$750 in a group of ex-combatants who would be displaying snakes at a charge of fifty cents per spectator. We had asked Eduardo to accompany them, but he refused, as he vividly remembered having been bitten once when young. Instead, he had come to tell me that he was going to get the surveyor general's department to construct a special map for us and our donors to show the location of all the cooperatives that we assisted throughout the country. That was really good news and made me very happy.

The difference between the former members of ZPRA whom I had seen that day and former members of ZANLA, like Eduardo, was profound. Former ZPRA were on the run, whereas for many former ZANLA, the future was shining.

Sharlottie, wife of Cephas Msipa, was related to Lookout Masuku, who was still locked up in Chikurubi Prison with Dumiso Dabengwa and others. A couple of months after the 1985 elections, she told me that, for the first time, Lookout and Du were in bad shape: depressed, very thin, sleepless, and Lookout was suffering from hypertension. She had been to see Minister Emmerson Mnangagwa, who said he would put a case to Prime Minister Mugabe for the release of Lookout, but that Dumiso was in forever.

Their misery and insomnia were fully understandable. They had been valiant, triumphant warriors against the Smith regime. Under the Mugabe regime they were helpless prisoners, unable to lift a finger in defence of the thousands of their fellow Zimbabweans who were being smashed into the ground by Zanu (PF)'s 'structures'.

There was hardly anyone who had stood for what were now abusively termed 'minority parties' in the most recent 'free and fair elections' who hadn't been detained or beaten up, or had their property burned and their family life destroyed. When I heard of the detention of Nevison Nyashanu, unsuccessful candidate in Harare Central for PF Zapu against Minister of Finance Dr Bernard Chidzero, I rang the Catholic Commission for Justice and Peace and said this was obviously a case where we could enlist Chidzero's help, as he would feel terrible if he knew his opponent had been detained. The director said, 'No, Judy. What is going on now is organised from the highest level. We all feel sick and powerless.' As early as 1985, knowledgeable and far-sighted people like him were becoming too scared to mention Mugabe's name on the telephone.

When people were 'picked', they were moved around so quickly that their lawyers, family and friends did not even know where they were. Stephen Nkomo disappeared from Chikurubi Prison and even his brother Joshua did not know where he had been taken. The same thing was happening with ZPRA ex-combatants. My heart clenched in horror when someone from Tsholotsho told me that white Land Rovers and white Peugeots – government vehicles – were moving around without number plates, collecting people who were not arrested as such, but were disappearing for good.

I started sending messages to a handful of friends, such as the writer David Caute in London. Writing helped me to get some of the burning out of my blood.

Friday 6 September 1985

I gave Edward Ndlovu MP a lift to Harare airport this afternoon. He told me about their trip to Canada last month to attend the funeral of his wife Mary's mother, Mrs Eleanor Krog. They were leaving Bulawayo when Edward was pulled off the flight to Harare by state security. Mary, leaving their three children on the plane, followed him doing the only thing she could to try and rescue him, which was screaming and screaming and thus attracting the attention of all in the vicinity until, amazingly, she got him released and back onto the flight. Edward told me the police had him by one hand and Mary by the other. The police kept saying quietly that they were sorry but they had their instructions and Mary continued screaming loudly about the Nazis who had also just followed instructions. Eventually Mary won. Edward, laughing, said Nkala, Minister of Home Affairs and thus in charge of the police, of course denies knowledge of this incident.

Tuesday 10 September 1985

I've proved, I think, that I'm not paranoid. I received a letter of thanks from a firm in London, Control Risk, for trying to help regarding the six abducted young tourists. This March Mugabe announced that their bodies had been found. Worried about the state of the letter, I sent it back with a query. Arish Turle's secretary has written back: 'Our previous letter to you certainly did not leave the office in the state in which it reached you. I can vouch for that as I certainly would not have unstuck it and then put it back in the same envelope.'

Monday 16 September 1985
All our newspapers, not just the *Sunday Mail*, have become almost unreadable since Willie Musarurwa was sacked. Talking to a friend on the *Herald* I was saying that never in my life had I seen such boring newspapers. He said 'Since Willie was sacked everyone is frightened to put a toe out of the corner.'

Thursday 19 September 1985
I have been feeling miserable about friends like Edward Ndlovu MP picked up this Tuesday at 5 a.m. and also the confirmation that Kembo Mohadi MP is in too, no one knows where. When I tried to ring Edward's wife Mary she wasn't there. Their little daughter Zanele answered the phone. She wept and said her mother was OK but 'daddy has been picked, and we don't know where he is'. Zimbabwe's venerable and valiant Edward Ndlovu picked, like a ripe tomato! It turns out that Edward is being held at Stops Camp in Bulawayo, one of the worst for torture, but I don't think they'll dare torture him physically as he is so ill, anyway. So many people are – high blood pressure as a rule.

Halfway through September, Dr Nkomo told me that his tiny secretary Primrose had been seen at the Bulawayo police's Stops Camp with her arms and legs shackled and that his brother Stephen and Kembo Mohadi were probably being held in Gwanda police camp.

I had learned that it is vital that authorities are made aware that others also know of the existence of their victims. So, without telling Nkomo, I rang Gwanda police from home. This kind of work I never did from the office. The policeman who answered was clearly flustered when I asked to speak to Mr Kembo Mohadi. He had to go off and talk to someone else. When he came back, he said he'd never seen Kembo Mohadi, didn't know him and he wasn't with the Gwanda police. I said, okay, could I then speak to Mr Stephen Nkomo? *Who?* I said well, you know, he's another member of parliament, and I'm told you are holding him too. He went off to get instructions again.

A new, rough voice came onto the telephone. 'Who are you?' I gave my name and telephone number. This man denied any knowledge of Nkomo and Mohadi, said they weren't in his custody, asked where I got my information from (I said 'friends'), and said he was going to check with the post office to see if I'd given the correct telephone number and address, and then tomorrow he was going to come and pick me. I said fine, but it's a long way for you to drive from Gwanda, and tomorrow I won't be here. I'll be at Great Zimbabwe. But, I said, I was going to be in his area the following week and I would call on him. What was his name? He wouldn't give it. Eventually he said, 'Ask for the member in charge.' I said I would, next Tuesday. What seemed to make him particularly angry was that I said: 'The information you have given me is important enough, anyway. I can now tell anyone that Gwanda police deny knowledge of the existence of these two members of parliament.'

It was just like old times under Ian Smith's Rhodesian Front, except now the abusers of power were black, although maybe there were still some whites helping to arrange the scenery. Another difference was that I couldn't recall any members of parliament being detained and tortured under Smith.

So, on the last Tuesday of September, I went to Gwanda police camp from Hokonui Ranch. I told my parents I was just going to drive around, which they knew I loved doing, especially at that time of the year with the delicate new leaves of the msasas and the mountain acacias shimmering in all their most brilliant colours. But I left a note in my bedroom saying that if I was very late returning, they should contact the officer in charge at Gwanda, as I was going to see him.

What a big camp it was. I was taken to a dour and bleary bloke, the one who had said he was going to pick me up in Harare. I tried to appear as light-hearted and breezy as possible. Eventually, when he again took my name and telephone number and asked where I was born, long-lost memories started tumbling in his brain. Was Mrs Judith Acton in fact Judy Todd? It turned out he had been a student at Dadaya. He denied any knowledge of anyone I said I thought was at the police camp. A young, much brighter policeman with him said: 'But she's come such a long way, shouldn't we find out from CIO …?' The beginnings of his kindly question were silenced with *such* a threatening look.

'I have the keys of all the cells. I know who is in all the cells. I've never heard of Kembo Mohadi and if Stephen Nkomo was here, I would know him. I've seen him. But he is not here.'

I spent about seven minutes with them and then retreated.

On the way home, I wished I hadn't been so scared, and that I had gone to CIO, especially when I later discovered that Stephen Nkomo had been there, at least during that week. Had our police been through a fast course on how to be fluent liars since the advent of Enos Nkala as Home Minister?

In the recent elections, PF Zapu's Naison Ndlovu had soundly thrashed Nkala in the Insiza constituency by 27 602 votes to 3 392. Mugabe then torpedoed the electorate by appointing Nkala to the senate and giving him the powerful portfolio of Home Affairs. Nkala obviously hadn't enjoyed his electoral defeat, and was now exacting revenge from the winners like Mohadi, who had thoroughly trounced his Zanu (PF) opponent, John Mbedzi. Stephen Nkomo had also won his Matobo constituency against Zanu (PF) by a dramatic ten to one margin.

I tried to call on an old PF Zapu stalwart in Gwanda, Sikwili Moyo, an uncle of Zimbabwe's future fighter, Jenni Williams of Women of Zimbabwe Arise (Woza). Sikwili had been kidnapped a few months previously by men from 5 Brigade, and, through a series of miracles, had escaped death, albeit with a bloated head and a tortured body. When he thought he was dying, a soldier had come in the night and smuggled him to safety. But now his house appeared deserted. Maybe I was at the wrong house. I looked round the back and found an old white man, so old he could hardly walk, staggering around. I fled. To me, everything that day appeared the stuff of nightmares. I got home safely and without my parents having been worried.

The previous week, in Bulawayo, I had seen the wives of three detainees, one, Mrs Agrippa Thembani, at the request of her father, SG Mpofu. Mrs Thembani was so young, so beautiful, and so new to politics that she couldn't cope. Her throat hurt, she coughed, her mouth was full of ulcers, she couldn't sleep and the skin around her eyes was terribly black. I told her a lawyer had been engaged and that she could go and see her husband at Stops Camp the next afternoon. I also told her who to ask for and what she could take for her husband, and advised her to get her doctor to prescribe sleeping pills. I rang her the next night and found she had seen her husband, got the sleeping pills, had slept and was feeling much better. I had to tell her that I had discovered that her husband was being detained for recruiting dissidents ... or so they said. It was said of everyone in detention, or that they had been in touch with foreign powers with the aim of overthrowing the government.

I managed to get hold of one of these incredible orders being showered like confetti by the detaining authorities. It was a ministerial (Home Affairs) detention order, and whoever served it on someone just filled in the gaps. It read, verbatim:

REASONS FOR YOUR DETENTION

1. Intelligence received from Zimbabwe African Peoples' Union (ZAPU), indicates that you posed a clear threat to the Public Security and

Public Order, in that between the month of June to July 1985 while within the country you … plus other persons yet to be identified, did hold several meetings on diverse occassions with certain members of the Zimbabwe African Peoples' Union (ZAPU) and did agree to supply (EX-ZPRA Combatants) now called bandits to further their activities in the Republic of Zimbabwe.

2. That during the aforementioned period on diverse occassions, you held meetings with certain elements of the former (ZPRA) (referred to as bandits now) against the Republic of Zimbabwe with whom you maintained close links and did plot and agreed that you would supply them (and did supply to them) at various points in Matabeleland North and South certain quantities of foodstuffs (which matters are under investigations.) The activities are clearly prejudicial and injurious to the maintenance of Public Order in the Republic of Zimbabwe.

3. You held these meetings with these elements whilst you were still in Matabeleland (Zimbabwe) area.

On the way back to Harare I met Mary Ndlovu in Kadoma, and we saw her husband Edward, overwhelmingly elected by his constituency to the parliament of Zimbabwe, but now confined to Kadoma police camp. He told us he was in a packed, lice-infested cell. Edward, one of the finest of our old strugglers, had diabetes, a transplanted kidney and a heart condition. He put on a brave display for us, but it was heart-rending to see him reduced to such grotesque captivity, unable even to shave.

I had been told, after my fruitless visit to Gwanda, that all detained members of parliament were being held at Kadoma. But, calling at Chegutu police camp later, where I was looking for someone who had been badly beaten up in Harare and who had since 'disappeared', I found, by accident, that the parliamentarian Sydney Malunga was being held there, not at Kadoma. I wasn't allowed to see him. But in the Chegutu charge office, the first thing I saw – which I found very revealing – was a handwritten note on the wall, instructing all police that there was to be a Zanu (PF) meeting at 10 a.m. the next day to discuss matters affecting 'our cell'.

My line with the police was: 'Have you ever been detained?'

'Of *course* not!' they would reply.

'Well, if you had been, you would want someone to be looking for you.'

One of my friends throughout these times was Ali Halimeh, the ambassador for the Palestine Liberation Organisation. Late on the night that Richard and I had first met him at a little party thrown by Zimbabwean journalist Michelle Faul, I said we had better tell him, before he learned the fact from anyone else, that Richard's great-great uncle was AJ Balfour, later Lord Balfour. In 1917, when he was British Foreign Secretary, Balfour had written to Lord Rothschild, promising a 'home for the Jews in Palestine' – not specifically promising the state of Israel, but paving the way. This letter became known as the Balfour Declaration. Ali staggered back, clasping his heart. 'You mean the author of all my misfortunes?' he said.

'I'm afraid so.'

Ali bore no grudge and appeared with Richard the next day in my office.

In 1985, people perceived to be opponents of Mugabe were not the only ones in Zimbabwe suffering great pain. That September, on Friday the thirteenth, I gave a small dinner party for Ali and his two beautiful young sisters. A brother of theirs had recently been killed in Beirut and another wounded. Ali just kept saying in his tired, dismissive little voice, 'Ah well, life is difficult.'

We didn't know it at the time, but it was early that month, with the people and structures of PF Zapu being mercilessly crushed throughout the country, that Joshua Nkomo accepted an invitation from President Canaan Banana to meet at State House to discuss the unification of PF Zapu and Zanu (PF). He must have concluded that there was no other way to stop the violence and repression being inflicted by Mugabe through Zanu (PF), except to succumb.

Simon Muzenda and Maurice Nyagumbo were present from Zanu (PF), and Joseph Msika and Naison Ndlovu accompanied Joshua Nkomo from PF Zapu. This led to a further meeting on Monday 16 September at State House, with an equal number of senior officials from each party for the first formal, but secret, talks. From Zanu (PF) there was Nyagumbo, their Secretary for Administration and member of the politburo, Emmerson Mnangagwa and Eddison Zvobgo; and from PF Zapu, Msika, John Nkomo and Ndlovu. This group formed what later emerged as a unity committee, chaired by Nyagumbo. He kicked off the gruelling discussions by stating that Robert Mugabe's leadership of the united party was non-negotiable. The name of the united party was also non-negotiable, and would be Zanu (PF). The purpose of this and any further meeting, he said, was simply to make the necessary political and constitutional arrangements for the assimilation of PF Zapu into the structures of Zanu (PF).

In October 1985, rugby legend Chris Laidlaw passed through Harare from New Zealand with a number of civil servants. New Zealand was contemplating the establishment of a High Commission in Zimbabwe, with, I thought, an eye on a future democratic state of South Africa. Laidlaw, to our great good fortune, was to be their first high commissioner, and was accompanied by his wife, the beautiful Helen Kedgley. One of my protections in the new Zimbabwe was the diplomatic circuit, where I was made to feel welcome, and Chris and Helen would soon add imagination and lustre to that level of the community, and comfort and friendship to ours.

One of those October nights I attended a cocktail party for the visiting head of Catholic Relief Services, and found that Michael Auret, chairman of the Catholic Commission for Justice and Peace, was going through an agonising time, as it was then totally against his nature to think ill of Comrade RG Mugabe. But Mike was being brought face to face with the violent repression being inflicted on the country, and the CCJP became the bravest and most forthright group in condemning what Zanu (PF) was doing. Eventually Mike left Zimbabwe broken-hearted. On another evening I met the former senator John Shoniwa in the tranquil garden of the Courtney Hotel opposite our offices. From time to time he needed someone to sit and listen to the story of his life without interrupting. That evening, Shoniwa casually said something I found amazing – maybe it's an old Oxford expression, or maybe he invented it himself. As he rose to go to the lavatory, he excused himself by saying, 'I'm just off to give a few little toasts!'

There was something both sad and touching about his Oxford manner and seeming vanity. His cousin, the writer Lawrence Vambe, told me that Shoniwa had been absolutely shattered when Mugabe did not reappoint him to the senate after the 1985 elections. One thing Mugabe could never be accused of was loyalty. Throughout his career he used people and tossed them aside when he was done with them.

The callousness with which the authorities treated their prisoners was appalling. Towards the end of October, Edward Ndlovu was still incarcerated in Kadoma, and even the prison authorities were beginning to worry about his condition. He had been taken to a doctor, who said he couldn't treat him, as he didn't have his medical records. The lawyer in Kadoma, Mr Palframan, was told by the police that they were taking Edward to Bulawayo, and Edward waited for police transport from 1 p.m. one Friday. But a relative saw him in Kadoma police station at about six that evening, and on Saturday morning, he was still there. He was suffering from angina, amongst other things. Mary had been checking with Bulawayo Central Hospital all day, and by 8 p.m. on Saturday, they still had no news of Edward being admitted.

I offered to ring Cephas Msipa, who was well connected to Prime Minister Mugabe and other high-ranking government officials, and did so. He tried to contact Simon Muzenda, acting prime minister, but he was in Gutu. He also tried Enos Nkala, but found he was in Bulawayo. He rang Nkala there, and also Callistus Ndlovu. They were both out, but Cephas left messages for them to ring him.

In the meanwhile I telephoned State House. I knew President and Mrs Banana reasonably well, having worked with Canaan in 1971 and 1972 against the Smith–Home proposals, which would have led to independence for Rhodesia under Smith if they hadn't been defeated. *Moto* was then a weekly newspaper and a useful vehicle in which to publish and distribute inform-ation. With future help promised by Baldwin Sjollema at the World Council of Churches, my father bought a second-hand VW bug for Banana, who set up a network of men on bicycles to distribute the paper throughout the country.

The men were meant to pay Hokonui Ranching Company for the bicycles from their proceeds, but by the time the Pearce Commission found the Smith–Home proposals unacceptable to the majority of Rhodesia's population and had left the country, Banana, my father and I were all detained, so luckily for the vendors there wasn't anyone around to pay.

I rang State House at about 9.30 p.m., and although I explained the seriousness of the problem, the receptionist was either unwilling or unable to contact the Bananas. Mary was agonising about the probability that Edward was still lying on a concrete cell floor at the Kadoma police camp, and neither she nor I thought government would like Edward to actually die in their hands.

After failing with State House, I rang the Kadoma police and had the most extraordinary conversation. The man on duty, who seemed deliberately obtuse, first tried to tell me that he thought I was ringing to report Edward's escape from Bulawayo Central Hospital. Then he said that Edward had been 'charged', so if he was still at Kadoma, the police would have to be performing guard duties, and they weren't, so he couldn't be. Then he said he didn't know whether or not he was there. At that stage, I said, 'My friend, if I were you, I would find out, because you may very soon be receiving a telephone call from your minister, Comrade Nkala.'

At that, obviously startled, he gave me the home phone number of the man in charge of the CIO, Mr Tekere. But when I phoned, Tekere was out. I left a message for him to call me, which he did the following morning. He said he didn't know whether Edward was still in Kadoma police camp, because Edward now fell under the Criminal Investigation Department, not CIO.

By now I was trying to get information through Richard Carver to Amnesty International, as well as through David Caute to anyone, and on 20 October I wrote to both that I had received a very happy telephone call from Mrs Agrippa Thembani to say that her husband had been released, along with 'quite a number' of others, but I had no details. I was confident that my letters to individuals probably couldn't be opened, but I nonetheless tried to camouflage any news.

Here is some more news from Harare. While our weather will probably be furthest from your interests I can't help mentioning that it is glorious, though a little too cool to augur well as yet for the rains. However, yesterday there was a crack of thunder, and the clouds are beginning to mass in the afternoons. I heard of three more detentions last week of senior army personnel. There is Colin Moyo, Commander of the School of Infantry at Mbalabala, and I'm afraid I'm not absolutely sure of the next two names as I've lost the scrap of paper I wrote them on. They should be Maflesto Sebata, Commander of the Military Police training school which was at Hwange, but was recently moved to Bulawayo, and Lt Col Rodwell Nyika, Second in Command of the Battle Battalion, Nyanga.

I managed to see Nevison Nyashanu. A man in plain clothes walked into my office some days ago, very ill at ease, to say he was a policeman on leave from Chakari police camp and that Nyashanu had asked him to come and tell me where he was held so that I could tell Nyashanu's wife. Nyashanu had been beaten up. The policeman was so anxious to leave and I was so anxious to see him go that I didn't ask him to sit down.

I was terrified that he may have been a plant but, nonetheless, went ahead that night to inform Nyashanu's wife, Shamiso, in Harare's suburb of Greystone Park. I told her I would do my best to see Nevison. I didn't tell her that Nevison had been assaulted but nonetheless, while I was with her, she rang Dr Nkomo and asked what he was doing about the situation. He was very sad and said that information was being kept from him.

The next day I drove straight to the police camp in the tiny settlement of Chakari about 160 kilometres from Harare. I hadn't been there before. It is a remote place, off the main road, fairly near Kadoma and also falls under Tekere of CIO in Kadoma as does Eiffel Flats where Welshman Mabhena is being held. Eiffel Flats is also remote and off the road. These are good places to hide prisoners. At the police camp I saw Nevison sitting in the sun in the wired cage outside the little string of cells they have there. His head was swollen.

We gestured imperceptibly to each other and without saying a word to him I went straight in to the offices to find the Member in Charge. He turned out to be a Mutasa. I asked if he was related to Didymus Mutasa. He said he was a nephew. I said I was a friend of Didymus and his wife Gertrude and I had come to see our mutual friend Nevison Nyashanu who had been a contemporary of the Mutasas when they were all together in exile in Birmingham in the United Kingdom.

The Member in Charge was so overcome by my claim of friendship to the Mutasas that he carried an office chair for me into Nevison's cage so I could sit in comfort while I talked to Nevison. This was such an incongruous set-up, me sitting high above Nevison while he crouched on the ground that Mutasa went to get another chair for Nevison.

While he was away Nevison told me quickly that he is being interrogated by three senior detectives who should, he said, be arriving any minute now to continue. They say the case will go to the High Court when they are finished. The allegation is that he organised several meetings with ex-ZPRA soldiers in the Zimbabwe National Army to overthrow the constitutional government of Zimbabwe. In other words, treason. He has not yet signed a sworn statement and is trying not to do so until he gets legal assistance.

Mutasa was almost back but I managed quickly to ask about Nevison's swollen head and he had time to say two words. 'Tekere. Truncheon.' Now Mutasa was back with us, in the cage. I didn't wait long. Forewarned by Nevison I heard the noise of a vehicle coming from afar, stood, thanked Mutasa very much, wished Nevison very well and was off in my car very fast as a police jeep roared in and about six men jumped out.

In later years, when PF Zapu had been thoroughly masticated and swallowed into the 1987 unity accord with Zanu (PF), Mugabe threw a few bones to some of those he considered to be his dogs now at heel. He made Joshua Nkomo a ceremonial vice-president, and appointed Welshman Mabhena governor of Matabeleland North. At about the same time, perhaps only by a quirk of fate, Tekere of the CIO at Kadoma was promoted to head the CIO in Bulawayo, where he had to report to Governor Mabhena.

Mabhena, like Nyashanu, had suffered under Tekere while detained at

Eiffel Flats. When I heard of their new relationship, I asked Governor Mabhena, 'How can you *bear* it?'

Welshman Mabhena looked at me with a still, steady, delighted grin. After a few seconds he answered my question with another.

'Shouldn't you be asking, how can *he* bear it?'

CHAPTER 12

Victory celebrations

NOT EVERYONE SUFFERED AFTER THE 1985 ELECTIONS. ONE evening I met the exiled South African, Patrick van Rensburg, at the Park Lane Hotel, and newly elected member of parliament Chen Chimutengwende bounced up to greet him. Throbbing humbly with joy, Chen invited us to his victory celebrations the following Sunday, 27 October. Patrick wasn't able to attend, but I did.

The celebrations were at a 'growth point' in the beautiful Mazowe area, for which Chen was the new Zanu (PF) representative. We spent the first couple of hours drinking in an open hall where cool breezes wafted through, sometimes scooping up crisps in passing. Kenneth Manyonda, an old boy of Dadaya, was a guest. In later years Zimbabwe's courts found him to have fraudulently won a rigged election at Buhera against his relative, Morgan Tsvangirai. He was made a provincial governor by Mugabe, another dog at heel with a little bone to chew. Even in 1985 he looked unhappy.

There were a couple of chiefs, a strong delegation of Maponderas, whose home region it was, an Egyptian lecturing at the Institute of Mass Communications and two of his friends from the Egyptian embassy. Someone asked later if I had been the only white, and I thought back. For the pre-lunch drinks and the lunch itself there had been three white farmers representing the Commercial Farmers' Union, and who had probably provided all the meat. Then there were the Egyptians, who, in that largely Zezuru company, appeared sparkling white.

People were warm and generous, and class seemed more important than colour. The VIPs (sheep being separated from the goats by the request 'will those invited from Harare please follow Comrade Chimutengwende') feasted in the secondary school on sadza, rice, sorghum, liver, chicken, beef and liberal quantities of beer, soft drinks and some wine. The guest of honour was Comrade Joice Teurai Ropa Nhongo. There weren't many old-timers in the political, nationalist sense, except for Michael Mawema. It was under his interim leadership, in the temporary absence from the country of Joshua Nkomo, that I had joined the National Democratic Party when it was launched in 1960. At sixteen, I was just old enough to do so. This was some time before the much older Robert Mugabe also threw his hat into the ring and joined the same party; my party, as it were. The National Democratic Party was soon banned, becoming the precursor of Zapu and then Zanu. It was because of the demonstrations and riots that flared across Rhodesia in July 1960 in response to the arrest of Mawema, Leopold Takawira and Stanlake Samkange that the colonial government enacted the vicious Law and Order (Maintenance) Act. After independence, the Zanu (PF) government took to the continued use of this Act like a duck to water.

After lunch we joined the people, massed in a large circle in front of our simple VIP shelter. The Egyptians were made a fuss of and, thankfully, all those introduced as dignitaries made very short acknowledgements: *pamberi ne* (forward with Zanu (PF)); *pamberi na Robert Mugabe*, and then a few *pasis* (down with), one being politely interpreted for me as 'down with the constipated gentleman', referring to Nkomo's girth. Mrs Nhongo spoke at length, captivating the audience with her beautiful voice. She was nice to look at too, so calm and young, and the braiding of her hair symbolised such time, patience and, probably, discomfort.

The governor of the province, a relatively young man, Kaparadza, looked intellectual in his large spectacles. My heart fell when, at the end of his brief remarks, he called someone forward who had been PF Zapu but had now recanted and joined the people's fold. A man of about thirty-five with burning eyes bounded up, his son, who looked about ten, wrapped in his arms. Michael Mawema, sitting just in front of me, turned and said: 'That man has captured the people's attention. Just wait and see. One day he will be the party chairman.' Alas, I doubt it.

The man took the microphone from Kaparadza, and perhaps he got carried away, because, after a few minutes, a hum started swelling from the crowd, and I sensed a commotion behind me. Turning, I saw an old man outside the VIP enclosure trying to restrain some angry youths. The former PF Zapu man was apparently implying that Zanu (PF) had forced its own candidate, Chen Chimutengwende, onto the constituency when voters had wanted one of the local people. The man, his eyes now really burning, relinquished the microphone to the master of ceremonies, shook a few hands and took to his heels, speeding, I hoped, far, far away. The hum grew and grew, and then a group of women, wearing dresses with Mugabe's face, rose in the VIP enclosure and started dancing.

'They are rejecting him,' my neighbour whispered. 'They want to beat him.'

Someone told me later that the man had such charisma that the women and youths feared and were repelled by him. Mrs Nhongo eventually took over the microphone, and with her beautiful voice soothed and swayed the crowd. She urged the people to be tolerant and said that the man was new to the party and only needed re-education. Kaparadza had also been trying to pacify the crowd, but ended by saying that the man had repented, 'but hadn't repented enough', which inflamed the crowd even more.

I asked a friend, seated next to me, if such intolerance had always been part of the local scene. He said no, but it had been growing in the past four or five years, especially before and after the 1985 elections. He said it was humiliating for men like him, but the women and youths had been told that they were the 'vanguard' of the party, and they interpreted this as meaning that they had all the power, and they enjoyed outclassing the men. When I saw women and young men peeling out of the reception area and running off into the distance after the man who had fled, I left too. My neighbour tried to stop me from going, mistakenly thinking I was enjoying myself.

'They won't hurt you,' he said. 'They like having you here. They will only burn that man's property. They won't kill him today.'

After that, the Zimbabwe Project staff had a break. Every few months we would go to government national parks and wildlife camps to get together, analyse our work and savour different parts of the country. On that occasion we went to Nyanga and had a wonderful time. We occupied three cottages at Mare Dam, which was just past Rhodes Hotel on the way to Troutbeck and the beautiful mountains bordering Mozambique. Most of our staff hadn't been to Nyanga before and were enraptured, loving the scenery, the fishing and horse riding. The national parks official who supervised the riding was obviously impressed to have so many blacks as clients, which, he said, was still unusual. He said the horses we were riding had also taken part in the liberation war, but on the other side.

Those who went fishing were initially driven nearly mad. First they were forbidden to use their own equipment – 'sticks', as their rods were contemptuously referred to – and then they were told that all the rules and regulations were stacked heavily in favour of the trout. The fishermen persevered for hours, and eventually managed to master fly-casting. In total one small fish was caught, a trout, but when Nkosana Mguni from Bulawayo proudly showed it to the wardens, it was laughingly dismissed as being a 'wild' one. They told him it was even smaller than the fish with which they stocked the lakes. But Nkosana cooked it anyway and had it for breakfast.

Nkosana was a survivor of 5 Brigade. He was a member of a cooperative we were assisting near Maphisa outside Bulawayo. They raised pigs. One day he was returning to his village from the sties and men wearing red berets asked him if he knew Nkosana Mguni. He said yes. They asked him where Mguni was. Nkosana waved his hand towards the pigsties, and said he had seen Mguni earlier, walking in that direction. They set off in pursuit and, without going home, Mguni headed fast for the main road, where he thumbed a lift to Bulawayo and to the Zimbabwe Project. He had been with us ever since.

There were many parties in Harare towards the end of 1985. At an EEC reception for the visiting mandarin, Maurice Foley, I was talking to the head of USAID when I felt a warm kiss on my left shoulder blade. I was wearing a strapless dress. I turned in surprise to discover the young-looking and handsome US ambassador David Miller.

'That was very nice,' I said, and added sincerely, 'but I'm glad it was you!'

The kiss impressed the head of USAID, and he continued our conversation with renewed vigour. Then it was off to Meikles for a reception to mark Algeria's Independence Day, where I found a lot of guests from the first reception. Some people had to attend four receptions that night, one of them being the Deputy Minister of Education Joe Culverwell. He was looking wonderful after a month in the United Kingdom and introduced me to the charming new Chinese ambassador. I could see from the card he gave me that his name was Zheng Yaowen, but had no idea how to pronounce it. He asked what I was doing, and I told him a little about the Zimbabwe Project. He said not to fail to ring should we think of any way he could assist us.

Then an old friend from university days, Tim Matthews, told me about a book written by Peter Stiff and loaned to him by someone in the CIO, titled *See You In November*, the recollections of a mercenary who claimed to have killed Zanu's Herbert Chitepo and Zapu's JZ Moyo. Tim said this chap also claimed to have nearly killed my father. He was flying once from Salisbury to Lusaka when he spotted my father on the aeroplane. He didn't have instructions to kill him, but knowing how much he was hated by the whites, thought of despatching him anyway. He tracked my father to his hotel, and then waited in the foyer while contemplating what he should do. The man was frustrated, however, as my father didn't leave his hotel room for more than twenty-four hours. At one point he thought of pretending to be a waiter, rapping on his door and then, when he opened it, clubbing him and chucking him out the window. I told Tim I had to go home as I was feeling wobbly.

That night I didn't sleep well. Various ideas were tossing around in my mind, which led me to pick up *Black Behind Bars* by Didymus Mutasa. It was published in Britain before Zimbabwe's independence, and, as it was launched at the Africa Centre in London by me, at his request, I suppose I must have read it then. Skipping through it this time, I was startled by a sentence that had either escaped my attention then or my memory since: 'It is surprising that Judith Todd and Peter Niesewand, those young whites who opposed the regime, were born and brought up in Rhodesia. Maybe they are opposed to Afrikaner domination.'

I was shocked and irritated by this, as well as half-heartedly amused, but maybe this weird rationale deserved some thought. Maybe Mutasa was genuinely puzzled about how we could break away from a sort of group loyalty. Maybe detention was wrong in those days simply because it was visited by whites, or by a colonial regime, on the representatives of the nationalist movement. Maybe today what is worse than that is disloyalty to one's peers in power. Maybe criticism of the way in which power is being exercised, once one has a popularly elected black government, is at least rude and wounding, and at worst, treasonable. I'm not being in the least ironic. I'm just trying to puzzle out how and why people adapt to the repression of their fellows.

The saga of Edward Ndlovu continued. Mary said he was getting very thin and had not yet been seen by a specialist. Bryant Elliot, our lawyer, rang her and said Edward was to be transferred from Chikurubi to Bulawayo, I supposed Khami Prison, at the weekend. I hoped there would not be a repeat of the previous two ghastly weekends when he was lost and no one knew where to find him.

Mary rang the doctor at Chikurubi and found him totally unhelpful. She said she thought that no one in 'control' had the faintest idea what a transplanted kidney meant. I promised to take Edward milk, bananas, oranges and tinned meat. He was eating sadza and rice, but couldn't take the bean soup. He had an aversion to beans since Zambia, where it had been their staple diet for too long. I also wrote to Eddison Zvobgo, Minister of Justice, Legal and Parliamentary Affairs, on Monday 4 November.

Dear Comrade Minister

Re: Cde Edward Ndlovu MP

As you may know, Cde Ndlovu is not in the best of health. He has a transplanted kidney and suffers from angina and diabetes. Just before the last election he was in intensive care at Bulawayo Central Hospital.

After his detention last September he was taken to Kadoma police camp where he lived in discomfort sleeping on the floor in a cell inhabited by lice.

Then the following sequence of events took place.

Thursday October 17: He was taken by police to Kadoma hospital suffering from angina. Doctor can't treat him as his medical history unavailable; Friday 18 CIO inform his lawyer that he will be moved to Bulawayo Central Hospital that day, or Saturday; Saturday 19 Mrs Ndlovu constantly rings Bulawayo Central Hospital. By 8 p.m. he has not arrived; Saturday 19 Kadoma police deny knowledge of whether or not he is still at Kadoma police camp; Sunday 20 Kadoma CIO deny knowledge of whether or not he is still at Kadoma police camp 'as he now falls under CID, not CIO'; Monday 21 Mrs Ndlovu is informed by Kadoma CIO that her husband will be moved to Khami Prison, Bulawayo today. Access will be given for his specialist to see him; Tuesday 22 Bulawayo Central Hospital and Khami Prison have no record of admission for Cde Ndlovu.

Wednesday 23 Bulawayo Central Hospital and Khami have no record of admission of Cde Ndlovu; Thursday 24 Lawyer sees Cde Ndlovu at Kadoma police camp and is very disturbed by his condition; Friday 25 Bulawayo CIO confirm that Cde Ndlovu is not in Bulawayo; Saturday 26 Kadoma police say Cde Ndlovu transferred to Chikurubi Maximum Prison the previous Thursday; Sunday 27/Monday 28 Mrs Ndlovu visits her husband and is distressed by how much weight he has lost; Tuesday 29, Wednesday 30, Thursday 31, Friday 1 November Lawyer informed by CIO that Cde Ndlovu will be transferred to Bulawayo over the weekend which will make it possible for him to be seen by his specialist; Saturday 2, Sunday 3, Monday 4 Prison authorities assure lawyer that Cde Ndlovu will be moved to Bulawayo later in the week when transport is available.

It is now nearly three weeks since Cde Ndlovu was taken to Kadoma hospital suffering from angina. He has still not been able to see his specialist.

Conditions of stress and ill-health can lead to the rejection of transplanted organs. Mrs Ndlovu is in near despair about how the detaining authorities can be made to perceive the extreme precariousness of her husband's health.

I thought the matter should be brought to your attention as Cde Ndlovu is at least partially now the responsibility of your Ministry of Justice as he is in Chikurubi Maximum Prison.

Thank you for your attention.

I delivered the letter by hand to David Zamchiya, the Permanent Secretary for Justice, Legal and Parliamentary Affairs, ensuring it reached his Minister Zvobgo before the weekly Tuesday morning cabinet meeting in case he had to consult colleagues about moving Edward. I had left the letter open for Zamchiya to read. When he had done so he leaned back and said: 'What exactly is your role in all this?' I said I was just a friend of Mary and Edward but I had done a lot of work trying to establish where Edward was. He thanked me for showing him the letter and asked me to wait for the minister in case there were questions. It was about 8.40 and the cabinet meeting was at 9.30.

Minister Zvobgo arrived shortly after and took me straight to his office although he didn't know what was up. He read the letter very slowly and carefully, and then said when he returned to the country on Friday he had come into the office only briefly. He heard that Edward wasn't in good health and that he was in Chikurubi. He phoned his colleague Emmerson Mnangagwa about the matter and Mnangagwa said he wasn't responsible for detaining Edward, it was Nkala. However, the minister said, the police denied this.

He promised me that he himself would go and see Edward at Chikurubi that afternoon. He also said the prison service was recruiting another 100 ex-combatants but that the Zimbabwe Project would not, this time, have to pay for their training. That was a piece of good news for a change.

Michael Keating, recently appointed assistant to Prince Sadruddin Aga Khan, passed through Harare on his way to Geneva to attend the Reagan–Gorbachev summit. He spoke very highly of the prince and of his gentleness and of the freedom his wealth had given him. 'He is very, very wealthy,' he told me. Maybe I didn't look impressed enough because he continued, 'seriously wealthy'. Michael was staying at the new Sheraton Hotel and conference centre and gave me a cursory tour. It was stunning. The stone carvings and marble floors were beautiful. The conference centre was terrifying, to me. Michael said he'd not seen anything to match it. I thought there was not only the danger of fire and Legionnaires Disease but also of hysteria, depending on who was using it. It would go to anyone's head to be surrounded by ranks of 4000 people mounting up and up to the ceiling.

Michael took me to see his bedroom which, although he said was single and must be of the humblest order, was luxurious. He was impressed by the fact that every time someone came to service the room, the radio was turned on. On the way up we were accompanied by two young men, one of whom rather aggressively asked Michael if he was a resident. 'Yes,' he said. 'Are you?' They must have been hotel security because they then relaxed and said: 'You see, our Zimbabwe citizens are very excited by the Sheraton. They come here, they get drunk and all night they go up and down in the lifts when our guests are meant to be asleep.' I was glad that the Sheraton was providing so much fun.

When I got home I was called to the gate where there was an old and shabby man, hat clutched in hand, wanting to see me. I wasn't going to agree but he disarmed me and gained immediate entrance with one shy sentence. 'I have come to see you Nicodemously.' He was an old-time member of Zapu and so a target and was on the move all the time. 'They are hunting us,' he said. 'What is happening to our Zimbabwe?'

I went to see Chris Andersen, Minister of State for the Public Service, about Nevison Nyashanu, under secretary (training) in the public service who had been detained on 14 August. He was one of the older Shona Zapu generation and had been detained under Smith for ten years. His wife's sister was married to Minister of Foreign Affairs Witness Mangwende. Nevison's wife, Shamiso, had been told by officials that he would automatically be fired after three months in detention on 14 November. His salary stopped at the end of September, they couldn't pay the mortgage on their house and risked losing everything.

Andersen was very courteous and helpful. He said he had been trying to get information from the police about Nyashanu's detention but was told only that he was helping with enquiries. He had the regulations governing the public service at hand. He said that Nevison had stood for PF Zapu in the elections earlier that year without seeking permission from the public service, as he should have, but he had been reprimanded and that matter was closed. He said the regulations stated that one 'may' or 'can' be fired after a three-month absence, not 'will'. I asked if I could give any reassurances to Mrs Nyashanu and he said yes, she need not fear waking up the next day to find her husband had been fired. He had been granted leave of absence, but no financial help was possible. If charges were laid against him and he was found guilty, that would be a different matter.

I went to tell Shamiso the relatively good news. Her church had loaned her Z$500 and I managed to raise some help for the mortgage payments. She had seen Nevison the week before and he was in good heart but getting thin. Quite amazingly, CIO Kadoma had taken him by car to the public service commission in Harare after he told them he might lose his job. Apparently they left him under guard outside in the car and went in themselves to ask that he should not be fired.

Edward Ndlovu was moved to Khami and at last saw his specialist, who said he was all right. Johnson Ndlovu was moved to Chikurubi on 18 November and his wife Connie was coming to see him. By chance I saw Ariston Chambati, an old colleague of Johnson's, who had just been informed by a friend at the Commonwealth Secretariat in London of Johnson's detention. This so well illustrated the position in Zimbabwe. A man in Harare learned well over three months later from London of the detention of his friend from Bulawayo.

Someone had come to tell me that Kembo Mohadi was being held in Beitbridge and had been roughly treated. I engaged a lawyer who hadn't yet located Mohadi but was trying. Even that would help, I hoped. I went to the International Committee of the Red Cross but the delegate was away until 6 January and nothing could be done in his absence. I got the feeling that they were unable to do anything anyway and were not permitted to visit detainees.

I collected Connie Ndlovu from the airport on Thursday 6 December and took her to Chikurubi Prison. I hardly recognised this little old lady. Only her laugh remained as free and gay as the rest of her used to seem. What a price, physically, the last few months had clawed from her, to-ing and fro-ing from the police camps trying to find Johnson, who, very close to Joshua Nkomo, was a special target.

I was finding that each time I did something I was afraid of, I became less fearful. I felt hardly scared at all as Connie and I approached Chikurubi. There was a dignified British diplomatic car outside the prison guard office and a chauffeur sitting on the visitors' bench at the guard post. I joined him after Connie had been admitted and asked if he had brought the British high commissioner, Ramsay Melhuish. 'To a place like this?' he said, highly indignant. 'Well, maybe the first secretary, Julian Harston?' I asked.

The driver, realising I must know his employers, relaxed and said usually he brought Julian, but not that day. Someone else had come to visit a British prisoner. He gave me the name of a man I didn't know and then dropped a few more, delighted when I picked them up. We went through them all, from the interim British governor, Lord Soames, to the high commissioners: Byatt; Ewans; Melhuish. Then we moved on to the second level. The game went on and on. So many British representatives had come and gone in the short years since independence. 'We have a very big foreign office,' the Zimbabwean chauffeur said proudly. 'Of course I haven't actually seen it, but it must be *very* big.'

When the guards were less busy I handed in a pile of newspapers for Dabengwa and company with no problems. After an hour or so Connie came out, glowing with relief. Johnson was wearing new, spotless white tennis shoes and prison clothes. He was clean-shaven and looked well. He was in a cell with seventeen other people, all from the same home area, Filabusi. It was crowded, but they had bunk beds, luxury after the floor in the police camps. They talked and talked and caught up on all the news of many years. They couldn't talk to Dabengwa and the others, but now and then they could wave.

I left Connie at home and went to the office, where I found an urgent message to ring the New Zealand ambassador in Athens, then their closest diplomatic office to Zimbabwe. My colleagues Petronella Maocha and Paul Themba Nyathi were curious, but just a bit blasé too. It had been our day for international communications. Paul had taken a call from the EEC delegate in Kampala who wanted another paper from us on demobilisation. He also wanted someone from the Zimbabwe Project to go to Kampala to give advice and had asked us to discuss the whole matter with the EEC delegate in Harare. There were telexes I copied for our Ministry of Foreign Affairs, saying that three government delegates would visit Zimbabwe from Guinea Conakry for the first three weeks in February to learn of the country's demobilisation experiences. This trip was being arranged by Bread for the World, the West German agency which had been helping us so much. Petronella was laughing with delight at all these happenings, but at the same time advising against inspiring jealousy in others.

I got through to Athens and spoke to Mr Harper, who said New Zealand was offering my father a knighthood in the Queen's New Year Honours, but he couldn't reach him to see if he would accept the offer. New Zealand needed to know urgently and he wondered if I could give my father's wishes by proxy.

I said that when New Zealand's prime minister, David Lange, had been in Zimbabwe earlier in the year, he had asked my father if he would accept an honour. My father, overwhelmed and delighted, had said yes. Mr Lange had said New Zealand would first have to clear the matter with the government of Zimbabwe and, as nothing had been heard since; my father had assumed that nothing more would come of it. Mr Harper said it had been cleared and would be announced in the New Year Honours List.

I rang home with the news and of course my mother was overjoyed. My father was weak and had been ill for so long with an undiagnosed disease. Maybe this was just the tonic he needed. It's too wonderful, she said, that the honour had also been approved by *our* government. My father was out when I rang. When he came in my mother said she had news but wouldn't tell him until he was tucked up in bed. He went to bed and waited expectantly. 'Did she think you were going to faint?' I asked him later. He really didn't know and she couldn't remember. When he was flat on his back, she said, 'Congratulations, Sir Garfield,' and kissed him. 'What on earth are you talking about?' he asked. She explained and then, she told me later, 'we had a little weep together'.

Connie Ndlovu told me about the recent funeral of the Khumalos, Luke, the headmaster of the famous Tegwane Secondary School near Plumtree and his expatriate wife Jean. They were shot dead. The official government announcement stated they had been killed by dissidents. Who were these dissidents? Connie said she was very scared of going to the funeral as she thought there would be roadblocks and army and police and people being arrested and questioned. But she went, and there were no roadblocks. When she reached the school she was told of the murky events of that night.

'Do you know about the spirits and hysteria?' Connie asked me. I nodded my head, but I didn't, really. Well, she said, on the night of the killings a woman at the school had started shrieking and others gathered around her. She was screaming and crying and doing acrobatics. Someone said the woman had a brother at the school. *Let's find him so he can tell us how to cope.* Some went to find him, including the Khumalos. The others waited and waited with the woman. Eventually a young man came in the dark. They thought it was the brother. Then they saw he was armed. 'Move!' he ordered. They started moving. They stepped over the bodies of the Khumalos. She might have been dead, but he was groaning. Maybe if there was help, he could have been saved. They were taken to a small room in a dormitory block and locked in. They waited and waited, then they heard a car moving.

The primary school headmaster was roused from bed by a man who ordered him to point out the Khumalos' house, which he did. The man poured paraffin everywhere and the headmaster thought he was to be burned. But as the Khumalo house was set alight he was told to get out. He did so.

The police eventually came at about 3 a.m. The shooting had probably been at about 9 p.m. A policeman asked a pupil: 'But there are so many of you. Why couldn't you stop them?' The student said: 'They were so hefty.'

There were about twenty-five of them. They were well dressed and well fed. They were big. They didn't speak much. When they did it was in Sindebele. And there were no arrests of the locals, no roadblocks. It was as though nothing had happened. A truckload of soldiers did come, but that was to make preparations for the visit of Prime Minister Mugabe. People were wondering...

Washington Sansole, who had been a pupil under the Khumalos, said they had been married a long time; they didn't have children of their own; they were no longer young and attractive but they loved each other so much that when you saw them wandering together through the school grounds, you could be sure they were holding hands.

On Christmas Day my father and I attended a wedding at Msipani in the communal lands about forty kilometres from Hokonui Ranch. The rains had at last arrived; the veld was emerald, the cattle sleek and content. The destination was quite far off the main road and so, wherever there may have been doubt about whether to turn right or left along the diminishing track, a beckoning tree fluttered with festive streamers.

The bride was dazzling in white lace, the groom stiff and proud in black tails. The guests, quite easy with each other despite huge disparities in dress, which ranged from ostentation to rags, were enraptured by the formal dancing, provided by eight young couples who had been practising since the school holidays began. They were beautifully dressed, smart suits, pretty dresses, high, high heels for the women and bright, pert little hats, dancing to music supplied by a nostalgic old wind-up gramophone. One of the dances was very provocative and had the audience in gales of laughter.

The eight couples followed each other in a line, a slow quickstep and highly decorous. Then, after about ten beats they would pause, heads high in the air, faces poker-like and averted from each other, and, quick as a flash of lightning, the hips of each couple played a swift staccato tune, male left hip against female right hip, then a twirl and then male right hip against female left hip twice, then on with the decorous quickstep and another repeat of the snaky little tattoo. What made it so hilarious was that the bodies appeared so disdainful and haughty, just the hips, alone and independent, completely subversive and naughty.

As we were leaving, Mr Raphael Baleni, head of the Department of Manpower Planning and Development in Masvingo, asked if he could introduce his daughter to me. She was beautiful and in Form Two at Northlea High School in Bulawayo. They both laughed with pleasure at my astonishment when I learned that at her birth sixteen years before, she had been named after me.

That night there was a horror story on the television news. A Comrade Moyo was shown under a tent-like structure in intensive care in Bulawayo. 'Dissidents' had forced his second wife to chop off his hands and feet. Can you imagine interviewing him on television? While he was telling the ghastly story and groaning and writhing in pain, my father was groaning and writhing in pain on the chair next to me.

The last day of the tumultuous year of 1985 was a Tuesday. Earlier that month my father had received a cable from New Zealand:

PERSONALLY I HAVE MUCH PLEASURE IN INFORMING YOU THAT THE QUEEN HAS BEEN GRACIOUSLY PLEASED ON THE OCCASION OF THE NEW YEAR TO CONFER UPON YOU THE HONOUR KNIGHT BACHELOR STOP PLEASE ACCEPT MY WARM CONGRATULATIONS STOP OFFICIAL ANNOUNCEMENT WILL BE MADE ON 31ST DECEMBER PAUL REEVES GOVERNOR GENERAL

Very few people knew of the impending honour until the morning of 31 December, when it was headline news throughout Zimbabwe. The front-page headline in the *Herald* was 'Todd becomes Sir Garfield – "I'm delighted"', and billboards all over town read GARFIELD TODD KNIGHTED. It was almost precisely fourteen years since the *Herald* billboards all over town had read TODD AND JUDY ARRESTED.

On New Year's Eve I accompanied Deputy Minister Culverwell to the annual Lonrho party at the Monomatapa Hotel and, because of my father's honour, there was a lot of joy and friendship. The veteran politician, businessman and scholar Stanlake Samkange said there had never been a more popular honour at any time in the history of the country. He also said, 'You may not know this, but when your father was prime minister, Africans referred to his government as "our" government.'

Stanlake's son and namesake was there too. He had finished his studies at Oxford University and was now studying law in the United States. Another Samkange, Nelson, came up to pat me on the back as though it was me who had been honoured.

Whenever I saw Nelson I remembered his escape from Gonakudzingwa detention camp, where he was held with Joshua Nkomo, Willie Musarurwa and others in the 1960s. I visited them there a couple of times. It was a hellish place, so dry, so hot, so far from anyone's home. Many years later Nelson told me that when he got out of the camp he hid for some time, growing a beard as a disguise. Eventually he started footing, as people say in Zimbabwe, in the direction of Zambia, getting off the road whenever he heard a vehicle. But once a vehicle came too fast for him to hide and so he just kept trudging along as though he was from the area. It was a police van driven by a white. There were two African Constables in the back. The vehicle skidded to a halt next to Nelson, the two ACs, as they were known, leapt out, grabbed him and threw him into the back, where he just sat, silent. They asked if he had seen any stranger in the area and he shook his head. Then they pulled out an old photo of Nelson and handed it to him. 'Have you seen this man?' He studied it closely for a long time while the van sped on and on, then shook his head and said no. One of the ACs rapped on the window separating them from the driver, the van pulled up and the ACs opened the door and threw Nelson out.

Years later President Mugabe appointed Nelson Samkange, a fellow Zezuru, governor of Mashonaland West, where Nelson took part enthusiastically in the uprooting and dispossession of commercial farmers, their employees and families. In November 2005 Nelson evicted the last eighteen, leaving only one white in possession of land in the province. This was Billy Rautenbach, reputedly a close friend of President Mugabe and wanted in South Africa on criminal charges. Eventually, he too was evicted.

CHAPTER 13

Survivors of Sekou Toure

I N 1985, STEPHEN ZACHARIAH ENTERED MY LIFE. A DEMENTED ex-combatant called Comrade Zuwa (Sunshine) used to come and agonise about searching for his mother's body. She had vanished during the war. Sunshine also talked about having been trained as a cobbler in Mozambique, so one day we took a chance and paid invoices he brought in for basic tools. He set up a shoe-repair stall in a high-density township and was soon making money.

On one of his visits he brought Stephen, a tall, shambling, wild-eyed guy who churned out ribbons of totally incomprehensible monologue. While Sunshine disappeared for good, Stephen came more and more often, sometimes astonishing sober citizens from places such as the Ford Foundation, who, while sitting talking to me, would feel a menacing presence and turn to see this derelict scarecrow, a sack of newspapers – his bedding – over his shoulder, swaying in the doorway. Invariably they would depart in haste, and Stephen would stagger in and take their place.

Over time I realised that with patience he would calm down and eventually disappear, especially if you gave him a dollar, ostensibly for food. People like Stephen have to buy the most expensive, processed food, like bread. Having no abode, they have no cooking pots. But in reality Stephen's dollars went mainly on *mbanje*, or dagga (marijuana).

I learned a lot from him. He got Z$45 per month from the Department of Social Welfare, and needed five balls of *mbanje* per day at thirty cents each. We gave him a blanket, which, unsurprisingly, was soon gone. He claimed he had been attacked and robbed, but he could see I didn't believe a word of it, and grinned. He had a nice smile.

One day I managed to make out that he was saying he was suffering, and that he wanted to work. I, too, was suffering, as he was scratching himself all over, tearing at his hair, and I was beginning to feel very itchy. I said we would help him, but, although I knew he could understand what I was saying, I couldn't understand what he was saying. Before we could help, I had to be able to understand him.

'True. True,' he managed to enunciate.

So, I said, he must come and see me early in the mornings before he started smoking *mbanje*. He was there at eight the next day, but I still couldn't understand him. Bit by bit he made an effort, and, in time, spoke relatively intelligibly. One morning he said, quite clearly, '*Try* to be good!'

'I *am* good,' I responded defensively.

He grinned and said with authority, 'You could be gooder!'

Stephen was originally from South Africa, of mixed race. He had no skills, but had been in the Rhodesian Army, guarding bridges. At least that meant he could shoot.

We were starting an agricultural cooperative on the edge of one of the high-density suburbs in Harare, and he said he would work there. Social Welfare put him into a Salvation Army hostel, and he bathed and started eating. We gave him clothes, and a different man started emerging. He told me that he had given up drinking and *mbanje*, as they were destroying him.

Initially Stephen was weak and his fingers were swollen. Just before Christmas 1985, he walked in, showing me a massive thumb, and I managed to work out that he was asking to borrow a razor blade. I took him off to outpatients at Parirenyatwa Hospital and left him there, hoping they would lance the thumb and put him into hospital for Christmas. I doubt they did, but the thumb got better. Stephen showed definite racist tendencies, and I knew we were in for a difficult time with him, but hoped that with perseverance there would be a happy ending.

We had a happy ending with Comrade Kissinger, another derelict skeleton, who used to torment me by sitting outside my office with his torso out of view but swinging his leg like a pendulum, up and down and in and out of my sight until I cracked, went out and brought him in to see me. One day we took a chance, bought him two new outfits, enough food and paid rent on a room for two months. This proved to be all he needed to restore enough self-respect to start managing his life. Soon he was somehow self-employed, and turned out to be well built and quite handsome. We didn't often deal with such cases, but expected them to increase as more and more school leavers each year flooded the job market.

It was often possible to tell by an ex-combatant's *nom de guerre*, like Comrade Kissinger, roughly when he or she had joined the struggle. The US Secretary of State Henry Kissinger had impinged on the consciousness of the Zimbabwean people when he discovered Africa in 1976, which was when this guerrilla was cloaked in his name. Comrade Lord Soames had become a freedom fighter at the very last minute possible.

An acquaintance released from the Bulawayo police's Stops Camp in January 1986 told me of a man there who had been so horribly beaten that some of his fellow prisoners found it difficult to eat or sleep. He had been working for a security firm and was suspected of being involved in an inside robbery.

I wondered what could be done. Bleak thoughts in the night used to wake me with a terror to which I suppose most of us are subject at some time – what if I was that man, helpless, in the hands of brutal torturers, no help available from any direction?

I rang the security firm, found out who the managing director was and made an appointment to see him. He was a tall, courteous man of English origin, in his late fifties. I told him what I had heard. He said this was a very dangerous subject and a political hot potato. One could not do anything on the basis of rumours. People might allege things because they had a particular axe to grind. While torture was something he abhorred, as most people would, it would be true to say that members of the police and security forces might have stepped out of line not only under this government, but past ones too. It was probably something that happened all over the world, regrettable though this was.

I said I didn't have an axe to grind. I agreed it was a very dangerous subject; one certainly couldn't take action on matters like this simply on the basis of rumour. But I wondered if perhaps he could find the man's name and give it to me. His security firm wouldn't need to be involved at all. Perhaps I could find a lawyer who could do something. There were still some brave lawyers around.

The MD seemed to start feeling more relaxed. It wasn't that he was at all hostile. He just didn't want to get involved. He said he knew of the case, and the man had been roughly treated. But there had been no complaints and the employee had just seemed to accept that this was the sort of treatment you could expect.

'Oh well,' I said, 'that's a great relief. If the man is out and okay, then I can forget about it. That really is a relief.'

I went on to say how awful it was to know that someone was being tortured, and there was no help available – and that if torture went un-hindered, it was likely to become more widespread, and one day even he and I might find ourselves victims.

We talked on generally about our agents of torture – the CIO (Central Intelligence Organisation) and PISI (Police Internal Security Intelligence) –

how in the United Kingdom a free press would act as a deterrent to torture, and his belief that fear was at the root of torture. Then a shadow crossed his face, and he said two men had actually been detained. Maybe the one I had been told about was the one who was still inside.

The MD seemed troubled but still unwilling to contemplate action. I left him my telephone number, and repeated that if he could give me the man's name, I would get a lawyer. He walked me out of his office and out of the building, saying that he hoped the unity talks would be successful, because then 'the fear that the authorities have of the Ndebele' might cease, and the cause of this kind of activity might be removed.

He also said that when things had been really bad in Matabeleland under 5 Brigade, some of his staff had disappeared. They would go home to the rural areas, and then eventually their wives or relatives would get in touch with the firm and say the men had disappeared. Obviously nothing was done about it.

I said, 'Maybe if we just even collected the names now ...?'

No, he said, decisively. That was all in the past.

Not long after this encounter, Isaac Nyathi, now member of parliament for Bulalima Mangwe, brought his fellow parliamentarian, Kembo Mohadi, home. I asked Kembo what he would like to drink. Isaac laughed. 'He drinks water,' he said. Then they told me what had been happening.

Mohadi had been released on 20 December 1985. Despite the fact that he was the MP for Beitbridge, he received the water treatment at Stops Camp. He was handcuffed, naked on the floor, hands behind his back. Prisoners carried in pails of water, with which they drenched a hood over his head, partially drowning him. Eventually he was taken back to Beitbridge, from where, he thought, he was released in error. He was formally released by the police on 6 December and signed out, but then put in the witness area of the Beitbridge police camp. He believed he was meant to disappear at that stage, but someone had seen him and alerted his wife, who found him and got the lawyers to kick up a fuss.

Kembo told me that this had become quite a common procedure. The prisoner was signed out and subsequently taken away and killed, 'disappeared'. Then, when no one could find him, the authorities could say, 'Look! He signed himself out on 6 December and so is no longer our responsibility.'

Christopher Hitchens stayed at the Sheraton in January, doing a travel piece. He naturally did a great deal more than that, nipping around the region, meeting with members of the ANC in Lusaka and explaining to readers of *The Nation* in the United States who the ANC were and what their goals were. That led to a television confrontation in Washington with the South African government's black public relations man there, who compared a possible release of Nelson Mandela with a possible release of Charles Manson.

While Christopher was in Harare, I saw more of the Sheraton, and one afternoon took along the Nyashanu children, who loved stroking the soapstone sculptures. Tawanda was about two. His sisters Tsungai, five, and Vimbai, four, were completely bilingual in Shona and English, all the better able to express what was going on in their sparkling minds. Their father had been detained since the previous August.

One day their mother Shamiso said, 'Oh! I have a beautiful dream for you!' Tsungai had told her of this dream. Tsungai and I were walking with Vimbai, and I had one little girl on either side of me. All of a sudden there was a strange feeling. I held their hands very tightly, and said, 'I think we are walking into danger.'

A big voice then said, 'Do you need help?'

I answered 'Yes, please,' and three lovely birds floated down from the sky, a little one for Vimbai, a bigger one for Tsungai and a big one for me, and we all sailed away into safety. I was glad I'd said please.

When writer Nick Harman came to Zimbabwe, I took him to visit Shamiso on a beautiful day after rain. The world seemed translucent. The sky was vast and tremulous, so washed with colour and freshness you could sense the earth breathing.

Shamiso told me of a terrible dream about her husband. She had walked into their sitting room and found the prime minister. Nevison was at his feet, weeping and weeping. The prime minister was quietly sitting on the edge of the sofa, looking down at Nevison. Shamiso couldn't bear the scene, so she walked outside. When she came back, she found Nevison alone and on his back, knocked senseless. His spectacles were gone and he was lying there blinded.

The last time I'd seen Nicholas Harman was in 1983, when he told me he was writing a book about an English trader in East Africa. This was eventually published as *Bwana Stokesi and His African Conquests*. I said then that it was rather strange to come to Harare to research a book on East Africa, but he said we had very good archives. Now he was visiting us again. I congratulated him on the good job he had done ghostwriting Joshua Nkomo's *The Story of My Life*, published by Methuen (London) in 1984.

Someone had smuggled a copy to me from London, as it wasn't available in Zimbabwe.

Nicholas didn't quite deny writing it, but he tried to appear totally perplexed. 'What *do* you mean?' I laughed. 'Nick, practically every fresh photo in that book states that it was taken by Nicholas Harman: *Nkomo in 1983 outside the last remaining house of the Railway Compound where he lived from his marriage until 1953* (Nicholas Harman); *Nkomo at Stanley Hall in 1983, the centre of Bulawayo's political life in the 1950s* (Nicholas Harman); *The home to which Nkomo was confined by government order in 1962. The picture, taken in 1983, shows …* (Nicholas Harman).'

Some people are just too honest by nature to be able to dissimulate, and I told him the story of Richard Lindley and Robin Denselow from the BBC in London who had come undercover to make a film of the guerrilla war in the late 1970s for *Panorama*. To make sure no one knew what they were up to they had even left their cameramen behind when they came to my father on the ranch to be introduced to guerrillas – *The Boys in the Bush* of the feature's title – and had shot the film themselves.

Some weeks later, a group of Rhodesian journalists visited my parents. They used a guest room a short walk from the main house and, when they returned, they said excitely that they saw Richard Lindley and Robin Denselow had been visiting. Despite all their precautions, Richard and Robin had at one point forgotten themselves and signed the guest book.

One Sunday afternoon I held a birthday party at home for Matenga Nyashanu. His father was still in Chakari police camp. I ordered a beautiful, massive cake from the Park Lane Hotel. It was white, covered with whipped cream, and flickered with nine pretty, coloured candles. I will never forget Matenga's face and his big, big eyes when he saw the cake and I told him that it was his. He hadn't known there was going to be a party. His little sister, Tsungai, hastily pointed out to me that her birthday would be in March.

There were twenty-five people present, including the South African Joan Brickhill and her husband Jeremy, our lawyer and friend Bryant Elliot and his wife Elizabeth, Mary Ndlovu, Shamiso Nyashanu, her four children and family. Her mother, Mrs Takavarasha, was touchingly grateful to me for trying to assist Shamiso, whose sister was married to Foreign Affairs Minister Witness Mangwende. I asked Shamiso if her brother-in-law and his ministerial colleagues couldn't help, as, after all, they *were* the government. She said: 'I suppose they helped us by saying that life would be tough after the elections. That we should be prepared. The problem is that Nevison didn't know how to go about preparing for being detained.'

To my great astonishment, I received a call from Mr Stannard, director, internal CIO, whom I had never met. How I wished afterwards that I had been able to record the conversation. I am almost certain he said, 'Please call me Danny.' I know he asked if he could call me Judy.

What had led to this was that eventually I got so heartily sick of all my mail being opened, most clumsily, even Christmas cards, that I decided to take action. The only item not being opened was *The Spectator* in its new plastic sheath. I tried to make an appointment to see the relevant minister, Emmerson Mnangagwa, but he was away a lot. So I wrote, enclosing a Christmas card heavily stuck to its envelope, and asked him please to find out who was opening my mail, and why. I rang his office again a few days later and was put through to him. He said he had received my letter that morning, and had immediately got 'Branch One' to look into the matter. He expected a report within two days and would let me know. We arranged an appointment for the end of the week, as I said there were other things that I would very much like a chance of discussing with him too.

I was on the phone when a colleague said there was someone, very impatient, on the other line, saying he wanted to speak to me on behalf of Minister Mnangagwa. Lo and behold, it was Mr Stannard. I said, oh yes, I've heard about you for years. We had our Danny–Judy exchange, and then got down to business. He wanted me to know that CIO was certainly not opening my mail ... well, maybe in the past a bit, but certainly not now. Who is it then? I asked. Well, you know, it might be the post office ... now and then they do open letters to see if there is currency smuggling and so forth and, well ... (he had what seemed momentarily an inspiration) well, it might be the other side. '*What* other side?' I asked. I could almost hear him kicking himself. He floundered a bit and didn't come up with a reply. Anyway, we agreed to meet some time and he gave me his direct number so that I could ring if any more mail was opened. I said every piece of mail was opened, and he said, 'They're very clumsy, aren't they?'

He agreed to write me a letter saying the CIO was not opening my mail, 'but I won't go into details like I am now'. I asked him please to keep up his investigations until he found out whom it was. The reaction in my heart to all this, had I expressed it, would have been very direct and Murdochian – GOTCHA!

As arranged, I went to see Emmerson Mnangagwa, Minister for State

Security in the prime minister's office, and took a little sheaf of envelopes from all over the world that had been opened. He looked at them with interest, and then told me there was quite an intricate procedure to be followed before someone's mail could legitimately be opened. Temporary permission for seven days could be sought from the minister, but authority finally had to come from the president (I suppose in reality that meant the cabinet or the prime minister), and the postmaster general had to set the process in motion. Permission had certainly not been sought from Mnangagwa. He said he would pass the envelopes on to Stannard to assist him with his inquiries. Poor Stannard must have been heartily sick of me.

It was a constructive meeting. I liked the minister, although I didn't really know him. He was relaxed and pleasant and told me how beautiful Moscow was – he'd recently returned from a visit there with Prime Minister Mugabe – and how Red Square isn't really red at all. We spoke about the forthcoming delegation from Guinea-Conakry, whom he said he would like to meet, and he didn't have any objection to the Zimbabwe Project taking up an EEC request to go to Kampala and advise on demobilisation. Then we got onto the subject of Makhatini Guduza.

Guduza had taken Joshua Nkomo over our border after, I learned much later, Nkomo had actually been tipped off by someone in government that he was to be killed. From time to time I heard from people who saw Mnangagwa that he always cited Guduza as being an organiser of dissidents. Sometimes friends in Holland sent small amounts of money for Mrs Guduza, which I passed on for food and school fees. I told Mnangagwa that I was in touch with Mrs Guduza, and that it really didn't seem as if Guduza could be an organiser, as he had apparently fled from Dukwe refugee camp in Botswana to Francistown. But the minister was adamant. He said Guduza was at Dukwe and that he was organising dissidents, and that government had applied to Botswana for his extradition. He also said that Nkomo smuggled information to Guduza, who sent it to Amnesty International, and then Amnesty sent the information back to Emmerson, so, he laughed, 'It's a vicious circle.'

I wondered if Mnangagwa was being deliberately fed false information. I didn't *know* that Guduza wasn't organising dissidents, but all I had heard pointed to the contrary.

I found it so hard to understand how people who had suffered at the hands of oppressors could so readily become oppressors themselves. Mnangagwa was jailed for years and only just escaped the gallows. I asked him about a few people who had been detained, but, according to him, most of them were detained by Nkala, Minister of Home Affairs, under whom both the police and the sinister PISI fell. Mnangagwa used CIO, equally sinister but maybe more intelligent. One of the detainees was Johnson Ndlovu, picked up the previous September. Mnangagwa seemed not to know him. I said Johnson had worked for some years at the Commonwealth Secretariat in London. Oh yes, said Mnangagwa, not long ago he had seen the Commonwealth deputy secretary general, Emeka Anyaoku, who had asked after Johnson. Mnangagwa had told Anyaoku he had no information on Johnson, but would get 'my boys' to find out what was happening. I knew that the Commonwealth Secretariat had been in touch with Ariston Chambati about Johnson. Ariston was reputedly a friend of Mnangagwa. So, either Ariston had not brought the matter to Mnangagwa's attention, or Mnangagwa was a good actor who, in his charming and quietly pleasant way, was stringing me along. And if he was stringing me along about that, then maybe he was stringing me along about everything. On balance, I felt strung along.

I said Johnson had been held at Nkulumane police camp in Bulawayo for ages but had been moved to Chikurubi Maximum just before Christmas. He thanked me for the information, and said he would telex Anyaoku and tell him!

Mnangagwa said I should try to see Nkala. I was dubious about doing so, although, like most people, Nkala was always charming when we met. Godwin Matatu had told me that his friend Eddison Zvobgo, sitting next to Nkala in parliament, had watched him sign a stack of detention orders without even looking at the names or reasons given. One of the people detained after the 1985 election was Mtshena Sidile, an old man who had worked with Christian Care for years and had spent much time and trouble caring for Enos Nkala when he was in detention under Smith.

Another case I raised was that of Edward Ndlovu. He was in hospital in Bulawayo, a really sick man and in constant pain, but he was being sent back to Khami Prison in a few days. Mnangagwa spoke of Edward with great friendliness and no apparent concern.

After receiving assurances that no authorisation had been given for my mail to be opened, I wrote to the Minister of Information, Posts and Telecommunications on 20 January 1986.

Dear Minister Shamuyarira

Opening of Mail

Sometime last July or August I became aware that mail addressed to me at 18 Masefield Avenue, Strathaven, Harare, was being opened. I sent an envelope to a security firm in London for testing, and in early September received their reply that the envelope had definitely been opened.

I was of course not happy about this, but my attitude has basically been that if the authorities want to open my mail, they can go ahead. But then mail addressed to me at the Zimbabwe Project started being opened, and then all mail to the Zimbabwe Project. This was a different matter. One of my duties as Director must be to safeguard the well-being of the Zimbabwe Project. In our last financial year we brought in over one and a quarter million dollars in foreign currency. If agencies writing to us learn that their mail is being opened, they may not be so keen to support development in a country where their good efforts seem to be regarded with suspicion.

So I wrote to Minister Mnangagwa and brought the matter to his attention. He immediately instituted an investigation, as he had neither authorised the opening of our mail nor had he been asked for such authorisation. As a result, I have received a telephone call from Mr Stannard, Director Internal, stating that my mail is not being opened by the CIO.

I suppose that this may mean that either a foreign intelligence is operating from within our post offices or unauthorised activities are taking place within our own intelligence and postal services. I am writing to you about this because I am sure that you may be able to find out what has been happening from the Postmaster General or other relevant officials.

Thank you very much for your attention.

Following my letter, I was visited by Comrade Robert Makoni, a youngish man from some recess in the PTC. He phoned to make an appointment and said not to worry about anything, as *lots* of people complained that their mail was being opened. He came to my office at eight sharp and was as uncomfortable a fellow as I had ever met. First he asked permission to close the door, and then to draw the curtains. Then he just didn't know how to proceed.

He drew me diagrams of sorting and receiving sections in the main post office so that I could see that a guy in this corner, or that corner, might be able to pocket a letter, take it away with him, open it and bring it back without any of his comrades being aware of the fact. He told me lots of stories about the perfidy of some customs officials. He told me how sorters of mail became so expert in their task that, quick as a flash, they could feel if there was money in an envelope. He told me stories of office employees filching from envelopes and their employers then thinking it was the post office. He went on and on and on, little white specks in the corners of his lips. Oh, he was uncomfortable. But he couldn't bring himself to admit to or recognise the fact that there must be some authorised surveillance of mail under the aegis of the post office. He had never come across it, never heard of it. He was quite sure that CIO had never asked anyone to open an envelope, but strange things did happen. He pointed out that my letter to the minister, of which he had a copy, was clearly marked *Confidential*. But the minister's secretary, according to a note attached, which he showed me, had written to the director-general, asking him to look into the matter on behalf of the minister. The letter had been misrouted and had gone to the wrong office, and then to another wrong office, and then to a third wrong office before it had reached the director-general. Now *everyone* in the post office knew that I was complaining about my mail being opened, and this was a cause of deep, deep embarrassment. He wanted some sample envelopes, and I told him that I had taken Minister Mnangagwa an assortment and that the minister had passed them on to Mr Stannard, director internal, CIO. So he made a note to ring Mr Stannard.

All in all I was glad I had complained. At the time I thought I was taking an awful risk. But everyone had been so nice about it and mail had started arriving in pristine condition. Probably the CIO had authorised its opening without realising that I might tackle their minister on the subject, and that's where all the embarrassment and wide-eyed bewilderment had sprung from.

Johnson Ndlovu, Lot Dewa and thirteen others were released from Chikurubi on Wednesday 5 February 1986. That same day Thabo Mbeki, passing through Harare, rang, and we met briefly so he could introduce me to a new ANC man in Harare. It gave me great pleasure to be able to tell Mbeki that the latest *Economist* was running an article by Xan Smiley, advocating sanctions against South Africa. He was really surprised and pleased. I liked him.

Not long afterwards, Roger Martin, deputy British high commissioner, and his wife Ann gave a lunch for James Allen, the newly appointed British ambassador to Mozambique.

Roger was fascinated by a point made by Smiley in the *Economist* article, namely that, when enough pressure was exerted, the whites in South Africa might lose their will to govern.

Veteran writer and musician Ian Mills was at the lunch and told us he had been at an extraordinary party given recently by the South African trade attaché. It was mainly for members of the Zimbabwe press, and Michelle Faul had been edgy about going, as she thought she would be the only non-white present. She was right. Anyway, there was incredible hospitality and Ian said everyone got drunk very quickly. He was playing the piano when his wife Heather came up and said he must quickly tuck his tie inside his shirt. He turned in amazement at the suggestion, and saw that the wife of the attaché was merrily frisking around with a pair of scissors, cutting off the ties of guests just below the knot. One guest, a businessman close to Finance Minister Bernard Chidzero, called Horstmann, was mournfully looking down at what had been a very nice silk tie. Someone then passed out and fell under the piano over Ian's foot, so he had to stop playing. Ian later learned that the faller was roused the next day by his host with coffee and a slug of good South African brandy and was none the worse for wear.

Roger was mesmerised by Ian's account. His eyes got wider and bluer and he kept asking careful little questions like: 'Would you say it was an evening devoted to Bacchus?' And Ian would say yes, carelessly, and continue with the amusing story. I think he was flattered by being given such concentrated attention by Roger. He didn't know, as I did, that burning behind Roger's fascination was the longing to pop the real question: *Do you think they have lost the will to govern?*

I was becoming a repository of many confidences, and this was not easy. Many years ago my father had taught me a vital lesson. At the time, it concerned the handling of funds for opposition to the Smith–Home settlement proposals. He said that if you had a secret, you must never confide it in anyone at all. Once you shared a secret, you were giving the other person a burden so heavy they would simply have to share it with someone else. Then there would be no secret left.

But some secrets, of course, were fun, like the one confided in me by the Tunisian ambassador. 'Do you see how the French ambassador is looking at Comrade Muzenda?' he asked me at a reception one night. He then explained that the French ambassador was very fed up with our deputy prime minister, for whom he had thrown a sumptuous banquet. The cream of Harare society had arrived on time, but not Comrade Muzenda. An hour after everyone should have been seated, the French ambassador rang

Muzenda and asked whether he had perhaps forgotten that this was the night of the banquet. Muzenda was shocked. Of *course* he hadn't forgotten!

'It's just that tonight I'm not very hungry,' he explained.

Just before he and others were formally charged with plotting a coup, I managed to see Edward Ndlovu. I went to the court and sat next to him for half an hour before the magistrate arrived. Amazingly, Edward kept on talking about the need for unity – PF Zapu must enter Zanu (PF) en masse; there should be a ceremony with Nkomo and Mugabe present, at which Nkomo should welcome PF Zapu into Zanu (PF), and then he should retire. Then the job of cleaning up Zanu (PF), stopping torture, detentions, etc., should start from inside. I'd heard the argument of working from inside before, and it didn't impress me, especially when I saw a man like Edward Ndlovu in the dock. It was amazing to hear a man facing treason charges under Zanu (PF) still advocating unity, especially after all he had been and was still going through.

Edward looked all right, but was desperate to get out of detention. Ten people were charged. I knew that William Kona, an old-time struggler, and Sydney Malunga MP had been tortured by being beaten on the soles of their feet. In Kona's case, medicine had been withheld and he had eventually collapsed and been admitted to hospital for two weeks. I didn't know what the other accused might have undergone.

One night, Gift Masuku rang. She and a sister-in-law had arrived in Harare and were stranded. I collected them in town. Gift insisted on trying to see her husband, Lookout, who had been admitted to Parirenyatwa Hospital the previous day. After lots of effort she was allowed in to see him at about 11.15 p.m. and had forty-five minutes with him.

Mrs Sharlottie Msipa had seen Lookout just after he had been admitted and never thought he would live the night. He was unconscious, and at one point, when she shook him and implored him to speak, he just managed to touch his head and his throat. He was in agony. She said when he opened his eyes, tears rolled down his face, so he kept them shut. Gift eventually got one of the doctors to write down what he was suffering from. The words she had were *Cryptococcal meningitis*. He was also suffering from nephritis, inflammation of the kidneys.

Lookout was guarded by four men from the police support unit who seemed to take pleasure in making it as hard as possible for Gift to see him. She stayed in Harare for three nights before taking the train back to Bulawayo. These wives, like Mary, Gift, Connie and Shamiso, wanted to be as close as possible to their suffering husbands, but they had children to look after and work to attend to.

The day after Gift left, Andrew Nyathi, chairman of Simukai Cooperative, came to say Jimmy Mbambo had been taken by CIO. I rang Comrade Shoko at CIO, and he said he would find out and ring back, which he did, with the information that CIO now also had Maplanka and Felix Msika from Simukai. Andrew then went to Harare Central police station to try to see them, and that night I was told the police had kept Andrew, too.

A delegation of three men from the government of Guinea-Conakry arrived on a private visit, financed by Bread for the World, to learn what Zimbabwe had done in the fields of resettlement, coping with refugees and demobilisation. I drove them around the country for ten days.

We struggled to communicate, as they spoke French and I did not, but somehow we managed. In Bulawayo, Stephen Nkomo helped, as he did speak French, having been Zapu's representative in Algeria. He had recently been released from detention. After they met Stephen, they told me they now wanted to meet his brother Joshua, and asked me to arrange it. They told me they were not afraid and they obviously assumed that I wasn't either.

Their delegation was headed by David Camara, who had been imprisoned under Sekou Toure. The other two were in exile for years. Camara was described as *Chef de Cabinet*, Ibrahima Sory Sow as *Conseiller* and Ibrahima Abba Diarra as *Administrateur*.

One evening at dinner, I asked Camara how long he had been in jail. He said about five years, and a pall seemed to settle over the table. He was very sombre, and shortly afterwards we all went to bed. The next morning he gave me a note, apologising for his poor English. I made some copies, exactly as he wrote it:

I was emprisoned twice in Guinea.
1. First time: From 22 February 1971 to 27 August 72.
   Accusation: They say that I have help the families of prisoners who were hanged (or killed) one month before.
2. Second time: I was emprisoned from 18/7/76 to 19/12/80.
   Accusation: They said I was with Diallo TELLI against the Government. We wanted to fall down they Party (PDG) and to take the power.
   Diallo Telli was the first General Secretary of 'Organisation de l'Unite Africaine'(OAU).
   My comrades were died by lack of food between 18 and 21 days. Very bad and sad things. It is not good for me to tell them.

They told me that under Sekou Toure about 25 per cent of their population became exiles. They were not so keen any more on 'socialism'. I think that is a word, like many others, that can be used to cloak many evils.

By 2006, President Robert Mugabe would equal the then President Sekou Toure in that more than 25 per cent of Zimbabwe's population was also in exile.

Swazini Ndlovu, ally of Dumiso Dabengwa, who gave important evidence for Dumiso in his treason trial, was released from another spell of arbitrary detention by the CIO, and Stannard arranged for him to return to Bulawayo, where I saw him. I was trying to fathom the role of Stannard, and so I asked Swazini if he could consider Stannard to be a friend.

'Yes, he is a friend of mine. They took me from office to office in Chaminuka Building and eventually they took me to his office. He said, "I know, it must have been hell for you." I said, "For God's sake, at least tell me what day it is today." He told me it was Friday. They had kept me for four days in total darkness at Goromonzi, and they had taken away the pills I have to control high blood pressure. I tell you, I was sick. I thought I was finished. They took me to a nurse. She refused to give me pills. She said I was critically ill and she would not be responsible for treating me. They took me to Parirenyatwa and ordered the doctor to give me pills.

'I was with them for eight, ten days. They drove me up from Bulawayo by car. My hands were manacled all the way. Yes, I knew them all. They said, "Now we will fix you," and "Did you think we had forgotten that you gave evidence for Dabengwa in the treason trial?" Yes, they interrogated me, but there was nothing for me to tell them. When they took me to Stannard, he said to them, "You see – I told you he knew nothing." They wanted to send me back to Bulawayo by bus. I told them I didn't have a Zanu (PF) membership card and the buses are stopped by people making sure everyone has a Zanu (PF) party card. Stannard said, "You brought him here, now you've got to send him back. Why don't you buy him a one-way plane ticket?" So they did.

'When I left Chaminuka Building, I looked at a telephone directory, but I discovered that these days there is hardly anyone in Harare that I know. I didn't want to come to your office. There are some people there that I don't like to see. That Sister – yes, I know the whole story and how she nearly finished you. So I just sat in the park and read a newspaper until it was time to go to the airport.

'No, I don't think there is anything that can be done for now. People are not widely enough affected by the suffering yet. They say, "Oh, I know so-and-so is having a terrible time. But I am all right." Also, I think government officials are still covered by the Indemnity Act. I don't think action can be taken against them in the courts.

'Yes, Stannard is a friend of mine, a real friend. I know he is very cunning. I am sure he is not working for the South Africans. He says he can't go there any more. They expected him to protect their operatives in Zimbabwe and he didn't. So they don't like him. He has thought through the whole thing. He knows very well that it is not PF Zapu responsible for all these things. He knows it is the South Africans. Maybe he can't get his colleagues to listen to reason.

'Maybe they will now leave me alone. I don't know. I started work again today at the Bulawayo City Council.'

It was reported in Bulawayo's *Chronicle* that a superintendent in the Ministry of Energy, Water Resources and Development, Anthony Peter van Beek, had appeared before a Plumtree magistrate facing a charge of contravening the Law and Order (Maintenance) Act, under which it was an offence to cause alarm and/or despondency.

The state alleged that he uttered words that were against the security forces and the state in general. On 4 January, Van Beek allegedly accused the security forces of murdering people in the area. He is alleged to have said this at the town's recreational club. Van Beek was further alleged to have refused both the army and the police escorts entry to his place of work at Ngwizi Dam, Mphoengs, because he apparently said the security forces would kill him on the way but later blame the dissidents for the murder. He was remanded on Z$200 bail.

In mid-March, my parents invited the Shamuyariras to dinner. Halfway through, Nathan said, 'Judy, I hope CIO is not still interfering with your mail?' I had to think on my feet, as it were, although I was sitting down. What worried me was any possible fright to my mother, so I tried to pass his question off as a light-hearted matter and said: 'Minister, I haven't told my mother about this, but everything seems to have led to vastly improved relations with the CIO, and Mr Stannard and I are even due to have lunch with each other.'

The minister seemed amused, and my mother and the two New Zealand visitors seemed unperturbed. I supposed, sitting warmly around the table, the possibility of the CIO opening my mail seemed unreal to everyone but the minister, my father and me. But of course, whatever I hoped, my mother would have known exactly what was happening. Her sensitivity was ultra acute.

Now and again, I thought that I had reached the age and the condition when nothing was so bad that it could shock me. That particular thought was in my mind on Monday 24 March when Michelle Faul rang to say that we must meet, which we did high above Harare on the Meikles Hotel pool deck at lunch time. She worked for Associated Press and was a stringer for the BBC.

Four days earlier, Michelle had been instructed to meet Nathan Shamuyarira. She was told that 'we' were tired of her reporting; she would have no further assistance from the ministry – which meant she would lose her accreditation. She couldn't be deported, as she was a citizen by birth of Zimbabwe, so the only way to deal with her was detention at Chikurubi.

She was rightly very frightened, and at the same time ashamed of being scared. She was leaving Zimbabwe within the next forty-eight hours, deprived of her home, her right to work and, basically, of her citizenship.

After our painful lunch, I got back to the office to find a white woman of about sixty who asked if I could spare a few minutes. Between Michelle and now this lady, I realised that there were still things that could profoundly shock me.

She sat down, introducing herself as Margie Schwing, and although she never actually wept, she was on the verge of tears and struggling for control throughout the awful story she told me. She had been in Park Street in November, and all of a sudden was surrounded by five men who said they were from CIO and took her off to Harare Central police station. From there she was moved to Chikurubi Women's Remand Section. She appeared once in a magistrate's court, and the CIO opposed bail because they said they were still investigating fraud.

From what Mrs Schwing said, it was CIO throughout, and not the fraud squad. She said she still didn't know why she had been held. She was released at the end of February, suffering from pneumonia, and was taken to Parirenyatwa Hospital outpatients. Due to one of those strokes of good fortune, Mrs Schwing had been alone when a member of her church saw her and came to ask what was wrong. She was accompanied by two CIO agents, one of whom had gone to get her prescription filled, while the other had gone to the toilet.

The friend was extremely practical and whipped out a notebook, and took down the name and address of Mrs Schwing's son, who apparently worked for Tabex in Malaysia, and then darted off before CIO reappeared.

The son then flew to Zimbabwe, got lawyers, got his mother out of jail and put her in a boarding house, where she had company. She had been living alone before, and no one had noticed she had gone, or, if they did, they didn't know where to look for her.

The conditions she described were terrible: women not knowing of any rights they might have; beatings by the wardresses; people having their hair torn out; a woman having teeth punched in; the use of hosepipes on the prisoners by the wardresses; malnutrition among the toddlers and babies picked up with their mothers. She said that on New Year's Day, as the women came out of the cell blocks, they each received a blow with a hosepipe and the accompanying greeting, 'Happy New Year!'

Mrs Schwing also said something that I thought might be the truth of the matter, although she apologised for saying it, because, she said, it sounded so unreal. She had been at a party before her detention, and Simon Muzenda was there. He had been very nice to her, and introduced her to a lot of people. Mrs Schwing heard a young man, who seemed to stay close to her all the time at the party, saying to someone else: 'It's just not fair! I'm also in business. Why doesn't Muzenda introduce me to all these people?'

So, she said, it may have all started with jealousy. To me, that didn't sound unreal.

Her lawyers were suing. I told her the only thing I could think of that might make her feel better and less shattered would be to go away and write down absolutely everything she could remember that had happened and to disregard how disjointed, incoherent or unreal it might seem. Not only would it help her lawyers, it might help her to get all the stuff out of her onto paper.

Naturally she had to be protected and, being white, she could easily be identified. But I thought I might give selections of whatever she wrote to Julia Zvobgo, after deleting anything that could identify her, in an attempt to improve the status of women in the prisons that Julia's husband Eddison was in charge of.

At Michelle's farewell dinner, a local journalist, Angus Shaw, confirmed what my acquaintance had told me. He had a friend who owed Z$300 to a boutique and was arrested, and so had a taste of the remand section at Chikurubi. Angus had written a report of everything to Eddison Zvobgo.

Something Mrs Schwing had said made me want to smile, but I restrained myself. She said: 'I actually saw them cutting up the hosepipe. And you know, I think something could be done about that. That's government property!'

CHAPTER 14

The death of Lookout Masuku

ON TUESDAY 11 MARCH 1986, LIEUTENANT GENERAL LOOKOUT Masuku and the veteran PF Zapu politician Vote Moyo were officially released from detention. As was the case under the Smith regime, the names of detainees could not be published, so there hadn't been news of them in the papers for the four years they had been imprisoned in Zimbabwe under Robert Mugabe. Now their freedom was headline news.

Lookout's wife Gift managed to get permission for me to see him on Sunday 9 March from 3.30 p.m. to 6 p.m. at Parirenyatwa Hospital. There were four heavily armed soldiers outside his room. I sat down with them, and said I gathered they had a permit for me to see Masuku. They were perfectly pleasant and said that was fine, so I walked into the private ward. Lookout was attached to two drips but sitting up in the bed, and he gave a small scream when he saw me, jumped up and hugged me hard. The drips were suspended from a wheeled stand, so he was mobile.

There was no awkwardness. It was as if we had known each other for years and had seen each other yesterday. But the joy was precisely because we hadn't seen each other for more than four years, and because it was so wonderful to see one another again. I couldn't begin to fathom the hell of uncontrolled suffering he had been going through. There were some days he had no memory of, which was probably just as well. The full story would probably never unfold, but if it did, it would be bleak. For example, it turned out that the 'specialist' the prison authorities had told his lawyer he had seen in December was neither a specialist nor even a registered doctor. I wondered, too, about the doctor at Chikurubi. I had learned he was a Russian Jew on contract, that he had worked previously in Israel and that he was very timid. I wondered if he had ended up in his position because he had such good qualifications.

We talked non-stop, an interested guard listening in the corner, until after six, when the soldiers very reasonably asked me to leave, as visiting hours were over. That was sad, because we didn't then think we would be seeing each other again in the foreseeable future.

I rang Gift the next day to thank her, and to say I'd had a wonderful time. Of course 'wonderful' was the wrong word. Lookout was skinny and his arms were very swollen from trying to find veins for the drips, and he was very, very sick. But he sat up all the time I was with him and was mentally as bright as a button. There was a heart-rending moment when he said: 'But what of the future? When I went to prison I got high blood pressure. Then I got kidney troubles. Now I have this. What is going to happen to me next?'

I said, 'Oh Lookout!' as though, how could he ask such a question?

But he said, 'No, Judy, I *mean* it. Let's be practical about the whole thing.'

I feared he was absolutely right. I had been consulting Professor Noel Galen, who was very gloomy about Lookout's future.

Late on Monday night I returned a call from Gift.

'Have you heard anything?' she asked.

I said I had heard a rumour that Lookout was to be released. She said it was true. I said, 'How do you know? Who told you? Is there a piece of paper?' She laughed and said the fact that she was telling me meant that it was true. She travelled up the next day from Bulawayo, and I spent half an hour with her and Lookout at Parirenyatwa. As he was now a free man, no permits were required to see him and the armed guards had been withdrawn.

At about six that Tuesday evening, an unknown man walked in and stood by the bed. Lookout was polite but cool. I kept thinking, what an odd doctor. He didn't ask how Lookout was feeling – he just kept informing him that he would be seeing him again, the next night, in hospital, in Bulawayo. Eventually, Lookout said, 'That is my wife,' and so distantly introduced him to Gift. Lookout never once referred to me. Gift asked what the man's name was. 'Maeresera.'

'That's a strange name,' she said. 'Could you repeat it?'

'Maeresera.'

'Very strange,' she said politely. 'It must be Shona.'

Gift herself was Shona.

When he left, they simultaneously said, 'CIO.' Then I remembered him. We had discovered at the Zimbabwe Project that Mike Mutsi, one of our colleagues at the time, was working with Maeresera of the CIO. Maeresera was one of those who had raided Grassroots bookshop and was believed to have introduced false papers into their office. He had a reputation of being obsessed with PF Zapu.

When we left the hospital and I took Gift home with me, she was depressed and quiet.

'I keep thinking of the future,' she said. 'There I am sitting having a drink, or eating, or watching television with my husband and my children – and Maeresera.'

She went to see Minister Mnangagwa the next day, and complained. Mnangagwa said he didn't know about it, and called in some white CIO officer and said the harassment must stop. He told Gift that Lookout's freedom was unconditional. Maeresera did not appear, as he had promised, the next day. Gift was wonderful: so calm, brave and clever.

Lookout was thinking everything through carefully and, after consulting with his lawyer Bryant Elliot, during which time he sent Gift and me out of the room, he showed us, in writing, what must be said if the press or anyone else asked questions. The statement was about his future. He said he was looking forward to being with his family; to discovering again what life was like in Zimbabwe; that he would be continuing his studies; and planning how he would be able to provide for his family. He was also thinking about a holiday.

Bryant was as quiet, steady and dependable as ever. After he left, we were saying how blessed we were to have him as our lawyer. I was startled when Lookout said: 'Bryant is such a brilliant man. It's a pity about his poor English.' Then I laughed. 'No, Lookout,' I said. 'That's not poor English. That's a Scots accent.'

It was marvellous that at least Lookout knew he wouldn't be going back to Chikurubi. Prisons came and dumped his belongings in the ward in a bag and two cardboard boxes. He wanted everything fumigated.

Lookout gave me copies of two letters to look after for him. They were both addressed to the Prime Minister, The Hon RG Mugabe, in his capacity as Minister of Defence. The first was dated 1 July 1980, less than three months after Zimbabwe's independence.

RE: Allegations against ZPRA

Whilst we appreciate the difficult task our Minister of Defence faces in moulding a Zimbabwe National Army, we would like to draw the Minister's attention to the following.

We are aware that a few former ZPRA elements have refused to go to Assembly Points. These few elements have refused to take orders from any quarter including those from the Minister of Home Affairs (Dr Joshua Nkomo). In compliance with the MOD's directive and appreciable spirit of reconciliation we at one stage managed to apprehend several of these elements and put them in Khami Prison.

We are still, with full vigour and determination, forging ahead with this exercise with an objective to obtain peace and tranquillity in our beloved land, and indeed create conditions for civil authority to function without let or hindrance.

In spite of this determination it has come to our attention that ZPRA has not been and is not being treated fairly and equally with other forces. The following examples serve to illustrate our case:

1. The appointments by merit to the Zimbabwe 21st Battalion was rejected by other comrades because the majority of the men recommended to be officers happened to be former ZPRA cadres.

2. ZPRA has revealed both to the Government and Joint High Command (JHC) Headquarters the number of cadres still undergoing training abroad but our comrades in ZANLA have not. We further understand that ZANLA has sent men to train in Libya, Romania and Yugoslavia without the knowledge of JHC. The intentions behind such a move puzzle us.

3. Incitement of the population against ZPRA and its Command by some political leaders and slogans such as 'PASI NE ZPRA' cannot make our determined effort to build one Army any easier.

4. Radio broadcasts give an impression that our full and well known participation in the struggle to liberate our country is neither appreciated nor recognised. FOR EXAMPLE only ZANLA and Chimurenga songs are played – a development which affects cohesion in the army and is indeed out of step with the spirit of National Reconciliation.

5. The presence of dissidents at Sanyati, Zvimba and Hurungwe has been blown out of proportion as ZPRA acts of organised rebellion while similar acts by ZANLA elements are not talked of. We hereby present a few cases of unmentioned ZANLA dissidents.

   a) On 22/06/80 ZANLA dissidents at Marenga Business Centre fired two (2) bullets destroying the fuel tank of the vehicle driven by Sgt Mjr Gava of Zvimba Police Post in Sinoia.

   b) In Chipinga Police are being assaulted by organised groups or gangs of ZANLA, making police patrol duties impossible. This includes an assault on Inspector De Lange at APX.

   c) (i) ZANLA shootings at Kachuta TTL on 17/06/80 (ii) shooting at Murambinda on 18/06/80 (iii) stealing of two (2) watches and $40.00 from a bus driver in Maranke TTL. Also threats to farmers in Maranke and Fort Victoria area on 22/06/80.

   d) ZANLA has been harassing and in some cases burning villages of the civilian population around Golf and Hotel Assembly camps for their refusal to provide them with food when they visit their villages. As a result people in this area are demanding the removal of these camps from this area. The above few examples involving ZANLA units exclude other wide ranging cases of murder, shooting, kidnapping, abductions and kangaroo courts by ZANLA or Zanu-PF cadres which are never mentioned.

6. We, in the ZPRA Command, wish to remind the MOD of the fatal incidences which led to near disaster in Zambia, Tanzania and Mozambique during ZIPA. [ZIPA, the Zimbabwe People's Army, was launched in 1975/6, an attempt to unite divided liberation forces, which ended in killings and disaster.] Integration of forces can never succeed if it means the absorption of one force by another; hence the shortcomings which befell ZIPA should be avoided at all costs.

7. The ZPRA Command calls for non-interference by certain politicians in Military Affairs. Military Affairs are the responsibility of the JHC and the Prime Minister in his capacity as MOD.

8. The ZPRA Command and the highly disciplined ZPRA cadres in the Assembly Points regard peace and cooperation with the Government as our first priority and an indispensable national duty – we sacrificed our lives for.

9. At present we have specialists in the country whose weapons still remain in Zambia. We understand the Government cannot permit entry of these weapons. We strongly feel that these weapons can be of better use in the defence of the state rather than left to wear and tear in Zambia.

10. We have submitted to JHC HQs figures of ZPRA personnel training outside the country but to our surprise those who have completed such training find it very difficult to return home. They have been made to wait under frustrating conditions in the country of their training. At the moment we have 1600 men in Angola who passed out two months ago and are still waiting for authorisation to enter the country.

11. On the other hand ZANLA cadres have no problems returning into the country after training for example the 2500 recent returnees from Mozambique.

CONCLUSION

In the light of what we say above, we hereby recommend the following:

a) The MOD to inform the nation that the Army is his sole responsibility and that any reprimands or praises are done by him and the JHC.

b) That politicians must leave military matters to military men, if the process of integration is to move with the desired speed.

c) The MOD to adopt a parental attitude to the Army and regard the three former armies as three children of one family, hence equal status.

D Dabengwa (ZPRA Commander)

L Masuku (ZPRA Commander)

The second letter was dated 8 September 1980 and was signed by Masuku alone.

We have again decided to bring to your attention, as Prime Minister and Minister of Defence our concern, resulting from a number of events and pronouncements that complicate the process of fulfilling our duties. These developments do not in any way assist us in our determined effort to mould ONE NATION.

1. We have found out that ZANLA, the military wing of Zanu-PF has been sending people for military training outside the country. This is contrary to the previously agreed position ie only those programmes already in process prior to the start of the integration exercise should be left to continue. ZANLA has been sending people for military training in Nigeria, Ethiopia, Yugoslavia, Romania and etc.

2. As components of the Zimbabwe National Army we have not been informed of the total of ZANLA Comrades still outside the country undergoing military training. On our part, with utmost sincerity, we have submitted this data in an effort to alleviate suspicion created by Western News Media on the numbers of ZPRA cadres and 'their intentions'.

3. We would Comrade Prime Minister, like to bring to your attention and consideration the plight of the demobilised comrades. As a result of absence of facilities provided for and means of livelihood for these Comrades, many have resorted to a number of anti-social activities like armed robbery etc. We recommend that these Comrades be absorbed into the army, firstly as a method of bringing them under control and secondly to give the government time to analyse the problem with a view to finding a lasting solution.

4. It is our observation that there is disparity in the provision of facilities to the war-disabled Comrades of ZPRA and ZANLA by the authorities concerned. We have, for instance, only heard of ZANLA disabled Comrades travelling to Britain and Tanzania for artificial limbs and none from ZPRA.

5. We would like to bring to your notice that despite constant appeals, there is no change on official bias against ZPRA and its contribution

to the liberation of our motherland which we pointed out in our first memorandum paragraphs three (3) and four (4). The ZBC and ZTV continue projecting only ZANLA's image vis-à-vis the liberation struggle. Only the massacres of Chimoio and Nyadzonia are projected and nothing on the massacres at Mkushi, Freedom Camp in Zambia and in Angola. This makes the ZPRA cadres question their very future and existence in the Zimbabwe National Army. We are aware, Comrade Prime Minister, that directives have been issued to the staff of ZBC and ZTV to project ZANLA's image only.

6. We have observed with great concern the increase in inter-parties rivalry, resulting in some cases in destruction of property and loss of lives. We would like to inform you that some of the victims regrettably have been members of ZPRA on their way to or from leave. The following examples serve to illustrate:
   a) A ZPRA cadre who was shot dead in Gatooma.
   b) The attempted kidnapping of nine (9) ZPRA Comrades when trying to board a bus for Mashumbi Pools at Harare.
   c) The injury of three (3) Patriotic Front members at Seke.
   d) The armed attack on the Administrative Secretary of the PF-Zapu in a Salisbury Suburb.
   e) Comrade Prime Minister, we are on record as having taken measures against those of our ranks who have defied orders, by way of molesting people. We now find it extremely difficult to continue with the exercise without any positive reciprocity from our counterparts of ZANLA.

7. We wish to point out that some of these unhealthy developments are a direct result of statements in our various mass media (Newspapers, ZBC and ZTV) or at meetings by members of the Government. These developments violate the spirit of reconciliation and the consequences thereof are too ghastly to contemplate.

8. Finally, Comrade Prime Minister, we wish to recommend that a meeting of the two major Parties in the Government be convened to discuss these sad and serious developments. The objective should be to create peace and stability and move forward with one spirit – a spirit to mould a strong and unbending nation.

We remain determined to play our part to the full.

LKV MASUKU
COMMANDER (ZPRA)   CC MINISTER OF HOME AFFAIRS
JOINT HIGH COMMAND

Neither letter was acknowledged, let alone answered.

As Lookout's condition deteriorated, more and more high-ranking people came to visit him. On Saturday 15 March, he dictated an outline of letters to be properly rewritten and typed up for him to sign:

1. To Emmerson Mnangagwa. Thanking him for visiting me in hospital. Thanking government for sending me to hospital. Thanking him for allowing my wife to go to GDR for treatment. Thanking him for recommending my release.

2. To Dr Sydney Sekeremayi. Thanking him for visiting me. Thanking him for expediting the arrival of the necessary drugs for my treatment.

3. To Enos Nkala. Thanking him for message of sympathy he sent and for his wishes for an early recovery. Thanking him for signing the revocation order for my detention to be lifted.

4. To Eddison Zvobgo. Thanking him for the quick arrangement in sending me to hospital when my condition was serious. Thanking him for visiting me in hospital. Thanking the government for allowing my wife to go to the GDR for treatment. Thanking him for looking into my problems while I was in prison.

5. Army Commander Lt Gen Nhongo. Thanking him for visiting me and the help he sent me after visiting. Batteries, fruit, toothpaste.

Now Lookout was getting tired and he dictated for only one more person:

6. Air Force Commander Tungamirai. Same letter.

Mary Ndlovu came up from Bulawayo to see her husband Edward in Chikurubi Maximum Prison and Bryant Elliot, whom I myself went to see. Bryant thought it unwise for Lookout to write any thank-you letters. Bryant really had his hands full. As I left his office, I bumped into Shamiso Nyashanu. Lookout couldn't understand why Bryant didn't want him to send letters. I promised to get Bryant to discuss the matter with him.

While I was with Lookout that day, the nurse gave him pills in a cup. He said he knew two of them, but the other two were new, and he asked what they were. 'I may not be a doctor, but I can see.' The new needle in his arm was a long one, and causing more swelling. As I left, I saw Joshua Nkomo, Isaac Nyathi and two others who were on their way in to visit Lookout.

On Thursday 20 March I was surprised to see that Lookout wasn't on the drip. I asked about this, and he told me that the medicine had run out and he had been told that the next consignment was at the airport awaiting clearance by customs. Both his other visitors and I were very concerned. One of them said, 'But doesn't this disrupt the whole treatment?'

Lookout, full of equanimity as ever, shrugged, smiled and said, 'Well, what can be done.' He was making a statement, not asking a question. I had been told the medicine was toxic, which was why it had to enter his system slow drip by slow drip over many hours. An interruption in treatment would surely be devastating. I said I would try to get to Dr Sekeremayi. Maybe the ministers didn't know about the situation. Lookout thought that there was nothing I could do.

He said the previous evening he'd had a hot bath and then sat by his window enjoying the breeze. But then he got very cold and he couldn't get warm in bed. He went to the staff on night duty and they heaped his bed with blankets, but he remained cold and couldn't sleep until that morning between six and ten.

I couldn't get the thought of the drugs sitting at the airport waiting to be cleared by customs out of my mind, so on the Friday I phoned Bryant Elliot and told him about the situation. I also phoned Dr Galen and asked if he could possibly speak to Professor Thomas, who was a colleague of his and in charge of Lookout's treatment, to see what could be done. I was constantly torn between the fear of interfering and the fear of being irresponsible. *For evil to succeed … it is enough to do nothing*. I also thought it might upset Lookout if he thought I was interfering.

I tried to telephone Professor Thomas myself, although I didn't know him and thought he might hate my intervention. He was out, so I spoke to his secretary, who was very reasonable. I said I was anxious not to be interfering, but was worried about the medicine at the airport awaiting clearance. The weekend would start the next day and customs wouldn't do anything on a Saturday or Sunday. She said she was sure Professor Thomas would know, as he saw Lookout every day, but she would make a note to tell him when he came back.

Later I talked to Jeremy Brickhill. He thought of the excellent idea of ringing a top official in the Ministry of Health, SK Moyo, who would certainly, if needs be, go to the airport and clear the consignment himself immediately, if he knew of the problem. So that was a relief.

I went to see Lookout that evening. Still no drip, but he said he had been told that the medicine had been cleared and was now available. They were going to give him different medicine meanwhile and put him back on the drip the next day. He showed me the needle in his arm, preparatory for the drip. Lookout said that after I left him the previous night, his temperature had shot up. Earlier in the day, he said, it had been 39°C. I noticed he was shaking slightly. He had been the previous day too. Maybe he had been all the time and I had noticed it only recently.

Lookout said a lot of blood samples had been taken from him. Both he and I used highly non-technical and unsuitable language, as we didn't know anything about medicine. He said they told him they were taking samples from different places in his arms and legs in case the blood was clear in one place, but there was a 'germ' in another. That morning he had been taken for X-rays because his chest was hurting, he said 'just as though I had been lifting weights'.

I felt we were nearing the end of a frightful tragedy of which neither he, nor Gift, nor I, nor the lawyer, nor lots of other people, knew the truth. Lookout, referring to the past years and to the authorities, said, 'They have mishandled me.'

At some point the week before, he had said to me: 'I have learned not to trust people.'

He also said: 'I always prefer to know the truth. If I have an hour to live, I want to be told, "Masuku, you have an hour to live."'

There were rumours around town. The previous week, Godwin Matatu had rung me. Somehow the name of Lookout cropped up, and Godwin said: 'Ah, yes, he is in his dying days.'

I said, 'What do you mean?'

He said Eddison Zvobgo had told him that Lookout's condition was incurable.

The night before, someone else had said to me: 'Do you think our friend has any chance of survival?' I said I didn't know, but on that Thursday, Lookout gave me an application to join the American Marketing Association. 'I am glad to let you know that I have been released from detention.' I had to post it for him the next day.

On Saturday 22 March, I took him a small tray with four slices of roast fillet and a very small roasted sweet potato. He had said recently that he could live on meat alone, but it must still smell of being meat. Meat in prisons and hospitals was always overcooked. Lookout was back on the drip. For a few seconds I didn't realise how horribly sick he was feeling. Visiting hours started at 3.30 p.m., but he had asked me to be there at two, while it was still quiet.

As I sat down, he said, 'A few minutes ago you wouldn't have liked me.'

'Why?' I asked.

'I was vomiting.'

I tried to slip the packet of food onto the windowsill, out of sight. He asked to look at it, and then told me to put it in his bedside drawer. I thought that was because the look of it made him feel more sick, and wished I could take it to the nearest rubbish bin outside his ward. He pushed the bedside drawer even more firmly shut. 'Later,' he said. 'I'll want it later.'

He lay still for a few seconds, on his side, and then said: 'Pass me the towel.' I did. 'Shut your eyes.' Momentarily I did, then found to my horror that he was hanging over the side of the bed mopping the floor at my feet, his head tangling with the drip. The floor was covered with globules of vomit. 'Please, please don't.' He struggled back to lying down, me helping to support him. 'I didn't even notice.'

'I know you didn't,' he said. 'I was glad.'

He lay there suffering.

'Lookout, today I'm staying for only a few minutes.'

The hand lying nearest to me was the one that was half shot away. He was silent. How could I tell whether he wanted me to stay or not? I put my hand on his arm. His skin was burning. 'Maybe today you shouldn't have visitors. If you don't want any, how will you tell them?'

'I could tell the nurse.'

I had taken him his application to join the American Marketing Association, with the label stuck onto the envelope as he had wanted, and a whole assortment of Zimbabwe stamps attractively arranged making up the required Z$1.40 postage. When he had given me the envelope the previous day, someone had already typed the address on it for him, but had made a mistake, which he wanted covered.

'Packaging is very important in marketing,' he said. He needed a US$55 membership fee to go with the application. I told him I had some money in London, so could send the equivalent for him. Then I had a better idea in terms of speed, and rang Molli Miller and asked if she could give me a cheque and I could refund their account from London. Lookout had told me that he became interested in American marketing when Molli's husband David, the American ambassador, had visited them in prison. 'American marketing is much more aggressive than British. I prefer their approach.'

There was no way of knowing whether he wanted me to go or stay. I told him I was going to the wife of the American ambassador to collect the cheque for his application fee. He didn't object.

I was expected at Molli's at 3.30, and it was now only about 2.20. I drove slowly past the house of Noel and Doris Galen. I wanted to talk to Noel. It was he who had first alerted me to how serious the whole situation was. But there was no car in the garage, which meant they must be out. So I drove slowly on, wondering where to go, what to do so that I was sure I'd be in control of myself when I got to Molli.

I ended up at Landscape Nurseries and found a secluded wall near the roses, where I sat quietly. A group looked at me curiously but then wandered on, leaving me alone. I looked up at the sky like any fundamentalist who believes that God is shaped like a man and sits on a throne up there, and flung my heart heavenwards. *I don't understand even computers and microchips and how electricity works so how can I begin to understand You?*

I don't know how to pray and I don't know how to ask for help for Lookout. I don't know what kind of help to ask for. But if it were possible for me to communicate with you in an acceptable way, please, please enfold Lookout with whatever would be the best thing for me to be able to pray for him.

On Sunday 23 March, I had lunch with Noel and Doris Galen. An American microbiologist, David Katzenstein, who was doing research in Zimbabwe, was present. He confirmed what Noel had warned me of. Lookout had AIDS and could not be expected to recover from his *Cryptococcal meningitis.*

David told me that in a case like his it would probably be best to stop medication. I confronted him with the age-old problem. Lookout didn't know of his situation. His family didn't know. But he kept asking questions. In fact, he had ordered me to go and find out what was wrong with him, because he felt something was being concealed from him. Now that I had found out, I didn't know what to do with the knowledge.

David's wife, Sharon Mayes, was forthright. 'He trusts you. He asked you to find out. You have done so. He wants to know. Now you must tell him.'

I said one doctor had told Lookout that they were going to keep him in hospital for another ten days. Then another doctor had said they were going to keep him longer. Lookout told me that they kept asking what countries he had been in. 'But what can what water I drank in what countries have to do with this? This I got in prison.'

David asked if he could possibly have had a blood transfusion in Zambia. I explained how Lookout and his family had been shot up in a Rhodesian attack in Lusaka, and how he had lost part of his hand. I said almost certainly he could have had a blood transfusion that night. I had been told that Zambians had poured out of their homes to give blood for the wounded. 'There you are,' David said. He went on to explain that research indicated that Zambia for some years had been a high-risk country for AIDS. So this meant that all those ex-combatants who had been wounded and received blood transfusions were a group at risk.

I drove home through rain after lunch. I picked two roses, one full blown, the other a bud, put them in a bottle and took them to Lookout. The rose was called Chicago Peace. I put them on his bedside table. He raised himself on one elbow and looked deeply into the rainy, full-blown rose. 'Now I am out of hospital,' he said.

Lookout said he was much better. His temperature had been 36°C that morning. Yesterday it was 39°C.

He said, 'Ah, I enjoyed what you brought me.' I thought of the fillet and sweet potato and felt sick and remorseful all over again. 'My stomach didn't know what was happening to it, such enjoyment. Because of that I'm going to ask Professor Thomas if my friends can cook meat for me.'

Then he explained he was allowed only hospital food, which was why he had hidden what I had brought him. I told him I had an oxtail in the freezer. When he was ready for it, he could tell me.

We talked for more than an hour, and I kept thinking what a terrible dissimulator I was capable of being. I was able to look him straight in the eye while knowing in my heart, beyond any hope or doubt, that he was dying. I told him I had a friend who knew all about this *Cryptococcal meningitis* or whatever the correct term was, and wondered if Lookout would like to talk to him. I said perhaps he could answer the questions Lookout had asked me and which I couldn't answer.

He said he would like to see David, but that I must come with him. Not the next day, because it would be another bad day, as he had to have a lumbar puncture, but Tuesday. I rang David. He said Tuesday would be fine, as he would have examined the fluid from Lookout's lumbar puncture by then. We would meet at 2.30 p.m. in David's office at the medical school.

I had planned to share the terrible news with Jeremy Brickhill on Monday night so that, together with David Katzenstein, we could plan how to try to help everyone cope. I'd wanted to talk to Jeremy ever since I knew, but each time there had been an interruption, and each time I was relieved to put off the sharing of such heavy knowledge. But now time was running out.

Jeremy came to the office on the Tuesday and I told him. We decided to postpone David's introduction to Lookout until after Jeremy had consulted

Dumiso Dabengwa at Chikurubi. Somehow Jeremy had managed to convince the prison officials that he was one of Dumiso's lawyers, and so magically gain access.

At 2.30 p.m. I went to the medical school and saw David Katzenstein. After he had explained more to me, I went to Lookout. He was dozing, and the arm attached to the drip was enormous. David had told me that there was still a *Cryptococcal* in the spinal fluid. I went and found a lavatory and tried to rid myself of nausea. Feeling better, I went back and sat quietly in the chair by Lookout's side. After some time he shook the drip cord with his hand and I looked up from my newspaper and said, 'Hello, Lookout.'

'Judy!' Weak but instant recognition. He said, 'Today they have drugged me.'

I said I would come back the following day with David. But when I got down to his office and told him of the swollen arm, he mentioned the possibility of a mainline drip. I took him upstairs and introduced him to Lookout, who was obviously pleased to meet David and to show him his arms. He said they hadn't been able to find a place in his non-swollen arm for the drip. He looked up at David and asked him straight: 'Am I going to recover from this?' David said that there was perhaps a 60:40 chance. Then I took David to Jeremy's home so that he could explain everything. Jeremy was ashen.

I couldn't concentrate on work the next morning. I was expecting to meet Jeremy for lunch after his trip to Dumiso at Chikurubi, and went home feeling cold and miserable. By the time Joan and Jeremy arrived, Julius Chikazaza had prepared oxtail for lunch, which instantly helped on this freezing day. Joan left, and Jeremy told me of his morning. Dumiso had said that Jeremy should be the one to tell Lookout, not me. This had to be done that day, that *very* day, Dumiso had emphasised, so that Lookout could start thinking about all he wanted done.

At about three, I took Jeremy to show him David's office, so that he knew how to contact David should he need help. Then I took him up to Lookout's room, leaving him at the door so that Lookout didn't see me. I heard Lookout's cry of pleasure at the sight of Jeremy.

Jeremy came down after about an hour. It was arranged that he and David would see Lookout the next day. There were to be no more medical discussions that day, but Lookout wanted to see me. I ran Jeremy home. He had told Lookout everything.

I went back to Lookout at about 5.30 p.m. He was shaking with fever and hardly able to speak. Jeremy had told Lookout that I knew the position. Lookout said to me that people had not properly informed him. He was not afraid of death, but he needed to be able to plan. He wanted to be the one to tell his wife, but Jeremy had said Gift might need a friend present. I volunteered.

While I was with Lookout, both Gift and Cephas Msipa telephoned and he motioned to me to take both calls. It was very, very difficult for him to communicate with me through the violent shaking and, as I left, he started vomiting.

It had already been arranged that Gift would come from Bulawayo on Thursday 27 March. She stayed with me, and I took her to see Lookout that night, knowing full well what Lookout was going to tell her. While we were with him, there were interruptions all the time by friends and nurses, and Lookout said to me, over their heads as it were, that the time wasn't opportune. I'm sure that by then Gift had a strong suspicion of what she was to be told.

After the friends had gone, Lookout asked me, in front of Gift, to take her to meet David, the specialist, and that the doctor would tell her everything. It was not necessary, he said, for him to be present. To be absolutely sure of what he wanted, I had to do the astoundingly presumptuous thing of asking Gift if I could have a couple of minutes alone with her husband. She left without demur, and I asked Lookout if he really, clearly meant that Gift must be told that he was dying, and he said yes.

When we got home, with Gift's agreement, I rang David Katzenstein in accordance with Lookout's wishes. He came round immediately with Dr Noel Galen. Noel and his wife Doris were my saviours, comforters and friends. Gift was sitting by the fire. I introduced her to both men, and then Noel and I left Gift and David by the fire and went to my study. Eventually Gift came out onto the stoep with David and, with the utmost composure, thanked him and Noel for their time, and they left. We went silently back to the fire. Eventually she sobbed once and heart-wrenchingly and fled from the fire to bed.

The next day Gift cooked lunch for Lookout and took it to him, then had to return to the children in Bulawayo. She came back on Monday 31 March to spend the last few days with her husband.

My father came to Harare at about the same time and managed to see Lookout, who said to me, 'I feel very proud.'

On Wednesday 2 April, a nursing sister put a chair for me beside his bed and twice tried to shake him 'awake'. 'Mr Masuku. There is someone to see you.' He tried very hard and rolled his eyes open, but they couldn't focus. I sat beside him for some time. He was shivering in his sleep. By that afternoon he was conscious but swinging here and away in his mind. I held his hand for a long time, trying to interpret what he wanted. He had said, 'Please try and pull me back.' He held my hand firmly, but in case he didn't really want to hold it, I gently detached it and just left it lying next to him. He groped for it, and held it again. Someone else came in and I left. Gift was now with him every possible minute.

I remembered my old friend and former Zapu representative overseas, Eshmael Mlambo, telling me that when I had rung him in a Geneva hospital to say hello, never guessing how ill he was, 'the sound of your voice pulled me back from very far away'. Both men used the word 'pull'. So dying can't just be like going to sleep.

That afternoon, Lookout said, as if he had just arrived at this conclusion, 'I think they knew.'

'Knew what, Lookout?'

'They released me because they knew I was dying.'

On Friday 4 April there was the third meeting on Zanu–Zapu unity, and Dr Nkomo, Vote Moyo and others were in Harare. One of the last things Lookout passionately wanted was a piece of watermelon. He asked both me and Jeremy to find him some. There were no watermelons in Harare. My father had been to see him the previous afternoon. He rang me about 5 p.m. in the office and said Lookout was asking for me and he had said I would be there by six. Nkomo was there and Vote Moyo and a whole crowd of people.

As I had got the impression that Lookout had said he couldn't hang on until six, I raced to the hospital. Dr Nkomo stopped me outside the building. He said he wasn't sure my father had understood what Lookout had been trying to say, but he, Nkomo, thought that Lookout was trying to say that I was bringing him some watermelon and that he couldn't wait for it until six. Nkomo said I had to find some.

I went up to ward C8. Vote Moyo was outside the door, and I explained that there wasn't any watermelon in Harare. Gift saw me and I motioned her out, without Lookout seeing me. I explained that there were no watermelons; they were out of season. She asked what *could* be done. I said I'd keep on looking, and sped off to the Holiday Inn and other places. Nothing! I went back to Parirenyatwa Hospital and explained the situation to Lookout, but said that Nkomo, who had gone by now, had told me there was watermelon in Bulawayo and so we would try to get some from there, as well as continuing to try in Harare.

Gift came out of the ward with me. The nurses let us use their phone, and Gift rang Colonel Tshinga Dube. He told us that at that very moment a driver with his car was scouring Harare for watermelon and he expected the car back at any minute. Gift asked me to ring Zodwa Dabengwa in Bulawayo when I got home. I also rang Dr Nkomo and asked him to please find someone in Bulawayo who had a piece of watermelon and have it flown up the next morning. Over the next twelve or so hours I was constantly in touch with Nkomo, now in Bulawayo, about watermelon, hoping that CIO didn't think the word watermelon was a code for something intended to blow up the country.

I learned later that Colonel Dube had walked into Lookout's room at about seven or eight on Thursday night with a piece of watermelon and that Lookout's whole face had lit up. Dube had gone to Meikles Hotel, quietly motioned a waiter outside, given him Z$50 and said he would be waiting in the lounge until the waiter found a piece of watermelon. Whew!

Zodwa Dabengwa also found a piece of watermelon in Bulawayo, and I collected it from the airport on Friday morning. It looked beautiful. I told Lookout it was from Zodwa, and he managed to say, 'Zodwa.'

On Friday afternoon, Gift told me that somehow Lookout was different. When I went in to say goodbye, he was wearing an oxygen mask. He motioned for my hand. I took his hand, the left one that had been partially shot away in Zambia, and he held it tightly and looked at me very steadily above the mask. Then his eyes started closing. But he still held my hand tightly until I gently took it away. As I was leaving, he opened his eyes and looked at me once more.

Lookout's father managed to come to Harare from rural Matabeleland and reached him not long before his death. Lookout wasn't able to speak, but with an apparently enormous effort he regained consciousness and his father was able to see his son gazing at him. He died at 2 p.m. on Saturday 5 April. The state of Zimbabwe would not give him a hero's farewell, but Bulawayo was already preparing.

Lookout 'Mafela' Khalisabantu Vumindaba Masuku was buried at the revered Lady Stanley Cemetery in Bulawayo on Saturday 12 April 1986. Tens of thousands of people converged to pay their last respects. The main orator was, of course, Dr Joshua Nkomo.

Those who rule our country know inside themselves that Lookout played a very big part in winning our struggle. And yet they let him die in prison. I say he died in prison because he died on that bed on which he was detained. It was not possible for him to leave that bed and it was not possible for you to see him. Therefore, I say he died in prison.

Why should men like Lookout and Dumiso, after being found innocent of any wrongdoing by the highest Court in this land remain detained? When we ask we get the same answer from the Minister as we used to get from the Smith regime.

Mafela, Lookout, after all his sacrifices, died a pauper in our own hands. We cannot blame colonialism and imperialism for this tragedy. We who fought against these things now practise them. Why? Why? Why?

We are enveloped in the politics of hate. The amount of hate that is being preached today in this country is frightful. What Zimbabwe fought for was peace, progress, love, respect, justice, equality, not the opposite. And one of the worst evils we see today is corruption. The country bleeds today because of corruption.

It is appropriate that the site chosen for Lookout's grave lies near a memorial to those who fought against Hitler. Lookout fought against fascism, oppression, tribalism and corruption. Any failure to dedicate ourselves to the ideals of Masuku will be a betrayal of him and of all those freedom fighters whose graves are not known.

Our country cannot progress on fear and false accusations which are founded simply on the love of power. There is something radically wrong with our country today and we are moving, fast moving, towards destruction. There is confusion and corruption and, let us be clear about it, we are seeing racism in reverse under the false mirror of correcting imbalances from the past. In the process we are creating worse things. We have created fear in the minds of some in our country. We have made them feel unwanted, unsafe.

Young men and women are on the streets of our cities. There is terrible unemployment. Life has become harsher than ever before. People are referred to as squatters. I hate the word. I do not hate the person. When people were moved under imperialism certain facilities like water were provided. But under us? Nothing!

You cannot build a country by firing people's homes. No country can live by slogans, *pasi* (down with) this and *pasi* that. When you are ruling you should never say *pasi* to anyone. If there is something wrong with someone you must try to uplift him, not oppress him. We cannot condemn other people and then do things even worse than they did.

Lookout was a brave man. He led the first group of guerrillas who returned home at ceasefire. Lookout, lying quietly here in his coffin, fought to the last minute of his life for justice. It is his commitment to fair play that earned him his incarceration.

Some of you are tempted to give away your principles in order to conform. Even the preachers are frightened to speak freely and they have to hide behind the name of Jesus. The fear that pervades the rulers has come down to the people and to the workers. There is too much conformity. People work and then they shut up. We cannot go on this way. People must be freed to be able to speak. We invite the clergy to be outspoken. Tell us when we go wrong.

When Lookout was in Parirenyatwa he requested to be able to say goodbye to his friend Dumiso. The request was refused. 'No!' By our own Government!

He is not being buried in Heroes' Acre. But they can't take away his status as a hero. You don't give a man the status of a hero. All you can do is recognise it. It is his. Yes, he can be forgotten temporarily by the State. But the young people who do research will one day unveil what Lookout has done.

The day after the funeral I wrote a letter to Byron Hove, who was increasingly in trouble with his party, Zanu (PF).

Over the years it has become almost customary for me to send you a message from time to time. Here is another small message of friendship.

Yesterday I attended the funeral of Lookout Masuku in Bulawayo. As the scores of thousands of Zimbabweans present were told by Nkomo, you don't give a man the status of a hero, you can only recognise it. Yes, a man may be temporarily and even deliberately forgotten by a state, or by a party, or perhaps even by people who he regarded as friends, but eventually the truth tends to break through.

We all walk roads which are very rough from time to time. Lookout's road was perhaps one of the roughest ever. Yours is rough too, but I'm afraid it's all part of the cost of having been given the privilege of loving and trying to serve Zimbabwe.

Yesterday, thinking of Lookout, I tried to find the origin of the saying 'the price of liberty is eternal vigilance'. I think it must have been drawn from the following.

'The condition upon which God hath given liberty to man is eternal vigilance: which condition, if he break, servitude is at once the consequence of his crime and the punishment of his guilt.' This comes from a speech John Philpot Curran, an Irish judge who lived 1750–1817, made on the night of the election of a Lord Mayor of Dublin.

Good luck, Byron, and look carefully after yourself.

Without knowing it, Lookout had left me a wonderful gift. I had once given him a lift from Harare to Bulawayo and, passing through the area between Gweru and Shangani, I had remarked that this was a boring stretch of the journey. Lookout had reacted with horror and surprise. 'How can you say that? Just *look* at all of Lobengula's cattle!'

Ever since, passing through that area, I thought of Lookout, unleashed my imagination and watched thousands upon thousands of cattle undulating across the beautiful land.

CHAPTER 15

Buckingham Palace

TO MY TOTAL SURPRISE, EDWARD NDLOVU WAS RELEASED FROM Chikurubi Maximum Prison on Tuesday 29 April 1986. He walked into my office with all his belongings in three plastic carrier bags, grinned hugely and said, 'Here's my shopping!' We rushed home so he could telephone Mary and have a hot bath, always the first thing required, if possible, when you leave prison.

I had a dinner planned for that evening. Guests included Ann and Roger Martin, Britain's deputy high commissioner; Jenny Hyland, secretary to Dzingai Mutumbuka, the Minister of Education; Julia Wood from the Attorney-General's office; and Bryant and Elizabeth Elliot. I offered to cancel, but Edward was very game for it to go ahead. I warned him that everything he said would probably go straight round the diplomatic circuit, the ministries of Education and Justice and then, through Dzingai, round the cabinet and the Politburo. Edward was delighted.

When the guests walked in, they were amazed to find someone who they thought was in prison, charged with plotting a coup against the state of Zimbabwe, sitting quietly in a corner. Roger did an initial double take, as if I had unkindly put him in thoroughly hot water, which maybe I had, but it wasn't deliberate. Roger was planning to leave the diplomatic service that year. Ambassador David Miller and his wife Molli had already left Zimbabwe. David was very cross with Minister Nathan Shamuyarira for alleging that South Africa's propaganda station, Radio Truth, was financed by the USA. When he was making his farewells, he said to Minister of Finance Dr Bernard Chidzero, 'The next time you want any aid from us, just send Nathan Shamuyarira to get it.' It was rumoured that the next US ambassador would be the incumbent head of Union Carbide, James Rawlings, and that the company might divest itself of some interests in Zimbabwe to help pay for the Bhopal disaster. After the saga of UN sanctions against Rhodesia under Ian Smith being bust through the Byrd Amendment on behalf of Union Carbide, I thought it ironic indeed for one of their top men to end up in Zimbabwe as an ambassador.

Edward was in good form and held everyone spellbound with his lack of bitterness and his continued insistence, despite all he had been through, on the desirability of unity between Zanu (PF) and PF Zapu. No one left that night remotely believing he was a coup plotter, if anyone ever had. That's probably why the police were so reluctant to let him go. They were still trying to serve further detention orders on him at Chikurubi after Nkala had announced his release pending trial.

When it was time for the guests to leave, we walked them to their cars in the garden, at the same time trying to spot Halley's Comet, which Edward had been longing to see but couldn't from prison. By then everyone was so relaxed that they were laughing and saying that, as a coup plotter, Edward would be sure to know where to find a telescope when he reached Bulawayo the next day.

Earlier in the year my parents were informed that the investiture at Buckingham Palace would be in June. The New Zealanders said families were not normally invited to attend private investitures like this one, but the Queen had made an exception and my mother and I would be present. Thursday 5 June 1986 dawned bright and sunny in London, the magic day on which my father was to be invested with the oldest order of chivalry, Knight Bachelor, and enjoined to 'protect the poor and punish the wicked' by Her Majesty Queen Elizabeth II at Buckingham Palace.

We waited with courtiers in a spectacular mirrored hall. When doors opened into a huge, gracious room, we could see this tiny, beautiful lady standing far away, next to lofty windows that overlooked lawn and lake, a long, slender, silver sword in her hand and a red velvet stool at her feet. My father rushed ahead so fast we were left behind. David Lange, the prime minister of New Zealand who had been instrumental in the knighting of my father for services to Africa and New Zealand, was with us. At the sight of the Queen, my father's inborn instincts of chivalry had instantly overwhelmed him and he had automatically sped to her side.

By the time my mother, Lange and I managed to catch up, she had already touched my father on each shoulder with the sword, he was rising from the dubbing and they were deep in conversation about South Africa.

'South Africa will be back in the Commonwealth very soon,' said my father.

'Oh!' said the Queen with joy. 'Do you really think so?'

'Perhaps not in my lifetime,' said my eighty-two-year-old father, 'but most certainly in yours.'

They beamed at each other and Lange joined in, also beaming.

'Remember what Diefenbaker of Canada said when South Africa left the Commonwealth? He said *we will leave a candle in the window for South Africa.* It's still there, shining in the dark.'

In later years, when Zimbabwe had been plunged into utter darkness and sorely needed a candle to shine for her in the Commonwealth window, it was snuffed out by South Africa and her collaborators.

From London I proceeded to Holland for a Novib conference, where, by chance, I met representatives from the Protestant agency Inter-Church Aid and persuaded them to make a generous and, of course, top secret donation towards the legal costs of the latest ten men facing charges of treason against the state of Zimbabwe. It was becoming clear to at least some agencies that things in Zimbabwe were going horribly wrong.

After the conference I had a few days to myself in Amsterdam. I visited the house of the Nazi victim Anne Frank, where I copied down the definition of fascism that is on display, and of which she remains an enduring victim. It helped me to understand what was happening in Zimbabwe.

> After 1933 Germany became a dictatorship based on fascist ideas. The most important ones are stated here.
>
> Central to the fascist's view is the principle of inequality. In their eyes there are better (superior) and lesser (inferior) human beings. Their own race, their own people are always the best. Other races and people are inferior.
>
> Every form of democracy is rejected. The entire society is dominated by the party, with one leader at its head.
>
> Fascism places the oneness of the people above all else. Each individual is completely subordinated to it. No unrest among the people is allowed. Groups who stand up for their own interests and rights are silenced.
>
> Certain groups are blamed for all the problems in the society. They are declared to be the enemy of the people.
>
> Fascists glorify violence. In their eyes it is the way to solve conflicts. The law of the jungle applies.

I returned home from Holland to find that Kembo Mohadi had successfully sued Minister of Home Affairs Enos Nkala and three named members of the CIO for torture and had been awarded damages. But Prime Minister Mugabe then announced that the state wouldn't pay such damages, as it would be a waste of taxpayers' money.

Mohadi warned me that Minister Nkala was very angry. He had actually said to Mohadi that he knew who was behind the whole thing: 'Todd's daughter.' He said I had been seen in court with Mohadi and had then driven him to the airport, and that he, Nkala, was going to 'fix' me. So I thought it prudent to inform Nkala that at the time I was in Holland, and wrote to him that July, thinking how extraordinary it was that the Rhodesian Front mentality about how there had to be a white behind any objectionable process had lingered in the minds of our new rulers. Ian Smith's Rhodesian Front and Robert Mugabe's Zanu (PF) were similar in so very many ways.

Dear Minister

Today I was visiting Beitbridge and so had the opportunity of seeing Cde Kembo Mohadi MP to whom I am grateful for telling me part of the conversation he had with you yesterday from which it is apparent that some inaccurate information is being passed on to you.

He said you were displeased with me as you had been informed that I had driven Cde Mohadi to the airport after his recent testimony in court on the appalling torture he endured, and that you indicated that you were going to fix me.

Firstly, I can't believe that my driving anyone to the airport could be considered an offence. Secondly, at that time I was in Holland. I returned to Zimbabwe on July 5 and heard of that court case only after my return. But thirdly, there is something on the positive side. Although this is a very small matter – whether I drove someone to the airport or not – it could provide you with a golden opportunity to track down the source of this false information, starting with the person who gave it to you, who gave it to him etc until you reach the culprit.

When my father was prime minister, information was provided to him on the basis of which he was expected to authorise action against Guy Clutton-Brock. Instead of taking action he tracked down the source of this 'information' which turned out to be a Special Branch plant who couldn't speak English, who had attended a meeting addressed by Guy, who couldn't speak Shona. The informer had simply concocted statements which had been dressed up along the line by his Special Branch superiors until the dossier arrived on the prime minister's desk. It seems, alas, that false information continues to be fed to ministers even in our new Zimbabwe, and unless some kind of action is taken to ensure that ministers are told only the truth I suppose innocent people will continue to suffer.

May I take this opportunity to offer you my most sincere congratulations on your very strong stand against the use of torture which was prominently reported in the *Chronicle* today? I hope your statement was also reported in the *Herald*, and that everyone in Zimbabwe learns of it.

Yours sincerely.

There was no reply, but on Friday 8 August, I joined nearly a hundred representatives of non-governmental organisations attending a heavy, heavy meeting called by four heavy, heavy ministers: Messrs Nkala, Home Affairs, Kadungere, Armed Forces, Chikowore, Local Government, and Mnangagwa, State Security. Minister Nkala asked each person to stand up and identify themselves and their organisations, saying, 'If you have no activities in the rural areas, we may not need you.'

Less than a quarter of the representatives of an astonishing variety of organisations had identified themselves before the process was stopped, as it was taking too long. Nkala waited until just after my turn. I said, 'Judith Acton, Zimbabwe Project,' and he said *Mmhmm!* loudly, as if he had turned over a stone and found a scorpion. Then he said we should proceed without further introductions.

The ministers were obviously appalled by the presence of groups such as the Society for the Prevention of Cruelty to Animals, Transcendental Meditation and the Ministry of Cooperative Development. Every non-governmental organisation registered with the Ministry of Labour and Social Welfare had received an invitation, and so had various other entities. When Comrade Muringisi identified himself as being from the Ministry of Cooperatives, Nkala said he should leave; why should he be there? Muringisi said because he had been invited. The ministers laughed and agreed he could stay.

Minister Nkala said that this presentation was from the highest level of government. Three of the ministers present were involved with state security, and Comrade Chikowore had to do with governance in the rural areas. They had been delegated by cabinet to hold mutual discussions with the NGOs, which, at the end of the day, would be of benefit to us all.

Amnesty International and the Lawyers' Committee for Human Rights, based in the United States, had been sent reports from Zimbabwe about military matters in Matabeleland, Midlands and, to a certain extent, Masvingo province, he said. These reports made negative claims about the CIO, members of the defence force and the police. They contained serious allegations that had been sent to almost all members of parliament, ministers, the prime minister, leaders of industry, company directors, even the manager of the football association.

Nkala said the documents suggested that the government was a government of scoundrels with no feeling, sitting in their offices planning activities against members of their own population. Names of highly placed people had been mentioned in the reports, linking them with activities such as murder. Government had investigated the allegations and they were lies.

It was true that Zimbabwe had some problems, like the dissidents who were murdering, maiming and raping. 'But we will not fold our hands and sit back and let them take over, come heaven, come hell, come Amnesty International, come the Lawyers' Committee.'

He said that once Amnesty International received information, it was circulated to members throughout the world, and in the process seemed to assume some kind of authenticity. So someone might be detained for a couple of days and then released and demands would come from Amnesty, demanding that person's release. Who, then, should be released?

According to Nkala, there was a man from Beitbridge, a madman, a member of parliament who had been assisting dissidents, and so had been taken in for a few days for questioning. He alleged that he had been tortured, but there were no marks on him. It appeared from the newspapers as though he had won a case against torture, but this was only by default, as government hadn't known he was going to court.

The dissidents and their sponsors, Nkala said, had certain objectives to achieve and it was known who and what party supported them. They were financed entirely from within the country, and the organisations that sponsored them were wholly Zimbabwean. 'One or two or three of you have taken it upon yourselves to champion the discrediting of government. We have an abhorrence of the activities of some of you. We can do without you, all of you, but we don't want to do that. We simply want to say, let us move in step. If there is anything wrong, tell us. Don't run to Amnesty International.'

Nkala further said that all NGOs would now have to register with the Ministry of Local Government, in addition to the Ministry of Labour and Social Services, already a requirement, and report all projects in all areas. 'If you want to spend money, you must first explain to the district administrator. Any one of you found in the rural areas without the knowledge of officials in the Ministry of Local Government will be reported to me and we will react. Those who are not Zimbabweans, we will deport. Those of you who are Zimbabweans know how we will act.'

Questions were invited. There were very few. Someone said his organisation received requests from all over the country. If, for example, he agreed to provide a roof for a school, should he consult the Ministry of Local Government before doing so, or should he just inform the ministry that a roof was being provided? Minister Chikowore answered: 'Just inform the ministry.' Earlier, there had been a ripple of uneasy laughter when Nkala said, 'and we know what you do at night'. Now, in conclusion, he said, 'a good lot of you have in your employment dissidents, perhaps as drivers or in other capacities. And we know what they do in the bush.'

The last questioner asked if we could be informed if we had dissidents in our employ. 'Identify yourself!' said Minister Nkala, and the tension in the room exploded in a howl of laughter when the questioner responded, 'Ian Hayes, director of the Zimbabwe Traffic Safety Board.' Minister Mnangagwa, himself laughing, pointed at Mr Hayes and said, 'We know you are innocent.'

Comrade Mugabe told a press conference at his residence in August that the unity talks between Zanu (PF) and PF Zapu had reached a sufficiently advanced stage to allow the Attorney-General to withdraw treason charges against ten men.

He said he had informed the Attorney-General, Godfrey Chidyausiku, of the 'critical stage' the talks had reached, and the latter had decided it would not be in the national interest to proceed with the case.

Mugabe emphasised that the release of the ten men was the decision of the Attorney-General, 'acting within the exclusive discretion conferred upon him by the constitution'. But, he said the government was not obliged to retain those who had been involved and who were in the army, and they were not going to do so.

Of the men concerned, Charles Grey, Kindness Ndlovu and Tshila Nleya were all army brigadiers, Joseph Z Dube and Eddie Sigogi were colonels, Brian Siziba a corporal and Leon Khumalo a captain. William Kona was Zapu's national chairman, Sydney Malunga a Zapu MP for Mpopoma and Edward Ndlovu a Zapu MP for Gwanda.

A few days after this press conference I was at the airport, waiting for the flight to Bulawayo, when I was approached by the Attorney-General. He was very friendly, and I responded, saying I was glad to see him and that he must now be the most popular man in Zimbabwe. Godfrey looked pleased but mystified. I reminded him that the prime minister, in announcing the dropping of treason charges against ten men, had said it was Chidyausiku's decision, not his, and that the Attorney-General had the constitutional power to release anyone. It was all nonsense, of course. The men were about to go to court, where it would have been revealed that most of them had been tortured, and government wanted to conceal this fact.

I said I hadn't known of Godfrey's power until I had read the prime minister's statement. 'And now,' I said, 'how about Dumiso Dabengwa? If you have the power to release anyone, how can we get Dumiso out? If I send you a bowl of red roses every day …?'

He grinned and said, 'You don't waste time talking shop, do you?'

Harare hosted a summit of the Non-Aligned Movement (NAM) in September 1986. My house was full throughout, and I was amazingly fortunate in who was billeted with me. Xan Smiley had arranged for the *Economist*'s Godfrey Jansen to stay. He was a gentle Indian based in Cyprus, and the magazine's expert on the Levant, cricket and the NAM. There were also journalists Allister Sparks from South Africa, Derek Ingram, and, for a few days, Patrick Bishop and Richard Dowden from Britain. Their company drew in many other visitors, such as Chris Laidlaw, New Zealand's high commissioner to Zimbabwe, and Emeka Anyaoku from the Commonwealth Secretariat.

Emeka was the essence of courtesy. He took me to dinner one evening. The restaurant proved disappointing, but he used the opportunity to teach the waiter how to pour wine properly. The young man was wide-eyed with pleasure and gratitude. The next day a sleek car arrived and the chauffeur emerged, carrying the most enormous bottle of Glennfiddich whisky I had ever seen, and a note: 'With compliments from Chief Emeka Anyaoku. Thank you for a most enjoyable evening last night in your home and in the pleasurable company of some old and new friends.'

Allister was on his portable computer all the time. I hadn't seen such a display of technology before. He wrote his story, stored it on a disk, plugged the computer modem into the telephone and the story flashed in seconds to the *Washington Post* or wherever. His machine was not exactly silent, but not as noisy as a typewriter, and it was attached to him by an invisible umbilical cord. Even sitting in the lounge with us for company he would have the machine on his knee. I'd never met anyone who worked so hard, and it was my theory that his work was his personal weapon against apartheid and all it implied, and that he wouldn't be able to rest until it was all over.

Some hours after Allister left, Derek, Godfrey and I were having a happy but nostalgic dinner together. Courtly little Godfrey, maybe about sixty, all of a sudden summed up what we were missing.

'God!

'Listen to the silence!

'That's Allister.

'Gone.'

Julius Chikazaza, who looked after 18 Masefield Avenue, delighted in almost all of my guests. Those he didn't approve of received silent, contemptuous backward glances over his shoulder. They tended to be black Zimbabwean journalists. Julius had worked all over the country. He was a Zezuru from Zvimba, Robert Mugabe's birthplace, and seemed to have proved what I was often told but always doubted, namely that Shona-speakers sometimes didn't pronounce the letter *l*, just as it was said Sindebele speakers often did not pronounce the letter *r*, so that for them, for example, Harare became *Halale*.

While we were having dinner, Allister phoned to say he had arrived safely in Johannesburg. Julius took the call and left a message on my desk. RASTA SPARKY SAFE.

Since Minister Nkala had ordered us at the NGO meeting to report anything amiss to government and not to Amnesty International, I had written a number of letters that had gone unanswered. Recently released detainees had come to see me, complaining of being beaten and, in one case, being given electric shocks. I had reason to believe that one of them was a plant, and, sure enough, the doctor who had examined him told me privately that he had found nothing to suggest the man had been abused. So I wrote post haste to Minister Mnangagwa, saying I was sorry to bother him during NAM, but, following instructions received, I felt I should let him know that a Comrade X was complaining about electric shocks during his detention and, if government wanted to investigate, he could let me know and I would forward the complainant's name and address.

Silence.

The front page of the *Herald* was sombre on Tuesday 21 October 1986, with thick black lines around the headline: 'Machel killed in jet crash'. The Mozambican president's Tupolev 134A jetliner had crashed on the Sunday night just after 9 p.m., and many were killed. A friend at Foreign Affairs had rung me on Monday morning around ten to tell me the terrible news. When I went out onto the streets, each seller of a special edition of the *Herald* was surrounded by a buzz of angry, tearful people who couldn't get copies fast enough.

On the Monday morning, after they must have known of the crash, I listened to a commentary on Radio South Africa, which was a vicious attack on Zimbabwe. It reminded me of their attack on Lesotho, broadcast just before their cross-border raid into that country. Things were moving fast.

We tended to regard beautiful Harare with its towering golden Sheraton Hotel and conference centre as a symbol of the state of the country as a whole. There had been dramatic improvements in many areas like health, water, roads and education since independence, but for too many, life remained a grinding misery of just eking out an existence.

Driving one day along the Botswana border with Godwin Matatu of the *Observer* and Albert Ngwenya from the Zimbabwe Project, we passed two schools, about fifteen miles apart, partially destroyed by 'dissidents' in one night. They were self-help schools, the bricks moulded and the buildings erected by the local community. I became suspicious. For people to have wreaked such havoc in one night they could either fly from place to place like Batman, or they had transport. The Batman hypothesis was as unlikely as the possibility that 'dissidents' had transport. This came at a time when the unity talks were said to be going well.

We delivered maize-meal to a man who was too weak from hunger to work. Then we met a businessman who was recently crippled. He had been forced to stand in boiling water by Zanu (PF) youths because they opposed the party he belonged to, PF Zapu.

Overall, the impression was that we were in a country totally different to what we in Harare knew. There was no grass. Cattle staggered around like hairy skeletons. People spent much of their energy collecting water from far-off places. There were so many who were barely getting by in appalling circumstances. But had the Lancaster House conference leading to our independence not worked, maybe many of them would already be dead.

The graduation ceremony for the comrades who had just completed a nine-month course in various skills at our training centre, Adelaide Acres, was a joyful occasion. Paul Themba Nyathi had sent off a lot of invitations to embassies and high commissions, which I thought would be politely declined. Not a bit of it. The New Zealand high commissioner came, as did the deputy British high commissioner and one other official; the Chinese ambassador; and the acting French ambassador. The United States sent their consul, the Ghanaian high commissioner arrived, as did an array of top civil servants from the new Ministry for Cooperative Development.

The charming new representative of SWAPO, Comrade Kapuka Nauyala, stole the show when he shouted the only three words of Shona he knew, three times. *Pamberi ne Chimurenga*! Forward with the armed struggle! He had already been to Adelaide Acres with a SWAPO delegation to meet the comrades and they all loved him, so no one minded a rather one-sided slogan, except that it made the American look a bit hot.

It was a lovely day. The permanent secretary for the new ministry, Dr L Chitsike, made a speech that was so full of praise for the work of the Zimbabwe Project that I thought I must be dreaming. The Soviets sent apologies and, in recompense, invited Paul Themba Nyathi and me to a reception celebrating the thirty-seventh anniversary of the USSR's formation. The caviar was fantastic. I enjoyed being non-aligned.

A young Tanzanian doctor passed through Zimbabwe after ten years of training in Cuba. He became a devotee of mine, but for only one reason: he had discovered that I knew the luminary and former Tanzanian minister, Sheikh Abdul Rahman Mohamed Babu; that I had known Babu for a long time, thanks to my friend the renowned Australian writer Murray Sayle; that I knew Babu's address; that I had shaken Babu's hand; that I was a *friend* of Babu. For him there could be no more exalted position in the world. A friend of Babu!

I didn't mention to him that Babu, whom he regarded as infallible, could actually be deprecating both about himself and about what he regarded as errors made in the governance of Tanzania. Not coming from the mainland, Babu always laughingly referred to himself as a 'Zanzibarbarian'.

The *Financial Gazette* carried a paragraph on its front page, 'No apology for riots', reporting that the University of Zimbabwe's representative council would make no apology for the physical violence that had occurred during demonstrations in Harare to mourn the death of President Samora Machel. 'No apology will be made for the physical justice prescribed upon retrogressive whites and blacks inclusive.'

In addition, a student action group called *Hokoyo* (Beware) had been launched to 'among other things continue conscientising the nation on the need to be vigilant, alert and critical of imperialist, neo-colonial and all reactionary machinations, and to consolidate the solidarity of progressive student politics worldwide'.

When I read that to Doris Galen, who lectured in law at the university, she laughed uproariously and said, 'Now translate that into rhetoric!'

On Friday 5 December 1986, Dumiso Dabengwa and others were at last released from Chikurubi Maximum Security Prison after all the cruel years of detention. Bryant Elliot took them to the Brickhills' house, and some friends were rustled up for an impromptu party at 4 p.m. Dumiso was surprised to hear that he looked well. People were pretty demanding, and some babies born in his absence were presented to him. Dumiso had a wonderful gift of appearing to be intensely interested in everything. At a certain point we gathered around him and he made a little speech and proposed a toast to … Bryant Elliot.

Bryant was standing on the edge of the circle, looking far away. When the toast was proposed and he was thanked for all his wonderful work, he appeared thunderstruck. Maybe he'd never been thanked for anything in public before. He tried to say something, but was tongue-tied. Unfortunately, Bryant's wife Elizabeth arrived only after that particular episode. I was touched by her too. She had never met Dumiso before, but when he took her hand and she looked up at him, her eyes filled with tears.

Julie, a Zimbabwean working for the Zambian High Commission, announced that she had two pieces of bad news for Du, one being the death of a friend in Zambia, and the second being that his wife Zodwa, who had returned to nursing, was going on night duty that very night for four months. Dumiso was appalled. He turned to SK Moyo from the Ministry of Health and said, 'You must order my wife *off* night duty at once!' But Simon Moyo said, 'Sorry, she's at the Mater Dei and the government has no influence on Catholic hospitals.' Sure enough, when Dumiso flew home to Bulawayo that night, Zodwa was not at the airport to meet him. She was dutifully at work.

By the time we'd piled into cars and left the house to go to the airport it was teeming with rain. I had Norman Zikhali in my car, who had been released with Dumiso. He seemed pretty shaky and was worrying about his future. He had been one of the Zapu officials Joshua Nkomo had sent to Beitbridge to rescue people from violence following the murder of Senator Ndlovu by 'dissidents', and had been detained in prison ever since.

When we got to the airport, there were another thirty or so people waiting to greet Dumiso. There was such joy. But a very sour note was finally injected by a man in a suit who walked up with outstretched hand just as Dumiso was going through the doors onto the tarmac. Maeresera,

CIO. The one who had come and stood at Lookout's bed. Dumiso shook his hand, I think reflexively, but he certainly realised almost immediately who Maeresera was and turned away. To me it seemed very deliberate and very unpleasant. 'Here I am, even in this seeming moment of freedom and joy.' Oh well.

Justin Nyoka, Ministry of Information, seemed happy enough, and Godwin Matatu from the *Observer* managed to keep moving along. Justin had a good intelligence network. A couple of days after a very enjoyable trip Godwin and I had had with Albert Ngwenya along the Botswana border, I saw Justin on a street in Harare, and he said: 'Why do you go together to Plumtree with Godwin Matatu of all people?'

Then I saw Godwin, who had been quite rattled when he'd bumped into Justin a day after our return and Justin had said to him: 'Why do you go together to Plumtree with Judy Todd of all people?'

I told Godwin he needn't worry. It was only Justin being fashionable and practising a little terror.

Some people came and stayed for a few nights from the eve of Monday 15 December. They were ANC and expecting cross-border raids from South Africa to mark the launching of the military wing of the ANC, Umkhonto we Sizwe, twenty-five years before. When there was a tip-off like that, all ANC personnel left their homes and got lost.

I found the following poem, by a Cuban called Roberto Fernandez Retamar, in one of their publications.

For an Instant
That glow in the night;
Is it one of *our* reflectors?
Is it one of *their* weapons?
(For an instant,
I'd forgotten
That there's a moon
In the sky,
and that there are stars).

On Wednesday 17 December I saw Guduza. A daughter of his, Nokukhama, had travelled from Bulawayo to Harare to try to renew her passport and came to see me.

Nokukhama was born in South Africa, and the Guduza family, along with so many others, was finding life in Zimbabwe such misery that she wanted to return to Soweto. It was so strange to know that, for many, life in apartheid South Africa was preferable to life in post-independence Zimbabwe.

No member of Guduza's family had been able to see him since he was returned by the Botswana authorities in February. Nokukhama, known by the family as Nobel, the diminutive of Nobel Prize, a proud nickname bestowed on her by her father, hadn't seen him since 1983, so I thought we must try to do something for her.

I rang CIO, but they said Guduza was no longer in their custody and was being held by the police at Chikurubi. So I rang the Director of Prisons and was given permission for Nobel to see him. We went to Chikurubi, but it turned out that he was being held at Harare Central. After waiting for ages, Nobel was let in to see him, but soon came out to say he wanted to see me too. So in I went. There were a couple of little cubicles. Guduza stood in one with a telephone, then there was a pane of glass, then a corridor where guards could walk up and down, then another pane of glass, then the visitor in a cubicle with a receiver.

The first thing he said was, 'For God's sake, get me a lawyer!' He looked all right, but he said there wasn't enough food and he was starving. He was to appear in court at Rotten Row the next day. He said they had tried to charge him with recruiting dissidents but couldn't make anything stick, so now they were going to charge him with taking Nkomo out of the country. In the middle of the unity talks? It didn't seem very wise.

Minister Eddison Zvobgo was having a very rough time indeed; very, very rough. When I saw him at Sandro's he took my hand and said, 'You don't have to worry about me. I'm a survivor.' I was amazed by his openness, and immediately answered truthfully, 'I'm *not* worried about you. I *know* you are a survivor!'

We set up an assignation. I told him I wanted to meet his father the next time I was in Masvingo. He said that that was not good enough. He would *take* me from Harare in the new year to Masvingo to meet his father. This would be worse for me than being recognised as a friend of Dumiso! I didn't tell him that, but I knew.

Zvobgo was being crucified on the basis of a secret CIO report which claimed that, at the funeral of Meyor Hurimbo's father in June, he was overheard saying that Nelson Mawema, a political enemy of his, was nothing more than Mugabe's *mujiba*.

A *mujiba* was a young boy who spied and ran messages, as young boys did for the guerrillas during the war. *Great* offence had been taken by the prime minister. In the past month, according to Godwin, there had been an attempt to assassinate Eddison. If the attempt had succeeded, I could just imagine the headline in the *Herald*: 'Dissidents penetrate Masvingo'.

My father was one of the happiest men I knew, savouring the sweetness of some of the fruits of the new Zimbabwe. On Christmas Day he attended a wedding in a village near our home. He was sitting watching the dancing when a boy of about four came up and leaned against his legs, arms folded and his back to my father, also watching the dancing but enjoying the support. A woman who was observing this laughed and said to my father, 'I'm sure you don't know who that boy is.' He didn't.

During the war, Christine Mukokwayarira, who worked on Hokonui Ranch, received a message to say that a ZANLA guerrilla had been shot by the Rhodesian security forces and help was needed. She drove as close to the village where he was hiding as she dared, then walked a long way across the veld to tell the villagers where the car was. They then carried the man to the vehicle.

Christine drove him to her home, and then called my father to treat his wounds. When the man was well enough, Christine and my father drove him to Bulawayo, where he was hidden in one of the high-density suburbs. All these actions were hanging offences. So far as I knew, that was the last my father heard of the man, until Christmas 1986. It was the rescued guerrilla's son leaning against him.

I spent Christmas Eve with Rita and Godwin Matatu, their sons Tendeka and Nicholas, and Fernando Goncalves, head of the Mozambique news agency AIM.

Godwin and Fernando were meant to have been on Machel's ill-fated aeroplane, but had gone on a binge and arrived at the airport too late to check in.

CHAPTER 16

We are flying

A FTER APPEARING IN COURT EIGHT TIMES OVER THE SPACE OF a year and being remanded in custody each time without anyone noticing, as he didn't then have a lawyer, Makhatini Guduza was released on bail of Z$100 on Thursday 8 January 1987.

Court 6 at the Rotten Row magistrate's courts in Harare was like a conveyor belt. The court was for remands only, and masses of people were shuffled through, often without the press, friends or family knowing. Guduza said some people had been held at Harare Central for five years and they were just remanded, remanded, remanded every couple of weeks, as they didn't have money for lawyers and didn't know what else to do.

I was in Bulawayo and my house in Harare was full of Ndlovus. Edward and Mary had brought their children from Bulawayo for a swimming competition. Paul Themba Nyathi, knowing that Guduza would be in court, paid his bail, then took him to my house to clean up and to stay. They were old friends, having been detained together under the Smith regime. Guduza's wife and two daughters were also in Harare, as they had heard he would appear in court and wanted a glimpse of him. Little did they know he would be released and that they would all land up in my home, where pressure on accommodation was so great that Guduza and his wife Poppy ended up in my bed.

His family left the following day and, when I returned on Saturday, Guduza had gone to a party at Dr Nkomo's house in Highfield, organised by local women to celebrate the release of Dumiso Dabengwa. About a thousand people were present.

Guduza left for Bulawayo on Sunday. I didn't think government knew he was out of jail. He had been in CIO custody at Goromonzi from February 1986, after being returned to Zimbabwe by the Botswana authorities, until October, when CIO had handed him over to the police law and order division. At the end of the day, despite whatever Mnangagwa was told, Guduza was charged only with leaving the country illegally. But how would Nkala feel? What would happen if they bumped into each other in Bulawayo? The lawyer didn't want any publicity at all until the whole case was over. Guduza was to appear in court again on 22 January.

He was at no stage physically tortured. For the first few days the warders had done the currently fashionable thing of soaking his blanket with water before locking him up for the night, but he was soon on reasonable terms with them and life eased. The bad thing was that, for all those awful months, there was no contact with his family.

Guduza was in fine form, mellow and gentle, but as straight-talking as ever.

When he returned to Harare from Bulawayo later that month, he had hoped to stay with me, but my parents were there with the Clutton-Brocks, whose trip to Zimbabwe from Britain was important. I therefore asked Ruth, widow of national hero Josiah Chinamano, formerly Nkomo's deputy in Zapu, to accommodate Guduza.

The day before Guduza had to be back in court he came to my office, but I was out. Shortly afterwards I received a message to say CIO was looking for him. I rang Ruth, and she said she didn't know what had happened. He had not contacted her, but five men from CIO had been to her place looking for him.

I went to court on 22 January, my heart in my mouth, fearing he may have already been 'picked'. To my great joy I saw him sitting there. If on bail you could sit with the public, and when your name was called for a further remand you stepped forward and were told on what date you should next appear. Guduza's bench was full, but there was a space behind him, where I sat. He looked splendid. His hair was snowy, but he was still physically vigorous. He seemed very pleased to see me.

I told Guduza that CIO had been looking for him at Ruth's, and he said they had been looking for him at Nkomo's too. He planned to see them after the remand, as they had nothing on him, and he didn't want them harassing other people while they were looking for him. I was still worried that they might spirit him away before he had formally appeared in court, but the magistrate walked in and proceedings started.

A well-dressed man came and sat at the end of my row, and I saw Guduza turn, smile and nod to him. Then Guduza's name was called, he stepped forward and was remanded until 26 February. As he walked out I rose, as did this man and one other, and we all left court together. One of them said, 'Don't worry, we're not going to detain you again. We just want to ask a few more questions,' and they took Guduza away.

When I told Paul Themba Nyathi what had been said about 'just a few more questions', he laughed and said that all those long years ago when he had been detained under Smith, the people who were picking him up had said exactly the same thing to Paul's employer. She had next seen him three and a half years later.

Later that day I received a message to say that Guduza was back in Chikurubi, detained under a new ministerial order.

I learned that after Guduza had returned to Bulawayo, the unelected minister, Callistus Ndlovu, had thrown a big party to celebrate the wedding of his daughter. Dr Nkomo was there, and he confronted the unelected Minister of Home Affairs, Enos Nkala, saying something like, 'Now we know you were lying in all you said about Guduza. He has been released on only Z$100 bail.' That must have spoiled the party for Nkala, and now he was having his revenge.

Guduza had told me that the roots of Nkala's hatred for him stretched back to 1975, when they had fought each other in detention and Guduza laid Nkala on the ground. Nkala also fought the future President Banana in detention, as well as the future president of the senate, Nolan Makombe. So a lot of people in high positions must have had mixed feelings about Nkala. I learned a lot when Guduza was staying with me. There was also a useful book by Robert Cary and Diana Mitchell called *African Nationalist Leaders in Rhodesia – Who's Who*, published in 1977, which had a chapter on Guduza. The last sentence read that Guduza 'describes himself as "not an Africanist or tribalist but a human being who loves all people in the world"'.

I thought Nkala might be angry with me again as he had probably discovered that I had gone to see Guduza in jail, found the lawyer who got Guduza out and had Guduza staying in my home, although I trusted Nkala didn't know that Guduza and Poppy were actually in my bed. But that was where God's Providence, or whatever we call what we hope is divine intervention, came in yet again.

To have the Clutton-Brocks staying with me at the time confirmed beyond doubt to everyone our deep friendship and love for each other. They were held in the most affectionate and respectful regard by practically every top leader in Zimbabwe. So I felt safe. But to have the privilege of feeling safe also, of course, increased the responsibility of trying to assist where possible the anonymous, the unsafe, the hurt, the incarcerated. I could do very little, but at least I was in a position to try.

Willie Musarurwa rang me, so sad for Guduza. They had spent a happy evening together at my home. That night Willie told me that at some point during their detention under the Smith regime they had slept so tightly packed together on the floor that when one man wanted to turn over, he had to shout aloud so everyone could turn over in unison. At that time, Willie slept next to Guduza.

Willie had attended Callistus Ndlovu's party in Bulawayo. Nkomo and Nkala were sitting next to each other, and when Willie and Ariston Chambati went up to greet Nkomo, Nkala moved away. Nkomo said to Willie and Ariston, 'I have been sitting next to a mad man, a mad, mad, mad man. He is so mad that I think he is driving me mad too.'

That January, Bob Schaplen, who wrote for *The New Yorker*, sent me a copy of his book on Vietnam, called *Bitter Victory*. I had met him during the Non-Aligned Movement conference and discovered that he used to be married to Lady Elaine Greene, my literary agent in London from 1972. When I was allowed out of detention, Elaine negotiated with the London *Sunday Times* publication of part of a book I was working on, which, she told them, would be called *Some Time, Some How, Something Better*, the title I had proposed, over her dead body. It was a quotation from the Pearce Commission's report, which had found that the terms of a proposed settlement in 1971/72 between the British government and the Smith regime were not acceptable to the majority of the people.

> Although statements by British ministers expressly disclaimed all hopes of any improvement in the terms or any future help if this settlement fell through (and we never gave anybody any reason to doubt this), some clearly persisted in the hope that some time, some how, something better would turn up.
>
> It may well be that such hopes were fallacious and that it was unwise to abandon some present advancement for the sake of them. But if people genuinely prefer hope to present realities they are entitled to do so. And if they reject on that score one cannot invalidate their rejection or even less turn it into an acceptance on the grounds that their hopes were likely to prove vain.

The book ended up being called *The Right to Say No*, and Longman Zimbabwe republished it in 1987. It was recommended by the Ministry of Education for the libraries of all schools teaching subjects at O and A level. When it was first published in Britain in 1972, it was banned in Rhodesia by special presidential decree, making it a criminal offence to possess a copy. We reproduced this decree, just for fun, as the frontispiece for the new edition.

Rhodesia Government Notice No. 1132 of 1972

Order Issued under the Provisions of Subsection (1) of Section 18 of the Law and Order (Maintenance) Act (Chapter 39)

WHEREAS, by Subsection (1) of Section 18 of the Law and Order (Maintenance) Act it is provided that, if the President is of the opinion that the printing, publication, dissemination or possession of any publication or series of publications is likely to be contrary to the interests of public safety or security, he may, by order published in the *Gazette* and in such newspapers as he may consider necessary, declare that printed publication or series of publications to be a prohibited publication ... AND WHEREAS I am of the opinion that the printing, publication, dissemination or possession of the publication specified below is likely to be contrary to the interests of public safety or security NOW, THEREFORE, under and by virtue of the powers vested in the President as afore said, I do, by this my order, declare the publication entitled *The Right to Say No*, by Judith Todd, to be a prohibited publication.

CLIFFORD W DUPONT
President
Issued at Salisbury this sixth day of December, 1972

Nice one, Mr President!

After eight days with me, the Clutton-Brocks were collected by Knotty, the esteemed Alfred Knottenbelt, former teacher of so many now in leadership positions. Guy was frail, but much better when he left than when he arrived. I heard him humming that morning. The week before, one of Didymus Mutasa's dogs had bitten Guy's hand, and that was a shock for Guy, as well as a nasty wound.

Enos Nkala had given parliament a long lecture the previous year about what a bad man Makhatini Guduza was, running Super Zapu, recruiting dissidents and generally working for the downfall of Zimbabwe. No one liked being proved wrong, and soon Guduza, back in Chikurubi, was charged with recruiting dissidents. I rang Willie Musarurwa to tell him, and he said Guduza would not be surprised as he had got used to such things. 'It's only when someone does something nice for him that he is surprised.'

It was incredibly hot in Zimbabwe that January, and in certain places crops were being blistered to death. It was reported in the newspaper that Dambudzo Marechera had been found in his flat in a terrible state and had been rushed to Avenues Clinic. John and Aelda Callinicos, who were in charge of catering at the Holiday Inn, said Marechera's friends were coming there to get food for him as he didn't like the clinic's food.

One day, John and Aelda supervised the preparation of a large trout for Marechera's send-out lunch. A waiter who took it reported that while Marechera was enjoying the trout, a nurse walked in and he seized a knife and threatened to throw it at her unless she got out fast. So it sounded as if he was getting better quickly.

I saw Eddison Zvobgo, and I told him some friends had repeated to me a marvellous story circulating about him.

'Every Friday evening, Comrade Zvobgo returns to his constituency.

'He travels with the people by bus.

'He sits at the back of the bus and drinks and plays the drums.

'His car follows behind carrying his chauffeur and his jacket.'

For once, Eddison was momentarily speechless. 'I haven't been on a bus since independence,' he said, then added hastily, 'but don't tell your friends.'

In February, there was an evening reception at parliament in honour of Guy and Molly Clutton-Brock. This was their first trip back to Zimbabwe since Guy had been deported in 1971 for his active participation in the politics of the people. 'I am glad to share in the fellowship of the dispossessed,' Guy said then. 'I take nothing with me beyond my love for many friends.'

Those friends abounded at the reception: Gertrude and Didymus Mutasa, the speaker of parliament; Stephen and Judith Matewa; Arthur Chadzingwa; Cephas and Sharlottie Msipa; Mike and Eileen Haddon; Anne Lewis; Patricia Chater; Cephas Muropa; Willie Musarurwa; Stella Madzimbamuto; and, looming large and looking well, Joshua Nkomo, whose hair was snowy white. Makhatini Guduza deserved to be there but had been locked up again. The Clutton-Brocks had just missed seeing him.

When it was time for speeches, Didymus called us all to order, with, seated on his left, Nkomo, then Guy and then Maurice Nyagumbo. I thought how typical of the Clutton-Brocks that, without even mentioning the word, they visibly and quietly created a friendly unity among those around them.

In a moving speech in praise of the Clutton-Brocks, Didymus recalled how both Cephas Msipa and Maurice Nyagumbo had gone to hide from the Smith regime at Cold Comfort Farm cooperative, where Guy and Molly lived, and had each been kept ignorant of the presence of the other as Cephas was Zapu and Maurice supported Zanu.

Fortunately, Nkomo had to leave before the final speech, which was by Nyagumbo. He nearly wrecked the whole evening, but he was speaking so softly I hoped that only those near him could hear what he said. He spoke graciously and warmly about the Clutton-Brocks, turned, looked at Nkomo's empty chair and said, 'Thank God he's gone or else I would have had to say this in front of him,' and then attacked.

He recalled the time when people had to choose the leader of Zimbabwe's African National Congress, forerunner of the National Democratic Party, which in turn gave rise to the Zimbabwe African People's Union (Zapu), from which the Zimbabwe African National Union (Zanu) split in 1963.

Nyagumbo said that Guy had pleaded with the then leaders – Chick (Robert Chikerema), George (Nyandoro) and Paul Mushonga – not to choose as leader someone who was a graduate, as such a person would feel that he had a lot to lose and wouldn't fight selflessly. But the mistake had been made, Nkomo had been chosen and the error was rectified only in 1963, when Zanu split from Zapu.

It would have been a strange statement for Guy to have made, as he himself was a university graduate. But no one took issue, and when Nyagumbo had finished, Willie Musarurwa and I went into the courtyard to breathe fresh air. Nyagumbo's attack on Nkomo was so unnecessary and he could not have chosen a more inappropriate occasion.

A man in plain clothes walked up to me at the Bulawayo airport one night and greeted me warmly. I couldn't recall his name, but knew his face. One side was slightly indented, from what kind of injury I couldn't tell, and one eye was smaller than the other.

He wanted to tell me that, after the Zimbabwe Project had helped him get his identity papers, he had secured a job with Air Zimbabwe. I asked him which section, searching for clues to remind me about him. Security, he said, and then he smiled even more warmly. He had managed to save some money, and with his wife had opened a small general dealer's store in Mutoko in November, and 'we already have Z$2 000 in the bank'. I congratulated him very sincerely and then remembered he had been sent to us by 88 Manica Road, a euphemism for Zanu (PF), for that was where they then had their offices. I couldn't recall exactly how we helped him, but he obviously thought we had and was very happy and proud of his achievements, and that made me very happy too.

At a dinner given by the Chinese ambassador, Zheng Yaowen, I was distressed by what other diplomats were saying about 'the black Russian', an unfriendly nickname for Dumiso Dabengwa, which stemmed from his training by the KGB in the Soviet Union.

We were seated at a round table, so it was easy to communicate. I said Dabengwa was a friend of mine, and wouldn't they like to meet him and form their own judgements instead of repeating about him what I thought was not true? They all enthusiastically said yes, and so I arranged an informal meeting at my house at 18 Masefield Avenue. Present were Dumiso and Zheng Yaowen; Baron Franz Mentzingen, PG Guyonnaud and Nils Larsson, ambassadors respectively of Germany, France and Denmark; and Ramsay Melhuish, Chris Laidlaw and Allan Edwards, the respective high commissioners of Britain, New Zealand and Australia.

Dumiso arrived with a friend, Krish Ragadoo. Krish and I sat out of the way, just listening, and although Krish was obviously burning to answer the questions being put to Dumiso, he managed to restrain himself.

It was all a great success. The guests were surprised and delighted by Dumiso, and later Ambassador Guyonnaud invited Dabengwa to his country as an official guest of the French government. Dumiso said to me that if he had been able to meet people like these before he was locked up, he didn't think he and the others would have been detained for so long.

Among many other things, Dumiso said there should be unity between PF Zapu and Zanu (PF), but under a new name. The old names should be placed in the archives. This was necessary if it was to be a properly unified party; even whites should be able to join without concerns about family or friends killed during the war by the forces of Zanu and Zapu. A one-party state should not be legislated. People who might eventually become dissatisfied with the performance of the new party should be free to form other associations.

Krish was a loyal and generous friend. He played an important role in Zapu during the struggle and so had excellent relations with the ANC, which had to keep a very low profile in the Zimbabwe of Pan Africanist Congress supporter Robert Mugabe. Krish ran a bottle store in Kensington, and very interesting people gathered in the back storeroom most evenings. Sometimes you could even find Joe Modise, head of the ANC's armed wing, Umkhonto we Sizwe, or MK, perched there on an empty crate.

Early one morning, Mike Munyati jogged to my house to get material on the Clutton-Brocks. He had interviewed them the week before for Zimbabwe television, and was amazed. 'Guy is the first man I have interviewed who is neither black nor white, Zimbabwean nor British.' He was still with me at 10 a.m. when a car arrived to collect me for a trip to Masvingo. The car was paid for by the London *Observer* and was being driven by Comrade Funero, who was ex-Dadaya, of SG Mpofu's generation. He was intelligence of some kind and was accompanied by Comrade Chisorochengwe, who was straight CIO.

We went to pick up the newspaper's local reporter, Godwin Matatu, who was still filing a story on being ambushed twice during his recent trip to Mozambique. The *Observer* was probably not aware that the purpose of our trip was to observe the offloading of Minister Zvobgo's first sixty-five heifers at the farm he had bought near Masvingo.

We met the minister at the Flamboyant Motel, which he now owned, along with the big Chevron Hotel in the middle of town. Then we set off in a police Land Rover and toured the farm. As we passed Masvingo Prison, the minister said that I would no doubt like to meet the female inmates, most of whom were on remand for dumping or killing babies, on our way back. There was nothing I would have liked less, and fortunately there wasn't time.

We watched the unloading of the beautiful heifers, and on the way back Zvobgo took us through a luxurious and modernised old house he had bought on top of a hill on the road to Great Zimbabwe. He was calling the house Juliana, after his wife Julia. The ceiling over the bed in the main bedroom was a mirror.

In 1950, Zvobgo's father, a cleric in the African Reformed Church, probably then still called the Dutch Reformed Church, was cycling to school with Eddison on the carrier. Outside this very property the father had suffered a massive nosebleed, and they went to the house to ask for water. Instead of helping, the white occupants chased the Zvobgos off with dogs. Ever since, Eddison had been working on a plan, and had now, to show his father, bought the house off the son of the man who had unleashed the dogs.

On the way back to town we passed a Red Cross vehicle, and we all waved at Byron Hove, now head of the Zimbabwe Red Cross.

I was very tired. I'd been at a meeting in Nyanga ten days earlier, followed by a staff meeting at Lake McIlwaine, where there had been twelve people, twelve beds, three to a room, and four women present. Petronella Maocha came up with the solution. It was obvious, she said, that the three directors of the Zimbabwe Project should share a room: me, Albert Ngwenya and Paul Themba Nyathi. Albert was the most reticent about the arrangement. The next morning, Paul said that all night he was aware of Albert's long neck helping his head rise to see that I really was in bed in the same room, near the door – quite far from them. But by the second of the three nights,

Albert had relaxed enough to start suffering from his terrible nightmares of being bombed at Freedom Camp outside Lusaka in 1979, so we didn't sleep well.

In April, Paul and Petronella held their engagement party. I counted this as another achievement of the Zimbabwe Project. At the beginning of that month, there was an interesting story in the *Herald*. It had been discovered that reception problems being experienced by television viewers and listeners to FM radio transmissions were being caused by their shoes.

> The problem was confined to some shoes made between July 13 1985 and Tuesday last week using hides from cattle and elephant that had been culled in certain drought stricken areas. Because of the drought the animals had been forced to eat a certain type of weed that contained an undue concentration of aluminium salts. This had contaminated the hides with what were, in effect, tiny transistors. The heavy static charges that could build up on shoes worn in dry carpeted rooms were causing these semi-conductors to activate.

> Fortunately the power of the transmission was minute. If viewers and listeners moved their feet back under their chairs or sat further away from the set the interference would cease.

> The 'radio shoes' came to light when a senior technical executive was dancing to FM Radio 3 in his living room and noted the interference growing and decreasing as he moved back and forth. Discreet enquiries with his colleagues in other companies and some detailed research confirmed his suspicion.

> Anyone requiring further information should phone the *Herald* on 702218 this morning. In the most serious cases, the shoes are being replaced.

The headline for that story was: 'Soft shoe shuffle gives you the best TV'. The following day the newspaper carried the headline: 'Dozens April-fooled by "Hot-shoe" story'.

I received further details on the position of Makhatini Guduza. He was still being held at Chikurubi, and was now being charged with recruiting, inciting and training dissidents, and trying to mobilise a foreign power to intervene after the government of Zimbabwe was overthrown.

Talking of which, I thought that once apartheid was overthrown we would be in for a lot of fun in southern Africa. Among those attending a conference of NGOs at the Chitepo training centre in Manicaland was a very impressive lawyer from South Africa, called Fink Haysom. I was intrigued by his name and asked for its origins. He laughed and said when he was born and his father was visiting the maternity ward, the baby was brought for his inspection. The father studied him, fascinated, and then said, 'But this isn't a little Haysom. This is a little Finkelstein,' and Nicholas had been known by his family as Fink ever since.

Fink was about the same age and size as Paul Themba Nyathi, and they made firm friends on the first evening of the conference. When work was over and people assembled outside on a beautiful evening, Fink struggled towards us all with a heavy tray of drinks. Paul calmly watched the slow and careful progress of this tall white man and, just as Fink was depositing the tray, announced with great satisfaction, 'Now *this* is what we were fighting for!' Fink exploded with mirth. A moment earlier he would have dropped the tray.

SWAPO was represented at the same conference by Dr Marcus Shivute, who wore a delicate gold heart in the hollow of his neck. I was chairing a session when the subject of the role of women in the struggle came up. Shivute was next to me and made a passionate speech about how SWAPO was constantly trying to involve women in all their affairs, but the women were shy and retiring and didn't want to be involved. He again called on all women to come forward and take their rightful place in the struggle. He said it was time for them to fight for their rights, as men, from the dawn of time, had always done. He sat down to lengthy applause.

I scribbled a note, to which he instantly responded.

QUESTION: Who did men have to fight for their rights?

ANSWER: MOTHER NATURE!

On public holidays, one could visit prisoners and take them food, so on Good Friday I went to see Guduza in Chikurubi, taking one cooked chicken, one cooked tongue, two avocados, a carton of yoghurt and one of cream cheese, and a packet of hot cross buns. I called on Phyllis Naidoo en route, and she contributed a tin of corned beef.

We met in the kind of telephone booth where you were separated by a sheet of glass. At least at Chikurubi, unlike Harare Central Prison, there were stools to sit on. Unfortunately the line was so bad you had to shout, and it seemed as if the conversation was being amplified somewhere else, so, from behind, you could hear yourself shouting in another dimension. Anyway, we managed. Guduza looked well but slightly crumpled. His little khaki uniform didn't enhance his dignity. He said there were thirty-four detainees at Chikurubi, five of whom were white. Three detainees, held since

1982, had been recommended for release by the Review Tribunal, but were still in custody. Guduza said he told the magistrate that the man who had detained him, Maeresera of CIO, had said that he would never be released from detention until he joined Zanu (PF), at which Guduza had laughed and said that however much he respected Prime Minister Mugabe, he would never join Maeresera's party.

In his speech to mark the seventh anniversary of independence, Prime Minister Mugabe said his Central Committee had decided to call off the Zanu–Zapu unity talks, 'for they are serving no useful purpose'.

I had dinner with Phyllis Naidoo, and among her South African guests were Eddie Webster and Luli Callinicos. Eddie was a university lecturer and much involved with the trade union movement in South Africa. He told of an incident some years before when he was arrested. There were two other white prisoners he could see through the wire mesh and, being lonely, he tried to strike up a conversation. 'What are you in for?'

'Dagga,' was the reply.

'And you?' Eddie asked the second.

'Rape.'

Then the first asked Eddie why he was locked up.

'Suppression of Communism Act.'

'Christ!' said the rapist in horror to the dagga smoker. 'He's a bloody Russian!'

I was trying to find out what had happened at the Zanu (PF) Central Committee meeting held on Friday 10 April. Eventually I gleaned that Comrade Kabasa had asked for a report on the unity talks. The matter was not on the agenda. I didn't learn the order of the speakers, or how many there were, but I was told Robert Marere spoke in favour of unity, as did Tekere, Ushewokunze and Zvobgo. Callistus Ndlovu gave an impassioned speech against unity. He said he knew the people in PF Zapu and they engaged in Soviet-style negotiations designed to wear down the other side.

Nyagumbo also spoke strongly against unity, and said comrades must heed what had been said by Callistus Ndlovu. Nkala kept quiet. When Zvobgo spoke in favour of unity, he was shouted down. There was no vote, but the prime minister himself decided what the consensus was. It seemed as if the Zanu (PF) hierarchy was gunning for Zvobgo. Maybe if he had spoken *against* unity, the prime minister would have discovered that the consensus was *for* unity.

My home was turning into a Front Line States/South African hostel.

Someone en route from Mozambique had been staying for ten days, and was leaving just as Peta Qubeka arrived from Johannesburg for two weeks. She was of the 1976 generation of turbulent Soweto schoolchildren and was working for the South African Council of Churches. A few days later, a young white ANC couple moved in. They had been teaching at the ANC school in Tanzania, but, after Kate Gardiner's fifth attack of malaria, it was decided it was too dangerous for them to continue. They were coming to recuperate and look for other options. Allister Sparks was hoping to come for a week in May, and then there would be Lombe Chibesakunda from Zambia coming for a rest. Allister called my home the Crossroads Squatter Camp.

I went to see advocate Chris Greenland, who, Bryant Elliot told me, might soon be made a judge. I hoped so. He was impressive. I contacted him because we had been requested by Alibaba Dlodlo, imprisoned in 1982, to help him study O-levels by correspondence. He, Davityne Moyo, Frank Nyoni, Samson Nhari and others in Chikurubi had been found guilty of attempting to attack the prime minister's residence in June 1982. Obviously helping Alibaba might be risky, and I wanted an opinion on him from someone who knew him. Greenland had represented this group pro Deo in a failed appeal to the courts.

I found a very troubled man. Greenland was convinced that Dlodlo and two other members of the group of about five were totally innocent. They had also been tortured. He said the failure of the appeal was something that he would have to live with for the rest of his life, and he kept wondering if there was something better he could have done for the prisoners. He said Alibaba was a splendid man. So now we could help with a clear conscience.

When I met Greenland, he was just about to get rid of the pertinent court records, which came to forty-four volumes. Instead, he gave them all to me. They were public documents. The records were those of the Supreme Court appeal of Samson Nhari and five others against their convictions and very heavy sentences. I was extremely alarmed to learn how one was expected in court to remember minute details of events that may have happened literally years ago. I couldn't even remember what happened the previous week, so I decided to try to remedy this deficiency by keeping just the briefest notes on each day, but in such a way that, whenever I read them again, I could actually remember what I had written about.

On the first night I had the court records, I made a mistake. I tried to go to sleep really early, at about seven, and asked my guests please not to call me for the telephone, no matter who rang. In the morning I learned that Masinga had rung from country unknown, but would try to ring back soon.

My house guests didn't know that 'Masinga' was Jacob Zuma, head of ANC intelligence. He had been forced out of Mozambique by the Nkomati Accord, and sometimes stayed at my house when he was en route from Zambia. I wanted to talk to him. We were about the same age, but while I had every chance of learning and reading while I was a child, he had had none. The first time in his life he'd had an opportunity to benefit from any kind of formal education was in 1963, when he started serving a sentence of ten years on Robben Island. He was twenty-one, very young to have been convicted of conspiring to overthrow the South African government, but quite old to start doing any studies. Zuma left South Africa in 1975. He didn't smoke and, although he didn't drink either, he seemed to be tolerant towards those who did, as he said he didn't mind looking after 'comrades' who got drunk. I shouldn't have thought that happened very often in his presence.

Another mistake I made was that before I switched off the light, I decided to dip into Volume 1 of the court records. Eventually I switched off the light after 1 a.m., by which time I was well into Volume 3. This was testimony from the state witnesses, and a shivery business. The inference was often clearly that the witness was under duress to give false evidence.

Are you happy in detention? *No, I am not.* Do you feel free? *I do not feel free.*

Do you feel free, that your spirit is free, that is your inward spirit? *My spirit would not be free if I am not at my house.* Would you say that you are intensely unhappy? *Well, presently where I am right now I feel free. I am giving my evidence freely, but my spirit is not free when I am in jail.* And you feel free in the witness box because the handcuffs have been taken off? Is that the position? *Yes, well when handcuffs have been taken off you can talk freely because they have been removed.* And you came to court in handcuffs yesterday? *Yes.* And today? *The same.* Do you know when you are to be released? *I do not know.*

And so on, and so on. Then there were lots of little, unwitting social comments such as this one, also from a state witness: How long had you been at the beer hall? *I arrived at the beer hall and I think I must have left at half past eight.* Did this affect you at all? *No, it's because I'm used to going to the beer hall to while away time. I would not fall drunk because of consuming, say, one sip of a mug because it was five people to one mug of beer.*

After what Greenland had to say, I felt completely easy about helping Dlodlo. I had been impressed by his letters and I regretted that initially my replies were so formal and careful. Dlodlo first asked us to pay for him to be able to study eight subjects: 'I have no doubt that you know that education is a liberating experience in which the individual explores, creates, uses his initiative and judgment and freely develops his faculties and talents to the full and therefore trust that you will consider my case with the greatest understanding.'

We suggested that he first try only two, and he responded: 'Of course, it is true that people who are not in a good school with good teachers and all the necessary text books usually don't do well if they take too many subjects at one time, but I wish and suggest that I can make it with more than two, say four. Though it is going to be my first time to study all but one, English language, I am sure that I will be able to work hard and to good effects. I know a lot of work will be involved and to achieve good results will require me to make myself an effective programme of work. But I assure you time is plenty here and I am confident I will succeed.'

We agreed to pay for three subjects. 'It is hard for me to write this letter, so overwhelmed am I with pleasure and delight at receiving at this moment from you the educational materials – complete sets of both Economics and Commerce lectures as well as incomplete English language lectures ... I cannot find words to express my grateful thanks to you for the assistance you have rendered me. Only what I can say to you now is that I will always be in touch with you informing you about how I am progressing ...'

Greenland told me that the court records should be a fiction writer's treasure trove – not his exact words, but something to that effect. When I read them, I found quite a few bells ringing from my memory of what was being trumped up in the treason case involving William Kona and Edward Ndlovu. Even in the Nhari case there was an attempt to implicate Joshua Nkomo in the attack on the prime minister's residence – and I was only on Volume 3.

I wrote to Alibaba Dlodlo and ended by quoting a poem by Eddison Zvobgo, which the prison censors absolutely could not object to, as he was the Minister of Justice, Legal and Parliamentary Affairs and in charge of prisons. I had started sending Alibaba poems, ostensibly to help with his English language course, but of course they were meant to be of spiritual consolation too.

Basil Sithole rang from the *Sunday Mail* to say goodbye. He had written a story on Cuba that Prime Minister Mugabe had objected to, calling for the punishment of 'the hand that held the pen', and so Basil was sacked. But he was lucky to have found a new job. One of our Bulawayo staff was involved in a car crash. The car rolled five times. No one was badly hurt, although the vehicle was a write-off. When Paul Themba Nyathi informed me of the accident, he was marvelling at the presence of mind of the occupants that they could keep counting as the car rolled. 'One … two … three …'

Godwin Matatu came back from Botswana, where, he said, they were really dreading an attack by the South Africans, who were trying to force them into a type of Nkomati Accord, à la Mozambique. Then, the South Africans said, they would round up all the ANC in Botswana and relieve the country of their presence.

Godwin rang me to say that he and Wilson Katiyo had *bad news*, and I joined them at the Quill Club.

Godwin had rung Justin Nyoka from Botswana and found that Justin had been instructed by his minister, Nathan Shamuyarira, to cancel Godwin's accreditation as a journalist forthwith, but with no publicity. I thought the no-publicity aspect might mean that Nathan had not consulted his cabinet colleagues.

Some weeks before, Nathan's friend, the British journalist David Martin, had returned from a trip to Mozambique. He went to see Tommy Sithole, editor of the *Herald*, to tell him Godwin was now persona non grata in Mozambique. The story, unsourced, was published on the front page of the *Herald* the next day. The *Observer* was now suing the *Herald*, and withdrawal of Godwin's accreditation might have been Nathan's way of exerting pressure to get the writ against Zimbabwe Newspapers dropped. Maybe he would say, okay, Matatu could keep his accreditation if the *Observer* dropped its case. But, although he laughed about it, it was obviously shocking for Godwin to think that this could happen to him, a Zimbabwean.

His friend, the writer Wilson Katiyo, had been unemployed for ages. He said it was Shamuyarira himself who told him that he had put round the word that Wilson was not to be employed in any capacity in the media. This would include even what Wilson was doing when I first met him – pushing heavy trolleys of tapes around the BBC's Bush House in London.

I didn't know specifically how Wilson had offended Shamuyarira. Wilson said that the only way to survive in today's Zimbabwe was not to take things to heart or else you got angry and unhappy and ended up as a dissident. I asked if he was writing anything. He said he was too hungry to write.

His two books, *Going to Heaven* and *Son of the Soil*, had been reissued in paperback in 1982, quite a long time ago.

In early May I went on a long trip with Max Kabasa, a member of our staff and a carpentry instructor, who lived at our training centre on the outskirts of Harare.

We were visiting Fungai Sithole, an ex-combatant who had used his demobilisation money to build a store in the Bikita area, ran out of funds before the store was completed in 1986, and had since been doing part-time work on the tea estates – Z$44 every two weeks for extremely hard work. He had told us that his uncompleted store was exactly 173 kilometres from Masvingo on the Mutare road.

It was a pale, bright, cool morning. I told Max that there would probably be plenty of roadblocks, as we were running up to the South African elections and, after their recent attack on Livingstone in Zambia, we could expect the worst from them. He had not even heard of the attack on Livingstone. Max was basically apolitical. It took three years after he joined us to discover that not only was one of his brothers a Zanu (PF) member of parliament, but also their deputy speaker. Max had never mentioned this.

A few kilometres along the Masvingo road, we saw a roadblock looming. 'Your information is good,' said Max. 'Better fasten your seat belt.'

The police were very courteous. All in all there were four roadblocks along the way, which meant eight by the time we returned. Most were mixed army and police, and all the personnel were pleasant. I had brought extra copies of the *Herald*, as people in rural areas were starved of news. Max picked up one of the newspapers from the back seat and there, all over the front page on Monday 4 May 1987, was the news that Edgar Tekere had been sacked as chairman of Zanu (PF) in Manicaland.

Apolitical Max was upset. 'Tekere is one of the few who can tell the truth,' he said.

At Chivu we gave a lift to a young policewoman, who travelled with us to Mvuma. She was uncommunicative, so not much fun. The only purpose in picking up police was so that you could get the latest hot news. At Masvingo we bought fuel and uninteresting meat pies and proceeded, having worked out that 173 kilometres must be 103 miles on my mileage indicator. The countryside was beautiful. Villages on the way out of Masvingo were crowded with fruit trees, especially mangoes and pawpaws. We saw two turkeys pecking along the roadside and thought they might be even better to raise than goats. Something else to explore.

As we got closer to Birchenough Bridge, the terrible drought became apparent. The brown earth looked as if it had been swept. Cattle had their ribs on display. The baobab trees started crowding in, with little tartar fruits hanging.

'Are they just starting?' I asked Max, but he thought they were small because of the drought.

By the time we saw the peg reading ten kilometres to Birchenough Bridge, Max thought we must be lost. We turned around on Devuli ranch and retraced our tracks, discovering that we had gone twenty-five miles too far. When we later complained to Fungai Sithole about his directions, he laughed uproariously and said that when the new road was built, they changed all the kilometre pegs. It *used* to be 173 kilometres.

We found him, and his little store, eventually, by which time our hearts were already dropping. He must have started building before he knew that the new road would bypass him by about a kilometre. The scene was lovely but hopeless. Villages clustered around koppies, a stream that was still flowing and people sitting around chatting to each other on the stoeps of the too many surrounding stores. Fungai had built every inch of the store himself, save the roofing, for which he had to hire people. He explained how he had carried each rock for the foundations from the stream. His store was a nice, neat little building, but it lacked a counter, shelving, a stoep, ceiling boards and two Blair latrines, without which he couldn't trade.

The simple Blair latrines were a wonderful invention, basically a long drop with a chimney-like pipe going from the pit up through the roof. The pipe was capped by a fine mesh. Flies laid eggs in the pit, and the young flew up the chimney, fell back into the pit and into the fermenting cycle of destruction. No chemicals were needed and there was no odour. They were named after the Blair laboratories in Harare, where they were invented.

Fungai had been waiting for us on the main road, but we hadn't seen him. So he arrived a few minutes after us, panting and sweating. I realised in the forty-five minutes we spent with him that his sweating wasn't only the result of his having run. He obviously had a high fever and was coughing dreadfully. He had brought his wife and their baby, whom he introduced as 'my firstborn'. His wife was absolutely beautiful and, thank goodness, was born right there, so, if we did manage to help Fungai, the surrounding traders with their empty little shops might not murder him immediately.

We left, emphasising that we could promise nothing. The decision would have to be made, as always, by our assembled staff at the next meeting. Fungai said he would sleep in the store until he heard from us. His horrible tea-picking job had come to an end, as the harvest was not good. The baby was sick too.

I got Max back to Adelaide Acres at about six. The round trip had been more than 500 miles and I had loved every minute of it. As I neared home, I caught a glimpse of the Heroes' Monument outside Harare, standing starkly against a radiant sunset, and in my mind I automatically saluted TG Silundika and others who lay there. My memories of TG were so fresh. I remembered having breakfast with him near my office in London before the Geneva conference and him telling me how sick he was, even then. He couldn't eat salt because of his high blood pressure. The loss of people like him, Tongogara, JZ Moyo and some of the others prematurely interred at Heroes' Acre had been too great for Zimbabwe. Tongogara with his gangling frame, huge smile and amber eyes had seemed to stand for genuine unity between Zanu and Zapu, whereas it was proving that Robert Mugabe could tolerate only a unity of supplicants worshipping upwards to him at the pinnacle. As Rugare Gumbo said on his release with other Zanu 'dissidents' from the Zanu pits in Mozambique early in 1980, Mugabe was in fact 'totally opposed to unity', as he and his small clique felt that only they were entitled to rule Zimbabwe.

I wondered what life in the new Zimbabwe would have been like for Jason Z Moyo had he survived, and I wondered whether his mother was still alive. Not long before he was blown up by a parcel bomb in Lusaka on 22 January 1977, I had asked JZ what the Z in his name stood for. He explained that, when his mother was pregnant and living in a remote village, she heard a loud noise advancing and her astonished eyes had fallen on an extraordinary vision. It was a white policeman passing on a motorbike. So, when her son was born, he was named Ziyapapa – *we are flying*.

CHAPTER 17

Standing for parliament

A GROUP OF US, INCLUDING MIKE MUNYATI FROM ZIMBABWE
Television, met at Sandro's to commiserate with Godwin Matatu. Mike
was 'shocked but not surprised' by the news that Shamuyarira was making
it impossible for Godwin, like Michelle Faul, to continue working as a
journalist in Zimbabwe.

It was now the turn of veteran Zanu (PF) politician Edgar Tekere to be
in trouble, and Mike told us what bits had been cut from his interview with
Tekere, screened that week. These were that the political leadership in the
country had 'decayed' and that Tekere no longer had any respect for the
Zanu (PF) Politburo, as it was now hand-picked, not elected. Mike said
his friends in CIO were expecting trouble in Tekere's stamping ground,
Manicaland. 'The ground is swelling,' they told Mike.

Mike, previously of ZANLA, asked me something about PF Zapu. I said
I didn't know, as I was not a member of Zapu or any other party. Mike
laughed. 'Don't apologise,' he said. 'It's not entirely a bad thing to belong to
Zapu.' Then he said, 'You see, Godwin, Judy loves underdogs. When she
came back to Zimbabwe, she was worried that she wouldn't have anyone
to look after. But then, fortunately for her, we started crushing Zapu.'

Mike wasn't very happy himself. I gave him a lift back to ZTV and, as
we arrived, his hands clenched and he beat a tattoo on the dashboard. 'War!'
he said. 'Whenever I come to work here I have to prepare myself for *war!*'
For the past two months there had been an instruction at ZTV that no
stories could go out without being cleared with the director of news. The
director was himself immediately under Zimbabwe Broadcasting Corporation's director-general, Tirivavi Kangai, brother of Minister Kumbirai
Kangai. Kumbirai had been appointed by the Politburo, through Minister
Nyagumbo, as Zanu (PF) chairman for Manicaland province in the place
of Edgar Tekere.

That first week of May 1987, Godwin Matatu for the London *Observer*,
Karl Maier of the UK *Independent,* Sully Abu for the Lagos *African Guardian*
and I visited Rusape and spent some hours with Edgar Tekere. I noted some
of his thoughts.

Was the removal a surprise?

I'm used to being surprised in the rough and tumble of politics. But I have always tended to be controversial and not many people like controversy, especially in a young country like ours, which is still trying to find its way.

Why were you removed?

Perhaps someone could find a very good *nyanga* (traditional sooth-sayer) to answer that question for me. But by way of guesstimating, it's probably because I'm very critical of the people up there. There is daily theft and corruption by our leaders. Compare this to our leadership code, where it is stipulated that our leaders cannot own more than fifty acres of land each. Perhaps some now own 50 000 acres. This is a collapse of our leadership code and it is my duty as a leader to criticise this.

Comrade Nyagumbo has said that I'm my own enemy. Well, I'm my own enemy because I'm not going to sit back and let them get away with what they are doing. They are violating every basic code of Zanu and of our beginnings. How can thieves talk about socialism? How can we talk about our own very poor people when their leadership is corrupted?

What do you feel about the collapse of the unity talks?

I was working in the very innermost Zanu committee on unity. I was made responsible for approaches to various groups. I was working from the basis that unity must not be only Zanu–Zapu, it must be national. And Zanu had accepted that concept. 'Let us work in togetherness and without recrimination.' As a governing party one of the obligations is to lead the nation in togetherness. But I'm not sure how many of my colleagues appreciate this. I describe the *pasis* (down with) as the slogans of yesterday, the products of minds that are bankrupt. Instead of *pasi* to Nkomo or to Zapu, can't we instead have down with laziness? Instead of *pamberi* (forward) with Zanu, can't we have forward with work or forward with the five-year plan?

I had done very well with the Muzorewa group, and so our leadership thought I could help with Matabeleland and suggested I go there for three weeks. I said no, I can meet Nkomo in parliament. I was getting on fine with them and I had even met Ian Smith. I was then going to get on with the Ndabaningi Sithole group, through Noel Mukono. The only problem was I thought I was going too slowly. So when it was decided that the unity talks had collapsed, I felt frustrated and embarrassed.

I had been doing the spadework single-handedly. How would the people I had approached in good faith now feel?

It is the obligation of this government to continue to toil for national unity.

What is your response to the statement that there is no Zanu (PF) in Manicaland without Tekere?
I really would not like to comment on that. That's for other people to say. I was a founder member of Zanu. They asked me to table the motion to get rid of Nkomo and then of Sithole, and I did. It was very dangerous then to try and get rid of Nkomo, but I did what I was asked.

I joined the Youth League in 1955. I am a political animal and I am going to die a political animal.

By way of national duty, I still know how to put on my uniform. If, for example, we are threatened by South Africa, I must remember to put on my uniform, not my tie and suit. I am fifty now, but I think the bones and muscles can still do the bush.

What is the future for yourself and for Zanu (PF)?
I leave that for providence to decide. However, it is not a privilege to be concerned about the future. It is a right. I am going to continue politicking.

Might you not step on the toes of those who are against you?
As I said at that meeting of our province addressed by Comrade Nyagumbo on Friday 1 May, you may yet sack me from the party, you might arrange for me to be gunned down in daylight, you might arrange for me to sit on a bomb so that I go up in smoke. In this game of politics one has to learn to wear heavy-duty shock absorbers.

What is your relationship with the prime minister?
There is no personal relationship. There is just a business relationship to do with management. I do not accept what has happened to me. We have a national disciplinary committee. This committee, in the case of Zvobgo, went to the Politburo, who then took the case to the full Central Committee. Why did this not happen to me? Because they are being dicey. This is where I get very, very hot. The Politburo is now hand-picked, not elected. I have no respect for it. It is the hand-picked people who are interfering with those who are popularly elected. What a mess-up in the party!

No one says the issue was clearly discussed, even in the Politburo?
No.

How do you think Comrade Nyagumbo had the authority to act as he did?
Political ineptitude. I'm not responsible for the activities of political fools. Although I myself am an April fool, born on the first of April just over fifty years ago, and I now have half a century of political foolishness behind me, I am not as foolish as some.

There have been allegations that you are running Manicaland as though it were your kingdom?
There is a lot of work to be done in Manicaland. I feel very lonely here in Manicaland. Most of my colleagues from here are to be found in Harare. I complain to them. How can you leave me here to do all the work alone? As chairman of the province I don't have an allowance from the party. I have an overdraft of Z$8 000 with Zimbank to keep our party vehicles on the road. This is my personal indebtedness that the party is running on. And I am not going to stop working for the party. I am a founder member.

What will your relationship now be with Kumbirai Kangai?
I'm going to say that I have respect for you as deputy chairman of the province, not as chairman. And I shall carry on with my work.

I have put together a consortium for development in Manicaland, particularly for the construction of a large dam that will benefit people as far as Buhera. When I went to that meeting in Harare with Nyagumbo, it was to report on my development plans. 'What wonderful work you are doing,' he said. 'The prime minister will be very pleased. But, by the way, will you excuse us? We also have an issue to discuss. We no longer want you as chairman of the province.'

I came back in the car laughing all the way. I laughed my lungs out.

But you know, it's not just Manicaland. We have tasks throughout the country. After the last general election, they said to me that if they had thought of it in time, they would have asked me to stand in Matabeleland because I would have won.

How will your reply to your dismissal be heard?
Ah, I don't know. How will Shamuyarira permit what I say to be published? But I have outstanding invitations to speak throughout the country. I even have an invitation from Nkomo to speak at Barbourfields in Bulawayo.

Are you going to raise your dismissal at the next Central Committee?
I am going to provoke discussion, in language they may not like. Then I may absent myself and not be drawn into the discussions. I'll just strike the match and light the fire.

I honestly believe that I must continue to make noises. The rules of our party are one thing. But how many people respect these rules? How many people are not in fact bully-boys, village bully-boys, in the upper echelons of the party? I must continue to make noises not so much about my removal, but about constitutionality, the bible of the party. If you can't obey the rules of your own party constitution – just a few pages long – how can you be trusted to obey the voluminous laws of your country? You are going to be the first to break them.

Speaking at the university on 13 April, I said one very caustic thing. I said that very soon we are going back to parliament and you can be sure that we will raise taxes. But then that taxpayers' money will be stolen. So don't we need some shouting about this? I will shout until death. Once corruption sets in we are in trouble. Uprooting corruption is a hell of a task.

We are degenerating not only into a society of corrupt people, but into a society of thieves. It is my obligation to shout about it; not my right, my obligation. Nyagumbo says I'm uncontrollable. Well, I don't want to be controlled in the wrong direction.

A one-party state?
A one-party state by decree, no. Our people would not like that. The Muzorewa group would be very angry, and so would Goodson Sithole in Chipinge. Why by decree? I don't like anyone trying to force something down my throat.

There are cliques in the party which have become operational – like Kangai. I said to him in a meeting: I want you to respond to this slogan, 'Down with going around like a snake.' Of course he couldn't reply.

It's not clear to me where we are going under this autocratic rule by an unelected clique. So I think my duty is to continue to be critical and try to ensure that people have a clear view of where they are going and how they are going to get there. We are worrying about individual survival when we should be worrying about national survival. I have confidence, and I derive confidence from my conscience. My conscience tells me that I'm not as bad as my accusers. This thing called conscience also has a role to play in politics.

Have you been asked to discontinue the task of the pursuit of national unity?
I haven't been given that courtesy. I've finished with the Muzorewa group but not the Sithole group. It is very embarrassing.

Is your party committed to unity?
At this stage I am unable to say whether they are committed to unity because they have not done what I expected them to. I have not enjoyed the courtesy of them saying that no, Tekere, the two committees we pushed you onto are not pursuing any useful function. I was sweating because I was fearing that I was not keeping pace with what was expected of me. But then I was ambushed.

The possibility of attacks by our powerful neighbour South Africa seemed ever increasing, and so was Zimbabwe's state of anxiety. One night I suffered vivid and frightening dreams of falling upon the preparations of an imminent South African attack. There were scores of young whites, male and female, in camouflage uniform, heavily armed, drinking and eating *braaivleis* before the sortie. At first I came upon them rather as if I were in a boat looking down into the water, where I could see them clearly below. Then I found myself amongst them, and knew that all was lost. But they started quarrelling and disagreeing amongst each other, and I felt slightly hopeful of escape. Then I woke up.

That day I went to see someone at Harare Central Prison. He was in a bad way, and so was the man in the next booth. Maybe a lot of the prisoners were in a state of shock or special dejection because of the seven hangings in the past fortnight. Prisoners were now day by day, night by night, living a nightmare from which, unlike me, they were unable to wake. I wondered if, post-independence, they still sang to the condemned en route to the gallows as they used to under Smith.

Thursday 21 May was full of sombre moments. Allister Sparks called from Johannesburg and said everything was absolutely terrible. I thought he was referring to the bombings in Johannesburg the day before, the probable aftermath and of course the heightened risk for us all in the Front Line States. But he wasn't. He had returned home from Zimbabwe to be absolutely shattered, as he put it, by the news that his wife Sue had cancer. She was to undergo surgery the following Tuesday.

In the evening, the ANC's Kingsley Mamabolo brought more supplies of food for Katherine Gardiner and Richard Jurgens, and we persuaded him to stay and eat with us. He cheered them up, as they had quite understandably been suffering from what Richard called 'the heebies' after South African attacks in Harare. So had I.

On Sunday 17 May, there had been an enormous explosion at 5.10 a.m.

As I woke, I could just imagine a building lifting up in the air and then settling down again, full of crushed people. I was anxious about some friends, including the Brickhills, but knew it would be unwise to speed off in my car when the security forces themselves would be rushing around. I set off at about 6.45 and checked on a number of houses, which were all right, and then went to the ANC offices just up the road from where the Brickhills lived, and realised that was where the attack had taken place. Not much damage was done and no one was hurt.

Tim Leech and two other journalists were arrested. I was slightly amused about Tim. He had been telling others that I was to be detained for passing information to Amnesty International. Now he was in, not me, but there was no need to worry. He was well connected, had lots of support and his many friends were arranging for gourmet food to be taken to him from Sandro's.

The ANC husband of the woman blown up by a TV bomb in Harare had also, unbelievably, been detained. I didn't know the man, Mhlope, but mutual friends said they could hardly recognise him after his wife Tsitzi was killed, he was so thoroughly psychologically smashed and miserable. To put a man in that condition into solitary confinement was beyond my understanding.

One evening, as I walked into 18 Masefield Avenue, the telephone rang. I rushed and answered. The voice on the phone was white, quite pleasant, and belonged, I thought, to a middle-aged man. The accent was Rhodesian or South African, which was perhaps why I was worried.

Is that 35209?

Yes.

Who is that?

Just hold on a minute. I want to put on the light. (This was to give myself time to think.) *Yes. This is 35209. Who would you like to speak to?*

Well, I was just trying to find out who lives there. You see ... the last digit of my number keeps slipping and ... well ... someone keeps getting 35209 and I was just trying to find out who lives there. I know it sounds a bit funny ... (laughter)

Yes, it does. But sometimes these 35 numbers can be difficult, so if you're having problems just ring 90 – that's telephone faults and they'll help you.

Yes. Thanks ... sorry ...

Not at all.

I was troubled by the call because of having had several ANC people billeted with me, the last group leaving just the day before.

On a trip from Harare to Bulawayo, my little Citroën turned 100 000 miles old. A policeman on the Bulawayo side of Gweru flagged me down for a lift, and I invited him to watch the milometer with me, as I didn't want to miss the event. But we reached his destination, a roadblock, at 99 999 miles, so he didn't witness the moment.

The policeman had been chasing a car in which he thought he had left his clipboard. He had found the car but not the board, but didn't seem much worried. As we took leave of one another, he asked for my name and gave me his – Masunga. Mr Masunga was obviously an absent-minded policeman, for he had almost shut the door and I was nearly on my way when he said, 'Oh, oh!' He had placed his firearm on the floor under his feet on the passenger side and left it there when he got out. What he or I would have done if he hadn't remembered, I don't know. I probably wouldn't have noticed it for a couple of days; someone else may have found it; I may have thought it was planted. Oh, oh, indeed!

'Zapu Rallies and Meetings Banned' read the headline in the *Sunday Mail* on 21 June 1987. I wondered how a 'meeting' would be defined: *Where two or three of you are gathered together in Nkomo's name?* It was also announced that in the recent Beitbridge district council elections, Zapu had won eight of the twelve contested seats. Minister Nkala was furious, and was reported as saying: 'If the current wave of killings is intended to intimidate the government, both Nkomo and the dissidents should think again. I am not threatening anybody, but as soon as things appear to go well, Comrade Nkomo poisons the atmosphere. This kind of thing we cannot allow.'

An ANC representative passing through Harare called in and it was very late, well after 2 a.m., when we managed to persuade him to spend the night. He was so tired he could hardly move. He gave me his car keys and asked me to collect some special cigarettes he had in his glove box and to please put them in the room he was going to use. I guessed exactly what was happening. I collected his gun from the car and put it under my jacket so as not to startle my guests when I walked through the lounge, and then placed it in the drawer of the bedside table in his room. I didn't enjoy handling the weapon, but I couldn't see what else he could have done. If he had gone out himself, the guests may have accompanied him.

In the morning, I was glad that no one had asked me what was so special about those cigarettes. How terrible to live with the knowledge that any minute an attack may be made on you. The former ANC representative to Zimbabwe, Joe Nzingo Gqabi, was shot dead outside his house in nearby Ashdown Park in August 1981. He was shot twenty-two times.

On her return from the Conference of Women in Moscow in July, Phyllis Naidoo brought me an exquisite wooden pen with a Russian doll painted on the top. She presented it to me in an envelope on which she had written, *To Judy – with love. A gift from the Soviet People. Phyllis.* I was very touched, but couldn't help smiling at the vision of the Soviet People getting together to decide what to send me.

My father turned seventy-nine on 13 July 1987. The date had been a significant one for him. On 13 July 1862, his father Thomas was born in Scotland. At the age of three, Thomas arrived in New Zealand on 13 July 1865. On 13 July 1908, my father was born, and named Reginald Stephen Garfield Todd – Garfield after the former president of the United States, not because he was assassinated, but because he belonged to the same church as did the Todds. On 13 July 1934, my father arrived in Southern Rhodesia with my mother Grace, who was twenty-three. On 13 July 1972, I was allowed to leave confinement in Smith's Rhodesia, although still as a detainee whose name could no longer be mentioned in the media at home. My father, tears in his eyes, said that, in the circumstances, my exile was the best birthday present he could possibly have hoped for.

As my father entered the last year of his eighth decade, I began to think that there was every reason to start feeling happy again. We'd had all those years of rough politics. Freud in *The Future of an Illusion* mentions count-less people 'who do not hesitate to injure other people by lies, fraud and calumny so long as they remain unpunished for it', and we experienced that in both Rhodesia and, more recently for me, in Zimbabwe. There were the years of defeat and detention and exile, culminating in the horrific civil war for all. Now most of the country seemed at peace. Rhodesia had given way to Zimbabwe. There was surely reason for joy.

The funeral of the tragic genius, writer Dambudzo Marechera, took place on 20 August. There were already six new graves dug next to his, two covered with planks so that people could stand on them.

The ranks of the ruling party were swelling a little. The speaker of parliament, Didymus Mutasa, announced that three of the sitting white members of parliament had crossed the floor to join Zanu (PF). They were John Landau, Tony Read and John Kay. A very old pop song – 'How Low

Can You Go-o' – echoed in my memory, recalled by both the three white MPs and by Zanu (PF).

For all my thinking life I had looked forward to the abolition of colour as the basis for parliamentary seats. This happened on Friday 21 August 1987, when parliamentary seats reserved for whites were abolished under a constitutional amendment. All citizens of Zimbabwe would henceforth be registered on a common voters' roll. I should have been rejoicing, but the way it had been done just made me laugh. The ruling party had tempted to their side the very whites who had either done nothing or had seemed to do nothing against the injustice of minority rule, or had actually been part and parcel of the Smith regime. The only purpose of this crossing of the floor was to cement the power and position of Zanu (PF). We were watching an unholy alliance unfold.

A politically high-ranking friend rang me that night, wanting to know what I thought of developments. I suggested that the ruling party, to which he belonged, should now be renamed Zanu (RF) in recognition of their new bedfellow the Rhodesian Front, the white supremacist political party that had led us into UDI and the war. He groaned and, realising he was in pain, I stopped teasing him.

At 4.20 p.m. on Tuesday 1 September, the telephone rang. I happened to glance at my watch. Someone said he was calling from the parliament of Zimbabwe, and that Dr Joshua Nkomo wanted to speak to Mrs Judith Acton.

I said Mrs Acton was speaking.

When Nkomo came on the line he was very gentle and a little jocular. It must have taken time to track me down to my parents' house in Bulawayo.

'What are you doing down there in the hinterland?' Nkomo asked.

I told him I was on holiday. We chatted a little about inconsequential things, and then he said he wanted to talk about the new structure of parliament. There would have to be members nominated to fill the seats formerly reserved for whites. 'Your name is down,' he said. 'What do you think of that?' He needed an urgent response. I said I was honoured. If I had been approached by anyone else, I would have needed time to think and to consult, for example, him. But since it was actually him asking me, I could just say yes immediately, 'if, of course, parliament means anything any more', I added.

Nkomo was pained. He assured me that parliament was important, even if at times it didn't seem to be. He said we must work hard at making it even more important. We agreed that I would see him on my return to Harare.

The last time we had spoken it was about getting watermelon for Lookout.

Minister Nkala was being tempestuous again and, in mid-September, ordered the closure of all PF Zapu offices, which were then ransacked by security agents. It was also announced that ministers Callistus Ndlovu, Chikowore, Nkala and Kadungere were in Matabeleland, and that they had dissolved all councils in Matabeleland North on the grounds that these structures were assisting dissidents, to whom they were diverting drought relief food. That month, Bulawayo's *Chronicle* inadvertently reminded its readers of how long Zapu had been under siege.

The Chronicle – 25 years ago. A look at History Highlights
From 26 September 1962

Miss Judith Todd (19), daughter of former Prime Minister, Mr Garfield Todd, was due to receive her Zapu membership card when the party was banned last week.

Miss Todd, first-year economics student at the University College, confirmed yesterday that she had joined Zapu soon after it was formed but had not received her card.

The card had been completed by Mr Stephen Lombard (19), a student at the University College. Before he could give it to her, Mr Lombard's room at the College was searched by security police.

Miss Todd's card and a number of Zapu documents were confiscated. Mr Lombard was served with a restriction order limiting him to travel within three miles of the College. Miss Todd said she had been a member of the NDP when it was banned.

Dr Terence Ranger and Mr John Reed, lecturers at the University College and officials of the banned Zapu party, have lodged an appeal with the Ministry of Justice against restriction orders served on them last week.

Twenty-five years and two days later, and with no prior announcement from Joshua Nkomo or from Zapu, the headline on the front page of the *Herald* was: 'Zapu lines up team for Assembly contest'. The story read, in part: 'The former ZPRA intelligence supremo, Cde Dumiso Dabengwa, and Sir Garfield Todd's daughter Mrs Judith Acton, are among seven PF Zapu candidates who will contest vacant seats in the House of Assembly that were created with the abolishment of white reserved seats.'

I telephoned immediately to alert my parents, as the publication was a bolt from the blue for me and would be worse for them. When Nkomo had rung me, he'd said there was some hurry as he had been asked to submit a list of candidates to the prime minister the following day, which was why he needed an immediate yes or no from me. The following week in Harare he told me it had been hoped Zanu and Zapu could have an agreed list for the former white seats so that there would be no need for a contest. Matters were still under discussion and, when appropriate, relevant announcements would be made. He also said that when he saw Prime Minister Mugabe, he had stressed that I was an independent and didn't belong to Zapu. I thought that was very kind of him.

In the subsequent searches of Zapu's offices, including those of Nkomo, state security seized the list of Zapu candidates, which was then leaked to the *Chronicle* and the *Herald*. This effectively torpedoed the whole apparent negotiation process between Nkomo and Mugabe. The way the announcement was made in the press gave the impression that the fielding of candidates was a unilateral and aggressive move by Zapu to fill the formerly white-reserved seats.

Karl Maier was the first person to ring. He sounded very surprised and quite glad. He had got the news that morning from the British journalist and publisher, David Martin. Karl was astonished to hear that I had been named as a candidate and was amazed to hear about Dumiso. He had got the impression from Du just the week before that he was weary of politics. Robin Drew rang from the Argus Africa News Service. He sounded pleased, but was worried that the news had been leaked before time. He was right. Anyway, he said, he was glad I had thrown my hat into the ring, and he hoped 'we shall see you there, and that we shall hear you'.

Moeletsi Mbeki rang me. 'Is this a typical *Herald* misprint?' I explained that it wasn't. He said if he weren't a refugee, he would have liked to be one of the people needed to sign my nomination form.

The best reaction came from Comrade Kapuka Nauyala, the SWAPO representative in Zimbabwe. A few weeks earlier, the Zimbabwe Project had received a card from him following his recovery from some strange and dreadful illness and his discharge from Parirenyatwa Hospital. As Paul Themba Nyathi said, it was written in Namibian English and was as exuberant as Kapuka himself.

The Namibian saying that 'your true friend or brother/sister is not seen born' has some scientific and, therefore, universal validity, now I do believe. When last August 17–29, I got critically hospitalised at Parirenyatwa Hospital, among my few friends and sympathisers who extended well-wishing recovery solidarity was the entire staff of Zimbabwe Project. What is more, was the bunch of precious flowers and a beautiful and moral-busting card and visits which were very much instrumental in my quick recovery.

Namibia being under colonial bondage, I can get no 1 million + 'diamonds' to befittingly express my thanks and deep-founded appreciation to you, comrades.

Long live Zimbabwe Project!

Kapuka seemed really thrilled when he phoned me on 28 September about the *Herald* story. He said that up to victory day he would be praying, *God, please let Judy into the National Assembly.* He said he kept his prayers short and concise and that they were usually effective. He even sang a little: *Ooh la la la la*, and signed off by calling me *bebby*.

Godwin Matatu rang and asked to speak to the MP for Nowhere. It was true that the new MPs would not have constituencies.

Two days after publication of the list, Prime Minister Mugabe announced that the closure and searches of the PF Zapu offices had uncovered 'immense evidence' linking Mr Nkomo's party to dissident activity. Joshua Nkomo was always referred to by Zanu (PF) as mister, or doctor, to emphasise that he was not a comrade. A close associate of Nkomo, PF Zapu MP Welshman Mabhena, detained in connection with the so-called treason plot in 1985, was detained again. It was all very sad, and I thought how the rulers of South Africa must be relishing these events.

Each nominee for a parliamentary seat was given a form to be signed by twenty people supporting the nomination. As I'd been nominated by PF Zapu, I planned to try to get twenty signatures from people who were not PF Zapu, and decided to go ahead despite all the grim news. The prospect of any PF Zapu nominees getting into parliament seemed remote. An unknown number of councillors from the dissolved councils in Matabeleland North had now been arrested.

Godwin Matatu rang to say he had something grave to tell me. We arranged to meet at Sandro's restaurant at 2.30 p.m. that day. Earlier I had asked Liberty Mhlanga, who headed the Agricultural Rural Development Authority, if he would be one of my required signatories. He generously agreed, as did the veteran writer Lawrence Vambe, and they gave me their signatures with warmth and good wishes. A number of people on the streets and in our office building wished me luck.

At noon I attended a reception given by the Chinese ambassador. He was among those who expressed pleasure at my nomination, others being Ali Halimeh of the PLO and High Commissioner Lugoe of Tanzania. Julian Harston from the British High Commission, who had been a contemporary of mine at university, introduced me to the white man who had served me with my variation of detention order when I left Bulawayo in July 1972. I remembered him as a young man, but now he looked much older than I felt. I recalled asking him what 'subversive' meant. He asked what he had replied. I said he had told me I should ask the Minister of Law, Order and Justice. He was standing with another white, who rather bitterly recalled that, at the time of UDI, he had been doing some government course in the UK and had been packed off out of Britain. I didn't express any sympathy, but said, 'Well, here we all are together now.' They used to be CID but now worked for a tobacco company.

Just after 2.30, I got to Sandro's. The first table I passed in my search for Godwin was manned by Oliver Chimenya, big business, Godfrey Majonga, public relations, and Justin Nyoka, Permanent Secretary of Information for the government of Zimbabwe. They laughed loudly when they saw me and then rose to greet me. For the first time in our lives, Justin went so far as to kiss me. They all obviously considered it a great joke that I had been nominated for parliament, but were so friendly. Justin said he would write my maiden speech for me. Then I found Godwin, who was sitting with Comrade Mau-Mau and Comrade Mao, both from the prime minister's office. I went aside with Godwin to listen to grave things.

He said that when he had accompanied Minister Zvobgo to the ANC Children's Conference the previous Saturday, he told Eddison it was rumoured that PF Zapu was nominating me for a seat. They joked about it, wondering how I could cope in parliament with my impossibly small voice. But, said Godwin, Eddison had now asked him to urge me to back down immediately, as I had made a serious mistake. I had become a pariah with the Zanu (PF) Central Committee. Zanu (PF) had no intention of allowing PF Zapu any more seats in parliament. They already had their own thirty candidates lined up, and there was no room for PF Zapu.

Zvobgo had told Godwin that when the prime minister had made my father a senator, it was with the blessing of the Zanu (PF) Central Committee. When Shamuyarira, Minister of Information, appointed my mother a member of the Mass Media Trust, he had the blessing of the Central Committee. If I had wanted to become an MP, I should have approached someone in Zanu (PF) to take it up with the Central Committee and my request would have been considered. But now I had accepted a PF Zapu nomination, people were looking askance. He was passing on this warning to me, through Godwin, to get out now because he wouldn't like to see me 'hurt'. He said that after Dumiso Dabengwa, the Central Committee considered me to be the most dangerous person in the country!

So, Godwin said, I have passed the message on.

I made no comment throughout, thanked Godwin for passing on the message and asked him to express my appreciation to Minister Zvobgo for his concern. But I left Sandro's inwardly boiling and thinking what a ludicrous role the minister was playing in the operation of his portfolio of Justice, Legal and Parliamentary Affairs.

I went to collect a signature from Ignatius Chigwendere, a long-standing member of Zanu (PF). When I entered his office, he had to excuse himself for a moment and I put the nomination form on his desk. Member of parliament Josaya B Hungwe walked in. He was the Zanu (PF) whip. We greeted each other. Ignatius returned and sat down. Hungwe picked up the form and looked at it. I asked, jokingly, whether I could have his signature. He said no, and I asked why not, still joking. He said, 'Because you are a Zapu candidate.' Then Hungwe spoke at length.

He wasn't pleased. He said there had been no agreement between the parties on any possible PF Zapu candidates. Zanu (PF) had the majority in parliament and, as the MPs would be electing the new members, there was no chance of a PF Zapu candidate being chosen. My nomination had caused embarrassment, and Deputy Prime Minister Muzenda had been speaking about it only the night before. Hungwe wanted me to know that they were angry that I was a PF Zapu nomination. They never knew I belonged to PF Zapu.

I said I didn't, which made me feel even more honoured that PF Zapu had nominated me. Well, he said, I might not belong to PF Zapu, but people would now go to their graves believing that I did. I said that was fine. Then, he continued, they couldn't vote for a PF Zapu candidate, but, because of the record of my parents, it was unthinkable that a Todd could stand and then be voted out. He himself came from the Chibi area, and all his brothers and sisters and friends had benefited from the fine work of my parents.

Ignatius was getting agitated. I turned to him and said if it was difficult for him to sign the form, that was quite all right. I didn't mind. But I had misinterpreted him. He ignored me and addressed himself to Hungwe. He, too, was angry. He said he didn't know and he didn't care whether or not I was a member of PF Zapu. But, he said, once, when I *was* believed to be a card-carrying member of Zapu, he had gone to me for help in setting up a committee in London to assist Tongogara and others who had been locked up and were being tortured in Zambia.

'Judy didn't say anything about people being Zanu or Zapu. She just helped us. And now she is asking me to help her and I do so with pleasure.' He signed the form with a flourish in front of Hungwe, who stalked out, slamming the door.

I said to Ignatius that whatever happened to my nomination, I would never forget this moment, and I thanked him very much. He brushed my thanks aside and said: 'They have forgotten what you did, and they need to be reminded.'

'Maybe they never knew,' I said.

'Then they need to be told,' Ignatius said.

The *Herald* reported that the Zanu (PF) Secretary for Administration, Comrade Nyagumbo, had said that the party was 'now emphasising very strongly national unity' following the failure of unity talks. The unity talks between the two major political parties were over, he said, and there was no reason for anyone to continue sitting on the fence. PF Zapu members and any other Zimbabwean who was not a member of Zanu (PF) were most welcome to join the ruling party, as there was nothing left to wait for.

This was published the day after the prime minister had left for the Commonwealth conference in Vancouver. The last time he went away, for the funeral of Lord Soames, Nkala had instituted a new wave of repression, closing and searching PF Zapu offices, and so I wondered what was now planned to take place in his absence.

Nevison Nyashanu, a senior Zapu official, told me that in discussions with the prime minister, Dr Nkomo had originally asked for ten seats in parliament and five in the senate. Mugabe accepted this, but then called him back and said he needed more room to manoeuvre. Nkomo then agreed on seven seats in parliament and three in the senate. So there was an understanding that was probably all along designed for scuttling. Nevison confirmed that it was believed by Zapu that their candidates were to be integrated into a Zanu list (thirteen for parliament and seven for the senate), that there would be no party labels and even no election. The list, totalling twenty for parliament and ten for the senate, would simply be accepted by the remaining parliamentarians acting as an electoral college, and this would be a further step towards unity.

Nevison had held a high position on the Public Service Commission. He was then detained and abused in an unsuccessful attempt to force him to give evidence against people such as Edward Ndlovu MP, accused of treason. When charges were dropped against the accused, Nevison was released but was sacked from the commission. I saw Ibbo Mandaza, who headed the commission after that, and said how unfair the sacking of Nevison was. Nevison himself had never been charged with anything, I said to Ibbo. His real crime had been to be brave enough to stand for PF Zapu against Dr Bernard Chidzero in the 1985 election.

Ibbo justified the action by saying that the fact that Nevison had been detained showed he was political, and no one on the Public Service Commission was meant to be political. I doubted that anyone in Zimbabwe could be classified as more political than Ibbotson Mandaza.

I went to get Byron Hove's signature for my nomination form. Byron was the first black president of the students' union at our local university, and he and I, along with two others, had been arrested, charged and found guilty in 1964 under the Law and Order (Maintenance) Act of organising a demonstration of students outside parliament to protest against the banning of the *Daily News*, Zanu and the People's Caretaker Council, which is what Zapu had renamed itself after it was banned.

Byron was one of the first to leave Zapu and join Zanu after the 1963 split in the nationalist movement. He was often brave and forthright and therefore in trouble with those to whom principle and free thinking were anathema. But now Zanu (PF) was giving him another chance to prove his obedience. I didn't realise until the Zanu (PF) list was published that Byron himself was a candidate. Sitting with Byron when I went into his office was the veteran journalist Farayi Manyuki, who, to my great surprise and pleasure, agreed enthusiastically to also be one of my signatories. That evening I was to meet Justin Nyoka at 5.30 at Sandro's to collect his signature. I was becoming quite brazen in asking people if they would support me, and no one yet had turned me down. The list of people nominating me to stand for parliament was becoming impressive.

Justin was late, and by the time he arrived at about 6.15, the news was already out that the Zanu (PF) Central Committee, which had met that day, had decided not to support any PF Zapu candidates.

Minister Eddison Zvobgo passed the table where I was waiting for

Justin, and I stood to greet him. Looking very grave, he asked how I was feeling. I said that I was feeling exceptionally well. Then he said, 'How *could* you have allowed PF Zapu to put your name forward as a candidate?'

'I was honoured.'

'But you could have been a Zanu (PF) candidate.'

'You didn't ask me.'

'We only ratified our candidates today.'

He moved on and Justin joined me. I said he really didn't need to sign if supporting me caused any embarrassment. He laughed, but then said quite seriously, 'Judy, you are much too young to embarrass me.' I couldn't fathom that remark. Ezekiel Makunike, Director of Information at the ministry, also signed.

I saw another PF Zapu nominee, George Marange. In his late fifties or early sixties, he was handsome and solid, with a beard turning white. He looked a bit like SWAPO's Sam Nujoma. But he didn't seem well, and kept shifting around as if seeking comfort for his body. He had spent the best part of his adult life in detention, and had been picked up again a few weeks before in the latest sweep and taken from his home in Gweru to Lalapanzi for four days. His wife, a nurse, went straight to CIO when he was taken, demanded his release and threatened to go to the press. CIO expressed complete ignorance and suggested she enquire at the police station.

Mrs Marange had managed to take the registration number of the car in which George had been driven away, and there, at the police station, was the car. First the police denied knowledge of him, but then, faced with her fury, the fact that she had the car registration number and that she was threatening to go to the press, they admitted having picked him up and agreed to release him. When eventually the police told Marange at Lalapanzi that they were going to release him and drive him back to Gweru, he refused, in case he really disappeared on the way. He found a friend to drive him.

He said his six-year-old daughter wept when they were reunited. She said, 'Daddy, they *hate* you. They came for you with guns. Next time they'll *shoot* you. Let's run away to the communal lands.'

He said to me that when he found his children so alienated, he wondered what he had fought and suffered for under white supremacy.

The previous Monday in Bulawayo, a young former ZPRA commander had said much the same thing to me. 'Even our own people laugh at us now. "What do you think you were fighting for?" they ask.' I tried to comfort him by saying that surely the achievement of Zimbabwe was in itself an important and necessary step on the way forward? Reluctantly, he seemed to agree.

The nomination court sat on the morning of Monday 12 October, and at noon announced the names of thirty-six candidates to contest the twenty seats in parliament. When eventually I left the court I was feeling slightly sick because of what I had learned and observed.

One of those I had spoken to was Fay Chung, a Zanu (PF) candidate. I discovered that the prime minister had called her in only the previous Wednesday and asked her to stand. She said to me that she hadn't really wanted to, but had agreed.

Fay, two years older than me, and I had overlapped for one year at university, from which she graduated in 1962. After teaching for five years, she went on to graduate from the University of Leeds with a master's degree in philosophy before going to teach at the University of Zambia. In 1975 she started working full time in Mozambique for Zanu in what was called teacher education and curriculum development. After independence, Fay became head of planning in the Education Ministry, and by 1983 had become head of the curriculum development unit.

I knew nothing much about Fay's background, save that she was born in Zimbabwe, was attractive, pleasant to me, obviously brilliant and hard working, but, whenever I thought of her, I was worried by her continued, even fierce, identification with Robert Mugabe and Zanu (PF). She must have known, for example, about 're-education' and the horrors that had entailed in Zanu hands in Mozambique. Rugare Gumbo and other friends of hers had been among the victims. It was difficult to understand how someone who had named her daughter Rudo, Shona for 'love', could support and promote the philosophies and leadership of killers.

On that unusual day, I said to Fay that I was surprised by Zanu (PF)'s inclusion on their list of Lieutenant Colonel Gaza, real name Mahlaba, as I had thought he was in Mozambique. She said he was, and had been called back by Mugabe only on Friday. Then I saw Major General Jevan Maseko, who had been called in by Prime Minister Mugabe on Wednesday evening and given only until the next morning to think about his nomination.

I laughed and said that I thought he probably hadn't slept that night. Maseko said gloomily that he hadn't slept since. He had consulted his wife, and she had said he had no choice but to accept the order to stand for parliament. He would have to take a drop in salary from about Z$40 000 to Z$18 000. Even Fay would have a substantial drop in salary. Looking on the bright side, she said she thought the prime minister wanted to improve the level of debate in parliament.

'Yes,' I said, 'by including people like Thrush and Elsworth and Reid, who hasn't opened his mouth since he's been in there.'

These were all people supported by Zanu (PF).

Fay was standing next to Minister Simbi Mubako, whom I hadn't seen for ages. He greeted me pleasantly. Nelson Mawema, one of Eddison Zvobgo's more powerful enemies from Masvingo, was by his side. Someone asked if Thrush, formerly a member of the Rhodesian Front and whose nomination to parliament had just been announced by Zanu (PF), was a member of the party. Mubako and Mawema both said yes, yes. 'When did he join?' the questioner persisted. Mubako and Mawema started racking their brains, so I tried to help.

'In 1963?' I hazarded, which was the date of the formation of Zanu. Simbi laughed his usual nervous laugh, but Mawema couldn't smile. What was going on in Zimbabwe wasn't actually very funny.

In trying to comfort Maseko a little, but very cold comfort this, I recalled that Shamuyarira had said only if army nominees were elected would they have to resign from the force. He grunted and said Shamuyarira hadn't consulted his notes properly. Once army personnel were even just nominated, they were automatically out. So, if Maseko lost the election to parliament, he would be left with nothing.

Nkala had started fulminating yet again. This was so much to be expected that it was quite inconceivable that the prime minister, before he left on his trip to the Commonwealth conference, did not know what Nkala and Nyagumbo would be up to in his absence.

Students at the University of Zimbabwe now referred to the prime minister as Comrade Vasco da Gama, forever sailing around the globe.

CHAPTER 18

A car bomb in Avondale

THE BLAST IN HARARE'S AVONDALE SHOPPING CENTRE ON Tuesday 13 October 1987 robbed other events of importance.

As Joan and Jeremy Brickhill left the Italian Bakery at 8.25 a.m., a bomb, detonated by remote control, exploded in a vehicle next to their car. Eighteen people were injured, Jeremy the most seriously. It was a miracle the Brickhills survived. Many people could have been killed. Five cars were destroyed. Those cars not full of petrol and with air in their tanks exploded and were burned out.

Joan, although badly shocked, was not seriously injured and was released from Parirenyatwa Hospital after two days. On Friday 16 October, Jeremy was moved from the intensive care unit to a private ward. He was expected to be all right, unless complications set in. His legs, arms and face were burned, and he underwent five hours of surgery. The bomb was packed with shrapnel designed to cause havoc. A steel fragment flew through Jeremy's ribs and stopped one centimetre from his heart.

All members of the Brickhill family displayed infinite courage and stoicism, Jeremy managing to flash his usual rays of humour. His mother Jean told me that on the morning after the blast, talking to him in the ICU, she had said that he mustn't worry about his legs, arms or body, as his face was as handsome as ever. Jeremy couldn't speak as he was on a respirator, but he scribbled a note: 'Lend me your mirror!' Fortunately, she didn't have one with her.

The Brickhills appeared to have been the specific target. There was great anxiety about their continued security and Jeremy was put under twenty-four-hour armed guard. The police detail changed every eight hours, and there was no briefing on exactly whom they were protecting, or why. So friends took it in turns to watch Jeremy around the clock. This gave the opportunity to impress upon the police that, as the would-be killers had failed, they might try again.

When Joan first visited Jeremy in ICU, she was distressed not to find a guard. The policeman had slipped out to buy cigarettes. The incident was reported, and the police had since been meticulous, the guard outside

Jeremy's door searching all visitors and even family. It was the first time in our lives any of us had hoped for overzealous policemen.

There was a tiny reception area with six chairs huddled around a table. On my first night's watch I found that the policeman on duty, Daniel Chisangowerotah, was young and bright. With solid talking, the hours from just after 6 p.m. to when he was relieved at about 12.20 flashed past. I asked how many shots could be fired from his firearm. 'Sixteen,' he said, then paused and added comfortingly, 'but one should be enough.'

When his relief, Constable Mbofanah, arrived, so did Comrade Rogers Makurira from CIO, who helped us pass the time to about 1.20. It turned out that Rogers was one of my homeboys, as someone from the same area is termed, so there were a number of people in common we could talk about. Many months later, I found that Rogers was probably deeply complicit in the disappearance of people, especially from Silobela.

Constable Mbofanah was young, fairly quiet and wonderfully alert. At about 4 a.m. we heard rubber footsteps approaching. Mbofanah's body clenched as they passed the door and then eased as they receded. 'Whew!' I said with relief. He turned to me. 'What for?' he asked.

'You didn't shoot!'

Getting on for 7 a.m., a very tired but gay and bright sister, Consolata T Zvirikuzhe, came in and flopped down with us for a few minutes. Her good humour was infectious, and we all had a happy, general conversation. Then she turned to me and tapped me gently with her bunch of keys.

'I never knew I would have the opportunity to thank you for all you did for my brother.'

Who? What? Where? It emerged that he was one of the students the Zimbabwe Project had managed to assist while we were in the United Kingdom. She was so warm and generous with her praise. Telling my father on the phone about this, and the pleasure she gave me, I said, 'We were only casting bread upon the waters.'

'Yes,' he said. 'Sometimes it comes back as ham sandwiches.'

Our lives were full of the word 'Parirenyatwa', but many knew nothing about Tichafa Stephen Parirenyatwa. Born in Rusape, he had qualified as a doctor at the University of the Witwatersrand in 1957, where two of his fellow students and countrymen were Silas Mundawarara and EM Pswarayi. I first read about him in the Bulawayo *Chronicle* in 1959, when I was sixteen and he was thirty-two. He had been appointed medical officer in charge of Antelope Mine Hospital in Matabeleland, and some of the local white farmers were horrified. A group of them wrote to the *Chronicle* in protest, the inference not quite spelled out but nonetheless clear that it was unacceptable to have a black man attending to their wives.

When he resigned from government service in 1961 to go into politics full time, there was another letter to the *Chronicle* from local white farmers. They were wholeheartedly thanking him for his services and the inference not quite spelled out but nonetheless clear was that a future without Parirenyatwa at Antelope Mine Hospital was bleak beyond words for the farmers and their wives.

In January 1962 he was appointed deputy president of Zapu, having proved his mettle by laying the foundations of a party network from grassroots to national executive level. On 14 August of that year, he reportedly died in a car crash on the Gweru–Bulawayo road. I heard the news in the foyer of Swinton Hall, my residence at university, and went away to lean against a quiet wall in shocked silence. That was the moment I learned how it was possible to grieve terribly over someone you had never even met.

Some months later, I listened, appalled, to Joshua Nkomo's lawyer Leo Baron telling my father that he had seen Parirenyatwa's body after the crash between his car and a train. The driver, Danger Sibanda, had survived. It was Baron's opinion that, when he died, Parirenyatwa's hands had been tied behind his back.

Joshua Mpofu was leaving when the telephone rang on a mid-October evening. The caller started gaily testing whether I knew who he was. First, in my mind, I thought it was Moeletsi Mbeki. Then, when he asked what I was doing and, as it was a Saturday night, why I wasn't out at a discotheque, I thought no, Moeletsi wouldn't have asked such a frivolous question. I wondered if it was Comrade Rogers, whom I had met at Parirenyatwa. To give myself a minute for reflection, I excused myself to see off my guest.

When I came back to the phone, I hazarded my guess that it was Comrade Rogers by saying: 'Are you still on duty?'

There was laughter, and he said, 'You are thoroughly confused, aren't you?'

'Thoroughly,' I admitted.

It was Thabo Mbeki. He invited me for dinner, and I accepted with alacrity. He, 'Auntie' Gertrude Mompati, Aziz Pahad and I had an enjoyable and peaceful dinner at the Jameson Hotel, not talking about anything profound. At one point the conversation touched on Jesse Jackson, and Thabo told us how, at a dinner in Chicago, Jackson had said, 'It's time President Reagan stopped looking at Rambo and started listening to Tambo!'

Thabo had an unusual trait. As he puffed on his pipe, he regarded you so steadily, unblinkingly, that you felt that, if allowed another few seconds, he would fathom exactly what made you tick.

When I got home, the telephone rang. I picked up the receiver. There was that moment of tangible silence that signals a transcontinental call, and then Richard Acton said: 'Hello. It's me.'

We hadn't had any communication for months.

He said he was so upset about what had happened to Jeremy Brickhill. I told him that the latest news was good. Richard himself was in good voice, and my news seemed to cheer him up further. Then he said: 'You must be careful of yourself. Next time it's going to be you, you idiot.'

I said I didn't think it would be me, but that I was being very careful. Was I? How could I be? The two rooms I used most at home were my bedroom and the study. Both faced the street and a vlei beyond. Both could, with the greatest ease, receive a rocket-propelled grenade or anything else through the windows. There was no way I could protect myself and the exiles who were lodged with me.

I seemed to fill people with doom. My father, talking about the car bomb at the Avondale shopping centre, had said: 'Next it may be this house.' I was stricken. He had built the house and he loved it. So did I. But I realised that, for so long, almost unconsciously, I had been regarding myself as so totally expendable that such matters as the destruction of the house didn't seem that important.

Richard continued. 'If anything happens to you, I want you to know that I'll do anything – it won't be much – but I'll do anything for you, the divorce or not.'

I asked if the divorce was through. He thought the decree nisi was, but then there would be other matters to clear up. We didn't touch on those. He said Johnny, my former stepson, was fine and very 'pro' me. I said I was fine too, and very pro both Johnny and Richard.

My electric typewriter was purring expectantly, but there seemed nothing more to say. I could feel grief gathering in storm clouds inside me, for so much, so much. I saw Jeremy lying on that bed with his burned black arms, his painful, twitching foot, his downcast mouth; Richard, still loving me a bit; Joshua Mpofu, indicating the perplexity of so many in Zanu (PF) about the frightening course of their party.

Zimbabwe was so fragile and so beset from outside and within, so tossed about with joy and sorrow. Oh, if I had allowed myself, if I allowed myself, what unhappiness! Instead, as usual in times of pain, I found myself giving a mental shrug and continuing with whatever, as usual, as usual, as usual.

Friday 23 October saw the election of twenty new MPs to the House of Assembly. I woke early, having dreamed that my name had been left off the ballot papers, and slipped into Parirenyatwa Hospital shortly after 6 a.m. to see Jeremy. The policeman on guard was sitting right outside his door so you practically had to step over him to get in. That was a relief. Jeremy was beginning to think about his future. It looked pretty bleak.

I helped the nurse to lift Jeremy, who lent a hand, as he was now able to use a swinging bar to manoeuvre himself, into a sitting position. Jeremy told me how to put my hand under the base of his neck, which wasn't hurt, and push him up. The smell of his body remained in the back of my throat all day. It wasn't a horrible smell; just the heavy, clinging scent of living, wounded, weeping flesh.

He was getting dramatically better. His courage was indescribable.

During the morning, Comrade Vambe came down to my office from the Ministry of Youth, Sport and Culture on the fourth floor. He said that he was a Zanu (PF) man, but he wished me all the best for the election, as government was doing some things which were very unpopular and it would be good to have some free minds in parliament. However, he didn't think I would win and so he had brought me a small consolation present – a ticket to the national fund-raising campaign being launched that night for Zanu (PF)'s prestigious new office block.

It was interesting to watch the events in parliament that afternoon. Most Zanu (PF) members seemed to be in a jolly mood. Prime Minister Mugabe was evidently very tired. He had flown back only that morning from overseas. First Eddison Zvobgo went and sat next to him and talked for some time while the voting procedures went on. The prime minister seemed most unenthusiastic about the company and the conversation. Then Nkala sat next to him. Mugabe seemed even less enthusiastic, and kept shaking his head and looking miserable. What I didn't enjoy were the few minutes when Nkala, Home Affairs, and Mnangagwa, State Security, sat next to each other and were laughing and joking, although I never caught Mnangagwa looking directly at Nkala. It seemed to me that whatever limited safety any of us had was largely dependent on as large a gulf as possible between Mnangagwa and Nkala and between Nkala and whoever else. Nkala was looking heavy and bullish and his eyes were windmilling, flashing white circles.

The candidates for parliament were watching from the Strangers' Gallery, and I was sitting next to Fay Chung. At a certain point, she nudged me.

'He is looking at you,' she said, as if somehow I should respond.

I glanced down, and there was Prime Minister Robert Mugabe draped over the front bench, arms folded, pointy knees crossed, elegant shoes on display, looking up at me with a little smile on his face. It wasn't a friendly little smile, more like a smirk, and I looked away with, I hoped, a poker face.

The elections for the vacant seats in parliament were for me, I suppose, an exercise in humility. I remembered in 1958, when my father was beaten by Ian Dillon of the Dominion Party, a precursor to the Rhodesian Front, my mother laughingly announcing that perhaps it was time she divorced him. She said that in an election voters would obviously choose the best candidate, and if Mr Dillon was a worthier character than my father, well ...

The results were of course overwhelmingly in favour of the Zanu (PF) list, which included former members of Ian Smith's Rhodesian Front. We learned that these former upholders of white supremacy, such as Chris Andersen (61 votes out of what could have been a potential 80, but it seemed a couple of MPs were absent); Duke (62 votes); Elsworth, whom I'd been told was a former Selous Scout (62 votes); Holland, former police anti-terrorist unit (61 votes) and so on were considered by Robert Mugabe's Zanu (PF) to be infinitely more desirable bedfellows than Dumiso Dabengwa, Ruth Chinamano, Vote Moyo and the rest of us, and this gave cause for reflection. At least none of us lost our deposits.

All in all it was an interesting and even a happy time for me. But after the contest was over, it was very odd to find myself being comforted – I didn't actually need any comfort – by Andre Holland, a founder member of the Rhodesian Front and inventor of an apparently lethal weapon used against 'terrorists' during the liberation struggle. This was known as the 'Holland Organ'. You pushed a button on your dashboard and bullets sprayed into the night from your vehicle. Now Holland was one of the new Zanu (PF) legislators. But, at the end of it all, I had absolutely no hard feelings, except that I regretted that PF Zapu had been misled and I hoped that the unity pact wasn't going to be just another exercise in cynicism, though this was doubtful.

There were fifteen PF Zapu MPs in the house, and three of the Zapu nominees each got sixteen votes, which meant at least one Zanu (PF) MP had voted for us, despite instructions not to. I told my Zanu (PF) friends that this was very fortunate for them, as I was now able to give each of them the benefit of the doubt – except, perhaps, for Enos Nkala. Nevison Nyashanu, ever hopeful against all possible odds, thought it might have been Robert Gabriel Mugabe who had voted for us.

My divorce was granted in the United Kingdom on 15 October on grounds of more than two years' separation, and I then went to Bryant Elliot for help in changing my name from the Honourable Mrs Judith Garfield Lyon-Dalberg-Acton back to Miss Judith Garfield Todd.

Jeremy fought for recovery inch by inch. I was overcome by the courage he displayed. He was even walking, and soon a faint little voice on the telephone announced that it was Jeremy. We were all so proud of him. He had been under contract to the Zimbabwe Project to establish our research, evaluation and documentation department, and, thank God, we'd put him on the CIMAS health insurance scheme just two months before the blast.

More information was emerging. The vehicle, its boot containing the bomb, was parked parallel to the Brickhills' car, with the boot on the driver's side. Joan was on the passenger side, facing Jeremy, as he was about to unlock his door when the bomb exploded. Jeremy said he had an image in his mind of Joan 'looking timeless', with blood on her throat 'like a jewel'. Then all was horror. His hair was on fire, and he was crawling round the front of their car with a sheet of flame behind him as cars were exploding. He was trying to hold in his guts. Joan found him round the front of the car and started shouting for help. Jeremy kept crawling until he found shelter behind a tiny, recently planted tree. I am afraid he was conscious throughout.

I tried not to allow myself to get on edge, but sometimes I felt my skin crawling. One night Jeremy talked about the 'ionisation of the atmosphere'.

'Shit,' he'd thought as the bomb went off, 'those bastards have got me.'

'Who?' I asked. 'Who did you think it was?'

He didn't know. It was just 'them'.

I wasn't questioning Jeremy, but maybe my face was. When he talked about the 'ionisation of the atmosphere', he struggled to explain. 'Maybe if someone has his finger on a button and was concentrating on you, you would feel it.'

He joked about the moment of explosion, then paused and reconsidered. 'No, no, it's not a joking matter. It's too serious. I thought I had been killed and I was full of immeasurable sorrow.'

It was a terrible time for him, but in other ways it was probably worse for Joan. She was endlessly gallant, but very pale and finely drawn. Someone gave their son Jason a miniature doctor's kit, and you could sometimes find him sitting on the end of Jeremy's bed, kit in hand, sheet-white, staring at his father's wrecked body with wide eyes. Jason was nearly seven and his little sister Linda was four.

Kwirirai Shoko, a lecturer at the polytechnic in Harare and one of the Shokos from Mberengwa near my home at Hokonui Ranch, came to enquire about my well-being. I would have presumed him still to be Zanu (PF), but he seemed to be in a state of fiery self-isolation. He said he didn't want to see those former friends or acquaintances who were now part of the power elite. He described them as totally self-interested and self-seeking, and then asked, as if honestly bewildered: 'Where did they all find each other?'

I received a comforting letter from Phyllis Naidoo. She still had shrapnel in her body from the parcel bomb she had received when in exile in Lesotho. Mhlope from the ANC rang. I hadn't met him face to face, but he had a nice voice. I thought of Tsitzi, his wife, blown up by the TV bomb in Harare a few months earlier. Now Jeremy was punctured and burned by a car bomb. How many different types of bombs there were and how close to my life they had come.

When I was lying sleepless in bed one night, I kept thinking again about how vulnerable the house was. I started thinking of putting up walls, at least in front of the bedroom and study. There were walls going up all over Harare. But then, I decided, walls might even attract attack. It was much easier and less expensive just to unload anxiety onto the typewriter.

Jeremy was in a lot of pain. There was a piece of shrapnel in his left knee, touching a nerve. One morning he said he felt raw. The rest of his body seemed to be healing well and the bandages were off his left arm. We didn't speak much and he dozed most of the morning. He told me of the conflicting medical opinions about whether or not to operate on his knee. He said there was a lot of jealousy in the medical field.

I knew practically from birth that there was rampant jealousy in the political field. Then I discovered it in the church and in aid agencies. Reading CP Snow, you could see it so clearly in the academic field. So maybe it was an integral part of any human organisation. If you became a solitary, as I was tending to be, you didn't suffer from it so much, I thought. Or maybe it was something you tended to overcome with age and experience.

Grace Todd

Judith and Garfield Todd, reunited in 1980

Dr Joshua Nkomo, General Sandy MacLean (Commander Rhodesian Army),
Lieutenant General Lookout Masuku (Commander ZPRA, military wing of Nkomo's Zapu)

Lookout Masuku and Isaac Nyathi
on Ascot Farm

Paul Themba Nyathi

Gijima Mpofu (centre, wearing white shirt) with men
from Vukuzenzele, building the first of individual homes

Justin Nyoka

Mike Munyati

Willie Musarurwa

Godwin Matatu and family

Edward Ndlovu

Garfield Todd and Guy Clutton-Brock
at Gelli Uchaf

David Coltart

Makhatini Guduza with his daughter
Nokukhama and grandchild

Emmerson Mnangagwa

Enos Nkala

Chris Andersen

Edgar Tekere

'Mafela' Lookout Khalisabantu Vumindaba
Masuku

Born: 1 January 1940
Died: 5 April 1986

IQHAWE LEMPI YENKULULEKO YEZIMBABWE
HERO OF ZIMBABWE'S WAR OF LIBERATION

Cover of programme for funeral
of Lookout Masuku

Gift Masuku at her husband's funeral

Bryant Elliot

Dumiso Dabengwa on release from detention.
Karl Maier in the background

Dr J.M. Nkomo and his wife Johannah (uMafuyana)

Eddison Zvobgo

Cover of invitation to celebrate Joshua
and MaFuyana Nkomo's 40th wedding
anniversary and his 72nd birthday

Helen Kedgley and Grace Todd
celebrating Garfield Todd's
80th birthday

Garfield Todd's 80th birthday.
From left to right: Joshua Nkomo,
Garfield Todd and Canaan Banana

Japhet Ndabeni-Ncube, Mayor of Bulawayo   Washington Sansole

Rod Donald and Henry Olonga

It was such a painful and destructive emotion. I was fortunate to be able to cast my mind around and fail to find anyone to be jealous of.

On a hot, still, shining early November evening – heaven for me, but others suffered from heat – I was sitting on Harare's airport balcony waiting for the flight from Johannesburg. A host of moths gleamed in the airport lights and made me hopeful of the possibility of rain. The moths were dancing all over the immediate sky, a delicate, floating curtain. I watched a little boy entranced with them. I was entranced by them and by his joy.

It had been a lovely day for me, though the start in the office was sad. A man came to me in rags and tatters, looking much older than I suspect he really was. But his face was alert and there were traces of happiness and hope in his smile. 'Do you remember me? We met first at Gonakudzingwa in the 1960s. Oh! I have been detained for years and years ...' Like others released from prison after independence in April 1980, he was completely lost. It was easy to adapt to the name of the country changing from Rhodesia to Zimbabwe, but the names of many towns, roads and provinces had also been changed, contributing to a desperate sense of total alienation in a strange and hostile landscape.

I found my cool and clinical mood overcoming me, which arrived when I knew a situation was hopeless. It was. The man was married and unemployed, and the little spaces of freedom granted to him by Rhodesia and now Zimbabwe were marked by the birth of many children. I was too frightened to ask for how many months the rent had not been paid. Somehow, we managed to help.

As arranged, I collected Moeletsi Mbeki to have lunch with me at home. He was kind, calm and thoughtful, despite, or maybe because of, his ever-erupting laughter. I tried to conceal from him the fact that my heart was aching for so many, many reasons. Instead, I revealed to him the other side of the coin of my life.

I told him of the marvellous and unexpected feeling of freedom and fresh air I had been enjoying ever since standing for a parliamentary seat and being defeated just because I was a PF Zapu nominee. Moeletsi was not surprised. He said that was because, in these difficult days when people didn't trust each other, they now knew exactly where I stood. He told me that people now knew I was independent of the powers that be, come hell or high water. They could feel free with me. They liked to feel free because that's what they had fought for. They know that's what you fought for too, he said, and they are hoping you will continue to be steadfast.

People were treating me so gently, as if being on the losing side was a new experience for me. It wasn't, of course, and I still had hope for the future. It was the future after the elimination of apartheid in our sad neighbour South Africa that I was counting on.

On Wednesday 6 November I was a guest of the PLO ambassador, Ali Halimeh, at a dinner he was giving to bid farewell to the Libyan ambassador to Zimbabwe. There were five other ambassadors – the USSR, Ethiopia, Nicaragua, Algeria and Pakistan – six wives and me. It was all such fun, so relaxed, and the people present so witty and urbane. There were only two very brief moments when I detected that maybe Comrade and Mrs Libya were racists rather than anti-Zionists. They passed, those brief moments, but I didn't like them.

Pakistan could have outdone anyone at London's Athenaeum Club in tone, refinement, wit and verbosity. He bored USSR almost to distraction. USSR couldn't get a word in edgeways 99 per cent of the time, and, when he did, although he was treated with respect, there was also a certain amount of jocularity accorded to what he said. No one behaved as if he was representing a client state.

Libya started the evening off by congratulating USSR on Gorbachev's recent speech in which he criticised Stalin and exonerated Khrushchev. But, said Libya, we must appreciate that, despite everything, Stalin had forced the Soviet Union into the industrialised age. Yes, said USSR, but the human cost was too great. 'I think we must put a full stop after Stalin.'

Francisco Campbell was, without any doubt on my side, Zimbabwe's most striking ambassador at the time. He was amazingly handsome and very tall, but his eyes seemed troubled. When Ali introduced us, he said to me, 'I don't think you know the ambassador of Nicaragua.'

'Know him?' I responded. 'Every day I see him on television, in the papers, at receptions ...'

'Ah,' said Ambassador Campbell gravely, outdoing me, 'but I have read about you in books.'

When we were placed at dinner, I found USSR on my right and Ethiopia on my left. I was in the middle of the table, neither to the right or left hand of my host, but somehow the serving of all courses started with me. The first was an awkward tureen of soup. As I was serving myself, the waiter whispered affectionately in my left ear: 'And how are you tonight?' I jumped, almost upsetting the tureen. Then, looking up at him, I recognised one of the old Callinicos stalwarts from the Park Lane Hotel, now with the Holiday Inn and doing the catering for Ali.

The Soviet ambassador was the next to be served. After he had finished, he tried to be diplomatic. He looked, as did his wife, so nice and unpretentious. He turned to me and smiled.

'Ah.'

'Ah,' I responded, also smiling, but not game enough to start a conversation.

'We are neighbours!'

'We are!'

End of attempted dialogue. Pakistan had struck up again. He complained at length about a surcharge that the government apparently charged diplomats for their children's school fees. I was puzzled by this, as I thought he had earlier indicated that he was a bachelor. Our host, dear Ali Halimeh, was silent practically throughout the whole evening, but when Pakistan paused, Ali waded in. He said that diplomats enjoyed such a vastly privileged life, why not graciously give a little to the host country? It was roundly pointed out to him what disadvantages diplomats suffered, such as climate, absence from dear ones and insecurity about future positions.

It was at that point that I realised how privileged I was to be part of their company that evening, treated as an equal, as one of them. They were speaking so freely. On the whole I was silent, just murmuring when necessary. But then, alas, and totally accidentally, I put my foot in it.

The Soviet ambassador said that if Zimbabwe really wanted foreign currency so badly, why was there no duty-free shop? I said there was. He asked, where? I said it was at the airport. No, he said, he meant a duty-free shop in the middle of town. *Everyone* had a duty-free shop at the airport. But Zimbabwe should be like other countries, like Mozambique, for example, and have another duty-free shop more accessible in the middle of town.

I said that, well, you see, Zimbabwe was meant to be a socialist country, and it wouldn't look good if we had a duty-free shop in the middle of town where only those with foreign currency could shop. I thought maybe such an institution would be against the leadership code. There was much laughter all round the table.

USSR persevered. No, he said. Such a shop would not affect the *leaders*.

It would be for diplomats only. I then found myself looking around the company. I suppose my silence, however innocent, spoke more than words, and each representative perhaps remembered that he was also supposed to be a socialist – whatever that meant. USSR addressed not another word to me all evening, except to say goodbye much later.

Both before and after dinner, although we were all within speaking and listening distance of each other, the men and women were arranged in two very distinct groups according to gender, but facing each other. Pakistan, before dinner, had entranced us all on the subject of whether or not his country had the capability to manufacture a nuclear bomb. As the evening waned, he pursued his thoughts in what became a monologue. He handled the topic of nuclear capability very well, and left us all even more in the dark by the end of the evening than we had been at the beginning. He said that as soon as anyone arrived in Pakistan, he or she was surrounded by offers of transport. 'You want to see bomb factory? I take you there very, very cheap.'

Eventually they got onto local politics. It was only at that point that the two groups merged conversationally, as by that stage I was in the midst of the group of women and, after the men had touched on unity, Ali addressed me directly. He congratulated me on my 'steadfastness' and for standing for parliament, especially as I knew there was absolutely no chance that I would win. I was quite overcome with pleasure.

I was also overjoyed by the release of Govan Mbeki in South Africa. My heart lifted every time I heard him being interviewed on the radio, and there had been quite a lot on the BBC. His voice was so strong, despite his age and his ordeal, and what he said was so generous and brave.

With the help of Bryant Elliot, my name had been changed by notarial deed. I thought my life could perhaps become more orderly and tranquil, but then I started having a series of terrible dreams that I was about to be hanged. I was shown a rack – like a tie rack in Harrods – where there were all types of hanging rope displayed, all at different prices. I would choose the cheapest, in the hope that it would break before it accomplished its purpose. Then I was taken to the death cells, but I always managed to escape. I didn't want to be hanged. I escaped all night, but there were dogs everywhere scenting me out and betraying my presence. I ran and ran. They could run faster. I would wake eventually, sweating, exhausted and sad.

Rhoda and Mervyn Immerman had a dinner that November in honour of Chris Beer, whom I had met in the seventies. He was at the International University Exchange Fund in Geneva, which was so totally smashed by Craig Williamson, the apartheid agent. Chris was now with Help the Aged. We all first gathered at a lunch given by the British high commissioner in honour of Alex and Jenny Boraine who had come up from South Africa for the premiere of Richard Attenborough's film, *Cry Freedom*.

Mervyn was one of Zimbabwe's top lawyers. He was endearing and exceedingly amusing, although perhaps he sometimes didn't mean to be. That night he told us of the time, a couple of years ago, when the North Koreans at their embassy in Harare got into trouble again and sought his help. It was something to do with collecting scrap iron in Zimbabwe and unlawfully shipping it off to their country. They made an appointment to see him. At that stage he had no idea what it was all about. They came in, sat down and looked at him inscrutably. Then one of them opened his mouth and Mervyn leaned forward eagerly.

'We deny everything,' the man said, and shut his mouth again.

Mervyn said the case was still pending and the North Koreans had changed their entire staff three times since it started. He got to know the actual initiator of the scrap-iron deal quite well. When the man was recalled, he came to say goodbye.

'Do you have the equivalent of Siberia in North Korea?' Mervyn asked. 'Because, if so, that's where I think you are going.'

I'm sure the poor man couldn't have been amused – in fact Mervyn said he looked miserable – but this was an instance of how he could appear to be funny unintentionally. I think it had been a genuine question.

In another example, he said that Jenny Boraine had been explaining to him at lunch how the Institute for a Democratic Alternative for South Africa, Idasa, was setting up groups of white Afrikaners and others against apartheid throughout South Africa. Mervyn pointed out that however many groups they set up, it wouldn't make any difference whatsoever to the state or to the institution of apartheid.

'That must have cheered her up,' I remarked, and Rhoda laughed.

'Whenever you have the faintest glimmer of hope about anything,' she said, 'just come to Mervyn and he will extinguish it for you.'

We were so fortunate to have Ken Rankin, an increasingly respected orthopaedic surgeon, in Bulawayo. He was a Scotsman, married to Joyce Sikhakhane of the ANC. There was a dispute about what next for Jeremy, and I managed to put in a word for the involvement of Rankin. Jeremy was eventually flown to Bulawayo in November so that Rankin could operate on his left knee. They arrived on a Sunday, and I was luckily at my desk when Joan rang, needing urgent help. The local security people in Bulawayo had somehow got it into their heads that Jeremy had been injured in a bomb blast that he himself had perpetrated. They wanted to shackle him to his bed in case he tried to escape. The only person I could think of who could come to the rescue was CIO's Dan Stannard. But it was a Sunday, and I didn't know how to reach him. I rang Julian Harston at the British High Commission, and he got hold of Stannard, who contacted me, and within a few minutes he had everything sorted out.

Jeremy had successive operations to remove shrapnel, but during recent major surgery it was found that a large abscess had formed around a wad of cloth that had been driven into his body, and the abscess was impairing a nerve. So it was decided that he would have to go to Europe to have a proper body scan. Harare's X-ray machines could pick up metal, but apparently in Europe they had machines that could pick up other foreign bodies, such as cloth.

Ken Rankin eventually achieved miracles. Jeremy's voice from Bulawayo Central Hospital on the morning of Sunday 22 November sounded quite different and almost happy. He had even managed to walk a few steps the day before. He thanked me very strongly for having insisted that they go to Bulawayo for the operation on his knee, despite the advice of the surgeons in Harare.

'I owe you a leg,' he said.

I didn't know what to say, so there was silence. Then he offered to send me the shrapnel extracted from the leg. I said that would be okay, so long as it was accompanied by a red rose.

I received a welcome Christmas present. Mildred Nevile from CIIR wrote to apologise for her role in trying to get rid of me from the Zimbabwe Project in 1983. 'When I look back to those traumatic ten days of several years ago I regret now the way in which I tried to steamroller you and your affairs. Not because I think I was wrong to have brought out the things which had been said to me and to try to do something about them but because of the way in which I went about things. If, as head of an organisation, I had been treated to a flying visit by a Trustee who tried to steamroller over me and what I had built up, I would have been beside myself with rage and humiliation. So, Judy, I do very much regret the suffering this long period of difficulty brought you.'

Of course I gladly responded with thanks to her gallant letter. There was no point in possibly increasing her pain by pointing out that all she had done was to quite unwittingly and innocently be used viciously by Zanu (PF) and their surrogates, whom she trusted.

After months and years of brutal pressure from Robert Mugabe and Zanu (PF), Joshua Nkomo and PF Zapu were at last forced into the Agreement of Unity, signed on 22 December 1987. It consisted of ten points that left no breathing space for any democratic values in Zimbabwe:

1. Zanu (PF) and PF Zapu were irrevocably united under one political party.
2. Unity was to be achieved under the name Zimbabwe African National Union (Patriotic Front), in short Zanu (PF).
3. Comrade Robert Gabriel Mugabe would be the first secretary and president of Zanu (PF).
4. Zanu (PF) would have two second secretaries and vice-presidents, who would be appointed by the first secretary and president.
5. Zanu (PF) would seek to establish a socialist society in Zimbabwe on the guidance of Marxist-Leninist principles.
6. Zanu (PF) would seek to establish a one-party state.
7. Zanu (PF) would abide by the leadership code.
8. The present leadership of PF Zapu would take immediate steps to end insecurity and violence prevalent in Matabeleland.
9. Zanu (PF) and PF Zapu would convene respective congresses to give effect to the agreement.
10. Comrade Robert Gabriel Mugabe was vested with full powers to prepare for the implementation of the agreement and to act in the name and authority of Zanu (PF).

The signing took place at State House, one of the last occasions hosted by the joyful midwife, President Canaan Banana. Amendments were then presented to and accepted by parliament under which Mugabe became executive president. The office of prime minister was abolished.

Mugabe appointed Nkomo chief minister in the president's office, ranked in status just behind Mugabe's deputy, Simon Muzenda, and gave him the task of overseeing local government and rural and urban development.

Despite this so-called unity between Zanu (PF) and PF Zapu, Guduza remained locked up. But the unity pact at least gave me the opportunity to move swiftly in getting our trustees to appoint the Zimbabwe Project deputy director, Paul Themba Nyathi, as director in my place. I had been with the project since its formation ten years before and it was time for a change in leadership. I had been hesitant about stepping down, as Nyathi was vintage Zapu and came from Matabeleland, and I thought there might be all sorts of problems. But now the time was ripe. He would take over from me, and I would carry on working at the Zimbabwe Project part time for as long as we continued to need each other, as, financially, I would.

CHAPTER 19

Into the hills with the guerrillas

C OMRADE GARIKAI CAME TO SEE ME IN JANUARY 1988. WHEN
the Zimbabwe Project receptionist rang to tell me of his presence,
I could hardly believe my ears. As I asked her to bring him to my office one
floor up, I instantly remembered the terrifying background.

One night during the war my parents were visited at their lonely house
on the ranch by a group of ZANLA, who stretched out and rested on the
stoep amid a large and heavy display of weapons. They were on their way to
Dadaya Secondary School, where they ordered the teachers to cook a meal
for them while they addressed the pupils. The import of their address was
that ZANLA now had enough recruits and it was the duty of pupils to stay
at school, do well in their studies and concentrate on training themselves
for the new Zimbabwe.

Despite this, the headmaster of Dadaya later received a letter, apparently
signed by a local ZANLA commander, Garikai, ordering that the school be
closed. My father thought the letter must be a forgery, but there was only one
way to make certain – find Garikai. He did so. The night after Garikai came
to my office, I found the letter my father had managed to send me about
this incident in July 1979, and it helped me to understand why I felt so faint
when Garikai was talking to me earlier in the day and nearly a decade later.

The headmaster at Dadaya found a pupil to accompany my father to the
village in the nearby communal areas, around which it was thought the
ZANLA guerrillas were based. Then, wrote my father:

> A group of four guerrillas approached and met us in the middle of the
> village. Two stood back and two came forward and shook hands with me.
> Garikai was short and thickset, carried a rocket launcher loaded with
> a rocket and had on his back a heavy load of three rockets. His second
> in command whom they called Tshaka was lightly built and carried a
> sub-machine gun with a 45 or so rounds magazine. People were rushing
> around to bring out a small table and four chairs which were set up in
> the middle of the village clearing in the warm sunlight. We sat down and
> a bottle of Bols brandy was produced. I was given an inch in a large
> tumbler ...

Everyone was being rather careful and we spoke of generalities for a few minutes. When I brought up the matter of the letters ordering the closure of the school Garikai immediately asked to see them but I did not have them. I had not thought it a good idea to carry them but I should have done so.

'So you received letters but you did not bring them. You are lying.' That phrase 'you are lying' Garikai used for the next hour. 'Mr Todd, there was a gap there …' and so on we went. 'Perhaps you have come to survey our place for Ian Smith.' I laughed and said I had 45 years of a reference and Garikai said yes, it was unlikely, but it was possible. He assured me that he had not written the letter but then I should tell him who would have written it. Maybe, he agreed, it was the Selous Scouts aiming at making trouble between the school, the people and the guerrillas. I was overcome with relief and just wanted to go home.

I was drinking my brandy too slowly but, in my estimation, Tshaka was drinking too much and too quickly. We turned to the equipment placed on the ground beside the chairs. I was handed the rocket launcher and had it explained to me with information about the types of rockets they had. Then we turned to the rifles and sub-machine guns, to what was happening in the area and conversation became easier although Garikai spoke sharply once or twice to Tshaka who was playing around with his sub-machine gun in a way which shocked me.

When the meal was over I made to excuse myself but encountered reluctance to let me go. I thought this rather nice but was soon to recognise that I wasn't going to be allowed to leave the guerrillas until it was too late for me to cause any harm by my reports.

'Now we will go and visit the bases. Would you like to see the soldiers at the bases?' I would like to see the bases and on we went, Maphosa, the headmaster of a local school, Garikai and Tshaka and a couple of other guerrillas. A mile on we came to the first base and a group of 4 or 5 guerrillas with one or two men and girls from the village. Into the hills and we came to another and then another. At the third one which was on high and rocky ground we obviously were settling in and there we sat on the rocks until about 2 p.m. Tshaka gave up and slept like a log while Garikai and I talked and talked. He was shocked that I knew no Shona and I used my limited Sindebele to the extreme. He started off at one point by saying 'Baba'. I replied 'Yes?' 'Oh no,' he said, you say 'Mwana.' So I said 'Mwana' and from then on he called me at each statement father, *baba*, and I replied my child, *mwana*.

Eventually three very pleasant looking girls arrived bearing a basin of water so that we washed our hands before eating. Then they set out sadza and meat and six of us sat as closely as we could get around the bowl of food. I was surprised that we ate like that together with the girls as it was basically very unAfrican but when I spoke to Ringpart (an employee on the ranch) the next day he said guerrillas now always ate with the people who brought the food since the time at our school at Sivanga where the women had been given poison to put in the food and some guerrillas had almost died.

One thing I had persuaded Garikai not to do, which he offered, was to fire a demonstration shot for me, as the Rhodesian soldiers could not be far away.

At the first village on the way back it was suggested that we dance, and music started. I said that it wasn't possible. I was too old and too stiff. Garikai then a bit abruptly said that if I wouldn't dance then all right, I could go on my way.

One thing I had not realised because I was not afraid myself was the reaction of the village people to seeing me taken off to the hills by the guerrillas. On our way back Maphosa said we must call at Siyape's village. We turned into the track to the village and saw a man of over 50 running towards us. When he was about 20 paces away he dropped to his knees and I came up to him and put out my hand. He seized it and shook it and shook it in a vice-like clasp and then I saw that he was going into a paroxysm. Maphosa said, 'He was so frightened when the hours passed and you did not return that he is now possessed by a spirit because of his joy. This sometimes happens to Siyape.' I turned back when I had gone 100 paces on and Siyape was still kneeling in the dust. At other villages people shook hands effusively with relief. I was overwhelmingly glad that I had persuaded Garikai not to fire that single shot up in the hills.

I have a very happy memory of my farewell. As Garikai held my hand he said, 'You can go with confidence and get on with your work for Dadaya is an important school for us. We will not close it.'

Over the years, since being back home, I had spoken to a number of former ZANLA commanders, telling them I would like to meet Garikai. When he appeared, I thought it was in response to one of my messages. But he told me he had read about the Zimbabwe Project in the newspapers and had come for possible assistance to further his education.

What Garikai told me was frightening. He repeated a number of times that 'Mr Todd is a blessed man. Mr Todd is a blessed man.' It emerged that he was saying Mr Todd was *very* lucky to be alive. He said that in fact Tshaka, not he, had been in charge. Tshaka could not speak or understand any English, and 'he had no history'. In other words, he knew nothing about my father. Garikai said that Tshaka wanted my father shot immediately. *Garikai spoke sharply once or twice to Tshaka who was playing around with his machine-gun in a way which shocked me.* He and another guerrilla pleaded with Tshaka for my father's life. Tshaka put my father through various tests, one being whether he would eat *rapoko*, brown sorghum sadza. None of them knew, of course, that my father loathed the taste of alcohol and that the hardest test of all was to force himself to drink that brandy.

At the end of the saga, Tshaka viewed Garikai with suspicion and he was sent to Mozambique for interrogation on his relationship with Mr Todd. Garikai used a word which I didn't understand. I didn't feel free to ask him what it meant, as he evinced such horror. He'd had five terrible days, he said, shaking his head and shivering, mentioning something to do with water. But then someone higher up had said that Todd was okay, so Garikai was released and sent back to Rhodesia to resume operations.

Paul Brickhill, on the advice of his brother Jeremy, came to see me about the cooperative he belonged to, Grassroots Books, which, among its wares, sold a lot of literature published in the Soviet Union.

Paul said that the week before a barefoot white man in handcuffs had been brought by CIO for questioning outside Grassroots. The whole block that Grassroots was in, near Meikles Hotel, was sealed off by the police support unit. Paul wasn't there, but, by the description, he thought this was the man he had told me about the year before. Paul had then thought the man was only masquerading as a professor from a black South African university, asking how books and literature could be smuggled into South Africa. Paul had said to me at the time that you get a feeling about these kinds of people.

Then, the day before Paul's visit to me, CIO had brought black barefoot captives in handcuffs on two occasions and gone through the same procedures, one of the men actually being brought into the shop while they questioned him. It was assumed that these suspects were being held in connection with the Bulawayo car bomb, which had exploded outside an ANC house in Jungle Road, Trennance. Paul and Jeremy wanted me to see Dan Stannard about it all. Paul needed to know if there was a plan to attack Grassroots, or whether it had simply been under surveillance.

I said I would try to help and phoned Stannard, but he was away. I told

Paul I would keep trying, but that I wouldn't want it known by anyone if I ever did manage to see Stannard. It wouldn't be good for me and it wouldn't be good for Stannard. Although I would have liked to be a friend of his, I just could not wholeheartedly trust the man. And I didn't think he really liked or trusted me either.

As a former prime minister, my father had the use of the VIP lounge at the airport, and so he arranged for it to be available for the Brickhills when they left Harare on 30 January 1988. The Algerian ambassador was leaving on the same flight, and so there was a phalanx of representatives from appropriate countries to see him off: Egypt, Ethiopia, India, Brazil, Iraq, Greece, Sudan and, joy of joys, Ali Halimeh, who immediately appropriated Jeremy and showed him off to everyone.

Jeremy rose gallantly to the occasion and insisted on getting up from his chair each time a new ambassador was presented. There was an Austrian envoy who looked like a Chicago thug, barrel-fashioned, with large square teeth clenching an enormous cigar. I winced when he clasped Jeremy's hand. Ali was introducing them and explaining about the Avondale catastrophe. 'They were aiming at *him*!' Ali said very proudly. The Austrian choked and moved as swiftly as decently possible to a far corner of the room.

Very early on Tuesday 2 February, I received a call at home from Dan Stannard, who said he had been failing to reach me for some time, and thus this early call. I said I would very much appreciate seeing him, and then, to give him a clue, said it was about Grassroots Books.

He said this was completely between us and he would be glad if I didn't tell anyone else – but he knew he could trust me! He said they had got the people responsible for the attack on Jeremy. In fact, they had got the people responsible for all the bombings and attacks since 1980. He said these people must have had a shred of humanity in them, as Jeremy had been in their sights on three occasions, but they had twice relented because he was with his children. He said they had also been planning to attack Grassroots.

Moreover, he continued, they were now trying to finger him, Stannard, and others within 'the organisation', as he called it, and I got the impression from him that he was under police investigation.

'However, I'm still here,' he said. 'I've got more intelligence in my little finger than they've got in the whole force.'

I said I supposed it would be in the suspects' interests to finger him. (I'd been fingering him in my mind since independence, but of course I didn't mention this although he probably very well suspected it.) He agreed with me. But he said that now the president had called off whoever was investigating him.

So, I asked, when could we see each other? The pressure was off regarding Grassroots as far as I was concerned, now that he had told me these things. 'That's why I told you,' he said. But I said I would still like to see him, and we fixed for 9.30 a.m. the next day. We arranged that I would come to him.

'You know where we are?'

'What used to be called Coghlan Buildings?'

'Yes, the pile of red bricks. The Kremlin.' He laughed. 'Now it's Chaminuka. Ninth floor.'

What interested me about this conversation, apart from its content, was that I thought it meant my phone wasn't tapped, and also, as I would be seeing him at his office, that he didn't mind being seen with me by his colleagues. Time would tell.

Overall I felt no less uneasy about him. I hoped I was being unfair. Paul Themba Nyathi had told me, from a source within CIO, that there had been a briefing at which it was said that one of Stannard's deputies had been arrested and that Stannard had fled the country.

I felt sick when Paul said this. My first thoughts were that I had been right not to trust Stannard, and also of how much danger we must all be in, as he himself, although knowing Jeremy, must have been aware that the attack was to happen. Instead of expressing my feelings, I said I just couldn't believe it. I knew Stannard was away from Harare. I felt we should wait until he returned before jumping to conclusions, as by then I would know whether I could see him or not. If I could, the rumour would be baseless. But the very fact of the rumour existing within CIO was bad enough and, by what Stannard himself had told me on the phone, it was based on at least some truth. Another thing I said to Paul was that if they had picked up the right people during the recent arrests, then Stannard must have been involved. Surely this should prove that he could not be a South African agent. But of course I was really just arguing against the apprehensions in my own heart.

I was at CIO headquarters in Chaminuka at the time we had agreed. The guard/receptionist rang Mr Stannard to say there was someone to see him. Yes, it was Miss Todd. 'Shall I send her up?' Then I was told to wait. Mr Stannard was coming down to collect me.

There were a lot of people in the reception area: two or three men behind the desk, about three or four messengers, seated, and a man in plain clothes, who I suppose was some kind of security. I took a seat, and one of the messengers asked to check my handbag. There was a constant stream of people coming in and out, flashing their identity cards. It was a public place.

Before long Mr Stannard arrived, greeted me by name very cheerfully and loudly, and leaned forward to kiss me. I was pleased but also taken aback, and quickly proffered my left cheek. He must have powerful kisses, because for hours I could feel my cheek burning.

On the way up in the lift, we engaged in trivial conversation. I remarked how aptly the building had been renamed, as wasn't Chaminuka, a historically very important spirit medium, Zimbabwe's chief spook? He said he hadn't thought of it that way before.

When we sat down, we quickly got down to business. No small talk. I had made notes of what Jeremy and Paul Brickhill wanted me to establish, and I said to Stannard that this was what I wanted to find out, if possible:

- Had Grassroots simply been under surveillance to establish who was using it? Paul said that, for instance, on one occasion a top ANC man had turned up there seeking assistance, as he had been stranded at the airport.
- Had an attack been planned on Grassroots? There was anxiety not only about the safety of the staff, but also, of course, for their customers. Recently, the former president of Zimbabwe had been there. Grassroots was often frequented by diplomats. An attack could have serious consequences for Zimbabwe's image.
- In the past there had been CIO investigations regarding Grassroots. Paul assumed that this was because of the political climate of the times and that they had been interested in possible Zapu links, or links with the dissidents, or links with the ANC. The investigations of the past might have obscured the common interests Grassroots presumably had with CIO, for example the apprehension of South African agents. Grassroots would be quite happy to have a CIO presence in the shop, as they themselves believed they were quite experienced in intuitively sensing who may or may not be an agent. They would be even happier to have a uniformed detail outside the shop for deterrent purposes.

Stannard then got out a large file, which, unobtrusively reading upside down, I could tell was obviously to do with the ring of arrested people. All the papers were marked TOP CONFIDENTIAL. He read me extracts, from which it became obvious that in their design to kill Jeremy, the suspects had indeed had Grassroots under surveillance and that they were indeed planning to attack it. It seemed they didn't know about the existence of Paul Brickhill as being distinct from Jeremy Brickhill, and they thought (i) Jeremy was an ANC activist; (ii) Grassroots was an outlet for Soviet literature, at which the Grassroots–ANC link became 'obvious' to them, and (iii) that Jeremy ran Grassroots.

From what he told me, there were two blacks involved, one a South African and one a Zimbabwean. I regret very much that I don't have a photographic memory but that, to the contrary, my mind almost immediately blots out all information I am told is confidential. And Stannard kept stressing that what he was telling me was top secret.

The agents had established where Jeremy lived and the registration number of his car. I think there were two whites involved in this operation, as well as the blacks. One of the whites was under arrest, but the other, as well as the controller, was in South Africa. At one stage in the planning, the South African black had gone into Grassroots and had asked to see Mr Brickhill, but the black female receptionist had made it difficult for him, so he had left. At another stage, the black Zimbabwean had gone into Jeremy's house in Natal Road and had asked if the Brickhills were there. The gardener had said no, they had moved to Hatfield.

Stannard asked me if that information had been correct. I said yes.

'So,' he said, 'you see what even domestics can give away?'

He indicated that this ring had been responsible for all the eruptions since independence – the bombing of the Zanu (PF) headquarters, the Thornhill air base, everything. The breakthrough had come with the Bulawayo bomb. He told me what I had already learned from Godwin Matatu, that they had gone to the Bulawayo Labour Exchange to hire a driver for the car bomb. Stannard said the poor chap must have thought it was his lucky day. The authorities had managed to get a fingerprint from the remains of his body. He was a Zambian. Apparently he had been told to go to the targeted ANC house in Jungle Road, Trennance, and hoot three times. On the third hoot, the bomb in the car he was driving was detonated by remote control.

I told Stannard that I must go and see Paul at Grassroots, and could we please agree on what I was permitted to tell him. Stannard said I could tell Paul that I had seen him; that I could cite him as saying, 'the danger has fallen away'; that when these people were at Grassroots they were looking for Jeremy; and also that, if at any future date people at Grassroots were concerned about anything suspicious, they could approach Stannard either directly or via me.

While he was reading excerpts to me, I was studying him, wondering if he could possibly be an agent and at the same time regretting that I could be pondering such things. Apart from his bluffness, there was a certain sadness about his face in repose, and he didn't look as if life has been particularly kind to him. I could well believe that he would be an assiduous and loyal servant of the state. My problem was how someone could be an assiduous and loyal servant of one state that had been replaced by such a totally different state. The answer to this, of course, was that it wasn't replaced by a totally different state at all.

At the end of our meeting, I said that the breaking of this ring must make the South Africans very angry, and that presumably they gave him much of the credit because of his position in the Central Intelligence Organisation, and that he himself must be at great risk.

Stannard shrugged and said that, yes, he was. The black South African had tried to implicate all the white officers in CIO, and they had also had to get rid of a man at the South African Trade Commission who was smearing Stannard. He said they had also smashed a PTC ring in Harare's telephone exchange working for South African agents, which had actually been tapping his telephone and that of Minister Mnangagwa. I asked if everything was all right now, regarding his position. Stannard crossed fingers on both hands, held them in the air and said, 'I hope so.'

Finally, I asked when we could hope for the release of Makhatini Guduza. Stannard had momentarily forgotten about him, or who he was. I explained. He said that if I wrote him a letter on this matter, he would raise the subject with Minister Sekeremayi, who was now in charge of security, and get Guduza out 'on grounds of unity'.

When I got home, I wrote to Stannard about Guduza without delay, saying that he was last detained in January 1986, and that I believed subsequent to that he was found guilty of leaving the country illegally and fined Z$100, which was paid. I said his family had been having a miserable time over the last few years and that his wife Poppy had come again to see me a week ago, wondering if in the new atmosphere of unity her husband might be released. I asked if Stannard would be kind enough to ascertain whether this might be possible.

Six months previously, prisons director Chigwida had invited me to another ceremony for ex-combatants who had graduated as prison officers.

After the passing out, I had sought and been given permission to see Makhatini Guduza. One of the senior prison officers on duty at Chikurubi Prison remembered me from 1971, when I had taken oranges to Willie Musarurwa, then detained in Gwelo Prison. On that occasion the prison personnel had made as much noise as possible, stamping on the concrete floor all around Willie and me while we tried vainly to talk through a glass pane and bars. This time the officers were very pleasant, and two of them accompanied me to see Guduza. We were treated to a fascinating history lesson, with Guduza telling us anecdotes about the different people he had been detained with over the years, from President Banana down.

On Thursday 25 February 1988, it was reported that the South African regime had banned seventeen more organisations, from the United Democratic Front to the Detainees' Parents Support Committee. Reddy Masimba, the local ANC chief representative, called round to see me. He was laughing at the news.

Some benefits were beginning to accrue from the unity accord. On Zimbabwe's eighth birthday, 18 April 1988, President Mugabe declared an amnesty for all dissidents and Joshua Nkomo urged them to lay down their arms and come in from the bush. In a *Government Gazette* published on 3 May, clemency and a full pardon was extended to all dissidents who surrendered their arms and reported to the police between 19 April and 31 May. Clemency was also extended to those who had assisted dissidents. And, at long, long last, Makhatini Guduza was released.

I received a blank postcard from Bulawayo with M Guduza typed humbly in the bottom right-hand corner. This was followed by a large card with a red and almost pulsating heart, saying THANK YOU! I gathered he was not eligible for the amnesty and that the release was in response to the appeal I had made to Dan Stannard. Bryant Elliot said the amnesty actually applied to very few people, but the ministers of Home Affairs and Justice could respond to appeals.

Julian Harston, my old friend from the British High Commission, was preparing to leave Zimbabwe later in the year. In the meanwhile he was delighting in some pre-departure mischief. When last I saw him, he said he thought I should be warned that Dan Stannard was a very randy chap. I was surprised that Julian should make such a remark with, as it were, no context. Then I visited the United States to deliver a lecture at the University of California at Santa Cruz. On my return, Stannard rang me to find out how Jeremy was getting on and enquired if I'd had a good trip abroad. I was covered with confusion when he laughed heartily and said Julian had told him I had left the country as I feared he, Stannard, was after my body.

Things seemed good but quite strange, with 'dissidents' giving themselves up and shaking hands with villagers in some sort of reconciliation. Very weird. This group included a man known as Tambolenyoka, who, together with a man known as Guyigusu, was thought to have been responsible for the grisly murders of many missionaries at New Adams Farm in Matobo outside Bulawayo the previous November.

June was such a lovely time of year for those who had beds and warmth and food. It was the beginning of winter, when the countryside was stark, the night sky blazed with stars, and the air was crisp and dry. I believed that, at least for the moment, Zimbabwe was blessed. I certainly was.

I attended a public meeting on cooperatives addressed by Dr Nkomo. He saw me in the audience and praised me. I couldn't believe it. He was surrounded by civil servants who now worked under him, but who, a few years, even a few months ago, had found it difficult to be polite to me, as they thought I was a friend of Nkomo and they had been informed that he was an enemy of the state. He told the meeting that people must never leave me, that I might not have money, but that I had ideas. He said I had worked tirelessly for Zimbabwe and that I had raised so much money for development, but had failed to keep even ten cents for myself. People must stay with me, he said, listen to me and talk to me. I would always be with them.

The civil servants came running at the end of his speech to shake my hand. That didn't give me much pleasure. I just thought how one couldn't depend on any of them, so easily could they change. But I was filled with joy that, after all the difficult years everyone had been through, Nkomo could publicly state that I was to be trusted. I never expected such a gift from him.

More good things kept flowing from the unity accord. Zimbabwean refugees, mostly from Botswana, were returning home, and dissidents were coming in from the bush. This was one of the topics addressed at our Zimbabwe Project staff meeting from 24 to 27 May 1988, held fifty kilometres from Bulawayo in the Matopos. We learned later that just a few koppies away, some dissidents too were meeting to plan their return to society. By the official deadline of midnight on Tuesday 31 May, 112 men had handed themselves over to the authorities.

At our meeting we agreed that we should be ready to assist with the amnesty, if necessary, and we allotted Z$4 000 to the Bulawayo office for emergency assistance. The subject arose because, the very morning we were to leave for the Matopos, Tennyson Ndlovu, whose pseudonym as a dissident was Tambolenyoka, came to the Bulawayo office looking for Albert Ngwenya, and help.

Over the years Albert had managed to find employment for a number of ex-combatants with National Foods in Bulawayo. Tennyson was one of them. The thought of assisting dissidents was my initiative, with, I hoped, the support, if so far silent, of Albert. It was very difficult for Paul Themba Nyathi, now director of the Zimbabwe Project, to stomach. One of Paul's brothers had been killed by dissidents. Another of his brothers had been killed by 5 Brigade. Most of the staff had been touched in one way or another by the brutalities of the past few years. But we were united in our support of the amnesty, and any efforts to bring peace and development to the entire country. The task of assisting dissidents, should this be necessary, was initially delegated to me and the Bulawayo office.

The dissidents had been ordered by the authorities to report to police stations. The majority had gone to the police camps in Gwanda and Nkayi, so it was strange to see Tambolenyoka openly wandering around Bulawayo looking just as wild and unattractive as anyone could expect a dissident to appear. We learned later that some of them were well connected with serving members of the Zanu (PF) administration, such as Mark Dube, governor of Matabeleland South. One of the most loathed, Guyigusu (Morgan Nkomo, also known as Morgan Sango), was alleged to have axed to death eleven missionaries and five infants at New Adams Farm, Matobo, in November 1987. It was widely believed that he had been assisted by Tambolenyoka. At the time of the amnesty, Guyigusu was wounded in a defensive attack while killing a Catholic priest at Empandeni Mission. On 31 May, as the deadline was running out, he sent a message to the police saying he was coming in, but due to his injury would be late. As Dumiso Dabengwa commented at the time, 'What kind of a dissident sends a message to the police?'

After our Matopos meeting, we consulted widely about what should be done regarding the men we now referred to as *returnees*, to try to detach them from the stigma of the word *dissident*. On Monday 6 June we met the Director of Social Services, Dawson Sanyangore, and the Commissioner for Refugees, Mr Mukwewa. The United Nations High Commission for Refugees was putting a programme together to assist refugees coming back to Zimbabwe, but 'returnees' would not benefit. Sanyangore said Social Services simply did not have any funds with which to assist, so any help from the Zimbabwe Project would be welcome. We were asked to liaise with Mr Naboth Choruma, in charge of welfare for Matabeleland North, and Mr Clement Mkwananzi, for Matabeleland South. We were also informed in no uncertain terms that, even if it had the money, government could not be seen to be doing anything for the returnees. There was no explanation for this. We immediately and officially informed the president's office, in other words, CIO, of our involvement. Quite understandably, the media was by then very hostile to the returnees, so we didn't draw public attention to our assistance, hoping the identity of those concerned would fade from the minds of people.

On Wednesday 8 June, Social Services requested us to provide clothing for seventy-six men, to be distributed from Gwanda and Nkayi police stations. This was the start of what became a close relationship. We now knew not only the name of each man, but exactly what size clothes and shoes he wore. As requested, we immediately bought them each two outfits of normal clothes, soap, toothbrushes, toothpaste and razors. It was difficult to find shoes big enough for Guyigusu's enormous feet.

We had also assumed responsibility for providing food for the men. We were fighting a running battle with the authorities, trying to keep the men in the police camps until a secure future had been carved out for them. Right at the beginning of June, a few hours after they had given themselves up, we heard rumours from CIO that they would be sent to their homes, where they would be followed and killed. We were sure that if even one of them was harmed, the others would return to the bush and Zimbabwe's troubles would start all over again.

We worked well with local civil servants, such as the provincial administrator of Matabeleland North, Zwelibanzi Mzilethi, and the district administrator of Nkayi, Stanley Bhebhe. We were also working with the Catholic Commission for Justice and Peace and the Commercial Farmers' Union, through a former president of the CFU and local farmer in Matabeleland, Ted Kirby. Along with the rest of the population in Matabeleland, the commercial farmers had suffered grievously during the 5 Brigade/dissident era, with a number being killed and more than half a million acres of their land abandoned. We were also appealing for funds to help make the amnesty work, and the first donation came rapidly from New Zealand through their high commissioner in Zimbabwe, Chris Laidlaw.

We visited the men in the police camps in Gwanda and Nkayi, and found some of those at Gwanda particularly strange. One looked like a withdrawn Clint Eastwood, with pointy boots, a wide-brimmed leather Stetson, dark glasses and amulets around his neck, sitting on a rock by himself. Where he could have got such clothing was difficult to imagine. By this time Tambolenyoka was back in Gwanda. He seemed to move to and fro as he wished. He had long hair that stood on end, a pendulous, heavy earring dangling from and permanently distorting one of his ear lobes, and the skin around his eyes was always flickering.

We had no idea what the agenda of these men had been and we weren't going to enquire. According to state security, through Minister Emmerson Mnangagwa, there were three groups. One consisted of straightforward former ZPRA. We knew that these were men who had been forced by Zanu (PF) to run to the bush for their lives, and that many of them had terrible grievances, such as having been forced to dance on the graves of their murdered relatives and friends. Another, Super Zapu, was said to be backed by South Africa. The third was a collection of criminals masquerading under any old hat. Mnangagwa did not, of course, mention the fourth element in the unholy mixture, which were the Zanu (PF) *agents provocateurs* from the security forces.

Mzilethi and Bhebhe totally agreed that the men should be kept in the police camps at Gwanda and Nkayi and provided with food until there was some safe place for them to go. But the local administrators were under constant pressure from government authorities, especially Governor Mark Dube, to disperse them. Governor Dube told Mzilethi to disregard any promises of assistance from the Zimbabwe Project. Long after we had established a steady and sufficient supply of food, Dube said about me, 'She is a very, very difficult woman and she will not assist with food for long.' So, he said, the men had better be sent to their homes before they started starving. It was obvious that we needed help and we needed it quickly.

Joshua Nkomo was away but expected back in Zimbabwe on Saturday 18 June. I enlisted the assistance of SK Moyo, one of Nkomo's aides for many years, and collected him from his home at ten that morning. We drove together to Nkomo's house and were waiting in his living room when he arrived from the airport. We didn't waste his time. I explained that the amnesty was in grave danger of being wrecked by those who wanted to disperse the former dissidents. It would take time to set up alternatives for the men, and we needed Nkomo to safeguard that time for us. He said he would. His mind was razor sharp and he immediately understood every implication of the situation.

When I got back to Bulawayo, provincial administrator Mzilethi told me that Nkomo had been in touch with the minister responsible for police, who said he was not aware of any moves to disperse the men from the police camps. Nkomo had laid down specific orders that people, any people, desist from dispersing the men. Governor Mark Dube was reportedly furious.

There was other good news. The Nkayi district administrator Stanley Bhebhe had come forward with an offer from the local community. If the Zimbabwe Project was willing to help with funds for development, they were prepared to offer the use of eighty-six hectares of land at Nkayi to the men now in the Nkayi police camp. The Zimbabwe Project was only too willing, and an initial eleven former dissidents, including one or two outsiders, such as a son of Stanley Bhebhe, started a little cooperative at Nkayi at the beginning of August and were soon selling vegetables to the local community.

Another group, some of whom had been mining in the Esigodini area near Bulawayo before their enterprises were wrecked by 5 Brigade, wanted to return to digging for gold. We agreed to help and assisted in buying second-hand equipment for their Green Light Mining Cooperative, within which they generously, but with trepidation, accommodated Guyigusu. Eventually, but many months later, the third group, largely from Gwanda police camp, set up an agricultural cooperative on good, well-watered land near Tegwane Secondary School in the Plumtree area. To our surprise this turned out to be the most successful of the three ventures.

On Tuesday 7 June, Makhatini Guduza came to see me for a couple of hours. He was not asking for any help, but I learned that when he went into detention he had had twenty-one cattle, and when he came out he had five. The same sort of ratio applied to his donkeys and goats.

Just after I returned from California there was a report in the newspaper that the courts had ordered the immediate release of two Bawdens from detention. I was petrified, as I thought they were responsible for the bombing of the Brickhills. But then Bryant Elliot told me that these were just members of the family who had been picked up along with the accused.

Guduza was telling me about one of them, Des Bawden, whom he depicted as a very old and helpless man. It turned out he was seventy-three. They had been detained together. Guduza was so glad Des Bawden had been released. He said the old man had been given sheets in jail, but that Guduza had said to him, 'In all your life you have never washed anything and it's too late for you to start now. Give them back and just sleep in your blankets like the rest of us.' So he did. Guduza used to wash Des Bawden's plate for him after meals. He said all Bawden could talk about, think about and dream about were his cattle, and Guduza became very fond of him. Much later I met Des Bawden himself, and he told me that Guduza was a wonderful chap.

Less than two years earlier I had observed people avoiding Dr Nkomo in public places. Now the same people would do anything to assure the chief minister in the president's office how they had always loved, lauded and revered him. He took it so well and always accorded them the same warmth my father accorded the whites who rushed up to him on the streets of Zimbabwe after independence: 'Garfield Todd! Do you remember me? We met twenty years ago … thirty years ago … I've often wondered what happened to you. Where have you been?'

I couldn't be as warm as my father or Nkomo were to the people who had damaged their lives, but I tried to be polite. A few days after 'unity' a senior Zanu (PF) man who had worked in the same building as me for years came to see me. 'I couldn't afford to be seen to be your friend. But I want you to know that I have always really been your friend.'

Today, yes, but, my friend, will the weather be fair tomorrow?

On the evening of 13 July, an unusual group assembled at the New Zealand high commissioner's residence to celebrate my father's eightieth birthday. Chris Laidlaw and his equally esteemed and loved wife Helen Kedgley hosted a relaxed and joyful celebration. Among those present were Joshua Nkomo, Enoch Dumbutshena, Canaan Banana and Nathan Shamuyarira. I said privately to Nkomo during the evening that, however worn out he had told me he was feeling, he seemed indefatigable in his pursuit of peace and development.

'Well,' he said, 'in 1982 I was cut off …' meaning that there had been a lot of wasted time which now had to be caught up on.

The expression in his little, sparkling, dramatic eyes was by now so permanently wounded that he was no longer able to conceal the reality of his breaking heart.

We had a very special present for my father, a collection of about fifty essays or reminiscences of how his life had intertwined with others, revealing just as much about the writers as about him. Included were also some brief letters, such as the one from Memory M'thombeni, recalling the delivery of her father. 'I write to say thank you to Sir Garfield Todd for what he did to save both my granny and my father in the year 1947. Just think of it! If it had not been for Sir Garfield Todd maybe two desperate lives would have been lost.'

The collection gave him so much pleasure, although, he laughingly protested, some of the anecdotes couldn't possibly be true, like the one from grand old man MM Hove about the 1948 elections, when my father won a seat in parliament. 'During or just after that election the bush telegraph buzzed ceaselessly. There were many out of the ordinary messages it delivered, not the least of which was that when you had addressed a farmers' meeting in the Greystone area you said *Let us pray*. The poor farmers waited and waited for the prayer and, when out of sheer curiosity they opened their eyes, you had disappeared.'

Another story, which my father did agree was true, came from Dr Baldwin Sjollema of the World Council of Churches. He recalled a meeting in 1971 of the Programme to Combat Racism in Le Cenacle, a Roman Catholic convent in Geneva, run by nuns. 'It was a rather dull place and one evening after very tough and emotional discussions, you and several others decided to go out and have dinner in town. When you returned to the Convent late in the evening all doors were locked and the lights out. You and Nathan Shamuyarira then decided to climb through an open window. When you jumped down inside, in pitch dark, you and Nathan fell on the bed of a sleeping nun. The poor woman, understandably, got the shock of her life and you probably did too!'

A contribution from John Mukokwayarira gave us all a fright. 'In 1980 after the war I met some young man who, on hearing that I was employed by Garfield Todd, freely confessed that he was one of the two assassins sent out by the Smith regime to kill two men in the Shabani/Belingwe area, Dr Zhou at Mnene Hospital and Mr Todd at Dadaya. One dark night they gunned down Dr Zhou on his doorstep – in cold blood. That was an easy task, he said. But Dr Zhou shall be long remembered by the Mberengwa people, in particular for his selfless dedication and devotion to serve his people. He died for his love of freedom.

'The next was Todd. Easy target, he said, as Todd was always driving alone on lonely dirt farm roads. One bullet would have done a quick job.

A landmine would have scattered him to smithereens. A believable story could have been readily tailored to incriminate the boys (guerrillas). On several occasions they lay in ambush, and surely Todd would drive into the ambush. But for some unknown reason they both lacked the courage or strength to pull the trigger. After a few trials they chose to give up – mission impossible – and had to face the wrath of their master. After this episode the witness said he resigned from the Selous Scout force. This story chilled me to the marrow for its callousness but I'm glad it was said for what it was worth today to the reader.'

There was also a reminiscence from Joshua Nkomo:

It was in March 1962 that I went to the United Nations to address the Committee of 24 on the question of Southern Rhodesia. I teamed up with Willie Musarurwa who was studying in New Jersey. The crucial issue was Rhodesia's 1961 Sandys constitution. The British representative argued that Rhodesia was not a colony and, in any case, this 1961 constitution was designed to bring about majority rule and that was going to happen sooner rather than later. Our salvation depended on destroying that argument and proving that the 1961 constitution would perpetrate white colonial rule for numberless years to come.

I thought that no one but Garfield could come and help me prove the 1961 constitution was dangerous for the black people. I asked Willie to send an urgent telegram to Todd to come and address the Committee of 24. Within two days Garfield reported to the UN in New York. I was so happy. I had heard him speak on several occasions and had been immensely impressed by his oratory. But on this day his oratory was devastating. Facts against the 1961 constitution flowed in fast sequence from his fingertips. I do not think that Garfield can ever repeat his oratory of that day. He spoke like one possessed and he got a most thunderous ovation from all the delegates except, of course, that of Britain. The eventual upshot of that and my representations was that on 21 March 1962 the Committee of 24 overwhelmingly voted in favour of the resolution that Southern Rhodesia was a British colony and Britain had an obligation to decolonise.

What Nkomo did not know was that the British delegate, Sir Hugh Foot, had got in touch with my father and invited him for personal talks that evening. They made firm friends and, in the same year, Sir Hugh, later Lord Caradon, resigned from the British delegation in despair at his government's policy on Rhodesia. 'It will be useless to continue patting ourselves on the back for past achievements and winning debating points against the communists if we are on the wrong side in the struggle between African nationalism and white domination in Africa. We show no concern for the subject African peoples, no indignation at their continued suppression. We are looked upon as the supporters, if not the friends, of Tshombe, Welensky, Salazar and Verwoerd. We may soon be regarded as their accomplices in a policy of repression in southern Africa.'

On Heroes' Day, Thursday 11 August, there were many visitors to the prisons, as on all public holidays. It was fortunate for me that Frank Nyoni was a top security prisoner, because that meant I could speak to him over a receiver in an internal booth. People seeing more ordinary prisoners at Chikurubi Maximum Security Prison now had to stand outside a barbed-wire barricade and shout across a very wide space between the fence and another barbed-wire fence, on the other side of which the prisoners stood, shouting back. The shouting grew louder and louder, more and more desperate, as people increasingly failed to hear each other.

Bryant Elliot had drawn up a petition to the president on behalf of Alibaba Dlodlo, Frank Nyoni, Davityne Moyo and others. They hadn't benefited from the 'unity' amnesty. Even Makhatini Guduza would have been left inside if Stannard hadn't intervened on his behalf. When I rang Stannard to thank him, he said 'that's what friends are for'. I was so thankful to Stannard that I didn't tell him how shocking it really was that a man can taste freedom again just because you happen to know the right people; shocking for all those with no strings to pull.

The petition started off once more affirming their innocence of the crime they were found guilty of (attempting to attack the prime minister's residence), then continued:

> The situation in the country now is materially different from what it was when we were convicted in that the Unity Agreement has been signed and Zapu is an integral part of the government.
>
> As previous members of ZPRA we owed allegiance to Zapu. We wholeheartedly support the Unity Agreement and would like the opportunity to take part in the development of the unified country. We would, therefore, humbly request our release on this basis.
>
> Another reason for requesting our release at this time is the recent General Amnesty. In terms of that amnesty, which was published in a Government Gazette Extraordinary dated 3 May 1988, a free pardon is granted to:

i) All dissidents at large on 19 April 1988 provided that they gave themselves up by 31 May 1988.

ii) Every person who had collaborated with dissidents before 19 April 1988.

iii) Every PF Zapu fugitive from justice.

In addition, we understand that some 75 members of the Zimbabwe National Army, the Support Unit, the Central Intelligence Organisation and Zanu (PF) Youth have been released from prison in terms of the amnesty ...

The only long-term hard labour prisoners who have benefited from the General Amnesty at Chikurubi are those who have a Zanu (PF) background. No ex-member of ZPRA who was serving a long-term sentence has benefited.

In our section at Chikurubi nine persons were released in terms of the amnesty on 27 May 1988. Four of these were SAMUAL CHAYANA, CHARLES SIMANGO, GEORGE CHIHWAYI and JULIUS GWATIRERA. These four were members of the Zimbabwe Army and had been sentenced to death for murdering Lt Ndlovu and three others in 1983.

Another two who were released were ISHMAEL MUTSUNGE and LEWIS GABA. They were members of Zanu (PF) and the Special Constabulary and had been convicted of murdering a PF Zapu supporter in Lower Gweru in October 1984. They had originally been sentenced to death but this was changed on appeal to twenty years in prison.

Also released on 27 May 1988 was JAMES ARIVERA. He was a member of the Support Unit and had been sentenced to thirteen years in prison for murdering a Zapu supporter in Bulawayo.

Another person released on the same day was ROBERT JAMU. He had been convicted of murdering a Zapu supporter in Chipinge in 1986 and had been sentenced to 22 years in prison.

The last person released in our section on 27 May 1988 was GEORGE JIRONGA. He was a Zanu (PF) District Chairman and had been sentenced to fifteen years in prison in December 1987 for leading a mob which had dragged a PF Zapu supporter out of the police station at Kwe Kwe and had beaten him to death.

They continued listing the names and circumstances of others released, and concluded:

It appears that it is a common feature of all those released from Chikurubi that they were previously members of the Security Forces and had been convicted of crimes arising from the serious political divisions within the country at the time. We were also members of the Security Forces ... and would respectfully submit that the same considerations should apply in our case and that we should also be released.

I was so anxious that people in Zimbabwe should have the chance to know more about Nkomo and his past. In the next few weeks he would be touring Masvingo and Mashonaland, and so people would have the opportunity to see and hear him again, but in the secret depths of my heart I couldn't believe that this could continue for long. As soon as people started laughing with him and loving him, the hatred of others, such as Nkala, Nyagumbo and Mugabe, would again be inflamed against him.

Nkomo's excellent biography, *The Story of My Life*, published in 1984, was still not available in Zimbabwe. It was dedicated to his wife, *MaFuyana, who has stood by me through it all*. The book was written after he had fled Zimbabwe and gone into exile, and he probably thought that his reflections on Robert Mugabe then would not promote unity now.

On the way back from Chikurubi Prison on 12 August, I gave a man a lift and asked what he thought about the unity accord. He said we would never have peace until Ndabaningi Sithole was included. To say that I was startled was an understatement. He said Sithole had never forgotten that it was he who had led the breakaway from Nkomo and that it was he who had formed Zanu. From what I had been told, Sithole had started going to pieces during his long detention in prison. He went into self-imposed exile among his few but very important fellow prisoners, one of whom was Robert Mugabe. Mugabe filled the leadership vacuum successfully for a very short time, then failed when Julius Nyerere and Kenneth Kaunda demanded the reinstatement of Sithole, and then finally succeeded for keeps. Sithole's first book, *African Nationalism*, published in 1959, was dedicated to his wife Canaan, from whom he was eventually divorced, and their children:

To my family
Wife Canaan (Land of Milk and Honey)
Daughters: Sipikelelo (perseverance); Sifiso (wish); Sikulukekile (freedom)
And Sons: Dingindlela (Find the Way); Zibonele (Do It Yourself)

The names of the children pretty well summed up Sithole's life. My mother said he was the brightest pupil ever to go through Dadaya. But poor Sithole lost his wife and then his country and was now in exile. He had to flee, as he was being accused of plotting to overthrow the sovereign state of Zimbabwe.

It was rumoured, without proof, that Sithole had links to the insurgent Renamo (MNR) of Mozambique, and that there was widespread but unreported violence in parts of Manicaland, Chipinge and Chimanimani, where people sometimes slept in the bush. I was at a dinner for which one of my fellow guests, a doctor, was late. When he arrived, he was very distressed. That day, he said, sixteen children had been brought in from Chipinge with their heads hammered in. Then a truckload of wounded soldiers was brought in. A few days afterwards, Karl Maier, now writing for the *Christian Science Monitor*, rang to say there was a rumour that one of the funeral parlours in town was inundated with the bodies of thirty soldiers, some brought in in their sleeping bags.

The hitchhiker who told me he thought Sithole must be brought into the unity accord was about twenty-nine, a worker with maybe two years of secondary education. He gave no evidence of remotely liking or admiring Sithole, but said that if people in Zimbabwe knew of the suffering going on at the hands of MNR on our border with Mozambique, 'they will stop liking our government and that's why our government doesn't give us the news'.

On Thursday 18 August I went to an American reception at their beautiful official residence in Tina Close, Chisipite. It was held upstairs on the veranda outside the lounge and we looked across at the American flag flying at half mast against a vivid sky. The news that morning had been of the shocking explosion that had blown President Zia-ul-Haq, the US ambassador to Pakistan, and others out of the sky, hence the flag at half mast. It was a more fortunate ending to suffer, however, than that inflicted by Zia on his predecessor Bhutto, which still appalled me in retrospect – the humiliation, the torture and the hanging.

President Zia-ul-Haq was one of the heads of state who had attended Zimbabwe's independence celebrations. At Rufaro Stadium on that night in April 1980 there must have been a momentary lapse in security as dignitaries left the stadium and, for a few seconds, I found myself next to him in a crush of people with no intervening bodyguards. He looked small and frightened and furious.

CHAPTER 20

Looting

TRYING TO FIND OUT WHAT HAD HAPPENED TO LAND BOUGHT
by government for resettlement with donor funds that had come
mainly from Britain, Chief Minister Joshua Nkomo travelled the country
in August and September 1988. It was said that, of the funds provided,
Zimbabwe had spent £47 million by 1985, with which well over three
million hectares had been purchased, and that £3 million that had not been
spent had been returned by a largely disinterested Zimbabwe government
to Britain. President Mugabe and colleagues had other matters on their minds
and weren't wasting much time or thought on the ownership or use of land
by their fellow citizens. I knew this at first hand. My father's Hokonui Ranch,
well watered and bordering crowded communal lands, had been offered
twice to government for acquisition, but no one was interested.

Before Nkomo left Harare, he assembled information on farms acquired.
Just before he arrived in Matabeleland South, Governor Mark Dube and the
head of the provincial police force based in Gwanda went on unscheduled
leave. That was a dramatic illustration of how little they respected the status
of the chief minister in the president's office and with what contempt they
viewed the unity accord. In their absence, Nkomo was attended to by the
provincial administrator.

When they met in Gwanda, Nkomo asked the provincial administrator
how many farms government had acquired in Matabeleland South. The
PA was obviously ill at ease and flustered, but said he thought there were
fifteen. 'Really,' said Nkomo, taking a list of farms from his pocket. 'This is
very interesting, because the people in Harare think there are sixty-four. So
let's just visit all the names on this list and see what the true situation is.'

On the second day of touring, the PA begged to be excused from accompanying Nkomo as, he said, he was beginning to feel very sick. Flu or
something. Nkomo assured him that he would undoubtedly start feeling
better as the day wore on and did not excuse him. The PA had already
admitted that he had been instructed by Governor Mark Dube to tell Nkomo
that government had bought only fifteen farms in the province.

As they travelled from farm to farm, the workers assembled, so happy to see Nkomo, who chatted easily to them, admiring the beautiful cattle and the wonderful farm. So when he asked to whom it belonged, they freely said, 'Governor Dube,' or whoever the chef in possession of the land was.

'How many cattle on this farm?'

'One thousand,' or however many there were.

'And to whom do they belong?'

'Governor Dube,' or whoever the chef was.

But there were not only cattle on these farms. There were government tractors, trucks from the district development fund, and where did all these cattle come from?

One of the farms turned out to 'belong' to the indisposed provincial administrator.

When Nkomo reported his findings on Matabeleland South, President Mugabe gave the impression of being stunned. Only one word could describe what had been going on, and that word was looting. Now we could begin to understand why people like Governor Dube were at all stages trying to sabotage the return of the dissidents to society. Their disruptive presence in the bush was a wonderful cover for the grabbing of land, animals and equipment and an excuse not to resettle the landless people for whom it was claimed the farms had been acquired.

Despite Nyagumbo and others who hated Nkomo, the integration of PF Zapu and Zanu (PF) seemed to be going quite well. One of the people being particularly friendly post-unity was Deputy Minister Amina Hughes. Just before the seventieth birthday in July of Senator Joe Culverwell, the Deputy Minister for Education, she told me that she had got hold of some fake rhino horn powder as his birthday present. Rhino horn is reputedly a powerful aphrodisiac, hence the plight of the rhinos.

I went to a small American embassy party in honour of the new head of the US Information Services, who was originally a Palestinian. I asked his American wife how they had met. She said her parents had sent her to Britain with instructions to come back with an earl, a duke or any other kind of British aristocrat. After quite a short time she had fallen desperately in love and wrote to her parents: 'Would you mind a refugee?'

Senator Culverwell was a fellow guest at the party, and we were on the balcony watching the most glorious sunset. It was the sort of evening that, depending on your circumstances, could inspire thoughts of rhino horn. So Joe told me of this wonderful gift that Amina had given him. He said, 'So many people want it! Comrade Marere (a fellow deputy minister) has offered me Z$10 for just a little pinch!' Of course, I didn't tell him that I knew about it and that it was fake. I just said I wondered how Amina could have got hold of it. Could it have been from Mrs Victoria Chitepo, Minister for Tourism and Natural Resources? Joe looked horrified.

I wrote to Dan Stannard to update him about the Zimbabwe Project's continuing activities with the returnees. The whole thing had been a complete mess. Dawson Sanyangore, Director of Social Welfare, kept delaying action with the promise that he was assembling a team of psychiatrists and doctors to interview them. What would happen then was not, it seemed, of concern.

Many of the returnees were still at police camps throughout Matabeleland and relations were becoming very strained. The only group resettled so far was the one at Nkayi, for whom we had provided picks, axes, food and so on. Past accusations in 1983 were that, under my leadership, the Zimbabwe Project was seen as a Zapu support group and that people suspected our relationship with dissidents – rotten innuendoes like that. And now here we were, feeding them and even providing axes. It was macabre. But somehow, I thought it would work.

I had written to the German agency, Bread for the World, appealing once more for help and submitting proposals for $250 000 for development projects for the returnees. A reply telex had arrived. *Bread For The World Prepared To Help.* Joy! I hoped the brave people of Nkayi would benefit as much from all this donor assistance as had the men at Vukuzenzele.

I would never forget Christmas 1981, sitting in a tent at Vukuzenzele with the disabled ex-combatants on their piece of land which they were physically, and most painfully, clearing, limping from tree to tree doing the stumping.

One of them said this to me: 'Some time in the future you will come back to us again, tired from your journey. And, instead of sitting with us in a tent, we will take you to a building and we will unlock our office. There will be a switch and we will turn it on and then there will be light. There will be chairs, and you will be able to sit down and eat at a table.'

It was at that stage, just before he was detained, that Lookout Masuku visited those men, praised their hard work and said: 'One day you will wake in the morning to the cry of a baby. Then you will know that indeed this is your home.' All these things had come to pass.

Early in September, we went to a Zimbabwe Project quarterly meeting at Victoria Falls. There we also delighted in two projects we'd had a hand in – Enos Dube's Guyu Safaris, and the Black Merchants, a band performing at the Makasa Sun Hotel. The Black Merchants were the former New Tone Sound Band, whose instruments were seized by the state in 1982. They were never returned, but somehow this band had kept battling on.

Two prominent members of the former PF Zapu were named as envoys, more fruits of unity. Isaac Nyathi, who was detained with Masuku and Dabengwa after Nitram was banned, became the new high commissioner to Nigeria and Ghana. Arthur Chadzingwa was the ambassador to Algeria. Arthur was someone loved by people in all groups. He was a candidate for PF Zapu in the 1980 elections, but was prevented from campaigning in his home area of Manicaland by members of ZANLA. At least they said 'sorry, Arthur' and didn't visit violence upon him.

During the time of the Pearce Commission, when thousands of people were locked up by the Smith regime, Arthur was for some time held in a cell with Charlton C Ngcebetsha. He helped the time pass by teaching Arthur cricket in a cell with no ball and no bat. Arthur said he got pretty good at shouting HOWZAT! Arthur also told me that Ngcebetsha had lamented the fact that most great men like Winston Churchill and Garfield Todd had disappointing children.

Charlton Cezani Ngcebetsha was born in the Transkei in 1909, and moved north to Ntabazinduna, outside Bulawayo, as a missionary for the Presbyterian Church. He became heavily involved in education, business, politics and the press, and was close to Joshua Nkomo. He founded the *African Home News* in 1953, which was closed in 1965 when he was detained in Gonakudzingwa. Charlton Ngcebetsha was quite irrepressible, and somehow, within a short time of his detention, the first edition of the *Gonakudzingwa Home News* hit the streets of Bulawayo.

Albert Ngwenya and I visited a gold mine near Gwanda. The man who came to ask for help for the miners said we must see for ourselves, as he couldn't describe all the hard work that had been put into the venture. Our arrival was unexpected and we found two youths in rags and an older man hastily putting garments over his skin as he saw us approaching. Everything had been done by hand. A shaft had been sunk about twenty metres. There was a series of heart-shaking ladders made of little branches going from level to level. The rock was then extracted, smashed with hammers by hand, sifted in a sieve with water and then, with luck, after hours of sifting and changing the water, there would be a tiny, milky glimmer, and that was gold.

Bit by bit a gram would be extracted from hundreds of kilos of other substances.

The background was unusual. Mr Ncube, who had pegged the site, had one night had a dream of the location – koppies on the left, arable land on the right, a path going round the koppies, a big tree growing just to the left of the path. In the dream he was told that he would find gold under that tree. Mr Ncube searched, found the site and the tree, uprooted the tree and started digging. For the first ten metres, all by hand, there was just clay, clay; heavy, uninteresting clay. He started digging in 1984. The local villagers thought he was mad, and laughed all the more the deeper the clay went. He persevered. He had struck rock about a year before and then, bit by bit, in all the sieving, came the first little milky glimmers. While we were standing around the shaft a villager came past on a bicycle, stopped, looked at us and laughed. 'Found gold?' The answer was presumed obvious, and he went on his way, laughing. Ncube had been very careful not to let others know of his little successes.

The marvellous thing about the Zimbabwe Project was that we had such freedom, albeit hard-won and thus infinitely precious. We could put small amounts of money even into dreams. Quite often the dreams turned into reality. Only recently I'd been sitting with the chairman of a successful agricultural cooperative about forty-five kilometres from Harare, overlooking four fish ponds they had dug and stocked with 3 500 bream per pond. Beyond the ponds were beautiful hectares of ripe wheat, and behind us were fat cattle and huge Brahman bulls. We were thinking back six years to when this cooperative was renting a farm and borrowing hand implements, and their medical orderly had taken me to their dilapidated house where about sixteen sick members were lying miserably on the floor with not even aspirin. Then troops moved onto their rented farm, as most of the cooperative members were formerly ZPRA, and they had a terrible time.

We helped in small ways to keep them going, and it was magic for me to sit on a mound of clay by the fish ponds, quietly talking to Andrew Nyathi, chairman of Simukai, *Stand up and Be Counted* Cooperative. Even a year earlier he had been at risk, as he was a former ZPRA commander. Now he was sought out by everyone, including the government, as an expert on cooperative development. Andrew's voice was even more difficult to hear and to interpret than mine. But he didn't have to say much. All I had to do was see his eyes moving over the successes of Simukai evident before us. All I had to say was, 'Sometimes our dreams come true,' and watch him nod.

A few years before, I had given a lift to a beautiful woman and her gorgeous son, who was about four months old, from that cooperative. I asked the boy's name, and when she laughed and said, 'Gromyko,' I knew his father had trained in the Soviet Union. She later had another son and announced to me that he had been named after my father, Garfield.

Shadreck BO Gutto, the Kenyan academic, was 'requested' to leave Zimbabwe, where he had been teaching at the university. He was given forty-eight hours to clear out and went to Norway. Paul Themba Nyathi, our director, returned from leave in Zambia, where he had bumped into some representatives of a group of 300 exiles who were still too scared to return to Zimbabwe. Eleven of their number had gone home the previous September and promised to write to their comrades to tell them what life was like. As the people in Zambia hadn't heard a word from them, they assumed they were either locked up in Stops Camp, or dead. So the safe return of these 300 would probably be a task for us in the New Year. We hadn't yet finished coping with the former dissidents. Forty-three of them were doing very well in the new cooperative in the Nkayi area, but the rest still had to establish themselves.

I went with my parents to see *A World Apart*. Barbara Hershey played Ruth First. Not many minutes elapsed before we were all trying not to cry. At the end of the film, my mother said, 'I couldn't have borne to see that without you both being with me.' Although we never had as tough a time as the Slovos, there were some uncanny resemblances to our own experiences.

I hadn't realised until after the film how much my hunger strike and force-feeding in jail in 1972 had affected my father. The strike was an attempt to get us out of jail or before the courts before the Pearce Commission, then testing opinion regarding a proposed deal between the British and the Rhodesians, left the country. Although I hadn't actually contemplated suicide – I thought at the time that other people were quite prepared to kill me without my help – the prison doctor had left me after the first afternoon's unsuccessful force-feeding with his instructions to the surrounding prison staff ringing in my ears: 'Don't leave her with anything she could use to commit suicide.'

There was a really terrible Anglican chaplain who came to see me in Marandellas Prison after I had started the hunger strike, but before I was moved to Chikurubi Prison, where the force-feeding took place. The

Reverend Bill Clark, chaplain general of the prison services, had a pleasant image, which, fortunately, he soon destroyed in front of me. He had come to my cell in Marandellas to try to persuade me to stop the hunger strike. He said he had been to see my father in Gatooma Prison and had told him that I was on hunger strike.

'And what did he say?' I asked.

'He said that if he could get his hands on you he would put you over his knee and beat you.'

That one sentence tore the scales from my eyes, and I was then able to observe this Anglican priest as the most dangerous of my enemies. I knew it was quite impossible for my father to have that reaction or to use those words.

Later I discovered that, after the priest had left him, my father had gone on hunger strike to support me. He hadn't said a word to anyone about it. My father was fortunate in that he had a flush lavatory in his cell, and so he flushed all food down it, in segments, as the prison staff kept checking on him. They were wiser than the Anglican priest in their knowledge of my father. He told me he was very worried about me and, as he was sixty-four and in bad health at the time, he thought it wouldn't take him long to collapse. Then, if he was found in such a state, something might be revealed about him that would lead to better conditions for me too. But thankfully, before he collapsed, pressure on the regime became so great that we were released to house arrest.

Writer Doris Lessing visited Zimbabwe in December. It was with mixed feelings that I agreed to a request by her friend, the brilliant university lecturer from Matabeleland, Anthony Chennels, to look after her for the first two days, as I thought she would be formidable. I found that I was completely enchanted by her. She was very direct and without pretension. She was beautiful, perceptive and kind. I introduced her to Kathy Bond-Stewart, who was 'animating literature' with women in rural areas. This was a great success, and resulted in the Lessing itinerary being amended so that she could go on a three-day tour of Matabeleland with Kathy and Talent Nyathi, wife of Andrew Nyathi of Simukai. Matabeleland was becoming so popular that I was now trying to steer people off to the misery of Manicaland and other places.

It was amazing how old myths still persisted and how they still hurt. A Canadian from an NGO/trade union background came to see me and explained how he had been informed that the Zimbabwe Project had always been pro-Ndebele, pro-Zapu, pro-Matabeleland. He related this to me as if these attitudes were totally praiseworthy. He wouldn't have, even only a year before, but now the Zimbabwe Project was apparently in vogue.

I found to my mortification that I was trembling and hoped he wouldn't notice. I carefully explained that this accusation had first been levelled at us while we were still in London, before Zimbabwe's independence. I said we had received a letter stating that Zanu was unhappy because most of the Zimbabwe Project's money was going to refugees in Zambia and Botswana, the implication being that most of our money was going to Zapu. I said our administrator, Brother Arthur Dupuis, had then analysed all our expenditure and found that two-thirds of our funds were being spent in Mozambique, and the other third was shared between Botswana and Zambia. Quite by accident, our funds had been correctly spent in terms of numbers of refugees, as about two-thirds were in Mozambique.

Then, I said, the same sort of accusations had been levelled in 1983 when I was director. To answer the accusations, our trustees had insisted on a breakdown of expenditure between former ZANLA and ZPRA. I had refused to participate in this exercise because it was totally foreign to our way of work. All staff knew they would probably be sacked if I found any one of them enquiring about the political background of anyone who came to us for help. So the trustees, without my help, did their own breakdown, and found that two-thirds of our money had been spent on former ZANLA and about one third on former ZPRA. Again this was by accident, not design, but again it correctly reflected the ratio, as there were about two ZANLA to every ZPRA.

So, said this guy, quite stunned, what I have heard about you is not true? In a way it was quite amusing to see someone so shocked and disappointed that we were *not* a Zapu front.

Doris McBride came up from South Africa in December and stayed with Phyllis Naidoo. Doris's husband Derrick was on Robben Island and her son Robert was on death row in Pretoria. These were nightmares made tangible.

Robert's fiancée, Paula Leyden, rang me from Pretoria. All avenues of clemency for Robert had been exhausted, except for an appeal that had been lodged with President PW Botha. Paula told me that at the end of the next week, the authorities would take a break from hanging people over the Christmas period and, if Robert was not executed by then, he should be safe for about another month.

His mother was roaming the world looking for support in bringing pressure on the South African authorities not to hang him. Robert was known as the Magoo's Bar bomber, and was responsible for an explosion that had killed three people in a Durban pub in 1986. His accomplice turned state evidence and had been freed.

I felt unutterably helpless when confronted with the brave misery of Doris and Paula Leyden. I knew you could multiply this misery, in one way or another, all over the world, but that didn't ease the pain for anyone. Once you had been sentenced to death in South Africa, I was told, you were kept in isolation. Robert had been kept in isolation for two years, since he was twenty-one. Each week you heard the sheriff coming. If he passed your door, you were lucky – you might have another week, or month, or year. If he stopped and came in, he would have either an affirmative answer from the president that he had granted clemency, or a statement that you were to be hanged within the week. Paula told me that some of those to be hanged screamed, cried and fought, and so they were somehow subdued sufficiently to be taken to the gallows.

Doris was at my place one night to meet people I thought, rather forlornly, might be able to help, such as Joe Culverwell, Deputy Minister of Education. I kept imagining what her tortured mind must be suffering, moving within her huge, ill body. She had no money and no employment. Whenever there was a pause in the conversation, I could almost feel her thoughts back with her son in the death cells of Pretoria; back with her husband on Robben Island.

'I am trying all I can,' she said. 'But I can't seem to do enough.'

We would all keep trying in our different ways. I had seen, and therefore believed in, miracles. But miracles demand a lot of hard work.

Paul Themba Nyathi returned from Zambia with the observation that we must save Zimbabwe from the one-party state at all costs.

'We?' I enquired. 'Save?'

Well, yes, I agreed, but how?

Part of the time Paul was in Zambia, he was doing an evaluation for Oxfam. Almost immediately he was introduced to the Oxfam person in charge of condoms. At that point, he said, he was deserted by any traces of libido. He was told that AIDS was no joke in Zambia. I hadn't heard of it being a joke anywhere. Then he was put in a tacky new Lusaka hotel where, he said, you could literally hear the person next door drop a newspaper. Unfortunately for him, the guest next door was not wont to just dropping newspapers. He was a soldier on leave with at least one new woman per night. Paul said *he*, not the soldier, got up red-eyed and exhausted each morning. The soldier got up bright-eyed and refreshed. So eventually the receptionist was beseeched for help, and she gave Paul the use of a television set. Paul asked what he should do when television went off the air for the night, because the soldier didn't. She was obviously impressed. 'You mean he continues *after* 11 p.m.?'

My father rang one night to say something serious had been tucked into the boring television news. Following allegations in the *Chronicle* about involvement of government ministers in what was termed the Willowgate scandal, Dr Sadza, head of the Mass Media Trust, had summoned Geoff Nyarota, editor of the *Chronicle*, from Bulawayo to Harare. Willowgate was essentially about the exposure of corruption, initially through the *Chronicle*, in the distribution of vehicles to cabinet ministers and others from Willowvale Motor Industries, and the forward sale at enormous profits of those vehicles. Among the ministers implicated through investigations under Nyarota's brave editorship were Maurice Nyagumbo (Political Affairs), Callistus Ndlovu (Industry and Technology), Dzingai Mutumbuka (Higher Education), Enos Nkala (Defence), Frederick Shava (Political Affairs) and the governor of Matabeleland North, Jacob Mudenda. Many others from different spheres of society were also involved.

I was a director of Hokonui Ranching, which held shares in Zimbabwe Newspapers. So, as a shareholder in Zimpapers, I dashed off a telegram to Dr Sadza:

RE: ZTV NEWS TONIGHT. THE CHRONICLE HAS GIVEN REALITY TO ZIMBABWE'S CLAIM THAT OUR PRESS CAN BE FREE, BRAVE AND HONEST. IF THE EDITOR OF THE CHRONICLE IS SEEN TO BE AT RISK THEN THE INTEGRITY OF THE MASS MEDIA TRUST WILL OBVIOUSLY BE JEOPARDISED, WHICH WILL BE A DISASTER FOR ZIMBABWE'S IMAGE ABROAD AND AT HOME.

On New Year's Day my father had formally married Talent and Andrew Nyathi at Simukai, and, ever since, had been referred to by Andrew as 'my priest'. Now my father was marrying Sly Masuku, chairman of the Vukuzenzele war-wounded cooperative, to Busi, who had been working in my parents' house for a couple of years. Anyone who had trained and worked in my parents' house was most marriageable, because my mother was such an expert in cooking, sewing, gardening and making a wonderful home in every way. The marriage was on Christmas Eve, and on Christmas Day there was a great celebration at Vukuzenzele, with hundreds of people singing, feasting and dancing. Sly was thrilled by the attendance of his former comrades-in-arms, Dumiso Dabengwa and Akim Ndlovu, among many other celebrities.

My sister Cynthia and brother-in-law Derrick Edge were visiting us from Australia. When I told Derrick about Sly's wedding, I learned that Derrick, then with the Rhodesian police, had been involved in 'mopping-up operations' after the Zapu/ANC group, including Sly and the South African hero Chris Hani, was routed in the Wankie incursions of 1967.

Derrick said he had had to take a commander of that group and others back to the Zambezi River to establish where they had crossed from Zambia. He said the commander was a most impressive man, and Derrick had always hoped he hadn't been hanged. One time, when Derrick was on guard, he saw the commander inching towards a cache of weapons, and Derrick slipped the safety catch on his own weapon. At the click, this man turned to Derrick, laughed and said, '*Why* couldn't you have gone to sleep like everyone else?' I consulted Sly, who said the man Derrick was referring to was Moffatt Hadebe, and that he was alive and well and living in Bulawayo. The news made Derrick's Christmas.

Some years later, Hadebe came to the Zimbabwe Project office to meet me. It so happened, I explained to him, that I was at that very moment writing a card to Derrick for his birthday. Hadebe asked for a piece of paper and the use of a pen, and also wrote a message for Derrick. Visiting Cyndie and Derrick in Queensland in 2005, I found they had kept Hadebe's message:

Happy birth to Derrick Edge on the 5th October 1992. Old friends meet as new friends. Yours sincerely, Moffat L Hadebe.

Zimbabwe is like an enormous kaleidoscope. People keep being shaken up and, each year, as if they were tiny pieces of coloured glass, they fall into different patterns.

CHAPTER 21

The Sandura Commission

S WAPO'S REPRESENTATIVE, KAPUKA NAUYALA, GOT 1989 OFF TO a positive start by ringing at dawn to joyfully sing 'Happy New Year to you!', adapted from 'Happy Birthday to you'. Later I set off for Chikurubi Maximum Prison.

Following the incarceration of South African agents Kevin Woods, Philip Conjwayo, Mike Smith and Barry Bawden, visible security had been massively increased. There were sweeps of new roads and army outposts and a stout security fence around the whole complex, so parking anywhere near the prison was impossible. At the main gate all but one of the benches for visitors had been removed. The officials were courteous, but much more inquisitive than in the past.

I was visiting Alibaba Dlodlo. Usually I knew some prison guards, but not that day. A seasoned-looking official told his colleagues that the local army chief would have to be informed of my visit, as Dlodlo had been sentenced for attacking the residence of the president when he was still the prime minister. While the official was ringing the chief, he asked for my identification disc. As he started explaining that Dlodlo was being visited by a white woman whose name was … I handed the ID to him, and he read, with rising voice … 'Judith *Garfield Todd*'. Whoever the army chief was, there seemed to be no problem, but a lot of laughter instead.

Alibaba wasn't looking well. His eyes were tired and despondent. No food parcels were allowed that day, and there were still no signs of amnesty being extended to any former ZPRA prisoners.

President Mugabe rather belatedly appointed a commission under the chairmanship of Mr Justice Sandura to look into the affairs of Willowvale Motor Industries, a wholly owned subsidiary of the Industrial Development Corporation. The commission was specifically directed to conduct a public inquiry into the distribution of vehicles assembled by WMI, the circumstances in which motor vehicles were allocated or supplied directly by Willowvale to persons other than dealers in the motor trade, and subsequent dealings with such motor vehicles.

This was in response to increasing demands for action against corruption and the abuse of privilege by powerful people first revealed in the *Chronicle* under the editorship of Geoffrey Nyarota. It was also believed to be a mechanism, unknown to Sandura, for Mugabe to get rid of people who he believed were becoming too powerful.

Kembo Mohadi, the MP for Beitbridge, called on me now and then when parliament was sitting. He had recovered from the violence of the 1985 elections, and the consequences – torture – of winning the seat for PF Zapu. But he still said, 'I'm not enjoying my stay in Zimbabwe very much.'

Another impressive man was Stanley Bhebhe, district administrator for Nkayi. It was because of him that the settlement of forty-three former dissidents at Nkayi had gone so well. But it seemed there were people still determined to do all in their power to disrupt the programmes for ex-dissidents and to wreck unity, and I had started getting anxious for Bhebhe about three months before he was arrested by PISI, Police Internal Security and Intelligence. He was refused bail on the grounds that he might tamper with witnesses and was held in Bulawayo's Grey Street Prison. Accusations against him were that he stole a length of piping 3 m × 40 cm; two bicycles, said to have been donated by Unicef; a new pump donated by the Zimbabwe Project to former dissidents, which he was said to have sold and replaced with an old one; and livestock – two cows, which he allegedly swapped for an ox.

When I heard the news I contacted the lawyer David Coltart, and he brought an application to the High Court for Bhebhe's release. I wrote to Coltart, saying: 'The Zimbabwe Project, of which I am the former director and for which I now work part time, has raised $250 000 for development in Nkayi. For us this is a large sum of money and we have a heavy responsibility to our West German donors to make sure that the development plans are implemented and the funds are not dissipated. The District Administrator is naturally a key figure to us in this regard.'

The police dropped the Zimbabwe Project charge. They never consulted us about anything. The pump we supplied for Nkayi was bought in 1983 and had been working on two cooperatives before Nkayi.

Bail for Bhebhe was turned down by Mr Justice Blackie in the High Court, Bulawayo. David Coltart telephoned, almost speechless with amazement. I wondered if Blackie, whom I didn't know, could be susceptible to pressure. David spoke most highly of him and said, no, he couldn't. But, almost as an afterthought, he said that one of the papers presented in the application for bail was the letter from me, and maybe Blackie didn't like my name.

His speculation was useful. Up to then I had thought of reconciliation only in a very one-sided way, as blacks being amazingly generous to whites, or, in another way, as 'us', those who didn't support white supremacy, to 'them', the Rhodesian Front. I knew I was bad at reconciliation. It took me years to be able to think kindly of, for example, Chris Andersen. But I'd never before considered the fact that there could be any necessity for anyone to be magnanimous towards me in reconciliation from their side. That was valuable if belated knowledge.

So we were in trouble again, and I tried to understand why.

- Former dissidents were successfully settled in Nkayi with the blessing of the local council. This could not have happened without the good offices of the district administrator, Stanley Bhebhe.

- All was going well. Positive attention was eventually paid by the media, both local and international, and Bread for the World had donated $250 000 for development in Nkayi, focused around the returnees.

- All kept getting better and better, except for people like Governor Mark Dube of Matabeleland South. Leases for government-bought land were cancelled in anticipation of resettlement programmes, as the area was now peaceful. People, mainly Zanu (PF) chefs, got notice to move their cattle off this state land. Governor Dube lost his temper and tried to shoot an investigating journalist, Gibbs Dube, from the *Chronicle*. Fortunately, Governor Dube's wife grabbed the gun before a bullet could hit the target.

- As things seemed to be under control in Nkayi, the Zimbabwe Project concentrated on trying to find land in Matabeleland South for the former dissidents who were still in police camps. Eventually, to our surprise and delight, permission was given for the resettlement of these men at Rustler's Gorge, land on the border of Botswana on the Shashe River. Paul Themba Nyathi, our director, was away at the time. I was overjoyed by the news, but nonetheless had a prickle of anxiety in the marrow of my bones about why, after being difficult for so long, Governor Mark Dube and Minister Enos Chikowore were now being helpful.

I rang Edward Ndlovu, who so recently had been a detainee facing charges of treason, lying on the concrete floor of a cell with no medical attention. But now he was Deputy Minister of Water and Energy Resources in the government of national unity. Rustler's Gorge fell within his constituency. Edward laughed. He said he knew the farm well. It was established in colonial times as an irrigation scheme, but had failed, as there were no local markets for the produce. Moreover, people on Rustler's Gorge had to be armed because of elephants. Finally, it was opposite a cattle station just across the Shashe River in Botswana. If you put active young men onto Rustler's Gorge and provided inputs, they would grow wonderful vegetables, find they couldn't sell them and had no money, and then, of course, they would start rustling cattle from Botswana.

The police, who on the whole had been very helpful, were all set to start moving men to Rustler's Gorge that week, and we had been making necessary arrangements regarding food and shelter. We halted the whole exercise. So the men were still scattered in police camps throughout Matabeleland South and probably getting very restive.

On Thursday 22 December 1988, I flew to Bulawayo en route to Hokonui Ranch for Christmas. The Zimbabwe Project offices in both Harare and Bulawayo were meant to be shut, but in Bulawayo I found a distressed Nkosana Mguni still working. He said Morgan Nkomo, also known as Guyigusu or Morgan Sango, had been in to say that two former dissidents had been arrested for past events and would appear in court on 29 December. Mguni was all set to go and rescue the men from custody. When I asked how the dreaded Guyigusu had happened to come to us, Mguni said he had been sent by the PF Zapu office in Bulawayo.

I suggested that we should be very careful, and that maybe Mguni should close the office immediately and go on leave. If there was injustice, it could be tackled after we reopened on 3 January 1989. The men concerned were used to being held by the police and would survive. I was deeply suspicious of what seemed a smoothly constructed triangle: Guyigusu, PF Zapu Bulawayo and the Zimbabwe Project. Mguni agreed and, with relief, closed the offices.

Since then I'd heard that Guyigusu and two other men might yet be charged with the murder of the priest at Empandeni Mission, which had apparently occurred the day after the amnesty expired at midnight on 31 May 1988. I rang Mguni, told him of this and suggested that he not have anything to do with Guyigusu. But this wasn't quite possible, as we had to be polite to those who we feared wielded great, albeit negative, power. People from the region discreetly told us that Guyigusu had allegedly been an agent of Governor Dube for a long time, and that Tambolenyoka was an agent for his relative, the politician Naison Ndlovu. And now we had heard that the senior executive officer of the Nkayi Council, Msibele, had been detained by PISI, along with the finance officer, Ndlovu.

After Christmas, two gentlemen from the president's office called on me in Harare, and I made them coffee. One, Comrade Renzo, had become a sort of friend. On one occasion I even penetrated the depressing CIO corridor at Harare Central police station to see him on behalf of someone in trouble. At the reception desk I asked for Comrade Renzo. The police seemed not to know him, and asked what section he was in. I said that he was in the president's office, the polite name for CIO.

One of the police laughed and said: 'Are you a new somebody?'

'No,' I answered. 'I'm an old somebody.'

'Then you should know that the president's office is not here.'

'How about CIO?'

'Oh!' and he gave me the directions.

To get to CIO, I had to go past homicide. In fact, as I walked along that corridor with different signs outside each section, I felt I was graduating in horror. At the very end I was peeped at through a slit in a steel door, which was then opened by people who looked thuggish and bored – a bad combination. Comrade Renzo was different. He was a university graduate, very smooth, and beautifully dressed from his shoes to his spectacles.

When he came to my office, Renzo was accompanied by Comrade Nyakanyaka, who wore dark glasses and was missing a front tooth, and thus tried not to smile openly. I asked what Nyakanyaka meant. Renzo laughed and said, 'Trouble.' I said to Nyakanyaka that I was sure he wasn't born with that name but, trying not to smile, he said he was. If so, he must have issued from a spectacularly unhappy marriage, as the dictionary definition of 'nyakanyaka' is provocation or public disturbance, or general disagreement.

The men were pleasant. Renzo did the talking and Nyakanyaka just listened, his hand covering his mouth. Renzo asked if I had anything interesting to tell them.

'About what?'

'About anything.'

I was appalled that they could think of me as a potential informer, but I did tell them about the arrest of DA Bhebhe. 'We have had a setback.' They were not in the least surprised by the news, which meant they had it already. Then I took a risk, based on my knowledge of the loathing that Mnangagwa, then State Security, seemingly had for Nkala, then Home Affairs, and Nkala's PISI. I said to Renzo that I gathered Bhebhe had been arrested by PISI. I hadn't heard of PISI since the last elections, when I was told they often posed as CIO. Who, I asked, were they really?

It was a risk, but it paid off. Bhebhe described PISI, their functions and their attempts in the past to become a sort of CIO with contempt. After that I felt emboldened enough to move on to Nkala, who had recently been Acting Minister of Home Affairs, and who, I speculated, might have tried during that time to reactivate PISI. On that they wouldn't rise. But Renzo did say how happy he was that the president had set up the Sandura Commission of Inquiry into Willowvale.

And here was the nub of present problems: there were so many very powerful people who once again needed to divert attention from their affairs.

The benefits of the amnesty that marked unity were being awarded in a very provocative fashion, with no respite in sight for the former ZPRA members still in jail. One of the beneficiaries was Sheila Hove, fiery wife of Minister Richard Hove. She had been sentenced to jail for kidnapping the baby her husband had by a mistress and for threatening the mother, but had not yet been locked up. A few weeks after being pardoned under the unity amnesty, she had a row with their farm manager, during the course of which it appeared that they had shot each other dead.

Details of that case never really came out. The sub rosa information circulating was that they were having an affair, she found out that he was also having an affair with another woman and threatened him with a gun, which he seized, she was shot during the struggle and he then committed suicide. Sheila Hove was buried as a Zanu (PF) heroine, with praises showered upon her by Mrs Sally Mugabe and others. I felt very sorry for her.

Sheila had come to me a couple of years after independence, asking for $3 000. I said the Zimbabwe Project couldn't help the wives of ministers. She said she wasn't asking for money from the Zimbabwe Project. She was asking it from *me*. Then she told me of her difficulties.

She and her husband had come back from Mozambique with nothing at the end of the war. All of a sudden he was a minister. They had to buy a house. The house was empty. They had to buy furniture on hire purchase. Then the relatives moved in. She said that after paying their bills each month, her husband was left with $300. They had young children. She was uncertain of their future and wanted to start a 'poultry project'. I regretted. Fortunately, she never seemed to hold it against me. She then got a job with the Bank of Credit and Commerce, but didn't do their public relations much good. There was one nice moment in the whole unhappy saga. When she went to court to face charges of threats and kidnapping, her husband, the minister, was by her side and holding her hand.

It was reported on the news one night that the Minister of Defence, Enos Nkala, had announced that all former ZANLA and ZPRA combatants were to receive a pension backdated to the day they had joined the struggle. I wondered if the Ministry of Finance, Economic Planning and Development had been consulted. At independence it was estimated that there were about 66 000 ex-combatants. Some of them had joined the struggle in 1963. Some could live another fifty years. The most derisory pensions, backdated, would cost Zimbabwe billions of dollars. The political consequences! For example, all ZPRA military records had been seized by government in 1983 and may have been destroyed. How would former ZPRA prove their credentials? The sheer mechanics of such an exercise, even if funds were available, were mind-boggling. It would essentially boil down to 'who can we exclude and how?'

I rang my father. He said the statement was so patently mad that he had dismissed it from his mind. But ex-combatants hearing about it would not dismiss it from their minds. For instance, the very next day a young man came in, requesting help to buy paintbrushes so that he could try to create work as a house painter. He had been unemployed since independence. Another wrote to say he was crossing to South Africa to try to find work in the mines. Thousands of these young people remained desperate. What would they think? What would they do? How could the state afford to disappoint them again? It all seemed dynamite.

Stanley Bhebhe appeared again in the Bulawayo magistrate's court on Friday 3 February 1989, and all charges were withdrawn before plea. I had kept in close touch with the provincial administrator, Bhebhe's superior, Zwelibanzi Mzilethi. We rejoiced at the news on the telephone, and then Mzilethi paid a great compliment to the tireless work of David Coltart. He said how much he liked Coltart, and then said that of course Coltart could never be a doctor.

'Really?' I asked, very puzzled.

'Really,' said Mzilethi. 'You see he is so much involved in his work that if he was a doctor, he would end up lying in bed with his patient.'

So that day started well but ended horribly. My mother telephoned late that night to say that, when my father had tried to coax his old Citroën to start by feeding petrol into the carburettor, it had caught fire, and his face, ears, neck, part of his chest, but particularly his hands, were burned. He was about twenty-five kilometres from Zvishavane, and a passing motorist rushed him to Shabanie Mine Hospital.

Zimbabwe was seriously hampered by the problem of insufficient transport of all kinds, largely due to a shortage of foreign currency. There were cars on our roads that, in the West, would probably be found only in museums. My father, approaching eighty-one years of age, had been spending a lot of time and energy trying to keep obsolete vehicles functioning, hence the accident. This was also the background to the work of the Sandura Commission. People were so desperate for vehicles that, to get hold of one, they would do practically anything, including bribing ministers.

I joined my parents at the hospital the next morning. The upper part of my father's body had been under the bonnet, leaning over the engine, when it burst into flames. Now his hands were in huge bandages, and his head was a swollen black football covered with a white salve. His little cap of white and brown burned hair would not be touched for some days. To stop the burning he had rolled in the soil on the side of the road, so all his wounds were filled with earth.

The excellent medical superintendent, Dr Mataka, said my father's eyes would be fine, but he would need skin transplants. Although Mataka was a surgeon, he said that one of his contemporaries in Bulawayo, Rosemary Hepworth, was particularly brilliant at this kind of work, and so we went in convoy to Mater Dei Hospital in Bulawayo on Thursday 9 February. My mother went first in her car in case it broke down, then came an ambulance with my father on a drip attended by a nurse, and I brought up the rear.

The only positive thing about some parts of life is simply our ability to forget them. Suffice it to say that after the accident my father was on a trek through hell, with my mother by his side, as always. For some days his mind was wandering, and it was difficult to pull him back out of nightmare and storm. I suspect he was immersed in the war. He certainly thought he had been attacked. Once he called for me, quietly, to discuss what arrangements there were for security; whether there would be another attack; if the women and children were properly hidden; where it was thought the attackers had gone and when they would be back. I couldn't give him any comfort, as my voice could not reach the level of his mind. But these bad days were tempered by waves of love to him from throughout Zimbabwe and abroad. In place of honour by his bedside was a card from one of the hundreds of children he had delivered, eleven-year-old Nokuthula Chazuzah.

To dearest Sir Todd

On behalf of my dear little family I send you this home-made little card – take it during your quite few moments when the doctor has had a look at your dear old hands which were the precious FIRST HANDS that welcomed my brother Nkosinathi Munyaradzi, me Nokuthula Hammond and Reginald Mufaro and were only the Dear hands that got my mother's mind to settle down by feeling our dear sister Gugulethu Thandiwe was the only baby in my Mum's tamie not TWINS. We are so thrilled to learn that you are much better. Get well soon and come back home. May God bless you.

One afternoon I was sitting alone in the grounds of the hospital, almost wishing that my father had never been born as he was in such agony, being fed water drop by drop from a teaspoon, his hands, covered with salve, suspended above his head in bags. Searching for a handkerchief, I found in my pocket an unread letter from Edgar Moyo in London. It was dated 30 January 1989, before the accident.

I thought I would share with you a small item of news which invoked your name on the BBC PM programme at 5.48 today. Gordon Clough is leaving the PM programme. Val Singleton who was probably on Blue Peter in your day is now a presenter there too. She asked Gordon Clough 'is there any particular PM broadcast that stands out in your memory?' 'Oh yes,' said Gordon Clough. 'I remember the day when I told Judith Todd that her father had been released from house arrest and the pure joy in her voice ...'

In a flash I thankfully remembered all over again that moment and the joy I'd felt, and a couple of days later, when my father opened his eyes in the morning, murmuring how glad he was to be alive, I felt properly remorseful about the gloom I had allowed myself to fall into. Not long afterwards, I received a letter from Chikurubi Maximum Prison.

I am verry sorry to what happened to our dear father, burnt by petrol. It had deeply pained my heart. I only came across the news after I had asked one of my fellow inmates to give me an old newspaper to write a letter on top of it to my wife whom I wanted to tell that I had failed to write O-Level exams. Please let me know if he is in good condition. Although I am a poor fellow without anything to contribute let this be my contribution – to seek Jesus Christ's mercy not to snatch away our helpful father. Your Deeply concerned Lovemore Mutsingo.

On Sunday morning 19 February, I was at Mater Dei and decided to briefly visit Edward and Mary Ndlovu, as my father was asleep, my mother attending him. I returned an hour later. My mother was giving my father his lunch, and he was looking startled.

'Things have been happening since you left,' said my mother. 'Bryant Elliot wants you to phone urgently. So does David Coltart. The police are trying to arrest David Coltart and he sounds very upset.'

I couldn't help laughing. Had the police been trying to arrest me, I would have been onto those two lawyers like a flash for help, but what was the point of lawyers leaping for *my* help? What could *I* do?

Although the charges against Stanley Bhebhe had been withdrawn as 'irregular', he had not been reinstated as district administrator, and his salary had been stopped by the Public Service Commission. I had already made an appointment to see the Minister of State for the Public Service, Comrade Chris Andersen, about this. Meanwhile, however, Inspector Kambira from Tsholotsho had arrived at Coltart's house with a warrant for his arrest on grounds that he had been interfering with state witnesses regarding charges against Bhebhe. Coltart rang Bryant Elliot, who spotted that the warrant had been signed by Superintendent Makosa, who was second in charge for Matabeleland (rural). If there had been any interference by Coltart with state witnesses, this would have been in his offices, and so the warrant would have to be signed by someone who had authority over Matabeleland (urban). So Kambira went off to get a valid warrant, and David told him he was going to visit friends.

Coltart and family naturally didn't return home that day or the following night. Instead he rang Dr Joshua Nkomo, who said he would try to speak to Moven Mahachi, Minister of Home Affairs. Bryant tried but failed to get hold of the lawyer Lot Senda, who was Deputy Minister for Local Government and also headed a commission of inquiry for Dr Nkomo into the goings-on in Nkayi. Bhebhe, of course, fell under the Ministry of Local Government.

I rang Edward Ndlovu, who said he would try to find Lot Senda. In the meanwhile, Mzilethi, the provincial administrator, was alerted, and Coltart also managed to speak to the provincial governor of Matabeleland North, Jacob Francis Mudenda, who cheered him up somewhat by saying he had already received a telephone call from 'up there' to say 'what on earth is going on?' All these linkages were quite strange. For example, Mudenda was a client of Coltart, and Coltart had been shocked the week Mudenda had had to admit to the Sandura Commission that he had given false evidence.

The allegation against Governor Mudenda was that he had used his position as senator and governor to purchase a Scania truck from Willowvale when he was not entitled to do so, and that he had sold it at a very large profit. Mudenda had provoked a lot of mirth in the public hearings by explaining that he had only been trying to help his father, who operated a refuse removal service in Dete Township, using a Scotch cart. This was a very small business, and so Mudenda had decided to buy a very large truck, which his father could use to expand his interests. But his father had died, there was no more use for the Scania and so he had sold it. The commission eventually found that Mudenda was an unreliable witness, and that 'he had simply discovered, as other people had done, that this was a simple way of making money for himself without spending a cent from his own pocket'.

Mzilethi phoned me at home to voice more concerns. Both his radio operator and his accountant had been picked up by police for questioning on what communications had occurred between Mzilethi and Bhebhe. They had subsequently been released, but Mzilethi was wondering whether whoever was behind this whole nightmare was trying to destroy him as well as Bhebhe. Trying to cheer him up, I said he shouldn't worry too much, and that his anxieties paled into insignificance beside the woes of writer Salman Rushdie. The orthodox Iranian leadership had on 14 February issued a fatwa, a sentence of death, against Rushdie, accusing him of blasphemy, and Rushdie had gone into hiding.

'What do you mean?' said Mzilethi. 'I *am* Salman Rushdie!'

Everything was in limbo. I telephoned Bhebhe, who hinted at frightening reports that were coming to him from Nkayi about plots against him. He was pleased that I was going to see Andersen. Elliot told me that the police had agreed not to arrest Coltart, but that they were still preparing a docket against him. There was a school of thought suggesting that Bhebhe and others in the local community knew too much about the horrors that had been inflicted by the former dissidents, as well as the horrors that had been inflicted by agents of the chefs, and that all of these strange events were actually manifestations of a desperate battle going on to save some guilty skins. This made sense to me. There was nothing more sensitive than the skin of a chef, except, of course, the skin of a guilty chef.

Returning to Harare, I settled wearily into the back of a Viscount, which had somehow managed to resurrect itself into the skies of Zimbabwe, and groaned inwardly when the last group of passengers, in sports gear and bonhomie, lurched loudly towards me. They sounded so much like a pack of former white Rhodesians that I decided they must be a pack of present white South Africans, closed my eyes and willed them all away from me. Alas.

The man who lowered himself into the seat next to me was about my age. He wanted to talk, and did. He also wanted answers to questions, and he got them. He was a former member of the Rhodesian Light Infantry, and had left Rhodesia in 1980 for Austin, Texas. This was his first trip back, for a golf event. He had been to Zambia and Mozambique and, as predicted, what disasters those countries had become. He must admit he was impressed by race relations in Zimbabwe. He couldn't himself, of course, live under a *munt* government, but he must say that Zimbabwe hadn't done as badly as he had expected, although the whole education policy had been a disaster, landing the country with an explosion of unemployment. He was doing well in Austin, and wouldn't ever come back here to live, but, well, you can't get Africa out of your blood and somehow he would have to keep returning for visits. After us, he was going to see some mates in South Africa.

He seemed astonished by my replies to his questions. He asked what I did. *Worked with a development agency.* In what fields? *All – for example agriculture, small business, education.* With whom? *Mainly with war veterans.* Where was I born? *Here.* Had I been here during the war? *No. I left in 1972.* When did you come back? *In 1980.* Where was I educated? *Shabani and Salisbury.* Oh. He had been in Shabani during the war. Did I know … and … and …? *No.* What was my name? *Judith Todd.* Judith who? *Todd.* Garfield Todd's daughter? *Yes.*

There was a serious silence. Really serious. I didn't try to break it. Then he said: 'A lot of blokes would get up and walk away if they realised they were sitting next to you.'

I didn't say anything, just smiled at him. Then came a hot and urgent question: 'These Afs, this government. They know you were always on their side. Do you get anything for it now?'

'Not really,' I said. 'My parents were honoured. My father was made a senator and my mother was appointed to the Mass Media Trust. But people in government tend to think that I'm Zapu, and Zapu has had a very rough time since independence.'

Then he was really hungry for information, and a barrage of questions followed until the aeroplane landed, all seasoned with his opinions, some of which I agreed with, which further astonished him. Like our mutual aversion to a one-party state.

He told me that his sister, who also lived in the United States, would always be affected by the war. She was thirteen when he collected his first landmine and came back to their house covered in blood. She had screamed, 'Who has done this to you? Why do they want to do this to you?' He had said, 'I don't know. They're out in the bush. I don't know who they are. I can't talk to them.' She had been sixteen the next time he was hurt.

He gave me a spiel about how he knew Afs and how, if the whites hadn't been messed around by outside interference, they could have brought the Afs into the future in good time and how this would have been the best country in Africa. I said that was rather what my father had thought in the 1950s. He said how all the whites, including him, had revered Ian Smith, and what was his status now? I said I didn't think he had to worry about Smith. He still had his farm and a nice house in Harare. Sometimes Smith said things which I thought were foolish and provocative and which might endanger the whites, but those in authority seemed to have kept a cool head about him.

What of the future? he asked, finally. I said I thought the greatest danger to Zimbabwe lay in the crisis and tragedy of apartheid South Africa.

Near the end of February, the inter-tropical convergence zone at last moved to the south of Zimbabwe and there was rain in Bulawayo, on the ranch and at Vukuzenzele. And, I hoped, also at Beitbridge, Masvingo and all the other thirsty parts of the country. My father was getting on quite well, although he was looking old and weak. He had a marvellous present when President Mugabe and Senior Minister Nkomo went together to see him, with an entourage, of course. Administrator Mzilethi told me later that when the dignitaries had arrived in Bulawayo, they went to State House to put the finishing touches to their itinerary, and Mugabe asked if Todd was still in hospital. He then said something like, 'He has done such a lot for us all, we must go and see him.'

My father was in the bath when they arrived, and there was pandemonium in the hospital, which had been alerted only by the strident sounds of approaching presidential sirens. One of the sisters said later that, when they were taking him back to bed, one of the security men said, '*Pangisa!* Hurry up!' She had replied, 'You do your job and I'll do mine. I will not hurry up my patient.'

They seemed to have had a gentle, warm time together, with Mugabe saying, 'Oh Gar! Oh Gar! What have you done to yourself?' and Nkomo beaming at my father over Mugabe's shoulder.

One week, while waiting to board the aeroplane in Harare for Bulawayo, a gentleman sitting along the bench from me shuffled up closer. He said he was from Zambia and had been invited to visit friends in Bulawayo. He was a farmer, and also ran businesses in Lusaka. Then he said he hoped I wouldn't mind him confiding in me, but he had a terrible problem.

His wife had died two years previously, and he was now heavily involved with a white woman, a Yugoslav, who was married to a useless chap in the Zambian army. He loved this woman dearly and they wanted to marry, but there were complications.

She and the useless army chap lived in a house he had provided and drove one of his cars, and she looked after him wonderfully and his children loved her. If only things could be sorted out and they could get properly married, but the fact was that he was a prominent member of the Methodist Church and so he really couldn't become a party to a divorce. And so the status quo would have to remain. Now the real problem was this.

Because of his involvement with this Yugoslav, he found that if he was ever with a black woman, 'I am completely flat.'

'Flat?' I asked.

'Com*plete*ly flat!'

'You mean,' I asked, 'that you are deeply depressed?'

'No, no, no,' he answered, exasperated. 'No, I don't mean deeply depressed. I mean com*plete*ly flat!'

He waved his hand horizontally in a deprecating way, and spelled out the problem for me in single syllables: 'I can not rise!'

'Oh,' I said, 'I understand.' Thankfully, at that moment our flight was called. 'Maybe this is a problem you could talk over with someone in your church?'

He laughed deeply and said no, no, because of his esteemed position in the church he couldn't possibly talk to anyone there about '*guruls*' – and the word rolled off his tongue in such a way that it embodied all possible deliciousness of sin.

In that case, I suggested, perhaps he could get his doctor to refer him to a psychiatrist, so that he would have someone completely independent to confide in. He seemed very satisfied with the practicality of this suggestion.

Earlier he had asked where I was born, and had then laughed at me in a mocking way for having obviously been a white supremacist. When I said, rather lamely, that not all whites had supported the Rhodesian Front, he laughed again and said, oh no, no, not *all* whites had, just *most* whites, looking at me in such a fashion that I felt the way Chris Andersen ought to feel.

A commission of inquiry had started work in March on where a new university should be situated, and we hoped that they would decide on

Bulawayo. As we then expected office rents to soar, we decided to find a house to buy for the Bulawayo branch of the Zimbabwe Project.

I spent a morning walking in Bulawayo, looking at available houses. Almost immediately a big lorry hooted at me from behind. I ignored it, but then it drew up at my side and the driver jumped out and offered me a lift. The truck belonged to Sekusile Supermarket, also known as All Are One Cooperative, and emblazoned on its side was *Another Battle Begun*. This was a reference to the physical war being over and the fight for economic development beginning. So I climbed into the cab and was driven to the first house, large and central and on a corner site, advertised for sale at Z$70 000.

I let myself in through the gate and was looking in dismay at a wreck of a building when a wreck of a man tottered out of it and joined me. Mr Middlemiss. He could have been any age between fifty-five and seventy-five, and suffered just as much from the scrutiny of the sun as the house later did from the scrutiny of electricity. The defiant-looking old tin roof, which made odd gestures from every angle, covered a medley of rooms. Mr Middlemiss walked me through his private quarters, which were a nest of bottles, and into the two professional offices.

Mr Middlemiss was a spirit medium and a hypnotherapist. One room served the mundane side of his life and looked quite normal, with a desk, telephone and typewriter, and the sort of atmosphere conducive to making appointments, writing bills and receiving money. The other was perhaps more redolent of mystery and the possibility of healing vibrations when the lights were switched off, but for me, of course, the lights had to be kept on. I thought how lucky I was to be able to see into the heart of both the spirit world and hypnotherapy without having to part with one cent.

There, in the corner of quite a snug little room, was a doctor's couch. I forgot to look up at what might be on the high ceiling above the patient's head. Along the walls, in whatever direction you looked, were cut-out pictures of a wide variety of individual images that might be assumed to have assembled in the spirit world, so long as you were not black. There was the rather glacial-looking head and shoulders of a nun with a rosary around her neck. Depending on the lighting, I suppose she could have looked concerned and even loving. Then there was a distinctly unloving-looking chief of the North American variety. His expression was such that you could only assume he was about to tomahawk you, but his hands were not visible. The other heads have faded from my mind, but what really caught my fascinated attention was the large tape recorder in a corner. I could just imagine the séances and hypnotherapy sessions.

In ventures the patient, groping through the gloom towards the couch, assisted now and then, no doubt, by a staggering Mr Middlemiss. Lights start gently picking out the nun on the wall, the chief, the ... and the increasingly bemused patient starts wondering ... while Mr Middlemiss craftily sidles over to the tape recorder, soundlessly turns on an appropriate tape, the little room fills with ghostly sighs and ethereal messages while Mr Middlemiss slips out of the door, leaving the poor old bat on the couch and returning to his bottles for a whole glorious, financially productive hour.

As I left, I asked Mr Middlemiss what he would do and where he would go once he had sold the property and collected his Z$70 000. He waved his hand in what I assumed was the direction of South Africa and summed everything up in two words. 'Out!' he said. 'Away!'

He didn't have to explain that he couldn't be sustained by the new state of Zimbabwe. There just weren't enough desperately lonely old white women with money left.

On Wednesday 29 March, a reception was held 'in honour of The Rt Hon Margaret Thatcher FRS MP, Prime Minister of the United Kingdom of Great Britain and Northern Ireland, and Mr Denis Thatcher'. As the Thatchers entered the reception area, I remembered the meeting my father had had with Mrs Thatcher six years earlier, in May 1983.

Passing through London, he was contacted by the British Foreign Office, who said that relations between Zimbabwe and Britain were at an all-time low, following the carefully disguised South African attack on the Thornhill air base in July 1982. Apart from massive physical destruction, the attack had resulted in the detention and appalling torture by the Zimbabwean authorities of their innocent top-brass personnel, Air Vice-Marshal Slatter, Air Commodore Phil Pile, Wing Commander John Cox and others, news of which, when it emerged, horrified everyone but Zimbabwe's government. However, life had to move on, and the Foreign Office thought a meeting between Thatcher and Todd might help improve relations. My father said he wasn't sure, but would be glad to try.

Coffee was arranged for him with Mrs Thatcher at 10 Downing Street. My father wasn't keen on coffee, much preferring tea, but was impressed by the fact that Mrs Thatcher was pouring the coffee herself. As she did so, she said: 'Now *do* tell me, Senator Todd, what *is* life like in Rhodesia today?'

My father laughed, saying only, 'Well, actually, Prime Minister, most of us call it Zimbabwe now,' at which Mrs Thatcher said, smiling at the man who was nearly twenty years her senior, '*Do* forgive me Mr Todd. It's my age, you know!'

I was chatting to Philippa Maphosa, who headed the local office of Oxfam (UK), when I saw the British high commissioner, Ramsay Melhuish, bearing down upon us with Mrs Thatcher, resplendent in the fresh blonde helmet her hairdresser had fashioned.

'Philippa! Mrs Thatcher is behind you,' I murmured, and, as Philippa turned, Ramsay introduced us all.

'Mrs Thatcher, Judith Todd, Garfield Todd's daughter, and Philippa Maphosa from Oxfam.'

Mrs Thatcher's smile wavered as he completed the word Garfield, and by the time he said 'Todd', her attention was fully concentrated on Philippa telling her, with great indignation, that MNR had just lifted three tons of food relief off an aid agency distributing it in Mozambique. Fortunately it wasn't Oxfam. I silently wondered where the British-trained Zimbabwe Army had been at the time.

The party progressed, and half an hour later Philippa and I met once more, when Aelda Callinicos came up.

'Have you met *her* yet?' asked Aelda.

'Oh yes,' said Philippa calmly. 'I was talking to Judy and she came up and interrupted our conversation.'

Towards the end of the reception I noticed that Mr Thatcher was standing in the garden on the fringe of the guests and talking to only three men, one of whom was Minister Chris Andersen. I joined them and said quietly: 'Chris, I would like to be introduced to Mr Denis Thatcher, please.'

Mr Thatcher overheard, nicely moved his head away from what appeared to be a monologue, glanced at me, shook my hand and then moved back into his monologue, all in one smooth glide. I was fascinated and impressed. To my surprise, Chris, on my right, and the gentleman on my left seemed not displeased to turn their attention from Mr Thatcher to me, and then I noticed that the eyes of the third gentleman, now receiving the monologue, appeared to be glazing slightly. Chris nudged me with his elbow and chortled quite loudly in my ear, 'He's *exactly* how they write about him!'

I then admitted to Chris that I had had a subterranean desire to say to Mr Thatcher, in the unlikely event that we were introduced, 'I'm so pleased to get this chance of meeting you, because I stopped getting *Private Eye* ages ago and I feel so out of touch.' The satirical publication ran a hilarious spoof letter from Denis Thatcher each week.

'You would have been spot on,' said Chris, beaming. So then I watched Mr Thatcher with even more interest.

Nkala has resigned! Nkala has resigned! Nkala has resigned!

Our mighty Minister for Defence was caught lying to the Sandura Commission. His resignation meant that he could no longer bluster, bully and threaten to set soldiers and police on anyone, as he did to Geoff Nyarota. When he announced his resignation, the packed courtroom of about 300 people rose to their feet in public ovation.

The allegations against Enos Mzombi Nkala were that he had purchased at least two motor vehicles direct from Willowvale and resold them at prices exceeding the controlled price, and that he and his wife had sold two second-hand cars at prices exceeding the controlled prices. The commission found that it was improper for Nkala to have purchased the vehicles, that he had abused his position and, along with other witnesses, had lied. The commission recommended that all who had committed perjury and lied under oath should be prosecuted.

Nkala phoned Dumiso Dabengwa after his ordeal and requested help in finding a good farm. He said he had told the Sandura Commission he was resigning only because he thought they would then stop asking him questions.

Dzingai Barnabus Mutumbuka, Minister of Higher Education, lost his temper when he appeared before the Sandura Commission. When Sandura asked him a question, Dzingai answered in a way the public found impossible to believe. They said, 'Hah!' and he turned on them in fury and said, 'One fool at a time!'

Mr Justice Sandura looked very surprised. All over Zimbabwe there were now people saying, 'One fool at a time!'

Allegations against Dzingai were that he had purchased three vehicles and sold two at a vast profit. The commission found that the minister 'was a very unsatisfactory witness. He was belligerent and hostile to the commission and appeared to believe, as he put it, that the commission was after his blood. At times he appeared contemptuous of this commission and had to be warned of the consequences of contempt, whereupon he apologised.'

It was found that a number of witnesses, including the minister and his wife, had lied, and the commission urged that criminal proceedings be instituted. Tapfumaneyi Maurice Nyagumbo, Senior Minister of Political Affairs in the president's office, was also a victim of his follies at the hands of the commission.

The allegations against him were that, 'on a number of occasions and using his position in Zanu (PF)' he had requested the provision of vehicles for Zanu (PF), knowing they were for onward sale to others.

The commission found that the minister was an unimpressive witness and that his evidence did not have a ring of truth, that he had abused his position and powers, and that 'it was highly improper and dishonest for the minister to tell Willowvale that the allocation of motor vehicles to the party had been authorised by the president when he knew that to be untrue'.

The *Financial Gazette* reported a physical assault on Nyagumbo soon after his appearance before the commission. There were lots of rumours circulating as to the reason. The most credible was that he didn't stop at an intersection and nearly hit a young white man and his friend, who were on a motorbike. They pursued Nyagumbo and, not realising he was a minister, punched him. But that wasn't an interesting enough story for the *povo*, and so it kept being embellished.

The latest version was that Nyagumbo had found out where his present desire was living and had gone there one night without his bodyguards. When he knocked on the door, she called out, asking who was there. He replied in a seductive little voice, 'Ndini Nyagu', at which point her furious husband burst outside and asked what the hell he wanted. In Shona, Nyagumbo then said something like, 'Young man, do not speak to me in that fashion! Do you not know that I am Senior Minister of Political Affairs in the president's office and that I am Number Three in the Politburo?' To which the husband replied, 'And in my house I am Number One!' POW! POW!

Politicians generally used the term *povo* for peasants in a Zanu (PF) way, interpreted as unreal and mindless people, like 'the masses'. It was a Portuguese word brought back from Mozambique, along with the word *chef* for chief or boss.

Journalist Blackman Ngoro joyfully came to the office with a new definition. He had been descending in a lift in the government Mkwati Building with a senior civil servant, who, each time the lift doors opened, said loudly: 'Come in, come in you POVO, you People of Various Opinions!'

One evening at dinner I was seated next to Robson Gapara, head of the Zimbabwe Farmers' Union, and opposite Julia Zvobgo, member of parliament, married to Minister Eddison Zvobgo.

'Tell me, Mr Gapara,' I said. 'What do you think of the word peasant?'

Even I, always dubious about applying terms such as peasant or capitalist, right or left, traitor or hero, black or white or whatever to the unique individuals who make up Zimbabwe, was startled by his response.

'I *hate* it!' he said with passion. 'Whenever I do anything *really* stupid, I go to our bathroom and look at myself in the mirror and say, "You, you, you *PEASANT*!"'

Julia was shocked. She said she thought 'you people' liked being called peasants. Gapara snorted. I silently remembered Ian Smith and how he also thought 'you people' liked being labelled. His name for them was 'tribespeople'.

Despite developments in the rest of the world, we seemed to be moving inexorably towards a one-party state, with increasing regulation of the media and strident calls from the *Herald* for action to be taken against restive and critical students, but the chefs were becoming uncertain about how to handle things.

I was deriving comfort from and gave all due credit to the president for the fact that the Sandura Commission sat in public and that he had promised to make available the commission's report as he received it. After the last Central Committee meeting, he had also made a statement in which he said people were baying for the blood of the leaders, and with due reason.

'We must now admit,' he said, 'that we are reaping the bitter fruits of our unwholesome and negative behaviour. Our image as leaders of the party and government has never been so badly tarnished. Our people are crying for our blood and they certainly are entitled to do so after watching our actions and conduct over the nine years of our government.'

But, for example, so long as 'Nyagu' remained Minister for Political Affairs, we had reason for fears. It might just be, as he stated to the Sandura Commission, that he didn't derive personal gain from his involvement in the Willowgate scandal, but, even if he didn't profit, what kind of Minister for Political Affairs was responsible for the distribution of about three dozen vehicles to his associates when the country was grinding to a halt for lack of transport?

Minister Nyagumbo inspired great loyalty in his friends, but when I thought of him, I remembered his virulence after independence for anyone non-Zanu (PF); the way his PF Zapu opponent in Dzivarasekwa was murdered in the 1985 election; and how, at his election victory celebrations, there was a mock burial of a bull, symbolising Joshua Nkomo and PF Zapu.

Overall, I thought the post-independence influence of Nkala and Nyagumbo had been negative in the extreme, both politically and, therefore, humanly speaking.

To celebrate the unity accord, Oliver Chimenya generously offered to buy a Zanu (PF) membership card for me. After the split with Zapu in 1963, Oliver became Zanu's representative in Tanzania, but now worked for Anglo American. He once told me that, in Tanzania, Zanu received funding through the local offices of the Israeli government. I didn't mention this to him at the time, but the news seemed to lend credence to what I had heard long ago about the origins of Zanu. People then speculated that Zanu and, it was also alleged, its counterpart, the PAC in South Africa, were nothing more than contrived, Cold War, anti-Soviet creations.

Oliver also offered to make good all the arrears of my years of non-membership since the formation of Zanu in 1963. I thanked him, but declined. When Zanu was originally formed, they wouldn't have whites as members anyway, so it would be difficult to work out the financial arithmetic. Someone else asked if, as we now had unity, I had joined the new united Zanu (PF). I answered that I was very fortunate in that no one had said I should do so. He appeared shocked, and said, 'But you will, won't you?'

'Why should I?' I asked.

'Because it will make an impact when you resign,' he said.

My father was much better. When he came out of hospital, he stayed on in Bulawayo for daily therapy on his hands. It was all such a ghastly time that I was trying to wash it out of my mind. His face was unmarked and covered with new skin, which, my mother said, made her feel jealous. She had just turned seventy-eight, and my father managed to find her a dozen red roses. I heard him saying that this awful episode must, he supposed, have been an experience of deep spiritual value.

'I'm glad it has been for you, darling,' she said. 'It certainly hasn't been for me.'

When I switched on television news on Thursday 13 April, there was a stern and huge picture of Maurice Nyagumbo, and I thought to myself, 'Can it be? Can it really be that ...' And yes, it was! He had resigned from government as Minister for Political Affairs, as well as from the Zanu (PF) Politburo.

The following day I flew to Bulawayo and proceeded to Tsholotsho. Until the same time the year before, Tsholotsho had been one of the most tormented areas of the country. Now there was development and hope, and Makhatini Guduza was hard at work in his home there, establishing an agricultural cooperative. Other good news was that the group of forty-three returnees who had formed a cooperative at Nkayi had done so well that they had just won the government agricultural extension award for the best horticulture in Matabeleland North.

When I returned from Bulawayo, I received a heartbroken telephone call from Phyllis Naidoo. I could hardly hear her voice as she said, 'My son has been taken.' So far as I knew, Phyl had two sons and a daughter, but she referred to a wide family of young men as her 'sons' – Jacob Zuma, for instance, and Ebrahim Ismail Ebrahim, who was back on Robben Island after having been abducted from Swaziland and then tried for terrorism. So my immediate response was, 'Which one?'

It was Sahdhan, one of her biological sons, who was helping to manage an ANC farm outside Lusaka. Phyl's friend Jack Simons, another illustrious ANC exile, had telephoned from Lusaka on Sunday 16 April to tell her the sad news. She didn't then know the circumstances. Fortunately her daughter Sukhthi was living with her, and also, by sheer chance, her other son, Sharadh, was with her for a month, so the three of them were together. Poor, poor Phyllis. Her voice was so tiny.

Sahdhan had been shot by an alleged South African agent on the ANC farm. He was cremated in Zambia on 22 April. A minibus full of relatives travelled to Harare from South Africa and that helped, because Phyllis's house was packed and they were all busy looking after each other. Paula Leyden came with them.

At the same time, an appalling tragedy was unfolding for the Nyagumbo family and their friends. Maurice had committed suicide by poisoning himself. One of the Sandura commissioners, Fernando Ziyambi, was feeling very low, as Nyagumbo had been a great friend of her late husband, Tarisayi (Frank). I was in court at one stage when Nyagumbo was being cross-examined. She asked him a question and he answered with such exquisite courtesy that you could tell he was banking at least on her.

Nyagumbo was buried at Heroes' Acre on Sunday 23 April. I had been rejoicing that at last – at last – he and Enos Nkala were out of government, but that didn't make the news of his suicide less awful. I had also been hoping that the country would no longer be subjected to threats and bullying, but, alas, Nathan Marwirakuwa Shamuyarira, now Minister of Foreign Affairs, had picked up the unsavoury habit and had been lambasting the

Zanu (PF) leadership in his constituency for being power hungry. This was because two rallies he was meant to address had flopped. People were getting bored stiff with Zanu (PF) politics, and Emmerson Mnangagwa said being a minister was no longer fashionable.

Many years later, a former colleague of Nyagumbo explained what, to me, had been inexplicable. He said Nyagumbo had watched the spread of corruption in Zimbabwe, initially particularly evident in various arms of the defence forces under the then Minister of Defence, Robert Mugabe. He had watched Mugabe cold-shoulder the parliamentary committee of accounts and divert any other attempt to bring accountability in government on board. Then, as the Sandura Commission's hearings proceeded unimpeded into the relatively small beer of Willowgate, Nyagumbo had recognised that, as with Tekere and then later Nkala, Mugabe had decided to dispense with him. He had found this fact unbearable and impossible to live with.

When I went to town one April morning, I thought the whole of Harare's transport system must have broken down, as I had never seen such queues of people jammed into the centre of town. It turned out they were lining up to buy the daily newspaper. I had already read the *Herald*, and was still feeling sick. I had never come across such a pernicious and sleazy piece of reporting in my life as the front-page story under the headline, 'Tekere and CAZ members form new party'.

The first couple of paragraphs gave the flavour. 'As the nation laid to rest nationalist hero Cde Maurice Nyagumbo on Sunday an assorted group were meeting in a Harare hotel to form a new political party under the leadership of Mutare Urban MP Cde Edgar Tekere and former Minister Cde Farai Masango. The *Herald* understands that some 50 people of diverse political opinion, including the top leadership of the Conservative Alliance of Zimbabwe once led by rebel Prime Minister Mr Ian Smith, and UANC supporters attended.'

The news from Namibia was also bleak as could be. Members of the Organisation of African Unity and the Front Line State observer missions who would oversee Namibia's transition to independence would first have to be accredited by Pretoria. Refugees were meant to start returning to Namibia in a fortnight, to South African Defence Force bases in the north. I couldn't imagine returning as a refugee to an SADF base, whether it was still full of South African forces or not.

The only positive news there seemed to be broke at the house of Phyllis

Naidoo. After Sahdhan's cremation, her friends and family had decided to stay on for a few days. When I went round, I found, to my astonishment, that despite her mourning, Phyllis was wreathed in smiles and Paula Leyden honestly looked radiant. There was no other word to describe her.

They had just learned that Paula had been given permission to marry Robert McBride! We all hoped and prayed that this meant that the South Africans were not intending to hang him. Wouldn't it be just too ghastly for even the South Africans to do that? Of course we couldn't put anything past them, and they seemed to be making the running these days. If they were allowed to legitimately act for the present and be for the foreseeable future the top dogs in Namibia, wouldn't they also want to crook their leg over Zimbabwe?

There were dreadful rumours around, the latest being that Dzingai Mutumbuka had tried to shoot himself. Paul Themba Nyathi was unmoved. 'In the foot, I suppose,' he said. The rumour turned out to be untrue.

Paul had gone to a party the week before and got lost. Seeing lots of cars parked outside a house he assumed must be the party venue, he walked in the gate, whereupon a large dog started barking and madly rushed at him. Paul froze and the dog reared up, putting its paws on his shoulders and ruining his suit, as it had been raining. A white man appeared and wrestled the dog to the ground. 'Sorry about that,' he said. 'He doesn't like blacks.'

'Neither do I,' said Paul gloomily, and went home.

I spent a lot of time on an open letter to Tommy Sithole, editor of Zimbabwe's main daily newspaper, the *Herald*, and delivered it by hand to his secretary.

Dear Comrade Sithole

This letter is sparked by the front page report in the *Herald* last Wednesday, 26 April 1989, 'Tekere and CAZ Members Form New Party' which made me think the time was ripe to draw your attention to and invite your comments on some of the important issues confronting the press in Zimbabwe today.

1. **Background**
    People in this country have always been intensely interested in news, even when they haven't had much formal access to it, and even when authorities have tried to suppress information. An outstanding example of this was over the attempted settlement between 'Rhodesia' and Britain and the subsequent Pearce Commission, 1971 and 1972. By that time the Southern Rhodesia African National Congress

(formed in 1957) had been banned, the National Democratic Party (1960) had been banned, the Zimbabwe African People's Union (1962) had been banned and then on that dramatic day in August 1964 the People's Caretaker Council (the new name for the banned Zapu), the Zimbabwe African National Union (1963) and the *African Daily News* were all banned in one fell swoop.

Just before UDI (1965) crushingly repressive regulations were imposed under the state of emergency, all news emanating within the country was censored and often distorted and there weren't many avenues of communication left to carry news to the population, particularly in the rural areas. Despite all this people gathered news, fed each other information and thus were able to rally together in that massive NO throughout the country to the Smith–Home proposals.

2. **Independence**

Eventually came Independence and the buying out of South African interests in our press through the newly established Mass Media Trust (MMT). Freedom of conscience, of expression and association was enshrined in the justiciable Declaration of Rights of the Zimbabwe Constitution where freedom of expression is defined as 'the freedom to hold opinions and to receive and impart ideas and information without interference'.

In retrospect, however, it is difficult to say that our freedom of expression has not been interfered with since Independence as, over the years, Government seems to have had a hand in the sacking of editors employed by Zimbabwe Newspapers (Zimpapers) leading, I am sure, to a sense of great insecurity for someone in your position. This may be the reason why when outrages in our country sometimes occurred, as they did, there was not a professional response from our press.

It must be conceded though, that there can never be any true freedom of the press while we still live under emergency regulations first declared in November 1965 to facilitate Smith's unilateral and illegal declaration of independence, and maintained for other reasons during and after Zimbabwe's legitimate attainment of Independence.

3. **Rumours**

The years up to Willowgate can be characterised in the Zimpapers' stable as being on the whole that of obsequiousness to the chefs. But that time has gone. Welcome or not there is now a new relationship discernible between the press and the people. The widely expressed resentment regarding Cde Nyarota's 'promotion' shows that those concerned with the press can no longer ride roughshod over the people in attempting to placate the chefs.

The day you published the report mentioned above I thought there must have been a complete breakdown of buses in central Harare. But no, people were queuing in their hundreds simply to buy the newspaper. They knew that Cde Tekere might be up to something and they wanted to know what, even if their own powers of deduction were required to sift what few grains of fact were discernible in the report.

It is reports like this that give rise to the extremely high rate of speculation and rumour there is, particularly within Harare. Lack of information and the absence of straightforward reporting are the direct causes of rumour mongering. A pertinent example of this was the failure of the *Herald* to report Willowgate until the President announced the appointment of the Sandura Commission of Enquiry. This lack of reporting in the *Herald* was naturally widely commented on giving rise to the rumour that 'Tommy Sithole is himself implicated in Willowgate'.

4. **Unhealthy and potentially dangerous situation.**

The months before us are of crucial importance leading through congresses to the elections of next year. The demand for news will escalate but may actually threaten a diminution in the ability of people to buy newspapers. Some shops now do not stock newspapers for fear of fighting over an insufficient supply. This is an unhealthy and potentially dangerous situation.

It is therefore urgently necessary to address the problems of supply and demand, the integrity of our press and its competence to provide people with information they will require to make informed decisions throughout this year and informed choices at the next election. Without accurate and untarnished information it is difficult for people to make correct decisions and this, at the end of the day, can damage the State.

5. **Crisis**

The crisis facing publications in general and Zimpapers in particular is mainly caused by shortage of newsprint, an imposed and unrealistic cover price, a controlled and unrealistic advertising tariff and, in the case of the *Chronicle*, obsolete equipment. These are the major reasons why Zimpapers' profits dropped so dramatically by 93% last year.

In order to ensure that their newspapers can perform effectively editors must therefore take determined action to solve these problems by bringing them inescapably to the attention of Government. For example it can be asked what logic there is in giving Bulawayo a new university and denying it a new press?

6. **Integrity of the press**

Recently the President stated that the people were crying for the blood of the leaders, and with due reason. An editor by virtue of the role he plays in society through his newspaper is a leader although I'm sure the President didn't have you in mind when he made this statement. But just as people demand and eventually get a certain standard in the conduct of Government, so people demand and eventually get a certain standard in the press that serves them. That's what the struggle for press freedom is all about. If the insecurity of editors makes it difficult to attain that standard then this situation must be redressed.

Questions that could be asked are, for example:

Is the constitutional right of the people of Zimbabwe to freedom of expression being fully enjoyed and properly safeguarded? If not, what can be done about this?

Who exactly appoints and promotes editors and what is the process of selection?

Is it in the interest of our newspaper industry to have the position of the Chairman of the Board of Directors of Zimpapers held by the same person as is the Chairman of the Board of Trustees of the MMT?

In retrospect, can the acquisition by the MMT of over 50% of the shares in Zimpapers be seen as a positive step in the long run for the freedom of our press? If not, can there be pressure for the sale of those shares to the public perhaps with the proviso that the shares be sold only to Zimbabweans?

The preceding questions naturally relate forcibly to the position of editors within Zimpapers and their ability to perform their duty to the people, that duty being to provide information. You can see from the long, long queues for newspapers these days that people are starving for information, and their hunger must be satisfied.

I look forward to your comments although this letter is so limited in scope. To broaden the range of discussion you might raise these issues and others for readers in the pages of the *Herald*. On my part I'll send copies of this letter to a few people concerned such as some of our Members of Parliament. As this is an open letter they could in turn if they wanted make copies available to others and this would help facilitate a general debate on the press in Zimbabwe.

Paula Leyden and Robert McBride were due to get married in prison at 10 a.m. on Wednesday 10 May. That was the good news. The bad news was that Phyllis Naidoo's loss of her son had been compounded by the brutal killing of her dear friend David Webster, shot in the back outside his Johannesburg home. Ten thousand people were permitted to parade under police escort through Johannesburg for his funeral.

I was coming to the conclusion that, although the findings of the Sandura Commission were damaging to government as such, they were damaging in particular to 'the ruling party', Zanu (PF). A result of a perceived weakening of Zanu (PF) was an unusual freedom in the air. Therefore, it had been revealed that we had an inescapable duty to make sure that Zanu (PF) was kept as weak as possible, while at the same time doing everything possible to strengthen parliament. But how?

Tommy Sithole was upset and angry about my letter to him, but for him to respond at all made me think that he was jumpy, and that, in turn, indicated that the effect of the Sandura Commission's findings had indeed been to weaken Sithole's power base, Zanu (PF). I invited Sithole for lunch or dinner, with anyone else he liked to propose, to discuss issues raised in the letter, as I was a shareholder in Zimpapers through Hokonui Ranching Company. Sithole replied that he wouldn't have lunch or dinner with me now or at any other time, and saw no reason to discuss issues 'about me and my newspaper' when my letter had already been distributed 'throughout the country'. He concluded by refusing 'to accord your circular any sort of decency' by replying to any of the matters raised, 'a number of which are pure insults against me anyway'.

What a monster Zanu (PF) had proved to be. At the Sandura hearings, one of the witnesses from Leyland said they had been asked for half a dozen or so vehicles by Nyagumbo for the party and had obliged, as they did not want to appear unwilling to assist the party.

Most of the crimes since independence had been perpetrated in one way or another by the party or through the party, and so I wished that the party could be thoroughly smashed, by peaceful means, of course. If the party was allowed to become the state, then action against the party would be seen as tantamount to treason, as it really already was, up to the functioning of the Sandura Commission. People were bored with the integration of Zanu

(PF) and PF Zapu, but the chefs were hysterical about Tekere and his new party, ZUM. This showed that the few official claims there were about anyone having the right under the constitution to form a new party were hollow.

At a diplomatic reception I saw Ali Halimeh, the PLO ambassador, a friend of mine and of Tommy Sithole. They had been together in Tanzania for about six years before Zimbabwe's independence. Nathan Shamuyarira was also there with them.

Ali took me aside towards the end of the reception. He had asked me to wait for him until he was free. We sat at a little corner table in a corridor at Meikles Hotel while the reception continued behind us, and he announced that he wished to discuss a letter I had written to Tommy Sithole. He hadn't seen it, but was nevertheless, although polite, livid with me. Initially I thought that was just because he was a friend of Sithole.

Ali said that he had interests in the development of Zimbabwe News-papers, and he wondered why I couldn't just have gone to see Tommy rather than circulate an open letter to members of parliament and so on. He asked if I had consulted anyone before I wrote it, in particular Elias Rusike, managing director of Zimpapers. I said I hadn't. He asked if I was trying to get at Tommy only, or at the government through Tommy. I said the latter. Ali asked if I knew that, in the latest reshuffle of editors at Zimpapers, only Tommy had maintained his position. I said I did. He said this indicated government approval of Tommy, and I replied that this was obvious.

Ali advised me to remember that I lived in a Third World country, and that I shouldn't place myself in danger by fighting for my beliefs – indicating that my beliefs were out of place in a Third World country. I said it was my country too. Then he said that he knew what was really behind the car bomb that had hurt Jeremy Brickhill, and that it had been contrived to look as if it was an attack by the South Africans, but it wasn't. I was stunned, and we came to the end of the conversation. I didn't quite understand the implications regarding Jeremy, but I thought I understood the implications regarding myself.

I had no idea that the PLO had a vested interest in our press.

I was very lonely and I was very scared. Tangling with Nkala was bad enough, but with Ali it was much worse. He was so intelligent and dedicated to his cause. I wouldn't previously have believed it possible for a man to censure you in such a way through just his eyes. They were incredibly cold.

Of course I was exaggerating madly. Zimbabwe was so beautiful, and I had driven 200 kilometres in my brand new Nissan Sunny, which, alas, I admit was an advertisement for divorce, as Richard Acton had had to pay for it for me. It was described as 'sea blue', and I swanned along listening to Verdi's *Otello*, much to the surprise of other people at red lights. I felt as if I was living in a film – fantastic car, fantastic music, fantastic hot winter sunshine picking out the poinsettias, the aloes, the red-hot pokers and absolutely blazing them at you. And I was feeling so ice-cold scared! It was all unreal – the car, the music, the blazing beauty of Harare, my fear. Everything was a bit too much at the moment.

I looked again at Eddison Zvobgo's poem 'A Time to Rise'. It was published before independence in a beautiful volume of photographs and poems titled *Under a Rhodesian Sky*, perhaps while he was still in a Rhodesian prison. As soon as I came across it I had it framed. It hung on a wall where I lived before independence in London and then, after independence, at my home in Zimbabwe.

> *without*
> *Turning to see who sees you, continue on your road*
> *Precisely as if nothing had ever happened*

So, to do this and to pretend that nothing was ever amiss and that I was not and never had been terrified, I sent Ambassador Ali Halimeh of the PLO, who had interests in Zimbabwe Newspapers, a copy of my open letter to Tommy Sithole:

Dear Ali,

I said that I would send you a copy of my open letter to Cde Sithole. Please find it enclosed.

With all best wishes, as ever …

CHAPTER 22

The unity accord and the people's congress

T HE FORD FOUNDATION OPENED AN OFFICE IN HARARE HEADED by Peter Fry. He was an expatriate postgraduate student at university when I was there. On a couple of occasions I went with friends, among them a fellow student Stephen Lombard, Peter Forbath of *Time-Life* and Richard Walker of *Drum*, to visit Joshua Nkomo and others held at the remote detention centre Gonakudzingwa (Where the banished ones sleep), set up near the border of Mozambique by the Smith regime long before the unilateral declaration of independence in 1965. On one of these trips, Peter had joined us.

Now he had arranged a party in Harare Gardens behind the Monomatapa Hotel to celebrate the opening of the Ford office, and sought my advice on how to ensure the presence of dignitaries such as Dr Joshua Nkomo. Ministers, and even people from the NGO world, like me, were becoming tired of exhausting, vacuous receptions. So I said to Peter that if he wanted someone like Nkomo, he should make sure the invitation was accompanied by a note, saying something unusual like, 'I haven't seen you since Gonakudzingwa ...'

When I got to the party, Peter seized my hand.

'All your advice worked! Nkomo came!'

I had forgotten about my advice and thought he meant Minister John Nkomo.

'You must come and see him!'

Hand in hand we advanced very fast to where *Joshua* Nkomo was sitting alone in the dark garden, facing the queues of people coming in. Peter was the host and had to rush back to continue greeting the guests, but breathlessly he said to Dr Nkomo, '*This* is who took me to Gonakudzingwa! Here is Judy.'

Nkomo laughed and said: 'All of Judy's problems have sprung from the fact that she loves me. She *loves* me, and I'm always scared to see her because I don't know what she's going to ask for next.'

Peter had to leave. There was an empty chair in the evening gloom next to

Nkomo, and I sat down to keep him company. No one else in the glittering throng had yet done so. Teasing Nkomo a little, I said, 'It's true. I love you, but ...'

He clasped his stick, pulled himself up a bit and looked at me. 'But?'

'But what are you doing for all those people still in prison who should have been released under the amnesty?'

He evinced shock, horror and surprise, and said he had been told they had all been released. I said they hadn't. Conditions at Chikurubi were getting worse. They were despairing and getting horribly thin. Would he please *do* something?

I asked about Mugabe and said I hoped things would be much better now in the absence of Nyagumbo and Nkala. He said Mugabe was okay, but the problem was that he always sought consensus.

'You can't govern a country by consensus.'

I said what a comfort it was that he, Nkomo, was there as senior minister, but he said he couldn't go on for much longer. Maybe five years, top. He found it difficult to walk, and if he walked too much, he had to have someone massage his leg. He said, as if it surprised him, that he found he didn't have his old vigour.

The Sandura Commission continued its work, and the latest star performer was Justin Votie Joel Nyoka. He had made it possible for a friend of his to acquire three vehicles but didn't benefit at all himself, although the vehicles were quickly resold at vast profits. Commissioner Robert Stumbles asked if the friend didn't at least say thank you. Justin seemed amazed by the idea, and assured the commission that at no time had the friend said thank you. I thought how the quality of even friendship had degenerated in Zimbabwe. If Justin had got one of his old friends, like me or Byron Hove, access to a vehicle, I'm sure we would have said 'thank you' to him. I may even have gone so far as to offer him a bitterly cold Castle.

Dzingai Mutumbuka said he hadn't been involved in the purchase of a particular Toyota. He probably never even saw it, as his wife had made the transaction, and he believed she had sold it, but he really didn't have any details. Most cars in Harare were very, very old, and I saw a particularly ancient and battered one with a sticker on its bumper that read: 'My other car was a Toyota but my wife sold it'.

At a dinner where the Zvobgos were present, I said to Julia that I had heard she was saying it was lucky they hadn't been in favour and so weren't able to benefit from Willowgate. She laughed and said she had asked Callistus Dingiswayo Ndlovu, Minister of Industry and Technology under whom Willowvale fell, to get her a car ages ago. He did nothing, and then started avoiding her. So she went to him and asked him to forget the request; she didn't want a car, and she didn't even want to hear about one from Willowvale.

Time rolled by and with it came the unfolding of the scandal and the appointment of the Sandura Commission. After the commission started sitting, Julia went to Callistus with a Z$20 bill and said, 'Thank you so much for never getting me a car from Willowvale.' Callistus got very angry and said, 'Don't insult me!'

Maybe if she had tried to give him Z$2 000, he wouldn't have been so angry.

Journalist Angus Shaw saw Minister Herbert Ushewokunze in Bulawayo, who asked Angus if he had noticed that there was no mention of him in connection with the Willowgate scandal.

'Yes, Minister,' said Angus, 'and why is that?'

'Because I can't *stand* these Japanese cars,' said Ushewokunze. 'If there had been any *American* cars available, that would have been a different story.'

Most people watching television news probably laughed aloud during an interview with the Minister of Health, Brigadier Felix Muchemwa, who was imploring junior doctors not to go on strike the following day. They did, and so the next night's news showed the Minister for Public Services, Brigadier Chris Andersen, ordering them back on duty forthwith.

The venue of Muchemwa's interview was puzzling. There seemed to be three or four journalists, who looked like they were freezing cold, sitting on the edge of a garden. The camera focused mainly on the minister, who sometimes appeared to have cacti growing straight out of his head. This wasn't consistently alarming, as most of the time he kept his head bowed, and all one could think of then was how perfectly symmetrically his head was balding and how perfectly polished it was. It was only when he looked straight at the camera that you couldn't help worrying about the cacti growing out of his head.

Towards the end of his impassioned plea – 'remember, you don't work for government, you work for your patients' – the camera panned back, and there, on Muchemwa's right, was SK Moyo, Permanent Secretary for Health, looking as if he was sitting both physically and spiritually on the verge of outer space. He seemed surprisingly thin and his eyes were darting up and down, left and right, as if he was thinking, 'Am I here? I can't be here! Help! How can I escape?'

At the end all became clear, as it was explained that the interview had been conducted in the minister's garden. SK Moyo must have been sitting on the edge of some elevated patio with no backdrop, so that it looked as if he were perched on the edge of outer space; the minister must have had a thin but lofty pot plant behind him, obscured by his body, so that when he looked at the camera, it appeared as if he had cacti growing out of his head; and the ZTV crew must have used the wrong lens when filming the other members of the press, which is why they appeared as forlorn and shivering midgets in some vast, empty rural setting.

By morning, sixty-six doctors were in custody for continuing their strike for better conditions. They had been charged under a section of the Law and Order (Maintenance) Act that carried a possible penalty of ten years in prison. At a reception later I saw a friend who worked for the Public Service Commission. I asked how he was, and he said he wanted to get drunk. I asked if his misery had anything to do with his minister, Chris Andersen. He said, exactly. It would have been better to have any other minister taking action against the striking doctors, but to have Chris Andersen, formerly of the Rhodesian Front, taking action on behalf of Zanu (PF) under the colonial Law and Order (Maintenance) Act was just *too* much.

Roel von Meijenfeldt, current representative of the Dutch NGO, Novib, pulled up next to me at a red light and, as if revving his own body, roared, 'ZUM! ZUM ZUM ZUUUUUM!' The Zimbabwe Unity Movement, or ZUM, Edgar Tekere's new party, was already in trouble. Four people had been detained in connection with ZUM, and Kempton Makamure, the deputy dean of law at the university, had also been arrested, why no one knew. Maybe it was because two people from Zimbabwe Broadcasting, now suspended from their jobs, had interviewed him on Zimbabwe's new Investment Code and he said he didn't like it.

It was becoming obvious that the air of greater tolerance and freedom in Zimbabwe since the unity accord had simply been a mirage, and that all the old intolerance lay under the surface. Mrs Joice Mujuru, whose surname had changed along with that of her husband when he altered his name from Rex Nhongo to Solomon Mujuru, had led a demonstration of Zanu (PF) women in Harare against the formation of Tekere's ZUM.

If I were the president, I would have been so embarrassed to see my face plastered across the active and overflowing bodies of these women, but he seemed to relish the sight. I remembered the late Eshmael Mlambo of PF Zapu once remonstrating with me on this issue. In October 1964, we organised a large party at university to celebrate Zambia's independence. A friend in Zambia had sent me a piece of cotton material featuring the smiling face of Kenneth Kaunda. I made a dress from it and wore it to our party. Eshmael was furious with me.

'You are a Zimbabwean, not a Zambian! How can you wear his face on your stomach? Don't you know he already has six children so far? You shouldn't let him get so close to you!'

Our papers had very little coverage of events in China, including the killings in Tiananmen Square, but eventually there was a massive editorial in the *Sunday Mail* excusing whatever was happening there because it had 'resulted from a premature relaxation on the ideological front'. My father was outraged and rang me to dictate a letter to take to Charles Chikerema, the editor, which I did.

Chikerema was very pleasant, calling me 'my sister'. I hadn't met him before. As I put the letter into his hands, I warned him that he wouldn't like it, and said I hoped he hadn't written that editorial. He said he wrote all the *Sunday Mail* editorials, then settled back to read what my father had written: 'I write to protest against your leading article ... I protest because of its prejudice and confusion.'

I sat there thinking about how this was the first and, I sincerely hoped, last time I'd ever physically given an editor a letter accusing him of prejudice and confusion. Naturally Chikerema didn't like it, and proceeded to tell me how much he hated missionaries and how they had brainwashed him about iron curtains and things. I tried to look sympathetic.

Chikerema also told me that my father had not started the armed struggle in Zimbabwe, which fact, I must say, had never been of much consequence to me before. Then he told me of his profound dislike of George Bush and Mrs Thatcher, and how anything they found acceptable, like Gorbachev, would naturally immediately become anathema to him. He was also much cast down by the success of Solidarity in Poland. I didn't say much at all, but I must have sighed and grunted enough in the right places, because I think we left each other on friendly terms.

Chikerema published my father's letter followed by a long comment, which was really another editorial. My father then wrote to thank Chikerema for publishing his letter, saying the editor's comment was fine, except for the arguments, which were prejudiced and confused.

Richard Dowden rang from the *Independent* in London to say they had heard that Ian Smith was about to 'turn up his little toes', and asking if my father would write an obituary. He needn't worry about dates and events, as they had those, but should give a 1000-word analysis of Smith's political career. I passed the request on, but it took my father only a short while to decline the offer on the grounds that he had never known Smith very well and that he had never had any respect for him. He also said to me, laughing, that he'd had the appalling thought that if Smith recovered, the *Independent* might one day be requesting Smith for an obituary on Garfield Todd.

Godwin Matatu telephoned from Windhoek, where he was now living and writing a book on Namibia. He was enjoying getting to know the UN representative to Namibia, a Finn called Martti Ahtisaari, who had the daunting task of overseeing the handing over of power by South Africa.

Godwin said it was being alleged that Enos Nkala was now living in Kent because of possible serious repercussions from a police inquiry into Zidco, the Zimbabwe Investment and Development Company. He said Zanu (PF), of which Nkala was the treasurer, was being investigated for buying shares in Zidco, worth £11 million, for £15 million, and that it was believed that the missing £4 million was enabling Nkala to buy sausages and chips in Britain. If there was anything amiss with Zidco, it would involve an awful lot of Zanu (PF) ministers and chefs.

My father was back in very good form. His right hand was in quite good order, but his left hand would always be problematic. He was driving again and behaving as if the accident had never happened. He kept pushing himself to his limits, but he had always done that. One night I spoke to my parents on the telephone and said I was going to have an early night and was going to unplug my telephone so I wouldn't be disturbed. 'That's fine,' he said. 'If we need you I'll just drive up to Harare.' Five hundred kilometres.

I, on the other hand, had been suffering from incredible inertia, and wondered whether I was in the throes of a dreaded and probably incurable new malady I had come across in an article on NGOs, called 'compassion fatigue'. The article, by William Shawcross in the *Spectator*, was on the awful plight of the boat people from Vietnam. A decade ago they had been regarded as refugees and acceptable as such. Now they were termed economic migrants and were unacceptable. They hadn't changed; it was the minds of the people who had to deal with them that had changed.

Frederick Musiwa Makamure Shava, Minister of State for Political Affairs, was another casualty of the Sandura Commission. He was making thousands of dollars a year dealing in cars and was jailed for perjury. Within a few hours Mugabe got him released through a hastily announced presidential pardon.

There was public outrage, and even the *Herald* editorialised: 'If there are those who support the pardon ... they are not saying so in public. What would apparently quench the thirst of those howling for Cde Shava's blood is a wholesale jailing of those disgraced Ministers.' I encountered Mutumbuka's former secretary Jenny Hyland out shopping, and she said Dzingai had resigned all positions, including his parliamentary seat.

I kept writing to the influential about those still in jail who had never benefited from the unity accord amnesty. I received a note from Didymus Mutasa. 'No. I am not aware that there are people in prison who did not benefit from last year's Presidential Amnesty. Please let me know who they are and I shall draw the attention of the Ministry of Justice, Legal and Parliamentary Affairs to the names.'

Allister Sparks rang from Johannesburg on the night of Tuesday 25 July with terrible news. The *Observer* had informed him that Godwin Matatu was dead. He had no details save to say that Godwin had been loading stuff into a car at his house in Windhoek and had collapsed.

Allister said Godwin had rung him a couple of times on the previous Sunday and was in a very excited state about the imminent arrival of SWAPO's Peter Katjavivi in Namibia. The last time Godwin rang me was just before Allister came to stay with me, which was on 12 July. Godwin had sounded frantic and said I must get Allister to ring him, and that Allister must come forthwith to Namibia to help put it back on the map. He said the South Africans had a *plan* to subvert the whole process of what should be happening there. I begged him not to reveal the plan to me over the telephone, and promised to put Allister in touch with him. I thought that surely the person Godwin should be talking to about the plan was his new friend Martti Ahtisaari. Maybe he had.

I was increasingly worried about the crucial elections due in 1990, and wondered what could be done about straightening out the whole electoral process and getting people to insist on having candidates from their constituencies. When would the delimitation committee finish its work? How would people be informed what constituencies they lived in, whether they were on the voters' roll and, if not, how they could register?

Hansard reported that parliamentarian Bill Irvine had said that the whole of Marlborough, his old low-density constituency, had been transferred to high-density Dzivarasekwa, but when people from Marlborough went to vote in the recent by-election there, they found they were not on the roll. He said that effectively the whole of Marlborough had been disenfranchised.

I hoped that PF Zapu was doing some very hard thinking. The next few months would, I believed, be of the utmost importance. I had moved from the position of half-heartedly tolerating the concept of a one-party state a few years ago to outright and adamant opposition to the concept. People like Ushewokunze and Zvobgo were party ministers. They were in the Ministry of Political Affairs, but they didn't attend cabinet meetings because they were party appointees. This meant that their ministry was simply a Zanu (PF) instrument funded by the taxpayer, and now women's and youth affairs had also been moved over to that ministry.

The *Herald* reported that Josiah Tungamirai had said that the war veterans should not have their own movement, but should be accommodated within the party. In the latest schedule of procedure, gazetted by the government, it was stated that the Politburo of whatever happened to be the ruling party (ha ha) had precedence over a whole lot of people, including the judiciary. In fact, the judiciary was ranked quite low, and the lowest of all were the heads of denominations and NGOs.

I had heard that Chief Justice Dumbutshena was upset when the Attorney-General announced that there would be no prosecutions of people falling foul of the Sandura Commission. Dumbutshena was said to think that the onus should have been placed on Mugabe, after pardoning Shava, to issue pardon after pardon, which would have meant more and more public outrage.

When no one except the chief justice and the headmaster, Mr Jemius Muguwe, turned up for a meeting of the Moleli Secondary School's board of trustees in Zvimba, I sat down next to Dumbutshena and said: 'You must be feeling a bit heavy-hearted.'

He nodded his head and said, 'What distresses people in my profession is that the due legal processes had not been exhausted before the pardon was granted.'

Nick Ndebele of the Catholic Justice and Peace Commission told me that Justice Minister Mnangagwa hadn't known of the general pardon until he had to announce it. But Dumbutshena said that 'they', by which I assumed he meant top Zanu (PF), had known about it for quite some time before it was announced. The insinuation in the *Financial Gazette* was that the decision for a pardon had been pushed through by Mutumbuka, and what Dumbutshena said seemed to tally with that.

Muguwe said the president must be badly advised. Dumbutshena sighed and said, 'I wonder.' I said I had written about three months earlier to Mnangagwa about people who should have benefited from the amnesty but were still inside, and I hadn't yet had a reply. Dumbutshena laughed, and said that President Mugabe didn't reply to letters either.

What I so much liked about the man was that, although he was of such elevated rank, he didn't appear affected by it. He was so natural, easy and kind, and he talked so directly and simply, so unlike people such as Mutumbuka or worse who flung their weight around and treated ordinary people as if they were inferior just because they were ordinary.

Sam Mpofu rang from the boardroom of Longman Zimbabwe, where he did a lot of entertaining. I asked what the judgment was regarding Dzingai Mutumbuka. He told me I could hear it from the horse's mouth, and handed the receiver to Dzingai, who told me it was 'a bloody disaster'. He would come and see me the following evening to tell me about it. I wondered if I dared ask him why Mugabe had pardoned Shava with such alacrity, and also why, in 1983, Dzingai had been so instrumental in trying to get rid of me as the director of the Zimbabwe Project.

Fred Shava was fined Z$120 000 before he was jailed for perjury but almost immediately released, and I supposed the Mutumbukas would be fined about the same. When I told my father Dzingai was coming to see me, he said: 'Oh, darling! Do you think you have enough money?' I could tell he was not pleased that Dzingai was coming to see me. Paul Themba Nyathi and company in the office would, I think, have been horrified. Julius Chikazaza would probably spit on any snacks he might prepare. I wondered if Dzingai and his fellows had any idea of just how deeply detested they seemed to be.

Paula McBride arrived for a week. The South African authorities had said everything to do with Robert's appeal for clemency had to be in by 18 August, which depressed her. She had been hoping that the process could be delayed until PW Botha was finally out of power. The good news was that she had seen Robin Renwick, Britain's ambassador to South Africa, and they had got on well together. I couldn't think of anyone more important for her to make friends with. Robin was such a tough man, whatever we all thought of British policy, and if there was anyone the South Africans might listen to, I thought it would be him.

Mary Ndlovu came for lunch. She had rung from Bulawayo wanting to arrange a time to see me, and her voice was so sad that I knew something was up. Edward had been on an official trip to Canada, where he'd had the kidney transplant, and, while there, had had a check-up as usual. They discovered he now had cancer of the liver. There was no treatment available. Obviously they had concluded there was no point in operating.

Mary's eyes filled briefly with tears when she told me, but otherwise she was allowing herself to be buoyed by Edward's perpetual optimism. His line was that just because you have been told by a doctor that you've got cancer of the liver doesn't mean the end of the world. But, from what Mary said, he had actually taken to his bed at home. Streams of people were visiting him and he got up for a few hours each day, pretending to have a good appetite but not eating much.

I wondered if Godwin could tell what we were all getting up to. There was a big item on the front page of the *Herald* announcing when his body would arrive in Harare and at the PAC/Ministry of Information seminar on information, all present rose for a minute's silence to honour him.

Godwin's funeral was simple, moving and direct. I don't think he would have found anything bogus about it. The little chapel at Warren Hills cemetery was packed, and many, including me, stood or sat outside listening to the service over loudspeakers. Mike Munyati was the master of ceremonies, and the speakers were the former president, the Reverend Canaan Banana, Willie Musarurwa on behalf of Godwin's profession, Herbert Munangatiri on behalf of his employers, the *Observer*, owned by Lonrho, and Eddison Zvobgo on behalf of the family. Chief Justice Enoch Dumbutshena was present. The only minister, apart from Zvobgo, was Joe Culverwell.

It was a bright day and it was hot in the sun. I wished that everything had been recorded, but it wasn't. The only person I couldn't hear was Munangatiri, but I was told he spoke from the heart. While the addresses by Banana and Musarurwa were outstanding, Eddison's was, as one would expect, really superb. He spoke of Godwin as being 'the most complex, the most complicated, the simplest, the humblest, the sweetest ...', and when he drew to an end, he said, 'I don't normally pray in public. But now I ask you to join me in a prayer:

Dear God.

Thank you for Godwin.
You gave him to us for free.
And now you have taken him.
Thank you.

Then there was a short walk from the chapel to the grave. Rita was composed and beautiful, and the children, Tendeka and Nicholas, were quiet and attentive. Tendeka was now almost as tall as Rita. There were so many flowers. As people were dispersing, Ibbo Mandaza came up and asked me to write a short tribute to Godwin for his *Southern African Political Economy Monthly* magazine, *SAPEM*. When I got home, I wrote it.

Godwin Matatu

No one could pretend that Godwin was an easy friend. Brave, loyal, generous, dogged, fun – all these things and more, but easy never. It was as though when he spotted a goal you had to see and pursue it too. All obstacles were there simply to be overcome; all objections to be brushed aside.

He liked to gather two or three friends, preferably colleagues, to journey off with him laughing and joking or anxious and intent to explore the trickiest situation or to find the most elusive person. That's when his sleuthing instincts would hardly ever fail. Contacts would be dug out of the lowliest to the most lofty of places, from pubs to the President's office; the quarry would be sighted then finally run to earth. And the quarry would most times turn out to be glad to see Godwin.

I write as though I was often with him although in reality I went questing with him and friends only four or five times. But one of the best things for me about our friendship was the other friends from many countries I made through him. Through them, of course, I learned more about Godwin's myriad journeys, mishaps, successes. His exploits will continue to be recounted and no doubt many who never had the good fortune to know him will come to feel that they did. They will learn of how Godwin was not only an observer but also a participant; not only a celebrant, but also a mourner.

One of the memories Godwin has left was of a time on a dusty back road in Plumtree where he met and listened to a man whose political misfortunes had been translated into physical devastation. When the terrible story was finished there was a short silence. Then, before the man's astonished eyes, Godwin bowed his head, cleared his throat and said 'I'm sorry. On behalf of everyone I'm sorry. Please forgive us all.'

Zimbabwe television news did Godwin proud. They used the most incisive bits of all addresses, including Eddison saying, 'Us politicians like craven, third-rate reporters who don't upset us, and that's why Godwin could never get a job in this country.' Willie Musarurwa said much the same thing.

ZTV simply could not have covered the funeral better. It was a first-rate job. There was a slip-up at the end of the item, when viewers could see the telephone on the newsreader's desk flashing and him picking it up before the camera moved fast to the other newsreader. One could imagine and almost hear Nathan Shamuyarira's deep, steady voice saying, 'This is the former Minister of Information and ...'

A letter arrived at home for me from the Ministry of Justice, Legal and Parliamentary Affairs. I looked at it for a long time, then made coffee, settled down in my study and looked at the envelope a bit longer before opening it. I superstitiously thought that the longer I took, the more chance there was that the letter inside would have some good news. I closed my eyes while I took the sheet out of the envelope, kept them closed while I smoothed the sheet open, and then I took a sip of coffee, opened my eyes, and read:

Dear Ms Judith Todd

People who did not benefit from the General Amnesty 1988

I refer to your letter of 18 July 1989 in connection with the above.

I wish to thank you very much for your letter whose contents will be considered in any Amnesty action the President may wish to take. But of course as you probably know, matters relating to Amnesty or the Prerogative of mercy are entirely within the discretionary powers of the President.

NA Cheda
Secretary for Justice, Legal and Parliamentary Affairs

So, before the amnesty was declared, the president must have called in the head of the army, Solomon Mujuru, and whoever was really in charge of CIO, and said to them, 'Here is the chance to get your boys out of prison,' and they went away and prepared their lists and got their boys out. I had been hoping, half-heartedly, it was true, but hoping nonetheless that the fact that all the ZPRA men had been left in prison was a mistake. I had written about this matter not only to Cheda, Mnangagwa and Mutasa, but also to the secretary to the cabinet, Dr Charles Utete. He was usually very good and efficient about acknowledging letters, but this time there was just a crashing silence.

The SWAPO representative in Zimbabwe, Kapuka Nauyala, told me that he was not a coward, but he wouldn't mind being the last man to return to Namibia. He was entranced with the Willowgate scandal and the Sandura Commission. I wondered why he was so avid for all the details, and he laughed gleefully and said it was because he didn't want to make any mistakes in the future. When the time came for plundering, he wanted to be sure he was smart enough not to get caught. But, he said, all of Namibia's resources had already been plundered – all the best diamonds gone, all the fish caught.

Kapuka had been in exile since 1964. He came from Walvis Bay. The way he described it, you would have thought it was one of the world's most fabulous beauty spots. Others told me it was quite the opposite.

It was public holiday time again, with Heroes' Day followed immediately by Defence Forces Day. A list had been published of the 100 people who were getting 'both the liberation decoration and the liberation silver medal'. The inclusion of S Mugabe (Mrs) might have made some of the recipients feel somewhat half-hearted about the whole affair.

The former president, now Professor Banana, telephoned on the eve of Heroes' Day. His voice was so sweet and so gentle. He said I was probably aware that he was working on a history of the independence struggle, with contributions from many people. However, he had just realised that there wasn't a section on white politics. This should be short, just five or six pages, and perhaps it could be called *The Mistaken Years*? But it was needed in a hurry.

My heart was already falling when I interrupted and asked who he had in mind to write it. There was a silence. It actually was clear whom he was thinking of.

'Were you thinking of me?' I don't know if I sounded as crestfallen as I felt. He said yes.

'But I was so alien to them,' I said. 'I couldn't write on their behalf. Why don't you get Chris Andersen?'

He said that Andersen was now associated with government, so that wouldn't be proper. I felt really sad. My colleague Robin Wild tried to comfort me by saying Banana was probably only thinking about trying to find someone who could write about the whites from his point of view. But of course Banana had thought *whites = Judy*. Simple as that.

On Heroes' Day, when food could be received by prisoners at Chikurubi, I went off on that usual run. My parents were with me in Harare. I told them that Alibaba Dlodlo, because he was alleged to have attacked Mugabe's residence, was top of the list, after the whites, of prisoners whose visitors were regarded with suspicion, and how difficult it was to think of a satis-factory reply to the usual question, 'What is your relationship with him?' My father suggested I should reply, 'I'm an admirer.'

Chikurubi was relaxed and friendly this time. There were whites bringing food for the captured South African agents Smith, Beahan, Woods and Bawden. Unfortunately for them, they did not benefit from the 1988 amnesty. On 28 April 1988, Clemency Order No. 1 of 1988 was signed by then Acting President Muzenda and Minister of Justice, Mnangagwa. This stipulated that all dissidents who reported to the police between 19 April and 31 May 1988 would be offered a full pardon. In June 1988, this full pardon was extended to all members of the Security Forces, but the pardon specifically excluded agents of foreign states.

I was behind the visiting whites when we got to the area inside where you could speak to prisoners on a receiver through the glass. There was a thin, attractive blonde of about thirty-five trying to visit Kevin Woods. By the time I was inside, she was informing the other whites that she had been there since 7.30, and it looked as if she wasn't going to be allowed to see him. I couldn't help but feel sorry for her. She was tough, but she was also close to tears and her voice was cracking a little. Before I left, a prison officer had come to say she could see Woods, and she was just so grateful.

The food the whites had brought for these prisoners! It went on and on and on being pushed through the bars to the warders. All the many other people, save a certain woman and me, were black, and they started getting restive. It must have felt painful not being able to bring similar amounts of food for the prisoners they were seeing. I managed, quite unwittingly, to lighten the atmosphere. I had brought four cooked chickens, some sweets, biscuits and cigarettes. All cooked food had to be tasted in front of the warders to make sure it wasn't poisoned. The warders weren't sure that I had sampled the third of the four chickens. I assured them I had, and added, 'It tastes very nice,' at which the blacks around me laughed and laughed. Others behind them asked what was so funny, and someone said loudly, 'She says her chickens taste very nice!' And so others started laughing too. That made me feel warm and included by them, not sad and excluded as Banana had unwittingly made me feel.

A white couple who had brought mountains of food for Beahan ('They share everything with each other,' the woman assured the blonde who had come to see Woods) seemed ordinary, except that the man, who was huge and about fifty, kept sighing loudly in a way that the journalist Howard Barrell had once described as the 'eye-contact syndrome'. That made me feel nervous, and I kept my back turned on him so that he couldn't eye-contact me. There was another white woman, who appeared to be on her own. She was from Chivhu, and she looked tragic. She was very thin, her skin in folds over her bones. Her hair was obviously dyed and was jet black. She looked as if she had given up smoking too late to save her health. I couldn't get her out of my mind, and wished I could. You could tell that she wasn't much used to this prison business, as she had brought ice-cream. She looked as if she had had such a dim life, and that now it was even dimmer.

I received a letter from our former Minister of Higher Education:

My dearest Judy

Cathy and I would like to thank you most sincerely for your support during the past traumatic months of our lives.

I am sure the worst is now over though God knows where we will get the $85 000 fine from. Do you know any bank that keeps lots of money which one can easily break into?

I have not yet decided on my future but hope to do something that will be of use to my family and hopefully humanity. After all life must go on.

With fondest regards
Dzingai

Edward Ndlovu died at home on Sunday morning 3 September with his family, and, I was told, in not too much pain. There was a lot to be glad about, even with heavy hearts. That kidney transplant had given him eleven more years of life, and in those years he had seen the birth of Zimbabwe and that of his son, Vu, at home, unlike his two daughters Gugu and Zanele, who had been born outside the country while he was an exile. He died in government, which was better than dying in Kadoma jail or Chikurubi or Stops Camp, and he had been pretty close to death in those places after independence. I was usually quite good at suppressing anger, but now I found myself at its mercy. How dare 'they' have inflicted all that misery and suffering on Edward and his family? And I bet 'they' would be at the funeral, lamenting.

I rang Krish Ragadoo. Unhappy as I was, I couldn't help but be amused by Krish. He always managed to be one rung higher than you, whatever the ladder. In the course of our conversation, I said how sad I was feeling about the loss of Edward. 'Sad?' he said. 'I'm broken! Totally broken!'

On Sunday 10 September, Edward Ndlovu was lowered into the heart of Zimbabwe at Heroes' Acre. President Mugabe, in a moving tribute, spoke of his concern that younger generations, particularly those at the university, whom he viciously attacked, did not know the story of the struggle and did not know enough of heroes such as Edward. He said he hoped the media could instruct us and that the full story of people such as Edward would be published.

Indeed.

Two days later I saw Emmerson Mnangagwa, one-time Minister for State Security but now Minister of Justice, Legal and Parliamentary Affairs. When I went into his office and said, 'Good morning, Minister,' he said: 'Please call me Emmerson. Being called Minister makes me feel uncomfortable.' I asked if he had been at Edward's funeral. He said of course he had. Not only was it a state occasion, but Edward had been a friend of his. I then wondered if Emmerson remembered that the last time I had been to see him, nearly four years ago, I had desperately been trying to get Edward released from jail.

'Edward?' said Mnangagwa. 'Edward was never in jail!' I said he was, and that when I had asked Emmerson about it, he had told me that Edward was being detained by Nkala, Home Affairs, not him, Emmerson, State Security.

Emmerson genuinely seemed unable to believe me. 'Not Edward,' he said. 'Edward was always so level-headed.'

So maybe the president had forgotten too. Should we all forget?

I was in general happier than I had been since 1983. But my heart and my mind were often in turmoil. That week on television I watched Dumiso Dabengwa, and then Gift, on behalf of Lookout Masuku, receiving medals, liberation awards, from Mugabe. I thought … well, I don't know what I thought.

I had spoken to Gift the week before. She said she had almost recovered from Lookout's death, that only now and then was she overcome by terrible depression, and that the intervals between the depressions became longer all the time.

We went to Bulawayo for the celebrations of the fortieth wedding anniversary of Dr Joshua Nkomo and his wife MaFuyana, and his seventy-second birthday. It was hard to believe that the lead story on the TV news on Sunday 1 October was President Mugabe calling on all Zimbabweans to emulate the life of Dr Nkomo.

It was a two-day affair, the greater part of it taking place at Barbourfields Stadium. I joined my parents for the dinner/dance at the Bulawayo Sun Hotel. After Advocate Kennedy Sibanda had detailed the major events of Nkomo's life, my father was the main speaker, and his conclusion brought much laughter:

I have made sure that I have not had to stand directly in front of Nkomo when speaking this evening, for in 1980 I was in such a position. I apparently had got carried away and was waxing either too eloquent or too ideological for I became suddenly aware that I was being hammered on my calves by the ceremonial stick Nkomo always carries …

and applause:

There are certain experiences Nkomo and I share. Tonight we celebrate not only 72 years of Nkomo's life, but also its best 40 years, the years of marriage. MaFuyana once said of her husband Joshua, 'When he is with people he makes them feel they are as good as anyone else.' So that is how they feel about each other. Now I can give an assurance from the vantage point of my 57 years so far with Lady Grace that, Joshua and MaFuyana, the next 17 years will be the best. So go along with the prayers and best wishes of us all.

Thousands of people turned up and only a fraction could be admitted. We were taken straight to a table for ten just below the main Nkomo table. With us were Ali Halimeh and his wife, and the three new representatives of Tanzania, Zambia and Mozambique, as well as the Egyptian ambassador, Badawi, and his wife. The company was bright and friendly, with Ali's beautiful wife trying not to explode with suppressed mirth when a waiter mistakenly poured gravy over the shoulder of Mrs Badawi.

The crush of people trying to get in was a real problem, although those seated comfortably were spared the anguish of being turned away or having the task of turning away. The large dining room held well over a thousand people, scores just standing along the walls watching the lucky ones eat. But at least some of them could participate in the dancing, and all of them could listen to what was being said. A file of people was allowed to pass through the dining room just to have a look. There were many old and distinguished people present. My father mentioned quietly to me that a great difference between now and when he had arrived in the country in the 1930s was that then you never saw anyone with white hair.

Another room behind our dining room was opened up and more tables brought in to accommodate people who had been left standing, such as Johnson Ndlovu, Aaron Milner and Ariston Chambati. Aaron had somehow been appointed Minister of Home Affairs in Zambia during the time many from Zapu were there in exile. His hair was now very long and sheet white, and stood dramatically on end. He had been so startled to be arrested and abused in Zimbabwe after independence and during the crushing of PF Zapu that his hair had probably started its upward journey then.

What a wonderful, joyful occasion it was, and, so typical of the Nkomos, it was an event for as many people as possible, not just the rich, famous and powerful. It also seemed to be an occasion for forgiveness, judging by some of the people present, such as Callistus Ndlovu and also Eddison Zvobgo, who looked battered and tired, but was friendly to everyone.

The presence of Zvobgo recalled the night that Nkomo had had to flee in his bullet-proof car from Eddison's fiefdom of Masvingo, where Nkomo had unsuccessfully been trying to hold a meeting. Violence was in the air. Eddison told him the route to leave town, which Nkomo took, and that route turned out to be past people positioned with guns, who shot at Nkomo and his entourage. Fortunately no one was hit. Late that same night, my parents, in their remote house on the ranch, were woken by their golden Labrador and the sounds of a vehicle. An advance party had come to say that Nkomo and others were on their way to seek help. They had fled Masvingo but hadn't enough fuel to reach Bulawayo. My father was able to come to their rescue. The following week Nkomo drove his vehicle, a great, wounded, pock-marked Mercedes, into the centre of Harare to silently demonstrate how precarious his life had become under Zanu (PF).

There were many other survivors celebrating. There was Sikwili Moyo from Gwanda, snatched from the jaws of death when an unknown soldier came in the night and rescued him from those who had abducted and assaulted him. There was Nevison Nyashanu, jailed and abused after he'd stood against Dr Chidzero in the 1985 election. There was Micah Bhebhe, an old Dadaya pupil, who had suffered so grievously from the 'dissident' attack that had left most of his family dead. And so on and so on ...

And they were all on the floor, joyously surrounding Nkomo and his wife when they stepped down from the high table to dance together. MaFuyana started dancing as she was leaving the table, long before they got to the floor. There was Kotsho Dube, still looking 'dangerously handsome', as he once described himself to me when young, but mellower now. There was Mary Ndlovu, very gallant but still visibly shocked and grieving about the recent death of Edward. Next to her was Connie Ndlovu, who looked fine but had been more physically scarred by her husband Johnson's tribulations than he had. Johnson, moving blissfully on the dance floor, face wreathed in smiles, had been the PF Zapu candidate chosen for the forthcoming Gwanda by-election, occasioned by Edward's death.

Of course everything took place much later than planned. The main course was served at about 10.15, although the dinner was meant to start at eight. When the Nkomos arrived and took their places at the top table, they summoned my parents to join them. I was sitting opposite the representatives of Tanzania, Zambia and Mozambique and was intrigued to see them putting their heads together. I discovered that they were trying to recall a particular biblical extract that turned out to be Luke 14 from verse 7, which records one of Christ's parables:

> When thou art bidden of any man to a wedding, sit not in the highest room lest a more honourable man than thou be bidden of him and he that bade thee and him come and say to thee Give this man place; and thou begin with shame to take the lowest room. But when thou art bidden, go and sit down in the lowest room, that when he that bade thee cometh, he may say to thee, Friend, go up higher ...

Harare is always beautiful. During a dramatic storm I found myself at a red light with a tempest of mauve jacaranda blossom behind it and, behind the red and the jacaranda, the blackest of skies slashed by brilliant lightning. I wouldn't have revelled so much in the drama of colour and commotion had I known that students were simultaneously being humiliated and hurt during the forcible closure of the university. As a friend of mine and former ZPRA commander, Andrew Nyathi, now of Simukai agricultural cooperative, said to me later: 'How can we unite with people who break the legs of our children?' I reported this reaction to SK Moyo, right-hand man of Joshua Nkomo, before a joint meeting of the Zanu (PF) and PF Zapu central committees. SK seemed quite unperturbed, and said: 'We will teach them not to break the legs of our children.'

The students had been trying to celebrate the first anniversary of the anti-corruption demonstration they had staged on 29 September 1988. Since then, every time they tried to assemble, state agents rushed onto the campus to break up gatherings. In July, the students boycotted classes in protest against being forbidden to demonstrate and were roundly attacked, particularly by the president. The Acting Minister of Higher Education, Fay Chung, also got in on the act and called the students 'drunkards and megalomaniacs', accusing them of acting in bad taste and being 'anti-patriotic and anti-nationalistic'.

The chairman of the students' representative council, Arthur Mutambara, issued a statement condemning the occupation by police of the campus from 7 p.m. to 3 a.m. on Friday 29 September in order to crush a planned seminar on corruption that had been banned by government.

'To enforce their decision, a 200-strong battalion of the Riot Squad was deployed and sealed off the Great Hall. They were armed with automatic rifle power, teargas, rubber batons and other forms of live ammunition. They harassed and terrorised students indiscriminately throughout the campus randomly teargassing halls of residence, wantonly clobbering and brutalising students and threatening to use gunfire when necessary.'

In reaction, government arrested Mutambara on 4 October. Students boycotted classes in protest and the university was closed. The secretary general of the Zimbabwe Congress of Trade Unions, Morgan Tsvangirai, sprang to the defence of the students with a statement describing the closure of the university 'and the action that preceded it as a demonstration of the fact that the authorities responsible have developed so much uncertainty in themselves that they cannot even show tolerance and rationality in dealing with our own children'. In response, Tsvangirai, too, was arrested on 6 October and denied access to his lawyers. Eventually the High Court ruled his detention unlawful and ordered his release, which was effected on 7 November.

While sorting papers from my father for the National Archives, I came across an essay written by a girl in Standard 6 at Mnene Mission near Mberengwa in 1953. Although this was a Swedish, Lutheran Mission, the coronation of Britain's Queen Elizabeth II was celebrated to the full and followed by compositions, one of which was sent to my parents. Unbelievably, the name of the girl wasn't given. I would still love to know her name.

I sent a copy to Lady Soames, thinking she would like the reference to her father, Sir Winston Churchill. She did. I also sent a copy to the resident British high commissioner, Ramsay Melhuish, and requested that if it was in order, perhaps he could forward a copy to the Queen. He wrote later by hand to my parents, saying, inter alia: 'Earlier in the year Judith sent me a lovely essay from a young African girl about the Coronation celebrations in Southern Rhodesia in 1953. I sent it to London with the recommendation that it be laid before Her Majesty. To my joy this was done and I have just received a letter asking me to let Judith know that the Queen "has read the essay with exceptional pleasure and enjoyment". She would like Judith to know what pleasure it gave her.'

> In order to honour our Queen we made our classrooms very tidy and hygienic the day before. Unfortunately the ink spots were too old to give

in to our trials though we worked with skill and real happiness. But I think that Queen Elizabeth would have been so happy to see how we tried. Perhaps she has some experience of ink. Then the Queen would understand why we did not succeed so well.

The Coronation Day was a very busy day because we started to pray for the Queen early in the morning about 10 o'clock and continued the whole day until 10 o'clock when some of us were quite exhausted. First we had a private prayer when we sang our National Anthem and said some words very nicely when we promised to help our Queen and our land. Perhaps she might have to come and see us girls and boys who promised to help her. Then we should cheer her up.

It was said in the radio that people had stayed for days in the cold and rainy streets, but never mind, when the Queen came there was a terrible noise. I never thought that a civilised person could shout and scream in such a way, especially not in the presence of a royal person. But it was said that Queen Elizabeth II just smiled and waved her hand. Honestly I did not hear her saying 'Keep quiet!' a single time. That tells you she can endure a lot.

It was a day of great excitement in the whole British Empire. The radio announced that it was a dangerous day too as 6 351 persons fainted out of 7 000. I think that was a very high percentage. Perhaps they died later, but that was not said.

As soon as the National Anthem was sung, or played, or just hummed, we stood up to attention and fancied we saw the Queen in front of us. We also arranged a concert in the evening to amuse ourselves and our teachers.

To honour our Queen we were allowed to remain without sleeping until she spoke. All the Ministers of the British Empire spoke and said very good words to the Queen. Our Prime Minister (Sir Godfrey Huggins) expressed himself in very good English. You could hear that he had been in England before. But the best speaker of the men was Mr Winston Churchill who is now a Sir, due to the kindness of the Queen. He spoke so distinctly that even a child in Standard 4 could understand him. I think that if I met him I should tell him that I liked his voice and his words.

At last the Queen spoke in a very girlish and smart way though you could notice her royal dignity through her words. I was near to weep when she said she had no parents, just a husband and two little children.

When I went to sleep I thought of our Queen and felt very proud that she though a woman had done such a lot in one day, and I said 'May

God keep a joyful umbrella over the Queen's bed this night as it is raining in London.' The next day I heard that foolish people had waked her up telling her that some adventurers had been successful in climbing a peak somewhere in Asia. I think that was very cruel as the Queen must have been very tired after her coronation day.

In November Mrs Ruth Mompati came to stay for a fortnight. She was a charming woman in her late fifties and a member of the ANC national executive committee. After I left London, she was the ANC chief represent-ative there for some time, and so of course, was a comrade of Ethel de Keyser, a pillar of the Anti-Apartheid Movement, Lombe Chibesakunda and other mutual friends. These days Ruth stayed in Lusaka, but she had recently undergone major surgery and so came to Harare to recuperate.

Apart from her thirty-four-year-old son doing training in the computer field, she said she really didn't want to see anyone. But on the first Sunday, Phyllis Naidoo rang to ask if she could bring a friend for a swim. Then Jaya Appulraja, a very bright South African working for the Ministry of Local Government and who had arranged for Ruth to stay with me, called round. The anonymous friend Phyllis brought turned out to be Reg September, who had been ANC representative in London during part of the time I was there. Jaya brought with him Barbara Masekela, also on the ANC national executive committee, in charge of culture. I was amused about Ruth coming to me in the strictest secrecy, wanting complete privacy, and landing up having drinks on the stoep with two members of the ANC national executive committee, Phyllis, Jaya and me.

Ali Halimeh invited me to a reception at Meikles for the International Day of Solidarity with the people of Palestine. After that I went directly to a dinner being given by Rabbi Ben Isaacson. If in Palestine/Israel the leaders were as in Harare, there wouldn't be any conflict. When Isaacson was installed as the new rabbi in Harare, the first person to tender his congratu-lations was Ali Halimeh.

The tragic death in a car accident of Kapuka Nauyala, until recently the SWAPO representative in Zimbabwe, was announced on 11 December. The accident had occurred in Namibia, but he died in intensive care in Cape Town. There didn't seem to have been suspicious circumstances. I was so very sad. We had become good colleagues and friends. I had assisted him with their publication *SWAPO News and Views*, trying to restrain his wild language and also helping him to put the pieces he requested from me into his turbulent language, which I then toned down again. He was very good about security and diplomacy and no one knew we were working together. I remembered one of his trenchant headlines: 'Mrs Thatcher in Namibia! What for?'

Paula McBride rang. She was pretty much down. I just couldn't imagine how she and Robert and all the others hung on to their sanity. He had been moved into the white section, and was opposite Barend Strydom, the right-winger who had shot and killed several black people on a street in the centre of Pretoria one lunch time. I was anxious about Robert's reaction to his neighbour. I was amazed when I heard it. He had said, 'We've got to get that guy some help.'

Another plea for help came from Chikurubi, this one from Matthew T Chizondo, Zanu, and in for murder. I wrote to Minister Emmerson Mnangagwa again, saying that I feared we would all be dead before the former ZPRA in prison would benefit from last year's amnesty, and adding this Zanu name to the list in the hope that he would get more interested.

The Unity Congress, to ratify amalgamation of PF Zapu and Zanu (PF), was held in Harare from 18 to 22 December. The new creature was to be called Zanu (PF). All Zimbabwe's high commissioners and ambassadors and their wives had been summoned back for the occasion, including Stan Mudenge, known by his subordinates as 'Jehovah', from the United Nations, and Arthur Chadzingwa from Algeria. Arthur was rapidly making arrangements to get married to a lady from Lesotho. When, a few months earlier, he was appointed an ambassador by Mugabe as one of the few fruits of unity offered to PF Zapu, Mugabe asked if Arthur was married.

'Not yet,' replied Arthur.

Mugabe said this situation would have to be remedied as it was difficult to be a diplomat without a spouse.

'Remind me to do something about this,' Mugabe said to an aide as Arthur was leaving.

When Arthur, an esteemed friend, told me, I laughed, and said that Mugabe might be thinking of the large and boisterous Shuvai Mahofa, who was currently available for marriage. Arthur, appalled, could see I was only half joking.

Mrs Mahofa, Deputy Minister of State for Political Affairs, had, despite her office, been charged with ordering two men, one a former bodyguard, to burn down the house of Abigail Huni, who had been vying with Mrs Mahofa for the favours of Phillip Chatikobo. While she was acquitted, members of her Gutu constituency made their disaffection with her very vocal indeed, and Mugabe had little choice but to ask for her resignation from government, although, to assuage her patron Simon Muzenda, she was permitted to keep her parliamentary seat.

Other Zimbabweans passionate about local politics, such as Edgar Moyo from London, managed to make their own way back to be in Harare at this time. Dumiso Dabengwa was one of the organisers of the conference, and I asked him to try to get me a ticket to what was being hailed as a 'historic occasion', but he hadn't managed.

In the nick of time, before the climax of unity on the morning of Friday 22 December, the high commissioner to Nigeria and Ghana, Dr Isaac Nyathi, telephoned to say that he had a ticket for me. I sped to the Sheraton Hotel, part of the international conference centre complex, and met him and others in his room. As he, like Arthur Chadzingwa, didn't have a wife with him at present, he had acquired a ticket with the obligatory security name tag for a friend, Elizabeth Siziba. But she hadn't been able to get off work, so I took her place. I put the bold name tag on my lapel and was rushing past security into the conference centre with Dumiso and Isaac when Edgar Moyo stepped forward and said loudly, 'You aren't Elizabeth Siziba!'

'How can you tell?' I responded, and proceeded apace while, thankfully, security scrutinised Edgar rather than me.

Edgar, on leave from his job in London, had managed to plant himself temporarily in the Kumalo Zanu (PF) Bulawayo branch, from where he had helped despatch himself to Harare as a delegate.

You would have had to be a very small human being to enjoy being squashed into the tiny purple seats of the vaulting conference centre, and I left as soon as was decently possible after President Mugabe's address. He was spilling over with excitement and pleasure, welcoming all present but, most especially, the fraternal delegation from Romania. He said how sorry he was that 'our good friends' Nicolae and Elena Ceauşescu had not been able to attend this conference, but that a state visit to Zimbabwe was being planned for them early the next year. I sensed a tiny shock throughout the assembly.

'Doesn't he listen to the news?' I murmured sideways to Isaac Nyathi. That very morning it had been reported on the BBC that Romania's President Nicolae Ceauşescu and his wife Elena, the esteemed friends of Robert Mugabe, were attempting to flee their country by helicopter. Later we learned that they had been captured by their own armed forces that had belatedly turned against them and whom they were trying to escape.

I wasn't there when the deputy Chinese prime minister made a speech in support of unity between PF Zapu and Zanu (PF), but Edgar Moyo was and reported later that, throughout the speech, delegates, despite themselves, had laughed uncontrollably and increasingly loudly. Edgar thought this was not necessarily because of the content, relayed by an interpreter with a broad American accent, but because the language pattern was so unfamiliar.

Edgar was also present at an earlier outburst of hilarity. It seemed as if that whole conference had verged on hysteria throughout. Edgar was chatting to a member of President Quett Masire's delegation from Botswana outside the conference centre, when the limousine carrying the president and Mrs Sally Mugabe pulled up. As they got out, surrounding members of the Zanu (PF) Women's League fell on their knees. The president of Botswana then turned to the man Edgar was talking to and said, 'M'na, if you boys ever want a revolution in Botswana, just ask the *basadi* (women) of Botswana to do this every time I turn up at a meeting!' At which, said Edgar, the whole delegation from Botswana teetered on the verge of collapse with helpless laughter.

The day before this peak of 'unity', I received a call from London. It was the BBC *Focus on Africa* programme, asking me to do a three-minute 'personal' profile of President Mugabe, which had to be ready early on the morning of the closing day of the congress. I asked them to give me half an hour to consider their request. Once again I found myself frightened. It was always so much easier to say no, and there always seemed to be good reason for doing so. But then I thought that this would give me the opportunity to mention some of the things Mugabe's friends didn't want to talk to him about – such as making peace with the students; letting former ZPRA out of jail; and apprehensions about his wife Sally and her rise and rise to power. With luck, I thought, he might listen to *Focus on Africa*, and of course while he wouldn't be pleased with me, it just might give him the opportunity to think about these things a bit. So, when the BBC telephoned me again, I said I would be glad to do the piece for them. Early on Friday morning, I dictated it to them.

PRESIDENT MUGABE – a personal view

President Mugabe has every reason to look as glad and as confident as he does at this week's Unity Congress. At Zimbabwe's birth a decade ago our future was desperately uncertain, and he personally had to overcome the vicious propaganda that was part of Smith's legacy. This he did, swiftly and gracefully gathering the whites into Zimbabwe's clan. Now he has skilfully coupled our two main political parties and is joyfully exhorting all Zimbabweans to join in the wedding feast.

Some can't. It's tragic that there are about 200 former freedom fighters convicted of dissident activity still in jail, unblessed by the amnesty that began the unity process. And it's sad to see the alienation of some sectors of our society by President Mugabe's continued dedication, in this day and age, to the goal of a one-party state.

We benefit in countless ways from President Mugabe's hard, hard work. It's said he often sleeps less than four hours. We profit from his intellect, his statesmanship, his flowering pragmatism. We are amazed by his ability to move seemingly effortlessly from one vastly different circumstance to another, without incongruity. Recently he was centre-stage in the sophistication of the United Nations. A few hours later he was back at Harare's airport where women kneel on the tarmac, their bodies heaving with his face printed on their clothes. But it's worrying that he can tolerate, and even seem to enjoy, this manipulation of women. It's also worrying that he himself seems to be one of few Zimbabweans un-troubled by his wife's unimpeded ascent up the ladder of power which bodes perils for him, for Mrs Mugabe herself, and for the rest of us.

Undoubtedly most of Congress will go home admiring him more than ever for his insistence on candour; his affectionate allusions to former opponents; his careful explanation for less literate delegates of the meaning of socialism and why it must have its exemplars, just as Christianity has its Christ.

I personally do not think we could have had a better President than Mugabe has proved to be. He has earned our respect, our gratitude, our affection. I'm also encouraged that he knows Lord Acton's aphorism 'Power tends to corrupt and absolute power corrupts absolutely' and that he has the ability to try to protect himself and his country from the ravages of distorted power. I hope for all of us that he also knows and would accept another of Acton's maxims.

'To be oppressed by a minority is bad, but to be oppressed by a majority is worse.'

On the day after the congress ended, I telephoned my father to tell him of my encounter that morning with Elleck Mashingaidze, a former Dadaya pupil and historian who now headed CIO. I was driving down Fourth Street in the Avenues when his car crossed in front of mine, and he motioned me to stop. I pulled up, we got out of our respective vehicles and had a short, friendly conversation.

He said he had been attending the Unity Congress and had walked out for a bit so as to listen to the BBC's *Focus on Africa*. He had heard my profile on President Mugabe, and wondered if he could have a copy. I said he certainly could, and that I would drop one off at his offices. I then asked what he thought of the profile. He considered my question and then said, 'It was very fresh.'

'Fresh?' asked my father. 'What did he mean by fresh?'

'I suppose he meant fresh as in milk,' I answered.

'I hope so, darling,' said my father. 'He may have meant fresh as in cheeky.'

Jane Parpart was doing research for a biography she and Ruth Weiss were writing on my father. Jane was a friend of Rob Davies, who taught at the university. Jane thus managed to interview his father, who for years was on the review tribunal for detainees in Rhodesia.

Mr Justice Davies had recommended the continued detention of my father and me in 1972, although neither of us appeared before the tribunal. We didn't know it was sitting, and we only heard of its recommendation for our continued detention on the radio. Jane said he had been very reluctant to be interviewed, but relaxed as the interview progressed. She asked why the tribunal had recommended our continued detention, and he said it was because they had been given evidence that my father was operating a bank account in Botswana through which arms and ammunition were being procured.

Jane told my parents this in a perfectly straightforward manner, as if it had indeed been a fact, and was, I think, surprised when my mother said that at no time in his life had my father operated a bank account in Botswana.

It had taken us seventeen years to discover this falsehood, and we were more than ever grateful for the existence of academics and researchers.

CHAPTER 23

The Zimbabwe National Liberation War Veterans Association

EARLY IN 1990, THE MIDLANDS EXECUTIVE OF A NEW BODY, THE Zimbabwe National Liberation War Veterans Association (ZNLWVA), met in Gweru. I was invited by Terry Shumba, one of the original Lido group of disabled. When I heard him decline the offer of a cigarette because 'I propel myself with one lung,' I remembered that during the war Terry had been shot in the chest.

We squeezed into an office of the Ministry of Youth and proceeded in a very formal and charming way under the chairmanship of Comrade Phineas Nyamunda. He was fetchingly attired in stonewashed jeans and was reminiscent of Minister Moven Mahachi, but less porcine. On his left was the secretary, Comrade Vasco Nyoni, who looked somewhat like the rising Zanu (PF) star Webster Shamu. It was rumoured that the Webster Shamu who had returned to Zimbabwe as a Zanu (PF) war veteran was, in fact, none other than Charles Ndhlovu, who had allegedly fled Rhodesia as a crook.

I sat opposite them with, on my right, Comrade Arthur Makanda, who took the minutes, and was also the treasurer of, so far, no money. Makanda was a member of the Zimbabwe Republic Police. We were joined by Comrade Ndiweni, a beautifully dressed little lady with a hot-chocolate voice. I made a mental note never to answer *no* when asked if I had met someone before, which I did when we were introduced, as she seemed hurt, and said we had met when I had visited the camps in Zambia towards the end of the war.

Comrade Ndiweni taught law and business studies at the Gweru technical college. We had so much reason to be thankful for Joshua Nkomo's insistence on education for as many as possible during those days.

Then there was Comrade Gumbo, a slightly desperate-looking young man who had come with Shumba from the far reaches of Mberengwa, and AR Chitefu, who worked for the Kwe Kwe municipality. A man came in very late, hot and tired, from Gokwe. I wondered guiltily if he had been one of the many hitchhikers whose appeals I had passed by. I suspected that he, Gumbo and Shumba were the only unemployed present.

My heart fell quite early on when architects' plans were proudly produced for the construction of a conference centre in Mberengwa, where people would be instructed about the war. Six hundred dollars were now owing for that plan, although, it was pointed out, it was incomplete, as it didn't portray the ten houses that would be built for the ex-combatants who would be administering the conference centre, and the attached piggery and poultry projects.

It was estimated that the centre would cost Z$500 000, and they were worried that unless we proceeded with it immediately, the Mberengwa Council would put up their own conference centre. Mberengwa was one of the poorest and remotest areas in the country. They asked for my comments. I tried to be as positive as possible by saying this must be a long-term project. But some faces fell.

I was cheered by another of their ideas, which was to start a security firm in Gweru. I said they could immediately nominate a couple of people to spend a few days each with Alarm Security in Harare and HABS, which was just getting off the ground in Bulawayo, and learn all about this business. HABS stood for hardworking, alert, bright and smart. Alarm Security, under the chairmanship of Paul Kadzima, had started off being called the Alarmist Security Cooperative. The name was altered when the meaning of the word *alarmist* was diplomatically explained. This group of about twenty men was brim-full of enthusiasm and energy and so excited when one day they managed to procure three Alsatians, German shepherd dogs from the SPCA, to beef up their operation. Less than a week later, a gloomy-looking Kadzima and two other executive members came to the Zimbabwe Project. Their dogs had been stolen. We advised them not to tell anyone in the world about this particular theft.

Another plan that seemed feasible was market gardening. ZNLWVA had been given a plot on a new irrigation scheme in Mberengwa, and they assured me that there was a vast market at the Mataga growth point, so that might be all right. But my heart fell again with the next proposal, which was to film the liberation war. This would be done by assembling former ZANLA and ZPRA, who presumably now would act as an integrated unit, on the one side, and former Rhodesian forces on the other, put them all in a game reserve and start shooting. I said that I thought that was probably also a long-term project.

I was pleased and honoured to have been pulled in with them, although astonished by the unreality of some of their proposals, and quite hopeful that positive things could be achieved. Above all I was delighted to find that, politely and as quietly as possible, they were refusing to become a wing of the party. In this regard they had pulled off a great coup by being registered as a welfare organisation, No. 1 of 1990. The Act governing welfare organisations stipulated that there be no party political activities.

The ZNLWVA executive said that individuals belonging to the association could pursue political careers, but they could not use the association for any purpose as political platforms, except that the president of the state could be the president of the association. The association was determined to consist only of people who had actually physically fought in the war, and this would exclude politicians such as Mugabe and Nkomo, as well as the *mujibas* and *zvimbwidos*. The authentic liberation war veterans did not want to be used. As an example of this, they said that when Edgar Tekere was in the area after launching ZUM, he had said, 'Come, all ex-combatants! We have always been together,' and it was difficult to decline, but they did.

Mrs Ndiweni was organising a variety show in Gweru to raise money. But she warned that there were many ex-combatants who didn't want anything to do with the new association. 'We will be registered with you, and then one day they will start hunting us again and you will tell them where we stay.' She said she felt too terrible, meeting some of them. They were poor, desperate and felt completely betrayed.

My only contribution was an idea I hadn't yet thought through. At the Unity Congress, Mugabe had apparently laughed and asked, 'Do you think you *own* the country? You *fought* for the country, but do you really think you *own* it? This country is owned by Lonrho, Anglo American, Union Carbide and Cluff.'

If people wanted part of the ownership, they must buy shares, he said. Government had bought a lot of shares, but did not have the money available to buy enough. When I told my parents this, my mother suggested that government put all the shares they'd bought into a trust, from which people could buy units at fifty cents or whatever and share in the dividends.

I said to the group that we'd had enough of people breaking their hearts over rearing poultry (what Mike Munyati called poetry projects), growing vegetables and sewing school uniforms over the past decade, and that we must now start thinking big – although I didn't quite know how. I told them what the president had said and suggested we try to find out what multinationals were operating in the province and what they did and then call a meeting with them. I asked about the Midlands Development Association, which was formed in 1989. They most politely and tersely made it known that this was an association of politicians from which they knew of no benefit so far. I asked about the new Zimbabwe Development Trust, apparently initiated by Joshua Nkomo. They said their impression was that it would be a trust benefiting a few politicians that would keep on sub-employing people in all the old ways associated with Rhodesia.

I silently agreed, but I didn't tell them of the recent occasion when I had visited Krish Ragadoo's Kensington bottle store and saw SK Moyo peeping over the steering wheel of the latest Mercedes, brand new, which he was intently driving away. I asked Krish where SK had got such a luxury vehicle, and he said it had come with SK's new position as executive director of the Development Trust of Zimbabwe. Thinking SK might be embarrassed by the Development Trust squandering money on such a car, I asked Krish what SK thought of the Mercedes. Krish pondered my question and then, laughing, said, 'SK thinks that the bullet-proofing is inadequate.'

The ZNLWVA so much loved the idea of talking to multinationals that I had to restrain their enthusiasm. I said multinationals such as Lonrho seduced people like Mike Munyati, who had joined their public relations and disappeared from our television screens, and offered all kinds of services to top politicians, who they thought would ensure their safety. They would not be polite or kind or helpful to a group like this unless they could see some kind of benefit, or some kind of threat, so it had to be most carefully planned.

I gave Arthur Makanda a lift back from Gweru to his work in Kwe Kwe, and was touched by the hot questions he asked all the way, for example, did I think the police had overreacted with the university students? What about their handling of prostitutes? I discovered that Arthur was in charge of community relations between the police and the people of Amaveni in Kwe Kwe, and he was obviously being hammered by the public on these issues.

Arthur told me that people really missed Mike Munyati. They used to see him on television talking as an ex-combatant one to one with the most powerful people in the land on *The Nation* programme. He had got really good. I told Makanda I would never forget an interview Munyati did with Nkala as Minister of Home Affairs. Mike drew him out bit by bit until Nkala, eyes rolling madly, said he was thinking of reintroducing curfews into Matabeleland, and then you could see him speculating aloud, maybe the Midlands too. I said I was sure it was because Munyati had enticed Nkala into such public statements that viewers were horrified and the curfews were not reintroduced.

With us in the car was AR Chitefu, who asked if I was connected to Garfield Todd. I said I was.

'He sheltered us,' he said.

When I dropped him off, Chitefu wished me a safe journey back to Harare, and said, 'We need you tomorrow.'

En route to Arthur's police station, we called at his new home so that he could show me his pride and joy, the first beautiful roses unfolding on five young bushes in his garden. Then I ran him to Amaveni police station, where there was a huge election poster on the wall of the charge office, instructing people to vote for Zanu (PF)'s Emmerson Mnangagwa, *The people's choice!*

A fortnight later, a welcome letter arrived from the man himself, Minister of Justice, Legal and Parliamentary Affairs, Emmerson Mnangagwa.

> Dear Judith
>
> I thank you for your letter dated 6 December 1989 requesting me to add the name of Matthew T Chizondo to the list of Comrades we intend to release.
>
> Kindly be advised that it is my belief that Comrade Chizondo will automatically be covered by the comprehensive amnesty we are working on now ...

The rains were good and my parents in high spirits. My mother was spending a lot of time and energy on the fabulous-looking cattle, even though they now belonged to SG Mpofu, who was buying the ranch.

My father had been in Harare three times over a six-week period, trying to rescue Zimpapers from total government control. He was also clearing laboratory equipment for Dadaya Secondary School, and was very fed up with customs over obstructions, announcing to the official who was dealing with him that such maladministration as was being uncovered would, in a civilised country, lead to someone being taken out and shot. The official was naturally very startled.

'In Britain?' he asked.

'Oh no,' said my father. 'Cuba.'

I had been thrown into the capitalist, private sector business world by the journalist Blackman Ngoro, and was full of trepidation. Blackman was a former protégé of Nathan Shamuyarira, and had worked for the Zanu

(PF) *Zimbabwe News* for some time. He left there after having – to his surprise – been pained by their distortions of truth. He then joined the *Herald* as labour relations correspondent, but eventually fell out with editor Tommy Sithole. Blackman was just not Zanu (PF) enough to fit uncritically into their organs. So he had been lost and moody and miserable.

I took him with me on a trip to Bulawayo and from there to see the enterprises of the returnees. Blackman was one of a number of former ZANLA for whom the Zimbabwe Project paid fees to study journalism. This encompassed photography, taught by the Australian Margaret Waller, and he took a camera with him on our trip. I hoped there weren't any CIO observers around when Blackman shook hands with some of these returnees and congratulated them on their courage in standing up against the government. He was thoroughly disaffected with Zanu (PF). I didn't really know anyone who wasn't.

Blackman presented me with a fait accompli. He went ahead with the help of a friend of his, who was a lawyer, and formed a company called Africa Network Publications (Pvt) Ltd, of which there were two directors, him and me. We each had one share worth one dollar. We were now in a position to accept offers of up to Z$32 000 in the sale of shares in our company. I wondered who could possibly be interested.

I wrote to Eddison Zvobgo, asking for clarification.

Dear Minister

I was watching you on television the other night addressing what I think was a group of civil servants from the Ministry of Local Government, Rural and Urban Development.

I know that the departments of Youth and Women's Affairs have been moved from where they were to under your Ministry of Political Affairs. Am I right in thinking, from what you said during that address I saw on television, that a section of Ministry of Local Government has also been moved under the Ministry of Political Affairs?

I wonder if you would be so kind as to explain to me what is happening? Is it not beyond our Government's legal power and authority to shift what sections of our life it feels like out of the sphere of national Government and into the sphere of a political party? And is it not unconstitutional to make our Treasury pay for what is quite publicly and unashamedly acknowledged as a vehicle of the united Zanu (PF) i.e. the Ministry of Political Affairs?

If it is unconstitutional then I suppose us taxpayers should deduct from the amount that the Collector of Taxes demands from us that percentage that is being spent on the Ministry of Political Affairs.

I very much look forward to receiving from you clarification on the matter as urgently as possible. I have a demand from the Collector of Taxes on my desk.

At a ZLWVA fund-raising variety concert held in Gweru, my father was guest of honour. Somehow his terrible accident had made him public property, and when he walked down the street people came up to look at his hands. He went to the government printers in Bulawayo, and the woman serving him took his hands and started soothing them with hers. Her boss then arrived and asked if Dad had had therapy for his hands.

'Yes,' he replied. 'Whenever I need a massage, I just pop into government printers.'

He drove into Zvishavane in a truck, jumped out of the cab, and a completely unknown young black man came up to him and said, 'I'm proud of you!'

Paula McBride telephoned, her voice filled with such relief. A moratorium on hangings in South Africa had been declared in February. I prayed they would never be reinstituted.

Phyllis Naidoo summoned me for lunch, and there was the South African exile Albie Sachs, whom I hadn't seen since before a terrible car bomb attack on him in Maputo. His missing arm was a grievous reminder of what he had been through, but his head looked fine. His recovery seemed impressive, but, he said, he still felt lost. He also said something that moved me greatly, starting off by stressing that he had no religious convictions whatsoever. When he'd met Nelson Mandela in Zambia and Mandela embraced him, Albie just wanted to remain in his arms, put his head on his shoulder and silently say to Mandela, 'Please, won't you heal me?'

A sad letter lay on my desk from another victim of politics who had been deserted by his wife. 'I am a frasted man.'

Rafat Mahdi, Pakistan's high commissioner, invited me to lunch at Sandro's. This central restaurant with its lovely open courtyard was one of Minister Zvobgo's favourite places, so it was no surprise when he wandered past and stopped to greet us.

'Good afternoon, Minister,' I said. 'Did you safely receive my letter?'

'About?'

'About the Ministry of Political Affairs.'

President Mugabe kept shifting Zvobgo from ministry to ministry in a seemingly vain attempt to dim his brilliance. At that time, Zvobgo was at the helm of a rapidly expanding Ministry of Political Affairs.

'Ah, yes,' said the minister, and began addressing the startled high commissioner and me on the subject of President Mugabe, whom he never mentioned by name, as if we were a crowd at a political rally.

As his voice increased in volume and rose in pitch, so a lot of people suspended their eating and turned to our table to enjoy Zvobgo's declamation.

'*You* think, Judy, that there must be rules and regulations to do with creating and financing ministries. But *he* doesn't agree with you. In fact, if *he* wants to, *he* has the power to create any ministry he jolly well feels like, even ... even ...' Zvobgo paused while he obviously tried to think of something totally absurd, then finished, '... even the ministry of astronauts in outer space! So there!'

And, laughing heartily, the minister proceeded to a nearby table to join friends, who were applauding him and also laughing heartily. But, despite all the evident good humour, I was pretty sure that Zvobgo was the author of the repellent party political advertisement currently being shown on television: *Vote Zanu (PF) and stay alive.* In the background there were hands shovelling soil over a coffin in a grave.

Willie Musarurwa died on 3 April 1990, my mother's birthday. He was at the Courtney Hotel in Harare at a lunch being given by the new American ambassador, a black man called Mr Rhodes. Chief Justice Dumbutshena retired that month. The double loss of these voices for freedom was serious. When I told our Zimbabwe Project director, Paul Themba Nyathi, about Willie, he was shattered.

'All the good people are dying,' he said in sorrow, and then, in a further rush of grief, he shouted, '*The bad have nine lives!*'

When my father turned eighty in 1988, tributes to him from friends were collected, bound and presented to him as his birthday present. They unwittingly revealed so much of the contributors themselves that there was no richer gift he could have received. From Willie's tribute we learned that, when he was born in 1927, he was named Wirayi Dzawanda.

> I first knew Garfield Todd when I was a student at Goromonzi Secondary. I used to derive great joy in reading his speeches in Parliament. When I became a teacher at Epworth Mission in 1952 I used, occasionally, to go to the House of Assembly to listen to Garfield Todd speak, particularly on matters pertaining to Native Education, as it was called in those days.

It was a great pleasure to listen to his polished oratory and articulation. His speeches were made more appetising because he spoke on behalf of the African people. He was, as it were, the representative of the African people in that lily-white parliament, even if he had not been elected by the African people.

As a budding nationalist in those days, highly critical of the white man's government and how it treated the African people as a whole, I was deeply touched to see a white man who spoke my mind and fought to see that justice was extended to the African community in the country.

It was a source of unspeakable joy not only to me but also to many blacks in the country when Garfield became Prime Minister of Southern Rhodesia in 1953. There was great jubilation among the black community, more so among black teachers most of whom were well acquainted with Mr Todd as head of Dadaya Mission. And Dadaya was not only famous because of Mr Todd but also because of the Dadaya schemes which were authored by Mrs Grace Todd and which were used by every black school in the country. It can be said that among teachers in Southern Rhodesia Grace Todd was more famous than Garfield Todd.

In 1957 I became Editor of the *African Weekly*. I achieved the distinction that I was the only black journalist at the press conference in February 1958 where Premier Garfield Todd announced that there was a rebellion in his cabinet and a group of Ministers led by Sir Patrick Fletcher had revolted against his leadership. The press conference was held in the Prime Minister's office and I attended the conference in the company of Mr CAG Paver, then Managing Director of African Newspapers. He had invited me for the press conference.

It was a most shocking piece of news for me and for the many Africans who worshipped Mr Todd as champion of the black people. I said so to Mr Paver. Naturally the whites had a different view of him. On our return from the conference Mr Paver tried to convince me that Mr Todd was not being ousted because he was too friendly to the black people, but because he was a dictatorial Prime Minister. He did not consult his colleagues on important issues. 'He makes the decision alone and then tells his colleagues after the fact,' said Mr Paver. 'That is the reason why his cabinet has revolted against him. Get that right and tell it to your readers. They are also going to draw wrong conclusions like you that he is being sacked because he loves Africans. So you should help them by telling them the truth,' said Mr Paver.

I could not argue stubbornly with my employer, but I replied politely and said that it would be difficult to convince the black people who knew almost every good thing that Mr Todd had done for them, apart from being a missionary and educator of the black people. They knew nothing about his dictatorship and about the rebels who had done nothing for the blacks. I said that it was dangerous for the *African Weekly* as a paper for the African people to be seen to be playing the role of apologist for rebel whites who had never shown for even one day that they were interested in the welfare of the African people, as Todd had done for decades.

I said in conclusion: 'The *African Weekly* has built a high reputation among its black readers as a factual paper and their champion. The circulation figures are rising every day. I wouldn't like to see that reputation ruined and the readership going down because of indiscreet reporting on Mr Todd and the rebels.'

A clever man, Mr Paver ended the conversation by saying: 'You are the Editor. You write what you believe is good for the paper and for your readers.'

I wrote a factual story about the rebellion and said it was believed the rebels did not agree with Todd on the pace of African advancement. Mr Paver challenged that, but he did not order me not to publish that story.

Back in my editorial chair I decided to write a eulogy based on Julius Caesar's Mark Antony. It was in actual fact a plagiarisation of Mark Antony's oration at Julius Caesar's funeral. For Caesar I wrote 'Todd'.

' ... O judgment! Thou art fled to brutish beasts
And men have lost their reason. Bear with me;
My heart is in the coffin here with Todd,
And I must pause till it come back to me ...'

I made sure that Mr Paver did not see it in advance, because I knew he would have ordered me to remove it. I inserted the story at midnight when Mr Paver had gone. I removed a news story and filled the gap with the Mark Antony speech. I knew that Mr Paver was going to be furious with me when he saw the story. So next morning I made myself scarce; he searched for me the whole day and could not lay his hands on me. I knew that by the time I would meet him the next day he would have cooled down. When eventually I met him he raved and ranted. I refused to borrow his mood. He was pained; I was not pained. Actually I was rejoicing, because I had triumphed. I replied politely and feebly that I had published the speech because I thought it was more interesting and relevant than the one that was there. That was the sum total of my defence. I was told to get out of his office. I went but triumphantly.

There was nothing he could do to undo what I had done because the newspapers had already gone round the country and he could not recall them.

Not long before his death, Willie told me that the event that had most pained him in his professional life was his sacking as editor of the *Sunday Mail* in 1985. He said a few months later Prime Minister Mugabe greeted him at a reception and said: 'How are you enjoying your new job?' Willie replied that he hadn't had a job since he was sacked and, he said, Mugabe appeared shocked.

'He told me that he had been informed that Ariston Chambati had offered me a position at TA Holdings and that I had requested to leave the *Sunday Mail!*'

Willie well knew that it was Mugabe who had ordered Minister Shamuyarira to fire him, but of course there was nothing for him to say.

In the last piece by Willie, published in *Parade* magazine, he defined what he had worked and suffered for but was never to see in Zimbabwe. 'The Press should be run and controlled by an independent body which is not answerable to anybody but to parliament. Press freedom and the independence of its editors should be enshrined and guaranteed in the constitution in the same manner as the judiciary.'

On the tenth anniversary of independence, I went to Chikurubi Maximum Prison to see George Ndlovu, whom we had been trying to help get an artificial foot.

I went via the Kensington bottle store to buy orange juice and cigarettes. Elias Mabhena, who had bought the bottle store from Krish Ragadoo, asked how I was going to celebrate the day. I said I was on my way to Chikurubi, and then I thought I would call on President Mugabe. The thought of me dropping in at State House electrified him for the two seconds it took to realise I was joking, and then he concentrated on Chikurubi.

'Who's there?' I reminded him, and he then started collecting more cigarettes for me to take. 'This isn't the way for you to make a profit in your store,' I pointed out, and he said, 'No, no, look ...' and pulled out his wallet and paid cash to his employee behind the till.

I was playing a collection of songs by Elijah Madzikatire and The Ocean City Band, which were all the rage in the 1980s. *The Boys are back in town!* This served me well at the army roadblock you now had to go through before you reached the prison authorities.

'You like Shona music?'

'Very much.'

'Where are you from?'

'Zimbabwe.'

He waved me through immediately. I'm sure this was because of my music, as I left a number of other whites waiting at the roadblock.

The prison officer who checked my papers at the next roadblock grinned. I suspected he was one of the ex-combatants the Zimbabwe Project had helped to get into the prison service.

'And who, Miss Todd, do you want to see *this* time?'

'Alibaba Dlodlo and George Ndlovu. Do you think I can see two?'

'I hope so.'

As I started the car engine again, I said, 'By the way, happy anniversary!'

He laughed and said, 'As the country grows older, the greater are the problems.'

The communication system at Chikurubi was breaking down. The many visitors had to crush their way to the window of the reception office and shout the name of the person being visited. The officer who caught the name from you then shouted on the telephone to some internal officer who couldn't hear him either so he shouted again, as in my case, 'Dlodlo! Dlodlo!' and put the receiver down. Then the telephone rang on his side, and he shouted, 'What? What?' Eventually, over the crush of people – maybe in about thirty minutes – you heard him crying, 'Dlodlo! Dlodlo!', and that meant it was your turn to go through the gate into the bowels of the prison.

While I was waiting outside reception for the cry of 'Dlodlo! Dlodlo!', a pleasant-looking white woman of about fifty-five approached me as she came out of the prison.

'Are you trying to see Odile Harrington?'

This was a young South African agent captured spying on the ANC in Harare. 'No, I'm not.'

She asked tentatively, 'Who …?' and I knew she was really trying to say who are you trying to see and who are you.

This was a matter of awkward etiquette. You didn't ask the name of the person someone was visiting and you didn't ask the identity of the visitor. This was information that had to be volunteered. I tried to help her.

'I'm trying to see Alibaba Dlodlo.'

The name meant nothing to her.

'Shame, Odile isn't well and there is no one to see her. I thought you were maybe from the South Africans ...'

'No,' I said, 'but if you like I'll try to see her. My name is Judith Todd.'

She was startled but pleasant and said no, I shouldn't bother.

'Maybe someone will come and see her tomorrow' – another public holiday.

After receiving a letter from George Ndlovu requesting an artificial foot, we got a lawyer to go and see him in Chikurubi as I had failed, having been allowed to see only Alibaba.

The lawyer came back quite shaken with the horror of the situation. Ndlovu, former ZPRA, had deserted the army in 1983, fled to Botswana, was returned and then tortured by each subsequent group who got their hands on him – police, CIO, army. Eventually he landed in military custody. He tried to escape in 1987, stepped on an anti-personnel mine and lost a foot. He was charged and found guilty of trying to escape. In all those years he had not seen a lawyer, until we sent him Bryant Elliot.

We did everything correctly with the prison authorities, and Ndlovu was taken to Parirenyatwa Hospital to be fitted with a prosthesis. A few months later we got another letter from him to say nothing had happened yet. I went to Parirenyatwa and found that nothing had happened because payment had to be made before the foot could be fitted. So much time had passed that the whole procedure had to start all over again. Ndlovu was taken back to Parirenyatwa, and we hoped all would be well, but this time we were leaving nothing to chance. I started phoning prison authorities well in advance, they checked with their people at Chikurubi, their people checked with George Ndlovu, who told them Parirenyatwa said he couldn't be fitted until he had boots, and he had only tennis shoes. And we didn't know! This time we were quite determined to succeed.

Signs were bad. Dr Hastings Banda, President of Malawi, had been in Zimbabwe being fêted, and President Mugabe had made a stinging attack on the Catholic Justice and Peace Commission for their stand against a one-party state. The new 'united' Zanu (PF) multi-storeyed headquarters had been opened, and ascendant on the top of the building was the old Zanu (PF) party symbol – the *jongwe*, a cock.

Dumiso Dabengwa was appointed Deputy Minister of Home Affairs. I watched on television as Mugabe announced this to the press. He laughed and said that Dabengwa didn't know of his appointment as yet. Apparently it was Dabengwa's daughter, having heard it announced on the radio, who informed her father of his appointment. The president seemed to enjoy flaunting his power and humiliating proud people.

I attended a meeting of the Kamfinsa/Greendale district of the ZNLWVA. We were about forty crammed into the little Zanu (PF) office at the Kamfinsa shopping centre. Halfway through we were joined by Margaret Dongo, the MP for that constituency. I found her enchanting, and the meeting was warm and lively. But I was depressed by the fact that, whenever anyone made a statement, they started off with *pamberis* (forward) for Mugabe and Zanu (PF) and *pasis* (down with) for Tekere and ZUM. Why did we always need an enemy?

Two days before the bomb outrage on Saturday 28 April, Father Michael Lapsley telephoned me, sounding happy and mischievous. I hadn't heard from him for ages, and so, when he announced himself as 'Michael', I said, 'Michael who?'

'You have too many men in your life, Judith,' he said in a priestly voice, and then laughed and identified himself.

Michael was a New Zealander, an Anglican priest, and supported South Africa's ANC.

He had just been on a speaking tour of Canada and a trip to Cuba, and was inviting me to a farewell party at his place on Saturday, as the following week he was going to take up a position with St Columbus Church in Makokoba, Bulawayo. He sounded as if he was really looking forward to it. I couldn't go to the party, as I was myself going to Bulawayo. I returned on Sunday morning and received a distraught message from Phyllis Naidoo. Apparently Michael had had a nice party, and afterwards ran some people to their homes at about 5 p.m. He then went home and seemed to have sat down to open mail, while at the same time either receiving or making a telephone call.

The bomb was in a book parcel, posted from South Africa. I gathered Michael had lost his left hand, the fingers and thumb of his right hand, and that an eye was gouged out. But the lower joint, the one in the hand, as it were, of his right thumb was still there, and there was talk of reconstructing part of that hand so he would have holding ability between the lower joint and the equivalent joint of the first finger. There was also increasing hope of sight in the remaining eye. Phyllis herself had been the recipient of a parcel bomb in Lesotho in the early 1980s. That bomb had flung shrapnel into her and blew off the hand of another Anglican priest, also a New Zealander, Father John Osmond, who was with Phyllis at the time.

People spoke very highly of the treatment Father Lapsley received at Parirenyatwa, and he was out of intensive care and in full command of his mind. He was also deaf, but that might be temporary. The blast must have been terrific. The ceiling was blown out and the TV set turned upside down. I happened to meet a physiotherapist who was with him, and she said he was in agony for about four hours before the operation, after midnight, as they couldn't give him painkillers, apart from the original medication when he was rushed to Avenues Clinic, because of the impending operation.

He kept saying to her, 'Please hold my hand,' and of course she couldn't tell him that there were no hands left to hold. She just said that she couldn't as they were covered with huge bandages, which they were. At that point of her account she briefly broke down, sobbing.

After the first forty-eight hours, the voice of Phyllis on the telephone had changed utterly from one of great distress to one of relief and confidence. She was meant to be part of an ANC group that was planning a meeting with President FW de Klerk in South Africa, but something had happened to delay her departure, which in the circumstances turned out to be a blessing for Michael.

I got a midnight call from Parirenyatwa to say that Brigadier Maponga, former ZPRA, supplicant to the Zimbabwe Project and a survivor, somehow, of Mugabe's regime so far, had been admitted and wanted to see me. Fortunately I was still awake, as I hadn't long been back from a Danish embassy dinner party (good fish, poor chicken). I asked what was wrong with Maponga and was told backache, so I callously told myself that he would last till the morning and went to sleep, setting off for Parirenyatwa not long after dawn.

His summons turned out to be most fortuitous, as he was in the military wing, B11, which meant I could ask him to take me to see Father Lapsley, who was also in that wing and under protection. Poor Maponga was in agony, and it hadn't been established yet what was wrong. He asked me for a hug, and I very much regretted not obliging when he stumbled through with me to Michael, as he immediately put out his stumps and enfolded me as much as he could in his arms. I hugged Maponga when I saw him again later that day. If it hadn't been for him, I wouldn't have been able to see Michael, who seemed really pleased to see me. His eye filled with tears. Oh dear. But we had a good conversation. He had been making a telephone call in the reception area when I got to see him, and then I watched him walk back to bed, quite steadily.

I had another appointment to see Minister Mnangagwa. 'Yes, Judith. What can I do for you?'

We didn't waste time. I said I had come to seek reassurance about possible beneficiaries of the 1988 amnesty, whose names we had at last been expecting to be announced on the most recent anniversary of Zimbabwe's independence, 18 April. It was now the end of June. What had happened?

Mnangagwa said cabinet had agreed that a list of those to benefit from the amnesty should be announced on the tenth anniversary of independence, but drawing up the list had taken longer than expected. It was ready only in May. The president was meant to announce the amnesty before he left for Malaysia, but lost the declaration that Mnangagwa had drafted for him. In the meantime Mnangagwa had gone to Swaziland, and the president couldn't get hold of him. Now Mnangagwa was back, but the president was on leave.

The impression he gave was that somehow the initiative for this amnesty had been lost. It could be put back on course again only if there was a question in parliament asking the president what had happened. I said there had been a parliamentary question the day before, on Friday 22 June, as reported in the *Herald* that morning: 'Free Zapu Dissidents'. Mnangagwa said that that question was an 'unguided missile'. So, I asked, did we need a guided missile? And he said yes.

Perhaps, I said, the amnesty could be announced the same day the *jongwe* was taken down from the Zanu (PF) headquarters. He looked at me as if he didn't know what I was talking about. Remember, I said, Minister Shamuyarira had said that the Zanu (PF) headquarters had been designed before unity, and that now appropriate changes would be made to that design.

'Shamuyarira had no authority to say that,' Mnangagwa said, and then he laughed. 'Yesterday I was there with Nkomo and he hit me with his walking stick and said, *take that down!* pointing up at the cock. I explained to him that I couldn't, as I had no instructions to do so.'

'Where do you get your instructions from?' I asked politely.

Mnangagwa explained that, as he was chairman of the building committee, his instructions had to come from the Zanu (PF) Politburo. In fact, he said, he was still actively pursuing the last lot of instructions he had got, which were to ensure the establishment of a crowing cock on top of the new Zanu (PF) headquarters. Such a crowing cock, apparently, could come from the Soviet Union. He had already been in touch with the Soviet ambassador about the matter.

I found it hard to believe my ears. He was laughing, and I wondered if he could be joking. I don't think he was. I asked if the cock would crow on the hour or just three times now and then. He missed the allusion.

The former dissidents were doing well in their respective ways, being joined by their wives and children, or getting married. There were now three groups of men, one engaged in market gardening in Nkayi; one in agriculture at Plumtree; and one in gold mining at Esigodini. The first entity in Zimbabwe to respond to our appeals for assistance in this matter was the New Zealand High Commission, which had also long ago assisted Vukuzenzele with their first cattle. Then we had a very large grant from the West German agency Bread for the World. I heard of a sticker on a car in Bonn that read: *Bread for the World – But the Sausage Stays Here!* I reckoned the Zimbabwe Project had managed to lift quite a bit of that sausage over the years.

In 1989, the Zimbabwe Project launched an initiative on unemployment. All the studies we had found lacked advice from the subject group. So, hoping to start a national debate, we assembled a group of unemployed, and also people who had created their own employment, to guide us. The name they came up with for their association was *Lifetime – Action For Jobs*.

I spent a morning in Harare's huge dormitory suburb, Chitungwiza, having received an invitation to the first formal annual general meeting of a constituent group of Lifetime. It read: *Confidential: Not for publication. Blind Rise Cleansing Cooperative Society Ltd. Notice is hereby given for a meeting to be held in Chitungwiza Blind Rise Depot on 28 July 1990 at 9 a.m.*

This was a very impressive cooperative that had started as a group of ten unemployed youths collecting waste paper, which they then sold to a recycling firm. There were now fifteen members paying themselves Z$400 each a month, and employing another twenty full-time workers to wash and pack plastic brought in by the scavenging poor in that area.

They paid twenty cents per kilogram for plastic, three cents per kilogram for paper and twelve cents per kilogram for bones. Recycling companies came and collected the tons of paper and plastic. Bones, which were a new venture, proved much more difficult, as they had to supply five tons per trip to the buyer, and they had collected less than one ton in a month, as evidenced by the flies and the smell in the area.

The Zimbabwe Project initially loaned them Z$15 000, which made it possible for Blind Rise to contract their first grass-cutting deal with the Harare City Council, as it allowed them to buy grass slashers and pay the first wages. They paid people Z$7.50 per day for cutting grass.

I saw from the Blind Rise accounts that they had been paid Z$91554.20 so far by the city council and had paid out Z$58010.07 in wages and other costs, such as transport. Overall, in six months, they had made a net profit of Z$2919.28 after having repaid us in full for the loan. This was the kind of endeavour that lifted our hearts, except that we wished they could pay people more per kilogram for plastic, paper and bones. A side product was that it was almost impossible now to see any scrap of plastic or waste paper in the town of Chitungwiza.

Blind Rise, together with two other groups, Karigamombe and Determination, had assisted the Zimbabwe Project in designing a leaflet for distributing, in the first instance, throughout Harare:

LIFETIME – ACTION FOR JOBS
We are experienced in suffering unemployment.
We want to share ideas with people throughout Zimbabwe on action for jobs.

This was followed by brief descriptions of the three groups. Blind Rise was followed by Determination: 'We are eleven ardent Zimbabweans. After failing to get employment we met together in April 1988. One of us had knowledge of bookbinding. We started operations on 1 June. With help from friends we are now engaged in bookbinding and we are training ourselves on the job.' Then came Karigamombe: 'We started in 1988 as eight. We were buying produce from farms then selling to the public. By 1987 we were ten but two cheated so we sacked them. Now we have a yard from where we sell vegetables, chickens and we also have a tuck-shop. We have a Honda (bicycle) to help with deliveries. Now we are doing very well, buying and selling.'

The leaflet concluded: 'Many Zimbabweans are experienced in some way and would be able to achieve their own employment if they knew where to get advice and small sums of capital. Let us get our brains working together and help each other.'

LIFETIME ACTION FOR JOBS
Wants to tackle unemployment
Wants to give a voice to the unemployed
Wants to share ideas with you
Wants action for jobs.

Krish Ragadoo, Elias Mabhena and I went to visit Dr Stanley Sakupwanya in Rusape. It was a business trip, but of course there was a lot of pleasure attached to visiting that beautiful part of the country. After our work on the first day was completed, we agreed to meet at the Brondesbury Hotel. It was empty and ours was the only car in the parking lot. Stanley, travelling under his own steam, was late. Everyone in the area seemed to know him, and he was obviously very popular. When he arrived, he said to the receptionist, a young black man, 'Have you seen three of my friends?'

The receptionist was quite definite. 'Oh no, sir.'

'Are you sure?' said Stanley. 'Because I can see their car outside.'

'Oh, there are certainly none of your friends here, sir. There is only one Indian, one white lady and one black man.'

Didymus Mutasa had sparked a new row by stating that all civil servants should belong to Zanu (PF). The latest *Parade* magazine carried a cartoon of him instructing someone to ask all civil servants who didn't like Zanu (PF) to resign. The man did as he was told and came back to report to Didymus. 'Now there is only one problem, sir. There are no civil servants left.'

While we were in Rusape, Mutasa's stamping ground, we were told that he had been booed at St Faith's school and had threatened to close the place down. People were wearing ZUM T-shirts at a rally he was addressing and he was incensed. 'Do you want WAR?' he shouted at them, and some of them shouted back, 'Yes!'

The Ministry of Political Affairs was going from strength to strength and had its annual allocation from the public purse vastly increased. It was known as the ministry that had been designed to carry Mrs Mugabe's handbag, and it was stuffed with more and more hangers-on from Zanu (PF).

At long, long last a presidential amnesty was proclaimed on Thursday 26 July 1990, nearly three long years after 'unity', and I hoped that all the former ZPRA men would benefit. It was taking a long time for the prison authorities to work out who should be pardoned, but I felt reasonably confident. I went to talk to the officer in charge at Chikurubi and enjoyed a friendly cup of tea. The next day Bryant Elliot went to see some of the men. And on 12 August, at long, long last, George Ndlovu was having his artificial foot fitted.

The *Sunday Mail* that week reported that Danny Stannard had been awarded the Gold Liberation War Medal for his role in foiling an attempt by South African agents to assassinate Zimbabwean and foreign leaders during the 1980 independence celebrations. They were all meant to be blown up together in Rufaro Stadium.

It was revealed that the deadly gadgets included two Strela heat-seeking missiles; four traffic light control bases containing explosives and chopped steel bars; and four giant claymore mines charged with explosives and chopped bars. These were apparently all intended for Rufaro and had been brought into the country aboard a one-ton Ford Cortina, covered by a tarpaulin.

That Sunday was also the unveiling of Godwin Matatu's tombstone at Warren Hills. Almost inevitably, the Minister for Information, Nathan Shamuyarira, who had destroyed Godwin's career in Zimbabwe, as well as those of Michelle Faul, Willie Musarurwa, Wilson Katiyo and many others, impinged on the event – at least in my mind.

The *Financial Gazette*, where Geoff Nyarota was now working, had run an account of what had transpired at the last meeting of the Zanu (PF) Politburo, during which the one-party state was discussed. I hadn't yet seen the story, but, unfolding the *Sunday Mail* prior to departing for Warren Hills cemetery, I found Nathan leaping off the front page to deliver a quick right-left across the chops to anyone who, like me, happened to be an admirer of Geoff Nyarota and the *Financial Gazette*.

'The statement in the *Financial Gazette* last Friday was both inaccurate and a breach of State Security. Like the Cabinet, all deliberations of the Politburo are strictly confidential. All newspapers know this. Publication of any material from high State organs, and more so material that has been obtained surreptitiously, is a breach of State Security.'

Then, so furious was he that he proceeded to tear off all his clothing. 'We are also disturbed by an element within the Politburo itself that seems to be briefing outsiders about the substance of our deliberations.'

The *Sunday Mail*'s centre pages were black with dense columns.

COMMITTED TO SOCIALISM

The Sunday Mail recently was granted an interview with Comrade Yuan Mu, the government spokesman of the People's Republic of China, on the future of socialism in China and its relationship with the rest of the world. *This is the full text of the interview.*

There was relief only as far in as page twelve, in an advertisement from the Municipality of Masvingo on Media Misinformation:

Notice is hereby given by all the councillors of the Municipality of Masvingo that recent Press and other media reports, indicating that the Mayor of Masvingo, Councillor PL Muzvidziwa, had been defeated in a bid by him to seek re-election as Mayor of Masvingo – in short – that he had been 'dumped' when he tried to seek re-election are, quite simply, untrue. The true facts relating to the election of the Mayor and Councillor Muzvidziwa's decision not to accept nomination for re-election to that office could readily have been ascertained by even a half-baked aspiring investigative journalist. One is left with no other conclusion than that these blatant, untrue and scurrilous reports have been published either for personal gain or for no other purpose but to endeavour to demean and embarrass, for no reason whatsoever, a man who has rendered fine public service to this community.

I drove past the new Zanu (PF) headquarters on the way to the cemetery. The cock was still resplendent. Someone had said recently that 'they' had better get a move on with taking the cock down or else one morning they might find its feathers scattered on the pavement.

At Warren Hills, a couple of hundred people had gathered with Rita around Godwin's grave. Mike Munyati, master of ceremonies, announced that this was a day of joy for Godwin, not grief. Godwin's sons Tendeka and Nicholas unveiled the tombstone. It was splendid – black marble with raised gold lettering proclaiming, in the utmost simplicity:

GODWIN MATATU

26-5-47

24-7-89

Eddison Zvobgo said when he felt down he came by himself to Godwin's grave and eventually left feeling renewed. He said he knew that 'this brother, this comrade, this fellow is very happy to see us all today', and that Godwin had taught him that life was beautiful.

'Alive or departed, a beautiful person remains very beautiful,' he said, and then, addressing Godwin, he ended, 'It was nice you came into my life.'

Among the guests at the lunch afterwards was the High Court's Mr Justice Washington Sansole. I asked why he had been named Washington, and learned that it was after Booker T Washington, whom his father, Josias Ndozwi Sansole, had admired for having achieved so much despite a background of slavery. His father, although having had the opportunity of only passing Standard 3 when he was already almost adult, had become a court interpreter, a very successful businessman and a pillar of many communities. He had also managed somehow to find a book on Booker T Washington for his son.

Washington Sansole remembered his grandfather Busaka as a small man, light in complexion and sporting dreadlocks. He had walked hundreds of miles to Kimberley from their home in the Hwange area, as he had heard that after so many years' service on the mines, you were rewarded with a Martini-Henry rifle. He achieved his ambition, and for some months of each year after his retirement from mining would go hunting. He couldn't write, but he made mountains of biltong and marked every tree where the meat was drying with a symbol denoting the kind of meat. He planted Virginia tobacco and *mbanje*, and, mission accomplished each year, would pack his ever-increasing fleet of donkeys with biltong, tobacco and *mbanje*, and go home to hold bazaars in his village.

All this started emerging when I was exploring how the Sansoles had forged their reputation for independence of thought. It transpired that the judge was one of three vaNambya cousins from the Hwange region of Matabeleland, who, despite a great deal of adversity, had all managed to go to university abroad at the height of white supremacy in southern Africa. Washington Sansole had enrolled at Kings College, London, Francis Nehwati at Oxford and David Kwidini at Cambridge.

The more I learned, the more I realised that the roots of their success lay not only in themselves, but also in the bravery, indefatigability and limitless vision of their parents and grandparents, who, despite their own lack of formal education, successfully urged the three cousins ever onwards and upwards.

Sally Roschnik, daughter of Molly and Guy Clutton-Brock, and her husband Roger were visiting Zimbabwe from their home in Switzerland and staying with me, and I was benefiting from the green lights that always flashed a welcome for the Clutton-Brocks. We were invited to dinner at the home of Gertrude and Didymus Mutasa, who couldn't have been more friendly, relaxed and welcoming. Sally and I were boarders at Queen Elizabeth School and had been firm friends ever since. She had taken me home with her to St Faith's at Rusape at just the time her parents were in severe trouble, with Guy being arrested under the then just declared 1958 state of emergency. That was when I first met Didymus Mutasa, who seemed skin-and-spirit close to the Clutton-Brocks, an apparently adoring disciple of Guy.

Now an enormous portrait of Robert Mugabe hung in pride of place over the fireplace in the sitting room, heart of the Mutasa family home. Nonetheless Didymus appeared to be feeling sensitive because, without any information being sought by us, he volunteered that the one-party state would not be legislated for, and also that he had been misquoted about demanding that all civil servants must belong to Zanu (PF).

After dinner I was astonished by the obviously unexpected arrival of Bishop Muzorewa with his son and daughter-in-law, a niece of Didymus. Half an hour after they had been settled with us round the fire Didymus made a little speech, saying we might be surprised to see the bishop there, and explaining how their families were connected. I felt uncomfortable then for Muzorewa.

He remained as smartly dressed as ever. This time he wasn't wearing the two-tone shoes that had been his trademark in the early 1970s, and looked even more dapper in a quiet corduroy suit, matching tie and handkerchief. He didn't pull any punches. Almost immediately after his arrival he started politely attacking the concept of a one-party state, and said how much harm all this talk was doing to the possibilities of investment and, therefore, employment. He obviously wasn't speaking just as an adherent of an opposition party – in fact, he used a phrase I won't forget, as I thought how differently it could be interpreted: 'I love this country to pieces.'

Didymus shook my hand as we were leaving and said we should embark on a new partnership. All I had really said all evening was that I couldn't understand why everyone had to keep talking about Zanu (PF). Why couldn't we just talk about Zimbabwe? That seemed to make him thoughtful and quiet for a few seconds, and he didn't seem to disagree. Indeed, he became exceptionally nice and warm, saying he wanted me to go around his Makoni constituency with him. I tried to look pleased, but didn't say anything. Didymus said we should travel alone so that he could have my brains to himself. I hoped I looked even more pleased, but I was actually recalling something Molly Clutton-Brock, half laughing, had said to me years previously, which, at the time, I didn't comprehend: 'Didymus scatters a lot of seed.'

Gertrude took me aside and said she had heard a broadcast on the BBC that I had done on Mugabe, and she wondered if she could have a copy. I promised to send her one.

I must have missed something. The piece I'd done, months ago, was anodyne, and I couldn't understand Gertrude's circumspection or why Anthony Chennels was so obviously upset by it. After he'd heard my Mugabe piece on *Focus on Africa*, Chennels, an erudite Zimbabwean who lectured at the university, said he was reduced to panic. Usually, he said, he loved hearing anyone he knew being broadcast on the BBC, because it gave him the feeling of being close to the pulse of what mattered, but not this time. This time he wished my piece had been broadcast on Radio Czechoslovakia or Zimbabwe Broadcasting, because then no one would have heard it.

I thought these reactions to my unremarkable piece on Robert Mugabe showed how terrorised we were all becoming without properly noticing it.

The Roschniks also spent a night with the Mutasas in their Rusape home. Sally said that in the half-light of evening she studied the face of Didymus in repose and found it sinister. Didymus had a nephew, an artist, named David Guy, after Sally's father. He had carved a life-size stone statue of Didymus, which was now on proud display in that home. The first night it was in place, the bodyguards hadn't been informed of its existence, and the Mutasas were in Harare when security started the routine evening inspection. The statue was spotted, reinforcements were called in and, as the police levelled their guns, the order was shouted: 'FREEZE!'

The release of former ZPRA detainees started on the night of 3 September, years after they should have benefited from 'unity'. The first five arrived in the office the next day. There was much rejoicing, but now we had to help them face the future. Of those five, one had heart trouble, one a peptic ulcer, one a problem with his eyes and the other two suffered from high blood pressure. Three had been deserted by their wives – not really surprising, as they all had sentences ranging from eighteen to twenty-four years.

The detainees had had to leave their prison uniforms behind, of course, and didn't have a change of clothes, and none of them had any money. One man who was released from death row had no clothes at all. They had been stolen by someone who, I suppose, reckoned he wouldn't be needing them again. Some had been imprisoned before independence for failing to go into assembly points, and all they had to replace their prison uniforms with was their guerrilla uniforms.

I received a letter from someone who hadn't benefited from the amnesty. It had obviously been smuggled from Chikurubi, as it had no official stamp.

'I was arrested in 1979, convicted and sentenced to death for murder the same year. Later I was reprieved to a life sentence. Since then I have several times petitioned the President for mercy but I got no reply. Maybe all my petitions were like a little voice which carried no weight. Please help me obtain my freedom.'

A list of eighteen remaining prisoners had been compiled by those who got out. I approached Minister Mnangagwa and received a very positive response. He asked for a report on the detainees from prisons, and said he would not fail to have the men released should it transpire that their crimes were politically motivated. So maybe this particular chapter could soon be closed.

Stopping at red lights at the intersection of Samora Machel Avenue and Prince Edward Street opposite the new Zanu (PF) headquarters, I looked up at the cock on top of the building, the visible symbol of the humiliation by Robert Mugabe of PF Zapu and Joshua Nkomo, indeed of Zimbabwe itself. I spotted that there was something seriously wrong with the bird, and thought exultantly, 'He's done it! The feathers must be on the pavement!'

The woman driving the car next to mine was also looking up, and then she looked at me. She seemed to be a Zimbabwean, and she didn't look like a member of the Zanu (PF) Women's League, but of course I wasn't sure. Then she grinned so joyfully at me – I must have been grinning at her – that I was confident that she really wasn't a member/prisoner of the hapless but violent Zanu (PF) Women's League.

The tail had dropped off the cock! All that was left, at least for now, was a scrawny little body with a head that, in the circumstances, looked as if it desperately wished for something to cower under.

There was a short item on television showing a few people just released from Robben Island at the end of September and stepping off the ferry. One of them looked as if he might be Ebrahim Ismail Ebrahim. I so much hoped it was, because, if so, Phyllis Naidoo would be filled with joy, and if anyone deserved some joy at last, that person was Phyllis.

There was also a sequence showing Zimbabwe's registrar general Tobaiwa Mudede addressing a workshop of his employees and looking even more ghoulish than usual. He was persuading the workers not to be susceptible to bribery.

Mudede said that if a murderer bribed one of them to give him a birth certificate, and then, on the strength of that certificate, got an identity card or a passport, he would move through the country killing people, and that member of staff whom he had bribed would also be guilty of the murders.

That cut very close to the bone with this viewer.

I had most definitely not been enjoying my conversations with one of the men released from death row under the amnesty. I mentioned this to Bryant Elliot, who asked if I would like to know why Lambert Tsikayi had been on death row. I said that normally I didn't want to know what people had been convicted of, because once they were out of prison, their deeds should lie behind them. But in this instance, yes, as I would like to understand why I was so appalled by the presence of this man. So Bryant sent me a copy of the Supreme Court's reasons for rejecting Tsikayi's appeal against the death sentence:

> At 8.30 a.m. on 8 January 1982 Mrs Frances Marie Clark was walking along Fife Street, Bulawayo, on her way to the bank. She was carrying an empty leather briefcase in her left hand and a cheque in her right hand. Proceeding along she observed a male African standing by a tree with a pistol in his hand. As soon as he saw her the man appeared to load the pistol. Mrs Clark screamed, dropped the briefcase and took to her heels. The gunman fired at her but missed as screaming she dodged in between motor vehicles parked in the centre bays in Fife Street, ultimately throwing herself down behind one such vehicle. Peter George Brice responded to the screams and rushed to offer aid. He was fatally shot by the gunman, just as the latter was departing from the scene in a motor vehicle.
>
> At 9 a.m. on 14 January 1982 Joseph Michael Fox cashed a cheque in an amount of $6 804.96 at the Standard Bank in Belmont, Bulawayo. He placed the money inside his briefcase. As he emerged from the premises he was shot at close range in the chest and abdomen. He was fatally wounded. A priest, Father Genera, happened to be passing by. He observed the gunman, who was a male African, throw the briefcase he had snatched from Mr Fox into a white Peugeot and jump into the vehicle. It was then driven away at high speed by a second African male.
>
> On 18 March 1983 as a result of information received concerning an armed robbery which had occurred earlier that day at Barclays Bank, Hillside, Bulawayo, Section Officer Chirowodza proceeded to the residence of Tsikayi who was not to be found, but as Chirowodza was driving away he spotted a blue Peugeot 404 open truck, the description and registration number of which had been furnished to him as belonging to Tsikayi, travelling along Pumula Road. He immediately gave chase and after a high speed pursuit managed to corner the truck and at gunpoint arrest the driver. In the hollow between the panelling of the offside door and the outer body of the truck Chirowodza discovered a Makarov self-loading pistol. It was cocked and had six rounds of ammunition in the chamber. It was found that the cartridge cases found at the scene of the previous murders had been fired from this Makarov pistol.

I had asked Tsikayi for a curriculum vitae. He provided a partial one. He didn't seem to have any background as a combatant and I couldn't begin to understand how he'd come to benefit from the amnesty. He immediately managed to find himself accommodation in Harare's high-density suburb of Kuwadzana, for which we were paying for three months at Z$50 per month, as for all other released prisoners.

The first time Tsikayi came back to see me, he was carrying a broken radio, 'a gift from a well-wisher', which he wanted me to get repaired for him. I declined. He had also started hunting for vehicles that he said had belonged to him when he was arrested.

I felt very sorry for the people he was among. They must have been terrified of him, as was I. But his requests were getting more reasonable. Initially he asked us for a minibus, a Land Rover, film projector, a mobile disco and a canvas tent so he could have film shows in rural areas. I explained our limitations. Now he was asking for $1 035 for lessons so that he could get a class one driver's licence, which would enable him to find employment as a truck or bus driver. This made me think of Mudede's strictures again.

One Saturday I went to two meetings in Gweru. The first, called by the Ex-Combatants' Security Company under the chairmanship of the founder Horuba, was characterised by a painful honesty – very rare – on the part of practically everyone who spoke. There were about forty present. Jostling for control had started, and one group was stating that this company had no right to use the name 'Ex-Combatants', which had, alas, actually been my idea, and were trying to dispossess them of everything.

My heart went out to Abdul Rahman Fernandez, a local businessman who had made premises available in Gweru for this group. He said he had been anguished by the plight of unemployed ex-combatants and had done his best to help, never thinking that he would be caught in a row.

Chris Pasipamire, CIO, I should think, arrived. He was reputedly very close to the president's wife, Sally Mugabe. She was known as the First Lady, but apparently no provision had been made for such a position in the constitution of Zimbabwe.

Pasipamire often wore a Che Guevara–type cap, promoting his revolutionary presence. He was a tall, quite impressive-looking man, and therefore was accorded an intellectual weight he might not actually have had. He simply stated that there was no use continuing to discuss the affair. While the ZNLWVA would not declare war on the company, it was illegal for them to use the name 'Ex-Combatants' or to raise money on the strength of saying they were assisting ex-combatants. He also said the ZNLWVA should put out a press release stating that they had no connection with this group.

I then said how unfortunate it was that we were sitting around discussing how something that was actually already providing employment in a dramatically successful way should be stopped, and how much better it would be if we were discussing increasing projects for employment.

I asked Chris how many people had been provided with employment by the ZNLWVA since its inception – at which point Horuba applauded loudly. His acclamation certainly didn't help.

Chris bridled and gave the impression that I had no right to ask that question, but that out of courtesy he would reply.

He said they were about to open a chain of hardware stores; about to start a national security cooperative; about to ...

He then went on to inform those present that the major donor agency these days was Amai (mother) Sally Mugabe's Child Survival and Development Foundation, and that a lot of support would be forthcoming from 'the First Lady'.

In other words, be quiet, Judith Todd.

When I got back to Harare, I found an item in the paper reporting that Charles Ndhlovu, aka Webster Shamu, had been chosen in absentia as chairman of the Mashonaland branch of the ZNLWVA. So here came the elite of Zimbabwe's new smash-and-grab generation, the Zanu (PF) CIO piranhas, and there went any hope of a vibrant and honest association of war veterans.

My mother once said the most important thing in life was to be kind to people, and increasingly I agreed with her. Hurting people was bad enough, but, I also found, hurting people unwittingly was even worse.

There was a dinner at the British High Commission for the visiting Lady Soames, who provided the guest list. Among the guests was Sir Glyn Jones, whom I hadn't seen since he and Lord Harlech had come to see me in Marondera Prison during the visit of the Pearce Commission in 1972, and his wife.

I described the visit in *The Right to Say No*, writing that the prison superintendent, Mr Darney, 'was very proud of being visited by Sir Glyn and Lord Harlech. He asked them to sign his special visitors' book and was disappointed when they declined to add a comment after their signatures. When I next saw him I asked what he had thought of the commissioners. He pondered for a moment and then said, "I wanted to show them the quickest way to the nearest barber."'

Sir Glyn came and sat next to me. 'You wrote a book!'

'Yes.'

'And you said my hair was long! Well, you see, Harlech and I played golf when we had time to relax, and we didn't have time to ... '

After all those years he was still upset! I remembered that section of the book well, and explained that the comment was Darney's, not mine, and I had included it because I thought it such a perfect example of Rhodesians having a view on how everything should be correct – even hair.

Sir Glyn was mollified.

Later I met his wife. They were both old now, and Lady Jones was another sad example of a bright spirit locked up in a frail and painful body. I really liked her. She said, 'Are you Judy Todd?'

'Yes, I am.'

'I rather thought so. You wrote a book?'

'Yes.'

'And you said my husband had long hair?'

I was anguished that these two people had obviously been hurt for eighteen years by a reference in a book to Sir Glyn having long hair. I explained again about Mr Darney, and she, too, seemed mollified.

As we all left after a very enjoyable evening, I was behind them going out. His hair was *very* short. I said, 'Sir Glyn, I do like your haircut,' and the three of us laughed. Then I turned back to say goodbye to someone else, and found the other guests within earshot looking at me as if I were quite mad. I realised that it must have sounded like the most absurd comment to be making to Sir Glyn, but I couldn't start explaining.

CHAPTER 24

Spirits of old men

OUR HANDS WERE MORE THAN FULL WITH 187 FORMER combatants belatedly released from jail. What was fascinating about many of them was the reversal of the usual desire to move from rural to urban areas. They wanted to go back to the communal lands and rebuild the societies that had been smashed by Robert Mugabe's 5 Brigade under his Operation Gukurahundi – 'the rain which washes away the chaff'. However, we still spent as much time as possible trying to help promote the positive aspects of the Zimbabwe National Liberation War Veterans' Association.

Through the chairman of the ZNLWVA in Masvingo province, Cosmas Gonese, we became involved with the Zimbabwe Institute of Religious Research and Conservation (Zircon) and the Association of Zimbabwe Traditional Ecological Conservation (Aztrec). They worked with Professor Inus Daneel, a member of the Dutch Reformed Church who was born at Masvingo's Morgenster mission, and with Fambidzano, the umbrella organisation of African Independent Churches. The leaders of these churches were being encouraged to incorporate the message of conservation into the sacraments, land as the body of Christ.

Aztrec combined in its membership traditional leaders (chiefs and headmen), spirit mediums (*masvikiro*) and freedom fighters. The *masvikiro* are responsible for preserving holy mountains, forests and other shrines, and for maintaining the fertility of the land for the ancestors and for present and future generations. This powerful combination of people worked in all seven districts of Masvingo, one of the most crowded and ecologically degraded areas of the country, planting thousands of trees.

I made the long trip from Bulawayo to Harare through Masvingo and Gutu to spend time with Zircon and Aztrec. I picked up a teenage hitchhiker who was going to Mashava, and he was good company. The teenager was at school in Bulawayo and said that he never wanted to set foot in Harare. I asked if this was because there were too many people there.

'Too many people and too much fun,' he answered.

I wasn't really concentrating, so I said 'yes' rather absent-mindedly, then, thinking I had misheard, I said, 'Too much *what*?'

'Fun.'

'Fun?'

'Yes, fun. Discotheques and noise.'

'Don't you have any fun in Bulawayo?' I asked, and he grinned and said, 'Yes, but in Bulawayo I can control myself.'

Later he asked if there were any private detective agencies in Zimbabwe. Criminal investigation was the profession he yearned to follow, but he didn't want to join the police force, as he hated uniforms. I told him about a group we were involved with, Cobra Security and Investigations, and he asked for their address. I said I would give it to him when we stopped.

Just as we came to the branch off the main road to Mashava there was a roadblock about a hundred yards further ahead, with police motioning us to stop. I pulled up at the turnoff to let the hitchhiker out, and was writing down Cobra's address for him when a tall, young and very angry policeman materialised at my window.

'Good morning and how are you?' I asked politely.

'How could you *do* this?' he cried, all agitated.

'Do what?' I asked, finishing writing the address.

'When a police officer tells you to come to him, you come! You don't stop!'

'But the police officer I saw was telling me to stop, and I have stopped.'

'But too soon! You are not meant to stop here. You could be getting up to something!'

By now I couldn't help laughing. The hitchhiker had his address and leapt out of the car and got away as fast as he could, while the policeman and I continued.

'What could I be getting up to?'

'You could be getting up to *lots of things!*'

'But I'm not and now I am ready to proceed ...'

'Next time you get an order from a police officer, you *obey*! Or else you will be in ...' He searched for appropriate words, and I thought he would say something like 'serious trouble'.

'*Shiiiit!*' he said.

In the rear-view mirror I watched him stalking after me the little way to the roadblock, where I found the other policeman grinning and motioning me on quickly before his angry colleague could catch up.

In Masvingo I had to see Mr Alexander Gugu, who wanted the equivalent of US$5 000 from the Zimbabwe Project to help him exploit a limestone deposit he had found, thus enabling the employment of precisely 140 school-leavers to use appropriate equipment imported from India to make cement. Very dubious.

When I arrived at his address, I found two men waiting for him under a tree and joined them. They were prospectors and had brought Gugu some rocks to look at, as they thought they might have struck gold. One of them was brother to Zaka's MP Chindanya, whom he wanted me to meet so that we could discuss appropriate and sustainable income-generating self-help projects for the poorest of the poor. It was too depressing that, even under innocent little trees in Masvingo, people were caught up in this appalling agency language.

But then I moved on to see Zircon/Aztrec, whose company was elevating. From Masvingo through Gutu I was accompanied by Comrade Cosmas Gonese and a young spirit medium, Lydia Chabata, who kept perking herself up with little pinches of snuff.

Gonese told me that Lydia had played a very important role during the liberation war, passing on messages from the ancestors to the fighters. I observed that in those days she must have been very young, as she appeared to be only about thirty now, more than ten years after the war had ended. Gonese said indeed she had been very young, but that didn't matter. The spirits that possessed her were those of old men, so they had the experience and the wisdom, and she simply provided the channel. I thought how exhausting it must be to be possessed by the spirits of old men, but didn't mention my concern for her. She looked strong and resilient.

It was a magic trip, looking at nurseries of bright green seedlings and plots of shooting trees in both rural and urban areas. One wood lot we saw had been planted the previous January, near a rural primary school, and consisted of 9 000 bluegums for timber, 1 700 indigenous trees and 1 000 fruit trees, and nearly a year later they were all still alive. Another wood lot we arrived at unexpectedly was being attended to by scores of men and women in a single, intent and eerily silent file, carrying water from a stream more than a kilometre away.

Water was a huge problem. Gonese said he had been in the Mwenezi district the previous month, where he had observed something he 'never expected to see in Zimbabwe'. In Chief Miranda's area he saw a borehole at which people were collecting water. He counted 500 buckets in the queue, and was told that it took two days to get from the back to the front of the line. He was told that people were walking to that borehole from up to twenty kilometres away, and that people were dying of thirst. Gonese went to see the district administrator to inform him of the situation. The DA said he was very aware of it, and had requested relief from the authorities, but no help had yet been forthcoming.

Leaving Masvingo eventually, I picked up two hitchhikers, one black and one white. The black hopped into the front. The white was about thirty-five, and was born in Zambia and brought up in Zimbabwe, but was now pretty well down and out. He had last held a job with Stuttafords a year ago. He told me he had noticed that money was missing and reported it, then replaced it the next day and was sacked for theft. He was still smarting.

'How could I have stolen money if I had replaced it?'

The black was a driver for Cargo Carriers whose passport was about to expire. As his job entailed driving to South Africa, Malawi, Zaire and Zambia, he couldn't wait to get a passport application processed in Harare, and so had hitched to Masvingo, where he had a brother in the passport office.

The driver said Zaire was hell for everyone, and that the army openly robbed people at roadblocks. The roads in Zambia were hell, but at least the army was okay. Malawi was wonderful because if anyone ever did anything wrong, they were punished so severely they would never think of doing anything wrong again. Zimbabwe used to be a good country, but now there were so many unemployed who had to turn to crime for survival that soon this country would be hell too.

The drivers for Cargo Carriers, he said, went to Zaire unprotected and got Z$300 danger money per trip. They dared not sleep anywhere but in their vehicles or else they would return to find tyres and fuel gone. And the army wasn't the only troublemaker.

He had stopped once to get some food, and an ordinary man said to him, 'Why are you looking at me?' He denied he was looking at the man, who said, 'You *were* looking at me, so you give me 100 Zaires now, or else you are dead.' So he forked out eighty and was still alive.

If the drivers refused to go to Zaire, they were immediately sacked. Every few months a top Cargo Carriers' official went to Zaire 'to give money to the politicians', and that's how they were able to keep operating. I mentioned a recent report in the *Herald* that a Cargo Carriers driver had disappeared in Zaire and wondered if he had been found. My passenger said that that driver had been travelling fast at night and didn't spot a roadblock until it was too late. He hit and possibly killed a soldier and, probably in terror, sped on. There was another roadblock ahead, where the army just hauled him out of the truck and shot him dead. Cargo Carriers knew what had happened, he said, as they sent another driver to collect the vehicle, but officially the poor man had just 'disappeared'.

We stopped to fill up in Chivhu. A middle-aged white man in long stockings, long shirt and a hat came up as I got out of the car, shook hands and greeted me warmly. His teeth were very bad and his eyes very small. I returned the greeting, wondering where on earth we had met, and guessed that he was an agency person, probably from Belgium.

He then walked round the car and warmly greeted the white man in the back. Then he started fussing with a money purse he was carrying, which seemed empty. I thought maybe he owned the garage and was going to collect our money for petrol. I went to the kiosk, just to get away from him.

The man then started walking towards the kiosk, very intent and looking troubled. When he got to the kiosk, he reached over the counter behind the attendant and pulled out a small *sjambok*, which lay coiled behind some packets of sweets. I slipped past him, back to the car, paid fast for the petrol and pulled out. The Cargo Carriers man said he knew him. His father worked for local government – or had – and this son was mad. He couldn't imagine how he had ended up in Chivhu.

We dropped the driver at Willowvale Road in Harare, and the white took his place in front for some final pleading. He looked healthy enough and his clothes were clean and not too worn. He said someone had given him fishing tackle, so sometimes he just fished for days on end. He was a stores' clerk by profession but was now desperate enough to do anything. It was already about 4 p.m., and he was hoping to catch the one friend he had in Harare before he left work, or else he was stuck.

He galvanised me inwardly by saying, 'You are sitting in my bedroom.'

Maybe he felt a huge, unspoken '*what?*' filling the car, because he continued, 'I sleep wherever I find shelter.'

I dropped him as soon as possible before he managed to elicit an address or my name, but I gave him some cash for food. *There but for the grace of God go I.* Missing teeth gave me the impression that he was probably riotous when drunk. I felt bleak about him. With most people you could hope that some wing of an extended family would afford some succour, but not any more with whites in his position.

I managed to persuade my reluctant father to take my Nissan Sunny in exchange for his incredibly old Citroën. He had been telling me how marvellously the Citroën had been doing. 'Came up from the ranch like a bird … twenty-five miles to the gallon … didn't take any water …' But after I had persuaded him to take the Sunny, the truth, unwittingly, started escaping him.

First he said that if the Citroën broke down, I shouldn't attempt to get it fixed. 'Just throw it away.' Then, an hour later, he said I wouldn't have to worry about it being stolen.

'Really?' I asked, amazed, as neither the driver's door nor the boot locked. 'Really,' he said. 'Anyone who steals it deserves to have it.'

We were still hoping for a pick-up truck for him, which had been paid for and should have been made available ages ago, but Duly's were behaving like people who had either been compromised in terms of whom they had actually given his truck to, or like unregenerate Rhodesian Fronters who still hated Garfield Todd. He called to see the sales manager, Graham Maugham, when he was in Harare, and Maugham sent his secretary to say he wasn't free. My father said the last time he was turned down like that had been by Ian Smith just before Smith first had him detained in 1965. It left a bad taste in his mouth – both times.

One who hadn't benefited from the amnesty was Matthew Chizondo. Imprisoned just before independence, he was deserted by his wife, and his two small children were brought up by his parents. When his father died, I received a desperate cry for help from his son, Shungu, who was about eleven. I answered Shungu, saying I would appeal once again to Emmerson Mnangagwa, the Minister of Justice.

Shungu wrote back:

> To say thank you is always in my heart but I will be grateful to hear from you again telling me the reply that shall be given by Mr Mnangagwa. Hoping to receive a successful reply from that Minister. Surely, it is a serious problem for me a young boy to live without father. I will keep on writing you for information. If possible try to write to my father telling that we are now in contact with you. Hopping to see my father in the near future.

Thanks to Mnangagwa, Matthew Chizondo was released on Thursday 10 October 1991, and came straight to the Zimbabwe Project office, but I wasn't there. He left a letter: 'Madam, surely I don't have enough words to thank you. My family were now on the verge of perishing but due to your sacrifice and your unexplainable love you fished me out of the deepest hole and now I am free.'

A fortnight later I received a letter from the address of Madziwa Primary School, Private Bag 956, Bindura. Throughout rural Zimbabwe, villagers use the address of the nearest school.

Dear Madam

I am Shungu Matthew, writing you this one madam. Madam, I am so thankfull that I told my old grandmother to make one small clay port for your flowers. My father is now free and united with us.

You have killed the greatest problem which was definitely aiming to destroy us. I cried a lot when I learnt that the man I was seeing was my father. Father shall send you our snaps.

Please give my greetings to all your family and I am happy that next year I will be going to school.

Thank you very much Madam.

Yours faithfull
Shungu Matthew.

His father had obviously taken everything he could from prison. Three letters of thanks from respective members of his family were all written on pages stamped 'Chikurubi Maximum Prison, Private Bag 7392 Greendale, Harare'. Chizondo himself wrote to say:

I had a very nice journey and before leaving Harare I bought one blanket at $39.99 a piece of soap and 1 bar green soap for washing clothes. Shungu and Darlington and my mother are all very happy. Everyone cried when they saw me. I am not married at this time being. I think it is better for me to find work for at least a year or so then I will be able to make the two ends meet.

We hoped to complete our programme with a hundred or so of the men who had come out of prison under the presidential amnesty by the end of 1991. For those who opted to return to the rural areas we had allocated Z$360 each, enough for the construction of a pole and daga hut under thatch, and we also provided a simple plough, maize seed and fertiliser. People were praying for rain, now frighteningly late.

I enjoyed getting to know the men, although sometimes I wished I had a crystal ball in which I could see an instant summary of their lives and future prospects. Elvis Mhlanga was only twenty-nine when he was freed. He'd been integrated into 4 Brigade after independence, and in 1983 he was sentenced to forty-six years in jail. What were the circumstances?

I never asked, as the past was the past and covered by the amnesty. But Enos Ncube, lying in Parirenyatwa Hospital, was unusually forthcoming. He was a cripple and told me that this was the result of being savagely beaten in his home area of Inyathi and then at Stops police camp after independence.

'I was unfairly arrested.'

He ended up on death row. He said he never had any medical treatment apart from now and then being given Panadol. I took him to Ken Rankin, the orthopaedic surgeon, who said his plight might also have resulted from malnutrition and sitting in one place for too long. He asked Enos if he had been sitting in one place for a long time.

'Yes.'

'How long?'

'Seven years.'

They were allowed thirty minutes of exercise a day.

A neurosurgeon in Harare eventually said he might be able to do something, which was why Enos was in Parirenyatwa. Were I him, I would have been full of foreboding, but he seemed happy.

My parents' friend and doctor, Paul Fehrsen, examined all these men for the Zimbabwe Project free of charge, and Paul was not a rich man. He was just extraordinarily compassionate and we were lucky to know him and Paddy, his wife, who loved and supported my mother with her unstinting friendship. When, on release from prison in 1972, my father and I were detained to the house at Hokonui Ranch, my parents started pining for my release. Paul, as their doctor, was able to get a police permit to visit us, and he brought Paddy with him. They also brought a blonde wig and blue-tinted spectacles for me, and proposed that I should accompany them in the boot of their car that evening when they left the ranch. They would help me get across the border to Botswana.

It was a brave idea, but I couldn't go with the Fehrsens. If I did, I would have put my parents in grave and unacceptable peril by leaving, without permission, our home, which was now an officially designated detention centre. The Fehrsens never stopped helping us.

One of the released men, Duke Moyo, came to the office painfully thin and sick as a dog. X-rays showed that he didn't have TB, and my heart fell. Blood tests were next. Duke kept trying to make me speculate about what he was suffering from, but I refused. He himself was asking colleagues of mine: 'If I have AIDS now, how long will I have to live?'

Three weeks later came the joyful news that the blood tests were HIV-negative, and Dr Fehrsen started treating him for malaria. Duke was grinning like a crocodile, shaking his head in disbelief and saying, 'I thought I had AIDS! But I am safe!' Another man off another kind of death row.

Clever Ndlovu was such a bright man, about thirty-eight, but wracked with abstruse thoughts. He got a job as a security guard, but was soon back in Grey Street Prison after stabbing someone. He was pleading for bail money from us, but had lost his job, and if we provided bail he might get into worse trouble. Others were struggling along, trying to create their own employment, hawking clothes and vegetables, sewing, repairing shoes, pushing Scanias – handcarts ironically named after the huge imported trucks. I was told that one of those pushing a Scania in Bulawayo had been trained as a MiG fighter pilot in the Soviet Union.

Some of the men could be difficult. My colleague Ska Nkomazana rather shocked me one day when she exploded and said that she had lost patience with them. She'd had another argument with Maseko, whose real first name was Lizard, but he called himself Farmer, as he hated being called Lizard. Ska insisted on calling him Lizard.

'Why?' I asked.

'Because he *looks* like a lizard,' she explained.

They really had a love–hate relationship, mostly hate but a bit of love too. I hadn't yet warned Ska that Maseko had come off death row and there might have been very good reason for him to be there. He was now studying motor mechanics at Speciss College.

Of all these men, Samson Nhari had done the best so far. First he got a temporary job with Fawcett Security and did so well that he was taken onto their permanent staff. He had also married a nineteen-year-old. Thuli Bhika got a job as a security guard in Plumtree. Ephraim Dube was exultant about the birth of his daughter. Davityne Moyo was helping with our programme for those released. Frank Nyoni and Alibaba Dlodlo were hawking.

Davityne accompanied me to the home of Enos Ncube about 100 kilometres from Bulawayo. When he introduced me to the ancient-looking mother of Enos, he paid the most perplexing compliment of introducing me as a Khumalo. Later I asked him why he had called me MaKhumalo.

'Because,' he explained, 'you are not a Kalanga and you are not a Shona. You are an Ndebele.'

I didn't tell Davityne that Tonga friends of mine referred to their neighbours the Ndebele as Mabhunu – the Boers.

In 1991 I moved to Bulawayo to be closer to my parents. My home was tiny in comparison to 18 Masefield Avenue in Harare, which was vast and being acquired by Dumiso Dabengwa. It had been beautifully built by my father and befitted Dumiso's status as a government minister. I loved it, but I loved my new home equally. It had a secluded little garden framed with elegant trees. I was within walking distance of the heart of the city, but I woke each morning to the songs of birds. Sometimes I slept in my little bedroom and sometimes I wrapped myself in a blanket and slept in the garden under the vast sweep of stars, hoping to tempt the rain. As usual, I was the most fortunate person in the world. Sometimes I found myself feeling slightly alarmed by all my good fortune. I could never understand the justice of Christ's statement 'to him who hath shall be given', but I found, at least as far as I was concerned, that it was true.

I was now on the board of Zimbabwe Newspapers, the culmination of a long saga, and heard something that amused me. In 1987, Nathan Shamuyarira, then Minister of Information, sued Zimbabwe Newspapers and editor Geoff Nyarota for printing allegations in the *Chronicle* that implicated Shamuyarira in the Willowgate scandal. At a board meeting towards the end of 1991, our lawyer, George McNaught, also a director, said the case was soon to be heard, and recommended that we settle out of court. Shamuyarira was demanding Z$50 000 and an apology on the front page of all the company's titles. McNaught said he could not find any witnesses to support Zimpapers.

Dr Sadza, the chairman of the board, always looked very tired when I indicated that I had something to say, but he usually let me. I said I was most surprised that no witnesses could be found. To start off with there was Geoff Nyarota himself, and then there was Elias Mabhena, who had been chairman of Willowvale at the time. I wondered if Mr McNaught had approached them.

The board decided to let the case proceed, and eventually Mabhena said he would be delighted to be a witness on our side. The case was due to be heard shortly afterwards, but at the last minute Shamuyarira requested a postponement, due to pressure of government business. This was granted. We had no idea when it would come up again, but I gathered that Shamuyarira was still being active behind the scenes, and so I wrote to Mr McNaught as follows:

> A friend of mine has just been speaking to Welshman Mabhena who is a relative and close friend of Elias Mabhena, one of our potential witnesses.

Welshman Mabhena gained a position in Government because of the Unity Accord between Zanu (PF) and PF Zapu. First he was Deputy Speaker and then, after he had criticised the existence of the Ministry of Political Affairs, President Mugabe made him Minister of State for Political Affairs. Welshman told my friend that he had recently had the most extraordinary conversation with Minister Shamuyarira which he couldn't make head or tail of. It went something like this.

Shamuyarira: I gather you are no longer interested in unity.

Mabhena: What on earth are you talking about?

Shamuyarira: I have been informed that Judith Todd has persuaded you to give evidence against me for Zimpapers.

It is extraordinary, as Shamuyarira must know the difference between Welshman and Elias Mabhena. But maybe it was just an implicit threat that Shamuyarira thought Welshman would pass on to Elias. For a top Zanu (PF) man this day to say something like 'you are no longer interested in unity' is a rough equivalent to saying 'I gather you are interested in treason'.

The most interesting aspect of the story though is that it reveals that someone on our Board has been chatting to Shamuyarira. There is nothing wrong with this, of course, but it sounds as though that someone found himself/herself in the position of having to make excuses to the Minister. It is that aspect that interests me.

I suppose the minister never dreamed that Zimpapers would do anything but meekly cave in.

Life continued to be fun for me, and also sometimes very surprising. Once I found myself sitting next to Enos Nkala at a wake. We were infinitely polite to each other. He had been born again and had calmed down, and only now and then did his eyes roll. But I hoped he would never again be in touch with political power.

People were not looking forward to the return from exile of Ndabaningi Sithole in January 1992. 'Just more of the same,' said my mother. Sithole had been one of the brightest of her pupils at Dadaya. But it seemed he also always had a great appetite for power, and we had enough – more than enough – people in that category already. According to statements published in what President Mugabe attacked as our 'yellow press' – independent publications such as *Parade* and the *Financial Gazette*, as well as the new *Sunday Times* and the new magazine *Horizon* – it seemed as if Sithole regarded himself as a sorely needed saviour, and that was not the wisest way to attract the electorate. Zimbabwe needed new faces and fresh brains, not a continuation of the old fights among the same antagonists who had started attacking each other when Zanu split from Zapu long before the majority of the present population was even born.

The backdrop to life in Zimbabwe – or rather the looming lack of life – was just too depressing for words. This was the punishment for putting Zanu (PF) before Zimbabwe, and the party ahead of the government.

I was appointed an unpaid consultant to the newly established Mafela Trust, named after the late 'Mafela' Lookout Khalisabantu Vumindaba Masuku, which was established to find the graves of those who had died in the liberation struggle on the PF Zapu side.

As the power went to Zanu (PF), and because of unfortunate political developments, Zapu's records of war dead had been seized and were missing. So this attempt to find the graves of and the circumstances in which about 2 600 of the missing fighters had died was primarily to honour them and to help assuage the continuing grief of their families.

The findings included entries such as: NDLOVU, Kwete Olivia (war name SIMPLICITY). Died 1978 at Mkushi camp, Zambia, during air and ground attack by Rhodesian forces. She was buried there in a mass grave. Came from Chief Mpini's area, Headman Sikhathini, Tshakowa area, Plumtree. Next of kin is ZONDO, Easter, of 61586 Pelandaba, Bulawayo.

A lot of the information was fragmentary, like: War name MAGUSWINI. Real name not yet known. Died 1974 at Sidobe area of Hwange in fierce battle while his unit was preparing to ferry recruits across the Zambezi. Next of kin not yet known.

All this research was intended to be published in the local press eventually to elicit further information from the public.

One Saturday I accompanied Peter Fry from the Ford Foundation and members of the Mafela Trust to Pupu, the site of the battle between Allan Wilson and his men and Lobengula's warriors near the Shangani River. It is about 45 kilometres beyond Lupane, and there is still a little memorial there to Wilson and his men, with a corner demolished during the liberation war. Resting next to the memorial is a circle of stones marking the mass grave of the Ndebele warriors. The local people wanted Wilson's memorial repaired and renovated and, within the same circumference, a memorial erected to Lobengula and his men, and to ZPRA. Preparations were starting to honour all sides by 1993, the hundredth anniversary of the Allan Wilson Patrol being wiped out by Lobengula's warriors.

The elders were gravely waiting for us on the verge of the road under the tall trees so that we wouldn't get lost. Opposite the Wilson memorial, which is very close to the road, was the work of one of the local dignitaries, an old man called Dube. It was a sign painted in rather shaky letters, reading: 'Welcome to the Dube bus stop'.

Sam Mpofu, who was in the process of buying Hokonui Ranch, deployed two security guards, armed with one shotgun, to wander over the land and 'protect' it. Part of their duty was to ensure that anyone caught fishing in the beautiful Ngesi River paid one dollar. I wished so much that my parents would just leave the ranch, which they continued to manage for him, and move to Bulawayo. But my father was determined to go on trading for as long as possible, and people were so grateful, especially as he retailed at normal prices and didn't indulge in conditional selling.

There were hundreds of people who sat outside the stores at Dadaya, Bannockburn and Zvishavane every day waiting for maize-meal. My father would go and tell them that he had been speaking to the suppliers and there wouldn't be any maize-meal that day, but they kept on waiting.

President Mugabe promised that not one Zimbabwean would die of hunger but many already had. One government administrator told me that when we read of children dying of measles, etc., this really meant malnutrition.

Sabina Mugabe, sister of the president, rose in parliament in April 1992 and said she was cancelling political rallies in her constituency of Zvimba because she had run out of things to say. People were asking her for even three kilograms of maize-meal to share, but she had nothing to give them. She said that 'we' had been telling lies to the people for too long and she now had nothing left to say to them.

Around the same time, I heard glad news in the rural areas that the president had absconded. For years, first according to Ian Smith's Rhodesian Front (those 'tribesmen') and then Mugabe's Zanu (PF) (those 'peasants' and *povo*), we had been told that the rural areas were packed with illiterate and ill-informed people. That had never been my experience. Two days after I heard that joyful rumour, it was reported in the press that President Mugabe had gone on leave and that Dr Joshua Nkomo was the acting president.

Nkomo's first move was to send Denis Norman off to South Africa to discuss the movement of maize. That was something Mugabe couldn't do. Then we learned on the grapevine that President Mugabe was in Ireland, guest of Tony O'Reilly, the Heinz tycoon. After that, rumour was rife. Mugabe had resigned. Mugabe was having trouble with his Ghanaian relatives, as they were demanding the money of his late wife, Sally. No one was sure when he would return from abroad. It would be better for Zimbabwe if he stayed away for ever and ever, amen.

Minister Kangai said people should effect citizen's arrests of anyone overcharging for maize-meal, as if there was any available to sell. I thought the first citizen's arrest should be of the president for putting Zanu (PF) ahead of Zimbabwe and for appointing such incompetent, self-serving people to his cabinet. Three years previously the Commercial Farmers' Union had warned that we were in danger of running out of maize.

A great scandal was unravelling at the Grain Marketing Board. When grain was bought and payment made, there was, in many cases, collusion between the buyer and the seller. If, say, I sold 100 tons, a nought would be added to the payment slip, and I would be paid for 1 000 tons, the difference then being split between me and the person who wrote the slip. So the authorities had been working on false figures, believing much more maize was available than was the case.

We were in a real mess. The police had activated a docket on the Attorney-General, Patrick Chinamasa, for fraud. The Attorney-General's department was prosecuting top police and other officials, and in that case the names of Solomon Mujuru (formerly Rex Nhongo), head of the army, and Minister Mnangagwa were appearing. Shirihuru, a top CIO boss, was at last being brought to book for organising the 'disappearance' of his girlfriend Rashiwe, who had jilted him. But when he was first meant to appear in court, he didn't, as he had been admitted to Parirenyatwa, rumour had it on the orders of President Mugabe. News leaked out from doctors at Parirenyatwa (not for publication, but just for thirsty individuals like me) that there was nothing physically wrong with Shirihuru. Eventually he did appear in court and was locked up, but then, as a consequence of pressure from high up in the Attorney-General's department, was released on bail.

Friday 3 April 1992 was my mother's eighty-first birthday, and I went to the ranch to celebrate with my parents. They were now leasing the house from Sam Mpofu, as my father was still trading. When my father got home that evening, he was exhausted and as white as a sheet. Four hundred pockets of maize-meal, weighing ten kilograms each, had been delivered to the eating house he ran in Maglas, Zvishavane, and there were 3 000 people waiting for it. The police had to baton-charge people off the veranda before the store could be opened. My father said the police were quite obviously afraid, so it was he – eighty-four next birthday – who had to go out among the people and organise them into a queue. He said the people, despite present circumstances, were so nice to him, and he seemed able to move among them with impunity when even the police could not.

I watched, with dismay, my father becoming more and more thin-skinned. He was devastated watching his beloved ranch, which he had built up so painfully, being wrecked not only by the drought, but also by the new owner. Fences weren't being mended. Pumps weren't repaired. Herders were not paid. Bulls were starving. So he was getting white and furious with government, with unscrupulous traders, with the Zanu (PF) chefs, and he suffered so abominably much for the people. I wished I could take the burdens of his heart onto my shoulders, but I couldn't. I am fatalistic and thus survive. He was not. But I was proud of him.

It wasn't just food; it was lack of water for people and animals. In the Kezi district of Matabeleland South, for example, 97 per cent of all wells, dams and boreholes were dry. There were only two government trucks, and one was out of order. There were seven water bowsers, and none of them had wheels. For those pumps that still worked, there was no diesel.

We received a letter from the district administrator of Kezi, Lancelot Moyo, who said the serious food shortages in that area were particularly affecting schoolchildren, 'who sometimes go for days without a meal, resulting in fainting at school and reduced participation in learning and other school activities'. He asked for help with supplementary feeding, and said the Ministry of Education had provided figures of serious cases at each of the primary schools in the district, 'which we consider as just the tip of an iceberg, as we believe more children than stated are affected. Could you please kindly consider our request and help save these little children?' The figure given by the ministry for that district alone was 6 393.

I went to see a family in the Hope Fountain area near Bulawayo who I suspected had no food. When I got to the village, I found that the children were cooking grass.

Life in Zimbabwe was like being in the midst of an unbelievable nightmare, praying that you would wake up to an acceptable reality. All the ecstatic rumours that Mugabe had absconded were soon dashed. He came back and cruelly sent Nkomo off to North Korea to attend Kim Il Sung's birthday party. But by then Nkomo and Denis Norman had arranged substantial deliveries of maize to Zimbabwe from South Africa, the USA and Argentina, so the situation regarding food was easing. The major problem now was distribution.

Our TV news showed President Mugabe back in State House, plush surroundings and plush visitors telling him how proud they were of what Zimbabwe had achieved under his leadership since independence. And there were long queues of people throughout the country, around the clock, who didn't believe shop owners when they said there would be no maize deliveries that week.

In July 1991 I was invited by the French Catholic Committee for Development and Against Hunger to a conference in Paris on Ethiopia and Eritrea, which would be attended by representatives of all their different factions. My role was to tell them about the experiences of the Zimbabwe Project in demobilisation and reconciliation, and presentations were also made by Vietnam, Cambodia, Colombia, Haiti and Algeria.

When the Ethiopians/Eritreans learned that I was from Zimbabwe, they were instantly united in their hostility to me, as Mugabe had recently given their former tormentor, Mengistu Haile Mariam, asylum. Firstly, although they were polite enough not to enunciate the fact, I could tell they were amazed that the representative from Zimbabwe was a white woman. After we jumped that hurdle, they quite obviously assumed that I was a member of Zanu (PF). They then wanted to know why we, Zanu (PF), had given asylum to Mengistu, but, even more urgently, they wanted Mengistu's precise physical address. They made it quite clear that Zanu (PF) would have to choose between friendship with Ethiopia/Eritrea and continuing to harbour Mengistu. It was a salutary lesson on how unpleasant it must be to be a member of Zanu (PF), but we made friends, I enjoyed the conference and all ended well.

Nine months after the conference, I received a call from one of the people who had been present, Dr Asrat Felleke, a former Ethiopian ambassador now living in Arlington, Virginia. He wanted me to pass on a message from him to Mengistu. I was appalled and said I couldn't possibly do that. Mengistu, it was reported, had been appointed to CIO as a consultant. He said, well, it wasn't actually Mengistu he wanted, but Mengistu's uncle, Asrat Wolde, who was living in exile in Harare with Mengistu. He had been the Ethiopian ambassador to Zimbabwe when Mengistu sought asylum, but of course he was replaced. Felleke just wanted Wolde to ring him and gave me his number. I said I would try.

Through Swazini Ndlovu, I found out that Danny Stannard was apparently still with CIO, under Elleck Machingaidze, and I rang him, explained the situation and requested help. He was charming and said, 'For you I killa da bull.' I said I would prefer a *jongwe*. Once again we promised to have lunch with each other some day. How times had changed. It was reported in the papers that a man detained in the 1980s had been awarded Z$40 000 damages. Enos Nkala, who had to give evidence, said he 'dimly remembered' signing a detention order.

Zanu (PF)'s telephones had been cut off, as they owed more than half a million dollars in unpaid bills. This was announced in the press, but then Didymus Mutasa appeared on television to say there had been a misunderstanding. PTC didn't just cut off their telephones. Zanu (PF) had *asked* PTC to cut the telephones, as people were abusing them.

Mutasa also took the opportunity to say that people didn't really understand democracy. They shouldn't be calling for the sacking of various ministers, as they had been appointed by the president and if the ministers were sacked, it would be a vote of no confidence in the president. The fact that people were calling for the sacking of these ministers showed that they did not understand the democratic system.

In June the *Government Gazette* announced the allocation of a further Z$500 million to the Ministry of Lands, Agriculture and Rural Resettlement. I assumed that this must be for the acquisition and distribution of more land, but then learned that it was for the importation of maize. What expensive mistakes we had been making. Government asked commercial farmers to release stocks of maize they were holding for their animals and for farm workers who, with their families, were said to account for a massive two million of Zimbabwe's population. The farmers had asked to be paid for this maize at the same rate that was being paid for imports. Because the maize price had been controlled, they made a loss on growing it. So the present crisis of hunger was a direct result of government policy.

Herbert Ushewokunze was now Minister of Energy and Water Development, which was one of the reasons that it was feared Mutare would be dry by July and Bulawayo by August. He had effectively helped to ruin five ministries since independence, and people simply didn't understand why Mugabe kept him on. It couldn't just be because of his undoubted charm.

On Thursday 11 June I was interviewed for an hour and a half by an Inspector Simango and a Mr (didn't get his rank) Ndlovu of the Law and Order (Maintenance) branch of the police. They had rung and asked for an appointment to see me at home. I agreed and gave them afternoon tea. When they left, they thanked me for the tea and said they hoped next time it would be dinner. There was a new group, the Forum for Democratic Reform Trust, which had started off as a think-tank but might transform into a political party. The police had erroneously thought I was one of those behind it.

There were meant to be nationwide peaceful demonstrations organised by the Zimbabwe Congress of Trade Unions, but they were banned by Moven Mahachi, Minister of Home Affairs, who cited the potential for violence, disruption of essential services and alleged political motives of the body.

'That demonstration is against democracy in the labour movement and is a recipe for disaster, because the unemployed and other misguided elements will commit acts which will cause untold harm and misery to our law-abiding citizens whose rights will be violated,' said Mahachi.

The atrocities of 5 Brigade were beginning to surface. In July I went to Antelope Mine in Kezi, where some people had opened up a disused mine shaft to find, to their horror, twelve human femurs and four human skulls above water level. The local people had known about this right from the beginning, of course, but an accidental discovery was needed to get the matter aired in the press.

I was accompanying a young man whose brother had been killed by 5 Brigade. One of the killers had come to him earlier in the year to seek forgiveness. The killer had been one of a group of four. The other three had since died. He was terrified of divine retribution and had sought help from a traditional healer. The medicine he was given was bitter. He had to seek out the relatives of those he had killed and publicly apologise. Only then would he be safe.

Local people were themselves feeling just safe enough to start planning a 'procession of prayer', to provide an occasion for proper and public grief. I was told it would be a protest against the government's failure to protect people from death and destruction, and a demand on government to acknowledge the crimes committed and accept responsibility for all reburials, reconstruction of destroyed homes and payment of school fees for children left fatherless. Finally, they wanted President Robert Mugabe, as commander-in-chief of the armed forces, to apologise to the people.

On Saturday 29 August, Zimrights, a group formed to promote and protect human rights in Zimbabwe, was launched. The two patrons were the former chief justice, Enoch Dumbutshena, and my father. The trustees included Morgan Tsvangirai, secretary general of the Zimbabwe Congress of Trade Unions, and John Deary, president of the Confederation of Zimbabwe Industries. Under them was a council of about twenty-two people, including doctors, nurses, lawyers, civil servants and the president of the Students'

Union at the university. I was deputy secretary for political and human rights.

The president appointed Perrence Shiri the new air marshal, head of the air force of Zimbabwe. Shiri, a Chikerema and a relative of Mugabe, was the founding and actual commander of 5 Brigade during their reign of terror in Matabeleland and part of the Midlands. The *Sunday Mail* carried a photograph of President Mugabe and Air Marshal Shiri toasting each other on the occasion of this appointment. Underneath the picture was a report on the launching of Zimrights, including a comment from my father that I'm sure was never intended for publication, saying he had learned from his daughter Judith that 5 Brigade, during the terrors of Gukurahundi, was under the command of one Perrence Shiri. Apparently this fact had not been published before. That afternoon, Jeremy Brickhill rang to ask if I had seen a copy of the newspaper. 'Air Marshal Perrence Shiri must be thinking of you most affectionately today,' he said.

A young man from Tsholotsho, who wanted to become a researcher for Zimrights, came to see me. In 1983 he had witnessed the killing of his father by 5 Brigade. He told me of a local man who had supplied a list of names to 5 Brigade of whom to hunt down in the area.

'I don't want vengeance,' he said. 'I know what happened to my father, but many people do not know exactly what happened to their relatives. I want to go to that old man and ask him why he wrote those names and if he can remember them all, and if he knows what happened to those who disappeared. Between us, we may be able to help the survivors.'

I had been speaking to a former member of ZANLA who had trained in Romania for seven years. I asked if he hadn't known what Ceauşescu was really like. He said that everyone had known, but there were so few people you could safely talk to. When I asked if there were any Romanian jokes about Ceauşescu, he gave me an example.

Ceauşescu was invited to an African country, where the head of state was just about to throw a banquet for him. In a fit of thoughtfulness, he asked if there was anything in particular Ceauşescu would like to eat. Yes, Ceauşescu replied. The brains of an African. They were duly served and enjoyed. A year later, on a return visit, Ceauşescu asked the African head of state if there was anything in particular that *he* would like to eat. The head of state grinned and said, yes, the brains of one of Ceauşescu's close-security bodyguards. The order was given. Hours passed. The African head of state got very irritated. Ceauşescu called for the head of the close-security unit and asked what was happening. The head of the unit was pale, sweating and profuse with apologies.

'So far, Comrade President, we have killed thirty-two of them, but we haven't yet found any brains!'

Our jokes were somewhat gentler. In Bulawayo there is a famous psychiatric hospital, Ingutsheni. In the usual fanfare of sirens that always accompanied the massive presidential cavalcade of armoured vehicles, soldiers crouched cat-like and at the ready over their guns in open trucks, and men on motorbikes, President Mugabe had arrived on a brief public relations visit to Ingutsheni. One of the inmates approached and greeted him, asking who he was.

'I am the President of Zimbabwe.'

The inmate grinned joyfully. 'Oh really,' he said, 'and how long do you think you will be here with us?'

Mugabe consulted his watch and said, 'About another seven minutes.'

The inmate shook his head sorrowfully and said, 'I'm afraid you may be in for a shock. I have been here for seven years already, and I was brought by only one policeman.'

On my most recent visit to Harare, I had watched the presidential entourage stream past and noticed that an ambulance had been added at the rear. The only vehicle still missing was a hearse.

CHAPTER 25

Plunder at Zimbabwe Newspapers

M Y PARENTS COMPLETED THEIR MOVE FROM HOKONUI RANCH
in good heart by the beginning of 1993. The acquisition of a computer
at just the right time helped my father bridge the chasm between the ranch
and Bulawayo. We were all undergoing major change in our lives, and that
March I completed a short-term consultancy for Core, the Reintegration
Commission in Mozambique, where I had never been before.

Core fell under the United Nations Office for Humanitarian Assistance
Coordination, and this in turn was part of United Nations Operations
in Mozambique. My brief was 'to assess the relevance of experience in
Zimbabwe in the reintegration of ex-combatants into civilian life and
examine how this can be brought to bear on the programmes now being
considered in Mozambique for rural occupations, vocational training and
job creation mechanisms for demobilised soldiers from Government and
Renamo forces'.

The assignment came at a good time. I had resigned from the Zimbabwe
Project earlier that year, when it was brought to my attention through a very
direct letter from my successor, Paul Themba Nyathi, that he really could no
longer bear the continued presence of 'a founder, ex-director, appointed
trustee continuing to be actively involved in the day-to-day operations', and
so I swiftly removed that presence. As I said to Paul, I was probably the kind
of person who needed a shove to make me move on, and he had provided
it. But I was sorely missing the work, the staff, the people off the streets,
everything to do with the Zimbabwe Project, including the salary cheque
each month, so the offer of this consultancy was welcome.

I returned from Mozambique feeling optimistic. I was wildly fortunate
in whom I met, one of the highlights being a morning with the officers of
the First Battalion, who wanted to discuss the nitty-gritty of demobilisation
in Zimbabwe. The first man to let fly with his opinions, which I thought were
really aimed at the men accompanying me from the Ministry of Defence,
was a Frelimo veteran of the colonial war who had spent practically all his
adult life in the army. He said that never, ever again did he want to hear
anything about politics.

The director of the Green Zones, the former showpiece of cooperatives outside Maputo, said that from 1987 they had realised that collective co-operatives were absolutely not what people wanted or needed. These former cooperatives had become 'associations', people working their own plots but sharing tractors and marketing facilities. It was my impression that people were sick and tired of ideologies and jargon, and I was amazed and heartened by the temperance with which members of the opposing groups, Frelimo and Renamo, referred to each other.

In 1966 at a World Assembly of Youth conference in Japan I had met a young man in exile from Mozambique who was studying in Algeria to be a doctor. He was one of the pioneering members of Frelimo, Mozambique's liberation movement. I hadn't seen him since but he was now the Minister of Foreign Affairs, and he called on me one afternoon in Maputo with his oldest son, who was also named Pascal Mocumbi.

They walked through the hotel lounge looking for me, totally relaxed, waving at friends and with no apparent bodyguard in sight. When Dr Mocumbi introduced me to his son, he told him of the dreams we had had in 1966 for our respective countries, and indicated, in the most subtle and diplomatic way possible, that he feared I may have been disappointed.

On 30 April, as a director of Zimbabwe Newspapers based in Bulawayo, I took part in a promotion drive at the *Chronicle*, handing over a water bowser to Ray Ndhlukula, provincial administrator for Matabeleland South. This was for the Msimbi community in Gwanda, who live on a bed of granite rock where boreholes can't be sunk. Also present was Tommy Sithole, editor in chief of Zimpapers, who escorted me to my car at the end of the presentation.

Sithole was extremely uncomfortable, but said he needed to talk to me. He had never before approached a board member and didn't like doing so. He had consulted his long-standing friend Ali Halimeh of the PLO, who said that Tommy should see me. Ali had offered to ring me and request a meeting, but then he had to go to London for health reasons before managing to do so.

I said we didn't need Ali as an intermediary anyway, and suggested we sit in my car and talk. Sithole declined, and instead we stood at the car for about half an hour in full view of *Chronicle* employees. They must all have been at fever pitch with rumour, speculation and anxiety.

Sithole wanted me to know that the company was in dire straits. I said I knew. He said he was doing everything in his power to rescue the company, which had been very good to him. It made him angry to have to tell employees there would be no thirteenth cheque for a Christmas bonus, and to see little people being retrenched when the cause of all this had been theft by the top people.

He had become sick because of the state of affairs at Zimpapers and had nearly lost his pilot's licence because of high blood pressure. He had been to see Dr Davison Sadza, the chairman of both the Zimpapers board and the Mass Media Trust, and had presented him with an ultimatum that action had to be taken by the end of the following week.

He had told Dr Sadza that the devastating scandal revealed at Hunyani Holdings (paper products), which also fell under the overall MMT, was a 'lollipop' in comparison to what had been going on at Zimpapers, and 'just for starters', he said to Sadza, here were photocopies of documents revealing theft of more than Z$800 000. Sithole demanded repayment of those monies to the company by 7 May.

Sithole said the police were aware that there was something amiss, but he had spoken to the permanent secretary at Home Affairs, Job Whabira, and asked that the police be kept out for the moment. Sithole first wanted to recover as much money for the company as possible, and then the police could act and take people to the cells.

Our editor in chief had been transformed by circumstances into investigator in chief, and I was impressed by his passion. It was obvious that he was really suffering, both physically and spiritually. Sithole was telling people that this was a fight to the death. They could choose sides. But if they wanted a future for Zimpapers, they had better cooperate with him and bring him evidence of all criminal activity.

I asked if he thought I could or should do anything. He said no. He didn't like talking to me, but as he was putting his head on the block, it was necessary for one member of the Zimbabwe Newspapers' board to have some idea of what was happening in case there was any attempt to conceal events from the board. However, he was confident that remedial action would be taken from the following week.

Jonathan Moyo told me there was a 'scary' paper circulating about the plight of Zimpapers. I was already thinking of reassembling the little group my father had instituted in Harare, which included Moyo and Luke Mahlaba, who taught at the university (both men were also writers); and journalists Geoff Nyarota, Tendai Dumbutshena and Tonic Sakaike, to plan ahead so that we could get the best possible board of directors elected at the next AGM.

These were people to whom my father had given a few Zimpapers shares each so that they could take an active interest in company affairs, especially at AGMs. I thought that when the financial scandal was revealed at the AGM, as it surely must be, the whole of the present board, including me, should offer our resignations. Unfortunately, Luke Mahlaba was in Cambodia.

Professor Reg Austin, originally from my hometown of Zvishavane, was helping to organise elections in Cambodia, hence Luke's absence. Reg had managed by including democrats with skills in the election process to help a few Zimbabweans like Arthur Chadzingwa gain temporary employment and earn some foreign currency. Arthur had fallen out with Foreign Affairs Minister Nathan Shamuyarira, and lost his diplomatic post. Swazini Ndlovu was one of those who, courtesy of Reg, had received, out of the blue, an offer of a contract to assist in the elections in Cambodia.

Swazini was overcome with rage and told me that he had *just* managed to survive the liberation war. He had *just* managed to hang onto his job with the Bulawayo City Council despite all the arrests and detentions he had endured since independence. He had even been promoted. So, he wanted to know, who was the lunatic who now wanted Swazini to go and get killed in Cambodia?

I didn't let on to Swazini that it was Reg Austin, to whom I was very grateful when he suggested my name to Bernt Bernander, head of UNOHAC, for the consultancy in Mozambique. It wasn't only Dr Sadza who benefited from the good offices of homeboys.

Throughout the first week of June, we were forced to read about, listen to and watch extensive coverage of President Mugabe touring Harare. He gave the impression of being spokesman for some vague opposition group, with no responsibility at all for government.

He thought the Harare City Council was charging too much for stands. He couldn't understand why bank interest rates were so high. He thought maize-meal was now too expensive, government subsidies having been removed, and hoped people would be able to use hammer mills to grind meal for sale in the rural areas.

He said multinationals had recouped all their investments and were now just 'scooping' money out of Zimbabwe, and both he and Dr Nkomo, depending on what mood and whose company they were in, were coming across more and more as anti-white and anti-Asian.

Most of us laughed at this, but some whose skins were more sensitive were becoming unsettled and unhappy. Nkomo, on behalf of his

Development Trust of Zimbabwe, kept urging whites and Asians to give up their commercial properties in towns to benefit blacks, and had been trying to pressure the local authorities in Bulawayo, Gwanda, Victoria Falls and Kariba – and no doubt elsewhere – into giving his trust land for free.

Geoff Nyarota told me there was 'a good black joke' doing the rounds, which was: 'If there are any business opportunities available, we would *love* to embark upon them with whites or with Asians, but not with the Development Trust of Zimbabwe'.

I overheard my mother saying, 'I do wish you would stop going on and on and on about Mugabe being mad. It gets so boring.'

My father laughed and responded, 'The problem is that he goes on and on and on *being* mad!'

A letter, dated 19 April, arrived from Doris Lessing. She said that writing her biography 'is quite painful, not least because it increases my conviction, always there, that there need never have been that terrible and damaging war, if a small section of the whites hadn't been so foolish. For I am sure if sensibly led and not by that rather stupid man Ian Smith, a war could have been avoided. And now today, at this very moment, there is Chris Hani's funeral, and he was killed by a follower of Terre'Blanche – a group of people so stupid and ignorant, and yet they can plunge all of South Africa into this misery.'

I attended the memorial service for Chris Hani in the large Bulawayo city hall. I went with my father, who, as soon as he was spotted, was elevated to the platform to join the Ministers' Fraternal, a body representing all the churches, and he offered the main prayer. Unfortunately people don't take notes of prayers, which is why they have so often been such valuable political weapons. It's difficult to bring as evidence to court what someone was saying aloud, but to God.

A number of Hani's contemporaries and others of the Luthuli detachment during the Wankie and other battles of 1967 attended the service, but unfortunately not Sly Masuku. Henry Ntsele (Nelson Linda), a South African, was the author of the main salute to Hani. He requested that it be read by Matthias Nyoni, a Zimbabwean, who had been with the ZPRA group in Wankie and who had been on death row in Bulawayo with Ntsele afterwards. It was a fine tribute. Thankfully some people remembered what that awful struggle had all been about – freedom, dignity, hope and justice. Maybe even love.

The Zimpapers saga rumbled on. I had felt very sad over the years for my father who, as a major shareholder, had battled hard to get information on the fortunes of the company but at every turn was consistently frustrated by the chairman, Dr Sadza, and his colleagues.

I hadn't been having an easy time of it either. If they hadn't been so intent on finishing AGMs in twenty minutes flat ('Have you given twenty-three days' notice of that question?'), and if they hadn't reduced the board to a rubber-stamp, Zimpapers might not have collapsed into such a mess. Davis Midzi, managing director, and allies had been skimming hundreds of thousands of dollars out of the company and neglecting to do such things as pay company tax. Midzi was responsible for all papers that came to the board, and the auditors reported to him, so maybe he felt his position was foolproof. Tonic Sakaike told me that Midzi was a homeboy of Dr Sadza.

Tommy Sithole collected a lot of evidence and took it to Sadza, who did nothing, so Sithole bravely published an account of the looting in the *Herald* under his own byline while Midzi and Co. were still in the building. I was the only one on the board who knew what he was going to do. After he published on a Friday/Saturday, I set about bringing pressure on Sadza and Co. to call an emergency board meeting, which took place the following Tuesday.

I had to sit and listen to Sadza lamenting the fact that Sithole had published without consultation, and managed to hold my tongue on the knowledge he didn't know I had, which was that Tommy had gone to him and he had done nothing. But when another board member suggested that Tommy be reprimanded, I really lost my cool and, shaking with fury, said that if he hadn't published we wouldn't be sitting there in the boardroom trying to save the company and Midzi and Co. would still be robbing away. People looked very surprised by my passion, but there wasn't another peep from anyone about trying to bring Tommy to heel.

Far from calling in the fraud squad, Dr Sadza and fellow members of the board, such as lawyer Honour Mkushi, ignored what had been published by the editor in chief. They ignored my protestations. All they did was set up an internal commission of inquiry, answerable, of course, only to themselves.

By September my time with Zimpapers was over, as I had been removed. Bill Saidi asked for a summary of the two years I had spent on the board for his *Sunday Gazette* magazine. It was published on 26 September, and included the following:

My two years on the board of Zimbabwe Newspapers (1980) Ltd were thanks indirectly to the now Minister of Foreign Affairs, Nathan Shamuyarira. My parents, Sir Garfield and Lady Todd, are long-standing friends of his. After Independence the Minister appointed my mother to the board of the Mass Media Trust (MMT) and from there she was appointed to the board of Zimpapers. The files of her time there prove that the board was a serious, concerned body meeting usually eleven times a year.

My parents had previously never been concerned with stocks and shares. Now they followed the fortunes of Zimpapers with keen interest. When the 1984 drought struck my father, then a rancher, sold cattle and spent the proceeds on Zimpapers shares. Our Hokonui Ranching Company became a major shareholder after the two giants, MMT and Old Mutual.

In 1985 my father retired from the senate and my mother from the MMT and Zimpapers. But they remained concerned shareholders. Zimbabwe, then on its way to a one-party State, was going through very bad days politically, and many people were suffering and scared. Something started happening at Zimpapers and Editors were removed, shifted or 'promoted' – Willie Musarurwa, Henry Muradzikwa, Bill Saidi, Geoff Nyarota – and were replaced with what Minister Shamuyarira referred to as 'true and trusted cadres'.

They had all contributed enormously to Zimpapers and to Zimbabwe. Every time I remember the then Minister of Home Affairs Enos Nkala confiding to Mike Munyati on ZTV that curfews might not only be imposed again on Matabeleland but would probably be extended to the Midlands, I give thanks for Nyarota and Zimpapers through the *Chronicle* bravely exposing Willowgate and giving Mr Mugabe the chance to restructure his Cabinet. But what was our board doing to protect these editors?

After Independence our Government had received a huge gift from Nigeria of about £4 million to buy out the South African Argus Press substantial, but not controlling, interests in our national papers. The MMT was instituted to receive these funds and was meant to act as a buffer between our Government and Zimpapers in order to ensure 'freedom' of the press. After 1985 the MMT secretly acquired a controlling interest (about 51%) in Zimpapers. The Stock Exchange did not report to shareholders, as it should have done, that Zimpapers was now a parastatal ...

It seemed as though our Government was continuing the Rhodesian

Front tradition of 'TOP SECRET! STATE SECURITY!' and I soon discovered that the same political culture was being applied to our Company through our Chairman. Dr Davison Sadza was the Chairman of both the MMT and the board of Zimpapers. AGMs were an exercise in concealing information. There was no conception that the share-holders, apart from the MMT, were the owners of the Company. You could have been forgiven for assuming that the board was responsible for the clandestine manufacture of chemical weapons rather than the production of newspapers.

But if, like my father, you see vibrant and healthy cattle being trans-formed into Zimpapers shares, you will try to follow those shares and their well-being just as closely as you looked after your cattle. You will constantly consult the herders of your shares.

An initial herder was Mr Elias Rusike, then Managing Director of Zimpapers. He told my father that it would benefit the Company if my father was on the board. So it was, in 1987, as my father was out of the country that I, representing Hokonui Ranching at a Zimpapers AGM, confidently proposed my father to the board. In those days very few independent (i.e. non-MMT nominees) shareholders attended AGMs. The three non-MMT shareholders present voted for my father. But the entire board voted against with the exception of Dr Sadza who said, with apparent satisfaction, that the decision was so clear that he did not have to vote. That, I discovered during my time on the Zimpapers' board, was his favourite position.

In 1989, my father in hospital after a terrible accident, I again repre-sented Hokonui at the Zimpapers AGM. Previous AGMs I had attended had been whistled through at top speed. But now so much was happening, for example the frightening physical assault on Gibbs Dube, a *Chronicle* reporter, by Governor Mark Dube that I rang Mr Rusike and asked if he could request the chairman for proper time to discuss important matters at the AGM. He rang back and asked if I could see Dr Sadza before the AGM. I did so.

Dr Sadza wanted to know what matters I had in mind. There was a variety, from dividend cover to the removal of Geoff Nyarota from the editorship of the *Chronicle*. Dr Sadza said he was glad to hear these questions now as he said he wouldn't have been able to respond to some of them frankly at the AGM as obviously the situation was extremely delicate. On Nyarota, for example, he said that Nyarota had gone too far. The forest and the grass had all been so dry that only one match would have assured a blaze. But Nyarota had struck several matches and thus, fearing for Nyarota's very safety as so many powerful people were after him, he had to be removed from the editorship of the *Chronicle*. I asked if it were the President who had demanded the removal. Dr Sadza replied enigmatically: 'He didn't have to.'

By the 1991 AGM my father, desperate about the well-being of the Company, proposed me to the board. When my name came up board members smiled kindly at this ridiculous suggestion. But my father had a card up his sleeve. He had discovered that most members of the board did not hold any shares in the Company as they were required to do under the Articles of Association. Only three did so and for the board to conduct business they needed a quorum of four. The chairman and his legal adviser were obviously thunderstruck and horrified. The AGM was halted and postponed. When it did resume the board had no option but to accept me as a member in order to legitimately conduct its business.

I took my time on the board very seriously coming to head office the day before my first board meeting to read board minutes so that I could be up to date. I found that the pages of the minutes had stopped being numbered about two years previously and that many pages had not been signed by the Chairman. So it was easy to slip papers in and out. At the time I thought that was just a mistake but, with hindsight, I am now not so sure. That was the first matter I brought to the board and it was rectified.

The second matter which may have damaged my long-term chances of staying on the board was my objection to the advice of our legal adviser regarding a suit being brought by Minister Shamuyarira against Geoff Nyarota and Zimpapers for mentioning his name in the context of Willowgate. Our legal adviser proposed settlement of the claim for $50 000 damages plus front page apologies. I objected on the grounds that we must protect Zimpapers' reputation. The Board accepted this.

I found that the plight of editors had not been brought to the attention of the board and that the board had become irrelevant, meeting now about four times a year. When I asked for more meetings this was declined by the chairman on the grounds that other board members were so busy.

I also found that Mr Elias Rusike had been replaced by Mr Davis Midzi as Managing Director by fiat of the chairman. The only role the board played was, at the request of Dr Sadza, to approve his action in retrospect which they did.

Even outside board meetings I tried as hard as I could to help

Zimpapers. Disturbing rumours were circulating regarding Mr Midzi being involved in a car racket at the dire expense of the Company. One day I mentioned this to him. He didn't blink. What I hate about rumours is that the person being rumoured about hardly ever knows. So then, about a year ago, I wrote Mr Midzi a letter putting the rumours on paper. There was no response until just before the Zimpapers' scandal broke. He asked me to come from Bulawayo to Harare to see him which I did. During the course of our meeting he touched a fat file on transport policy which was on his desk saying 'I always keep myself covered'.

Just before last July's Zimpapers' AGM at which I was voted off the board by Dr Sadza (who, through MMT, exercises 51% of the shares) I went once more to read the board minutes. To my great astonishment I found 'Board Resolutions' slipped into the minutes and signed only by the Chairman, the then Managing Director Mr Midzi and one also by the Board's legal adviser George McNaught although board activity demanded a quorum of four. These resolutions had never been presented at a meeting of the board. One gave the chairman power to determine the salary of the Managing Director (far greater, I'm told, than that of the President of Zimbabwe although still, I believe, not actually known to board members apart from the chairman) and the MD's terms of reference which included the hiring and firing of editors. One, signed only by Sadza and Midzi, authorised the Managing Director to borrow, on behalf of Zimpapers, $4 million from the Zimpapers' Pension Fund. Another gave him power to sell Zimpapers' properties. I made copies available to all board members, most of whom appeared to be shocked.

After the AGM at which Dr Sadza removed me from the board I received a fax from the Zimpapers' legal adviser saying that Dr Sadza was interested in getting a 'minority shareholder' onto the board but that 'in view of recent developments ... there is unfortunately no possibility of a harmonious relationship between you and Dr Sadza as board members. So the representative should not be yourself. There is nothing personal in this suggestion.'

There is also nothing personal in my suggestion here that in view of recent developments Dr Sadza must step down from the Zimpapers' board in the best interests of the company. Maybe it is not Dr Sadza's personal fault that everything MMT has touched has turned to ashes – like the Hunyani paper and board company.

Maybe it's the fault of those who appoint 'true and trusted cadres'. Loving, so much, the Party, they sometimes forget to love Zimbabwe.

The Shamuyarira case against Nyarota and Zimpapers was partially concluded by the first quarter of 1994 in that Mr Justice Robinson stated that Nyarota need not reveal his sources. He said that 'where the press has publicly unearthed corruption in government circles … our courts will lean over backward to declare a journalist's sources to be privileged'. He also said that 'until Zimbabwe establishes an independent commission against corruption … the Zimbabwe press has a vital role to fulfil in making government officials fully accountable for their actions'.

My father pleased me by saying he believed even this interim indication from the courts had vindicated my time on the Zimpapers board. He said that just having managed to stop the board from settling out of court with Shamuyarira was worth all those painful months, as the consequences of the case were proving so important.

Towards the end of February 1994, I received an invitation from the Commonwealth Secretariat to join their election observer team to South Africa. I accepted with pleasure and enthusiasm. Later I had a personal call from the Commonwealth secretary general, Emeka Anyaoku, as he was passing through Harare, and I was able to ask if my nomination had been cleared with our government. Anyaoku and I had been distant friends for many years, and I had always thought he was an admirer of both President Mugabe and Minister Shamuyarira. Anyaoku said he had simply announced to the president and Shamuyarira that he had invited me, leaving no room for objection. Other Zimbabweans would be selected by the government.

Those days in the April during the South African elections unfolded in a shining sequence of what could only be described as miracles, but I soon discovered the miracles were rooted in months of incredibly hard work by representatives of almost all sectors of South African society. This started with the Peace Accord of 1991 signed by the ANC, the South African government, the Inkatha Freedom Party and sixteen other bodies.

The Commonwealth observer teams were in place some days before the elections. We were dispatched in pairs, each with a car and driver. Whoever selected our areas seemed to have done so on the basis of the hotter the better. So my colleague, the Honourable Oki Ooko Ombaka MP from Kenya and I ended up among those covering Mpumalanga, a sprawling, partly rural, partly urban area, which started about fifty kilometres from Pietermaritzburg and sections of which fell under the governance of KwaZulu-Natal.

When I first saw the ballot paper presented to the voters, many of whom were said to be barely literate, I wondered how they would manage. There had been a lottery for the extremely important position at the head of the list. This was won by Zanu (PF)'s ally, the Pan Africanist Congress, so this meant that the PAC, its logo and a photo of the leader, Comrade Clarence Makwetu, white-haired, smiling and looking just as much like Nelson Mandela as possible, was right at the top of the ballot paper.

What a lot of parties! After the PAC came the Soccer Party, the Sports Organisation for Collective Contributions and Equal Rights. This was led by a young man pictured in dreadlocks, who had spent a long time on Robben Island after being found guilty of belonging to Umkhonto we Sizwe, the military wing of the ANC. Then there was the Kiss Party – Keep It Straight and Simple; the Freedom Front of General Constand Viljoen, offering a safety valve for the white right-wing; and the WRPP, Women's Rights Peace Party, which seemed to have two members, one white lady and one black lady, and I'm not at all sure that one of them was not the employee of the other. Next came the Workers' List Party; the Ximoko Progressive Party; the African Muslim Party; the African Christian Democratic Party; the African Democratic Party; the African Moderates Congress Party; the African National Congress; the Democratic Party; the Dikwankwetla Party of South Africa; the Federal Party, which may have been a breakaway from the Democratic Party; the LUSO-South African Party, trying to represent the Portuguese section of the population; the Minority Front, led by an Indian, and I rather suspected that it was he and his wife who provided the broad base of its support; the National Party; and, at the bottom of that long, long list there was just enough room left to add a sticker accommodating the breathlessly last-minute inclusion of the Inkatha Freedom Party. The South Africans were certainly exercising their democratic rights.

One thing that struck me forcibly was how ineffably proud most people seemed to be to have voted. I couldn't help smiling at one poor, thin young man, marching like a soldier out of a dim little schoolroom in KwaZulu after having cast his vote. He caught my eye, looked very startled to see me smiling at him, then grinned back and raised his arm in a brief salute. That moment was indelibly printed in my mind.

Another was the final minutes of the elections at Woza Moyo School. By the afternoon of Thursday 28 April, we had watched the last of a little group of people getting their temporary voting cards to enable them to vote at Charles Memorial, a remote school set among the green and chocolate mountains of Mpumalanga. All was in order, so we climbed into the car to go off to the next voting centre on our list. At that moment, a young man in a white T-shirt, with Pierre Cardin emblazoned in pink across the front, came to the car and said something to our driver.

'He says,' reported our driver, 'that if we've got a camera we might like to go to the Woza Moyo School, where we will find the chairmen of the local branches of the IFP and ANC having lunch together. But we don't have a camera.'

'So what?' said Oki Ooko Ombaka. 'Let's go!'

Procedures at Woza Moyo seemed to have been completed, although officials were still at their places in case any last-minute voters appeared. And there, on the stoep outside the voting area, stood Victa Sibisi, IFP, and Lucky Zwane, ANC, the chairmen of their respective parties in the Shongweni area of KwaZulu-Natal, sipping Cokes and eating a plate each of sadza and meat. Someone had honoured obviously only them, as no one else had food.

We learned that as far back as 1989, the two men had brokered peace for their area amid the then surrounding carnage in KwaZulu-Natal. The peace had held. Sibisi had just sent a message to IFP headquarters in Ulundi that he was satisfied with the conduct of the election. The two men were now talking about consolidating peace and embarking on development whatever the outcome of the election. We left them, our hearts filled with hope and pleasure.

I carried with me a poem from the Catholic religious and poet James Baxter, which he had given me in Jerusalem, New Zealand, in 1969. At that time I was touring New Zealand and then Australia, trying both to raise money for the International Defence and Aid Fund created by Canon Collins in London, which supported political prisoners in southern Africa, and also to raise consciousness about the plight of my country, then called Rhodesia.

I had also got caught up in a new movement, Halt All Racist Tours (Hart), with Denis Brutus, Trevor Richards, Tom Newnham and others, which tried to stop rugby tours to or from apartheid South Africa. Passions on this subject were high and some of the public meetings quite rough.

For Judy
The high pear tree is loaded with white flowers
At the centre of the paddock – this morning I knelt
In the church where the Maoris do not come much
And thought of you Judy – how is it with you, my love,
Out there in the bull ring? I would like to say –
'Wherever you are, anywhere,

When you are most tired and wear the bloody crown,
Put your head on my shoulder' – which is no
doubt to be
A very foolish, fond old man,
But you will understand it – we are not
quite jars of stone
But the ones who have to fill them; whether
wine or water
Flows out of them can hardly be our doing –
That is the point of peace – the love of one to one
Is a dark fire, but the love of the Many
Burns in these Maori houses where they have the
light on
For a child's fear of *te taipo*, all night till dawn,
And in the open space, neither accepted
Nor unaccepted, we are permitted, my storm bird, to
watch with them.

I carried the poem with me for consolation and reassurance, and to keep reminding myself that 'We are not quite jars of stone but the ones who have to fill them. Whether wine or water flows out of them can hardly be our doing.'

It was tough and disappointing to be back in Zimbabwe in May after the stimulation and joy of South Africa. Immediately missing was the glorious wealth of debate on television, radio and in the newspapers, and the sense that whatever their background, citizens were each now an intimate part of the vivid, exciting nation of South Africa, and that their leaders were not constantly scrutinising them on public occasions to determine whether they were white or Asian or black or whatever. They were South Africans, full stop, just as we should be Zimbabweans, full stop.

I was saddened by the inappropriate comments Minister Shamuyarira and Vice-President Nkomo made on their return from that great non-racial event, the inauguration of President Mandela. Shamuyarira and Mugabe must, of course, have been devastated by the poor showing of the PAC – they got 1.2 per cent of the vote – after all that had secretly been poured into them by Zanu (PF) from Zimbabwe since independence and without our permission. But Nkomo should have been wiser.

Minister Shamuyarira said the whites in South Africa seemed to welcome their new democratic order, whereas the sulky whites in Zimbabwe had not.

Vice-President Nkomo apparently said he had been impressed by the almost equal numbers of whites and blacks celebrating down south, something he said had never happened in Zimbabwe. He even warned of a racial civil war in Zimbabwe if parents kept 'hiding' their white children. He was referring to what he thought was a deliberate absence of white children at public gatherings, obviously not comprehending how drastically the white population of Zimbabwe had declined, how tiny it now was and how few white children there actually were. Both Nkomo and Shamuyarira seemed totally unaware of how vastly dissimilar were the statistical profiles of each country. Excluding the former 'homelands' of Transkei, Ciskei, Bophuthatswana and Venda, it was estimated in 1993 that of South Africa's population of 32.5 million, 23 million were black, 5 million white, 3.5 million Coloured and one million Asian. So, for every twenty-three blacks, there would be nine whites/Coloureds/Asians, a highly visible percentage of the population.

In Zimbabwe the situation was utterly different. The 1992 census figures were not yet available, but it was estimated that whites made up about one per cent, if that, of a population of more than ten million, and of course those of Asian, Coloured and other descent numbered far less than the white population. In 1982, only 21 635 of what the Department of Statistics referred to as 'Coloureds and others', and 10 805 people of Asian descent, were living in Zimbabwe. So, if Nkomo's nightmare of a racial civil war ever came to pass, the one good thing was that it would be incredibly short. It would be statistically impossible for every group of 100 blacks to find more than one white and .03 per cent of a Coloured/Asian/other person to confront.

Once again President Mugabe was inciting his party to violence. How I yearned for the peacemakers of South Africa. The *Sunday Mail* of 29 May, the biggest circulation newspaper, carried the front-page headline: 'Go house to house, President urges party youth'. The split by Zanu from Zapu in 1963 had occasioned appalling violence, especially in the capital's high-density suburbs. Now Mugabe was re-invoking that time of terror:

> President Mugabe yesterday called the members of the youth wing of the ruling party to undertake a 'house to house action' campaign to mobilise support for Zanu (PF) in preparation for next year's elections. He said the party had now to resort to the methods used in the early 1960s where party cadres moved from one house to another recruiting membership. He said the youth and women's leagues were the real wings

of the party. 'It is these two which will send a message to the opposition, to those little parties that think the opportunity is ripe to take over and destroy the revolution. Make them think twice before doing that,' he told the cheering youth.

CHAPTER 26

Moving on

I N JANUARY 1995, MATTHEW CHIZONDO WROTE TO ANNOUNCE the birth of his daughter:

> I named the baby girl in respect of you; to honour you. My family is longing to see you. They sometimes argue to each other, one saying, let us have special chairs first, then we tell father to invite her, but Mum and Shungu said no to that idea. So may you kindly visit us.
>
> Shungu passed form one last year and his young brother Darlington passed grade seven.
>
> Warm greetings from young Judith and the whole family.
>
> Yours sincerely
> M Chizondo

Hokonui Trading Company, the residue of my father's ranch and stores, bought a house at 39 Fife Street in Bulawayo to let rooms as offices. We named it Edge House after my sister and brother-in-law, Cyndie and Derrick Edge, as the assets they left behind when they were forced by the war to leave Zimbabwe also went into this house. The drab building started looking lovely as it was painted cream and mellow gold, the little front lawn was established, flowers started blooming, awnings were erected over the hot front windows facing the street, and curtains and pictures were hung.

The house had belonged to Dr Elliot Gabellah, one of the participants in the 1978 internal settlement with Smith, Muzorewa and company. It was said that, after independence, he went to the PF Zapu offices in Bulawayo to apologise for his collaboration, and to say, referring to the internal settlement, 'I really never knew I was selling out. Of course all the *others* knew that they were selling out, but I really didn't know.'

Then, in the horrible years of the 1980s, when PF Zapu was being smashed, it was rumoured that if you wanted to join Zanu (PF) but didn't want your friends to see you doing so, you just limped into Dr Gabellah's surgery at 39 Fife Street and he would secretly sign you up and hand over your protection, a Zanu (PF) membership card. I don't know how much he charged.

Dr Gabellah had died some years before his house went on sale in 1994. The house itself was very secretive and gloomy, sealed off from the street by shrouds of privet. The walls were adorned with portraits of the doctor and many pairs of praying hands, some of which were positioned under and pointing upwards to the portraits. Now the privet was gone, the portraits had gone, the praying hands had gone, and we were there.

There was a detached office block in the backyard, with a large conference room, where Gabellah used to teach nurses homeopathy. This was now occupied by the Zimbabwe Human Rights Association, Zimrights. A portrait of President Mugabe had adorned the conference room once, but that, too, was now gone.

We also housed the local office of MCS Printers, which had started out as the Memorial Cooperative Society. They wanted to call themselves the Heroes' Memorial Cooperative Society, but this was not allowed by the registrar of cooperatives, as he probably thought they were honouring the wrong heroes. They had brought all the PF Zapu printing equipment from Zambia and had weathered very hard times, but still survived.

We had been together a long time, since independence, and in 1991 they presented me with a dignified certificate stating: 'The Management Committee and members of Memorial Cooperative Society have awarded the title of Hero of the Memorial Cooperative Society to Judith Todd, Hero of Socialist Labour, in recognition of her outstanding Service, Sacrifice and Contribution to the cause of unity, socialism and cooperation, to which the Memorial Cooperative Society has dedicated itself.' The certificate was handed to me in my office privately, quietly and proudly by the chairman, Kiva Tshuma, and the secretary, Albert Ndindah. People's attitudes were naturally affected a great deal by where they had spent time in exile from Rhodesia and during the war. Ndindah, by now an old man, had spent years in East Germany, where he had married a member of their Politburo, raised a family and learned about 'Socialist Labour'.

Other tenants at Edge House were Multi-Tools, importers of machinery, Petman Chemicals, importers of veterinary materials, and Home Renovators, belonging to a seasoned builder called Teacher Moyo from Filabusi, who thought it would be a good thing to have an office in town but seldom used it. Finally, there was Khatshana (Far away) Tours and Travel. This was Malcolm King and his entourage, who ran minibuses within Zimbabwe and to South Africa. It was all a lot of fun.

That September a sad letter reached me from former chief justice Enoch

Dumbutshena, visiting South Korea. He had been looking over the border into North Korea and contemplating Zimbabwe. 'We think of the past and the hopes we entertained for a future we thought would be pleasant. For those now in power and those who have made it, in whatever manner, life in Zimbabwe is indeed enjoyable. But for the millions whose hopes have been shattered, the present is not for them. I am in this group. It is good to keep on hoping. For me, personally, my condition cannot be improved. But I hope that there is time to put things right for you, the young, and for my grandchildren.'

Dr Jocelyn Alexander stayed with me intermittently during 1995. She was a colleague and former student of my friend Professor Terence Ranger and was based, like him, at St Antony's College, Oxford. She hadn't read any John le Carré before and became an instant devotee of his character, intelligence agent Smiley. I had all of Le Carré's books. Jocelyn was doing research in Matabeleland, and over the months she took the books, two or three at a time, to Nkayi, where she stayed in a lodge called Panke, erected thoughtfully by the local council as 'an income-generating project'.

She said the cook there, Mr Mpofu, was a charming man, although not a good cook. Jocelyn was pretty sure that Mr Mpofu had never travelled far beyond Nkayi, but he liked reading. Naturally Jocelyn passed on the books she borrowed from me. Naturally Mr Mpofu, too, became a devotee of Smiley. One night, waiting and waiting for dinner, Jocelyn decided to investigate the delay. She ventured into the kitchen, where she found Mr Mpofu stirring something on the stove with one hand and clutching his latest Le Carré in the other. 'Oh!' he said, shivering and disarming Jocelyn. 'This one is really *sinister*!'

How I wished we had our own Smiley acting in the best interests of our little nation and chucking out all the dubious Russians and others who were extracting diamonds and minerals and God knows what else from our land. They were even being given rights to pan gold, thus to tear up our rivers. The Development Trust of Zimbabwe was one of their many entrances to the economy of Zimbabwe. The Russians were apparently mostly former KGB, allies from the struggle. There were also the Serbs, who got all the building contracts that didn't go to the Chinese, and yet we had our own builders available. Now the Malaysians were in on the act, and were going to build essential police housing while they looked around for other opportunities. With each new wave of 'investors', our ministers seemed physically to swell like warm balloons, now and then lifting slightly from the ground to emit incredible statements.

The leaders of the nation, at vast, personal profit, were excelling in giving away what should belong to the people of Zimbabwe.

Brave people under the aegis of the Catholic Commission for Justice and Peace and the Legal Resources Foundation compiled and published a detailed report on atrocities perpetrated by 5 Brigade in Matabeleland and the Midlands from 1980 to 1988, titled *Breaking the Silence*. The report consisted of 260 pages, text and photographs, recording some of the sheer horror visited upon helpless citizens of Zimbabwe. Attempts were made to prevent publication of the report by, of all people, the Zimbabwe Catholic Bishops' Conference, but when it became apparent that censorship was looming, someone thankfully and, again, so bravely, put it on the Web in Johannesburg at the *Mail & Guardian* and it could no longer be suppressed. The hideous facts in the report, which could now be read across the world, were so painstakingly corroborated that even the author of the atrocities and the subsequent cover-ups, President Robert Gabriel Mugabe, could no longer attempt to deny knowledge.

Fortunately, people working for the state press sometimes managed to smuggle news into their stories. An example of this was the headline story in the *Sunday News* on 11 May 1997, published in Bulawayo under the headline: '5 Brigade atrocities a mistake'.

HARARE – President Mugabe said yesterday that atrocities perpetrated by the army's 5 Brigade during anti-dissident operations in Matabeleland and the Midlands should be regarded as a historical mistake which should never be repeated.

Addressing mourners gathered for the burial of veteran politician Cde Stephen Vuma at the National Heroes Acre in Harare, the President took time to respond to the allegations detailed in a report of the Catholic Commission for Justice and Peace and the Legal Resources Foundation which has been leaked to the Press.

Cde Mugabe warned that such reports threatened national unity brought about by the merger between PF Zapu and Zanu (PF) in 1987 which brought to an end a five-year insurgence by mostly disaffected members of the former ZPRA, the armed wing of Zapu.

'If we dig up past history, we wreck the survival of the nation and can tear our people apart into tribes and villagism will prevail,' he said.

The report detailed killings and rape of villagers in the two provinces by troops of the North Korean–trained brigade which was under the command of then Colonel Perrence Shiri who is now the commander of the Air Force of Zimbabwe.

'History should be a register that will remain as what never to do. If that was wrong and went against the sacred tenets of humanity we must never repeat we must never oppress man,' Cde Mugabe said.

The President has in the past said there was no need to apologise for the killings and sufferings as it was a war situation.

A Catholic himself, Cde Mugabe warned people to be wary of detractors of unity, who disguised themselves in religious garb.

Giving himself as an example of true reconciliation and forgiveness, he said people should not go by the happenings of the past.

'If we go by the past, what cause would compel us to keep Ian Smith (former Rhodesian Prime Minister)? Perhaps I would be first to cut his throat,' he said.

The *Sunday Mail* published a fuller version under the headline: 'Beware of mischief makers – President', and was more explicit about his thoughts on Ian Smith: 'If we go by the past, would Ian Smith be alive today? What cause will there be to impel us to keep him alive? Perhaps I will be the first man to go and cut his throat and open up his belly but no we shall never do that.'

While I no longer had any connection with the work of the Zimbabwe Project, I had by chance become involved in trying to help South African agents Barry Bawden, Kevin Woods and company in Chikurubi Maximum to sign applications for amnesty so that they could appear in front of the Truth and Reconciliation Commission in South Africa.

This saga had started years before, when I visited people such as Frank Nyoni, Alibaba Dlodlo and Makhatini Guduza in prison. Guduza's wife Poppy died in Bulawayo on 17 May 1997. Nkomo, now an old man, attended Poppy Guduza's funeral, and stood hunched by Makhatini's side. Makhatini had quite recently recalled Nkomo's escape from Zimbabwe. He laughed and said that, although there was no truth in the story put about by Ushewokunze that Nkomo had been disguised as a woman when he fled Zimbabwe, it was still very difficult indeed to hump him over the fences into Botswana. Such an activity would have been quite beyond either of them now.

Once, when I was visiting Chikurubi, I had been approached by a woman who asked if I was there to visit the South African agent, Odile Harrington.

She turned out to be Barry Bawden's mother, Irene. A week after our brief encounter, my mother telephoned and asked what I had been doing at Chikurubi. She had been to the hairdresser in Bulawayo and an old friend of hers, Mrs Cecil Goddard, sat next to her and said how touched Irene Bawden had been that I had offered to see Odile. Cecil and Irene were old friends and farmed at Shangani.

After this, Irene came to my office to see me. She had been persuaded by Cecil that I might be able to help. Irene was so nervous that she couldn't speak, her mouth was so dry. I got her some water, and that was the beginning of a friendship that was abruptly terminated some months later with a bowl of lovely flowers and a card. The printed words on the card read: 'Your thoughtfulness meant so much!' And inside Irene had written: 'To dear Judith, Just a small gift that I hope you will enjoy to say a very big "Thank you" for trying so hard to help me and all the trouble you went to. With love and God bless, Irene Bawden.'

Initially, Irene had shown me a letter from her son Barry, who had been sentenced to forty years. The other South African agents, Kevin Woods, Philip Conjwayo and Michael Smith, had been sentenced to death, since commuted. Barry wrote: 'I see you want to see "Judith Todd". I think she could be a big help. She has helped a lot of people in the passed. If you see her please tell her we 5 have written one PETITION through Rob Hartley in 1993 and in 1996 through the PRISON both to President Mugabe.'

Rob Hartley was their lawyer and, it turned out, a nephew of Cecil Goddard. The fifth person Barry referred to was Sam Beahan, who was caught trying to spring the others. They never received acknowledgements from Mugabe. Barry suffered from clots in the leg, so was in pain and scared of thrombosis, and so was his mother. Rob Hartley had got amnesty application forms from South Africa, but had told Irene that when he took them to Chikurubi, the prison authorities wouldn't allow the men to sign them. Minister of Justice Emmerson Mnangagwa had also said he would never think of letting the men go to South Africa, and they should stop trying to do so.

So it was against this background that I, probably foolishly, was trying to ensure that they were at least able to sign the applications. The new government in South Africa seemed helpful, and had accorded the men South African citizenship. During our first meeting, I suggested to Irene that they should give their lawyer power of attorney so that he could sign the applications on their behalf. She thought this a good idea, but told me later, with a smile, that when she had put the idea to Hartley, he said he didn't need 'that woman' to tell him what to do.

I heard from Peta Thornycroft, at the time an assistant editor of the *Mail & Guardian*, that the cut-off date for the amnesty was 10 May 1995. I rang Irene, only to find that she was in South Africa. I had met her husband Des, who had been detained with Makhatini Guduza years ago, but didn't know him well enough to talk to him. So I sent Cecil Goddard a letter, in which I wrote:

> Finally, I think I should tell you something the possibility of which worries me very much but I haven't mentioned this to Irene. I leave it to your discretion about whether or not to do so, and if mentioning it would in any way be useful.
>
> It seems to me to be pretty obvious that whoever Barry and Co were working for/with (and who presumably are the ones that made/make finances available for the legal costs, maintenance of wives etc) will do everything possible to stop any application by them to the Truth and Reconciliation Commission. I should think they would be bending over backwards to block any possible mention of their involvement or that of any further agents or collaborators in Zimbabwe. Thus it could also well be that they would try to subvert any attempt by lawyers to get the forms to Chikurubi for signature. I don't want to offend you or anyone else, seeing that Mr Hartley is your nephew, but I think it should be taken into consideration that legal firms usually act on the instructions of those who pay them. We may also, then, need to set up a parallel operation to Coghlan Welsh and Guest and get someone else *also* to take the necessary papers to Chikurubi for signature.

I discovered later that Mrs Goddard had faxed this letter to Irene, who was staying with her daughter in South Africa. But Irene was away, so the daughter dutifully faxed the letter to their South African lawyer, Adolf Malan, who then faxed it to Robin Hartley.

Hartley was naturally not amused, and wrote to me, stating: 'I write to record this firm's strenuous objection to the fourth paragraph on page 2 of your letter. The statement contained in this paragraph is a deliberate, unqualified and intentional defamation of this firm and until such time as this statement is retracted and we receive an appropriate apology, we must reserve our rights in this matter.'

I couldn't help but feel alarmed. However, I remembered a couple of very nice letters that DJ Lewis, the senior partner of Coghlan, Welsh & Guest, had written me over the years. One was to do with my appointment to the board of Zimbabwe Newspapers and the other was again to congratulate me, this time on my appointment to the Commonwealth observer team for the 1994 South African elections.

I therefore tried to make my reply to Robin Hartley light-hearted, if not actually flippant. First I said I was enclosing for him further copies of application forms for amnesty which I'd had forwarded to me by the legal firm of Scanlen & Holderness. This gave me the opportunity to copy the letter to Bryant Elliot. Then I wrote, 'Thank you for your ... objection to ... my private letter to ... I would never dream of defaming anyone, let alone the prestigious firm of Coghlan, Welsh & Guest, whose senior partner is held in such high regard by so many sectors of our community.'

This gave me the opportunity to copy the letter to DJ Lewis, who I was pretty sure didn't have a clue about the threat Hartley had made to me. It seemed to work, as there was a wonderful silence afterwards. But I suspected that Irene Bawden's farewell message to me was the result of pressure Robin Hartley had placed on her through her son, Barry.

Sam Beahan was eventually released in November 1989, and Barry Bawden in November 2000. Kevin Woods, Mike Smith and Phillip Conjwayo, all in poor health, were released at the beginning of July 2006.

There was so much misrepresentation going on regarding the status of ex-combatants that, in August 1997, I wrote an article on the subject and distributed it to all local publications, underlining the fact that there was no copyright. I emphasised that the self-styled leader of the ex-combatants, a former Zapu junior representative to Poland, Hitler Hunzvi, was a dangerous extortionist who might well inflict great damage on Zimbabwe unless someone managed to bring him under control. He was making outrageous demands on behalf of an ever-increasing band of ex-combatants with which Zimbabwe's economy couldn't possibly cope.

As someone who worked exclusively for ex-combatants from 1980 to 1993 I wish to remind the public of some facts regarding State and other assistance to Zimbabwe's ex-combatants since 1980.

Ex-combatants were attended to by the Demobilisation Directorate set up in July 1981 under the Ministry of Labour and Social Welfare. The first Director was John Shoniwa, Zanu, and the Deputy Director was Report Phelekezela Mphoko, Zapu. Their task was to coordinate activities and programmes for the ex-combatants with relevant Government Ministries. An Inter-Ministerial Committee was established for liaison with the Directorate. Ministries represented on the Committee were Agriculture, Labour, Finance, Education, Health, and Manpower Planning and Development.

Those men and women who had gone into the 45 Assembly Points (APs) scattered throughout the country at ceasefire were eventually attested into the national army to make possible the process of demobilisation as the first attempt, which took place within the APs, had been unsuccessful. An offer had been made of between $400 and $600 depending on rank for people to leave for good. (The Z$ was at that point the equivalent in value to the £ sterling.) The few who took this option soon exhausted their funds and went back to the APs.

The total number demobilised, according to the records of the Demobilisation Directorate, was 41 000. These were entitled to a grant of $185 per month for two years to help them build new lives. This was distributed through the Post Office Savings Bank.

Further figures from the Demobilisation Directorate showed that 3 000 declared themselves too late to be included in the demobilisation exercise and 25 000 had found employment before the demobilisation programme started and were not, therefore, included. The only ex-combatants not provided for were therefore those who had been kept out of the APs clandestinely for electioneering purposes, their places being taken by many who were patently not ex-combatants but to whose presence the authorities turned a blind eye.

Of the 41 000 demobilised, 5 000 went to school, 1 000 took vocational training, 5 000 formed cooperatives of one kind or another and a further 4 000 found employment. The Zimbabwe Project soon had another 1 200 enrolled in correspondence courses and raised money from the European Economic Community to hire seven 'experts', some now in SEDCO (Small Enterprises Development Corporation) to vet the enterprises ex-combatants wanted to embark on. If the enterprises were thought to be viable ex-combatants were then allowed to receive their money en bloc and to pool their resources. From this scheme, for example, 87 ex-combatants pooled their funds and bought a commercial farm, Simukai, outside Harare. (See *Tomorrow is built today* by Andrew Nyathi with John Hoffman, published by Anvil Press, Harare in 1990, ISBN 0-7974-0934-3.)

Those who had been disabled were carefully examined and awarded pensions, still being paid today. In one particular case the ZPRA war-wounded, isolated at Lido Hotel in Bulawayo, were given 3 000 acres of land next to the ever-flowing Ngesi River near Zvishavane where they established Vukuzenzele agricultural cooperative. Their cattle were provided by the New Zealand High Commission; their housing by the German agency EZE; transport by a Canadian agency, CUSO.

Kushinga-Phikelela, the agricultural training institute set up near Marondera by the then President Banana was specifically intended for ex-combatants who had become a very popular group for aid agencies, and the entrance level was only Grade 7. The German agency Bread for the World made available to the Zimbabwe Project $100 000 to enable our Ministry of Justice to train 100 ex-combatants for entry into the Prison Service. Many, many agencies such as Zimfep (Zimbabwe Foundation for Education with Production), Christian Care, Glen Forrest, Hlekweni assisted ex-combatants and outside agencies such as Oxfam poured millions of dollars into schemes to assist ex-combatants through local agencies such as the Zimbabwe Project.

It can therefore be safely said that no other group in this country has, since independence, received greater assistance than the ex-combatants. The Registrar of Welfare Organisations in the Ministry of Labour and Social Welfare should, from the annual copies of audited accounts required from NGOs each year, be able to work out roughly how many millions/billions of dollars have been spent through NGOs on ex-combatant programmes since Independence.

In 1993 I went to Maputo having been asked by the United Nations Operation in Mozambique to advise on 'Reintegration mechanisms for demobilised soldiers in Mozambique' based on my experience in this field in Zimbabwe. One of the points I made which I think holds true was that 'Zimbabwe's political leadership has placed too much emphasis, verbally, on the role of ex-combatants. A war affects everyone, particularly in the rural areas. It is not helpful to the overall development of a community to assert that one group (the ex-combatants) is more important than any other. This leads to ex-combatants believing years after conflict has ended that they still have the right to special resources from the State and this, in turn, stirs up resentment in other sectors of the community, especially among unemployed school leavers.'

The truth of the matter today is that many ex-combatants have now plunged into the depths of poverty experienced by the majority of our population and they need exactly the same kind of help as do the rest of our people. But, unlike the rest, the 'ex-combatants', a mixture of real and fake, have wealthy and therefore mobile leaders such as Dr Hunzvi, who know how to exploit their situation, terrorise the Government, and thus jeopardise the economic well-being of our country, Zimbabwe, for which the real ex-combatants once purported to fight. Our economy is thus put in extreme danger and, if the false claims made by 'ex-combatants' are acceded to, we can expect a ripple effect throughout the region and consequent strain on the economies of South Africa, Namibia, Mozambique, Angola and so on if their ex-combatants start demanding what ours are demanding.

The independent press published the article, and so, to my pleasure and astonishment, did the *Chronicle*, a member of the Zimpapers stable. But it made no difference. An unbudgeted 'gift' to ex-combatants of Z$50 000 each, extorted from Mugabe's government by Hitler Hunzvi, was paid out in November 1997, and an allowance of Z$2 000 each per month thereafter from December. A lot of people who had been feeling very worried about the ex-combatants were now directly damaged financially, as was the entire economy.

After what became known as Black Friday that November, the value of Zimbabwe's currency plunged and has continued to plummet ever since. By July 2006, the extent of the damage suffered by Zimbabwe from Robert Mugabe was explicit in terms of currency exchange rates. At independence in April 1980, one Zimbabwe dollar was slightly harder than one pound sterling. Twenty-six years later, to buy one pound sterling, a Zimbabwean would need one million dollars. By then the currency, like a lot of Zimbabwe's ex-combatants, was fake, dollars having been replaced by spurious 'bearer cheques'.

A new group, Associated Newspapers of Zimbabwe, of which I was a founding member and very small shareholder, launched five regional newspapers under the overall management of Wilf Mbanga and the editorship of Geoffrey Nyarota, designed to lead to the national launch of the *Daily News* on 22 February 1999. ANZ had assembled a team of some of the best journalists in the country, and we longed for their success and for sufficient financial support in what were increasingly dark political, social and economic circumstances.

As intended, everyone had been frightened by the military arrest, detention and torture of Mark Chavanduka and Ray Choto of the *Zimbabwe Standard*, and the subsequent arrest of the publisher Clive Wilson. They were released, but then Mark and Ray faced charges under the Law and Order (Maintenance) Act. This Act had been on the verge of being scrapped, but was hastily resuscitated by the Minister of Home Affairs, Dumiso Dabengwa, and the government while they put more teeth into the Public

Order and Security Act, POSA, designed to replace it. Worst of all was the daily, grinding poverty that was rapidly escalating and the hopelessness of an estimated 70 per cent of Zimbabweans. How humiliating it all was for those who had actually looked forward to, worked for, and believed in a 'free' and 'democratic' Zimbabwe.

The *Chronicle* reported an announcement made by the Minister of Information, Chen Chimutengwende, that government would soon introduce stringent measures to regulate the operations of the media. In an obvious reference to ANZ, he said proposed measures included the introduction of a legal framework under which foreign investment in the media sector would not be allowed.

'We know that the owners of these papers are being funded by right-wing Rhodesians and other fascists internationally, so we cannot sit and watch while they destroy us,' said Chen.

Another report on current government thinking came from Minister of State for National Security, Sydney Sekeremayi. Addressing the joint command and staff course for senior defence force officers from Zimbabwe and other countries in the region, he said that some foreign countries were forming an informal coalition with the press to try to remove the Zimbabwe government from power, and that, given the morbid hatred of the Zimbabwean government by some elements of the foreign press, it was not surprising if such organisations tried to ferment dissidence in Zimbabwe.

I remembered a nursery rhyme from the dawning of my life.
They huff and
They puff and
They blow our house down.

CHAPTER 27

Respect for the dead

I MISSED THE FUNERAL OF BYRON HOVE. ACCORDING TO A PIECE
by his cousin Sekai Hove Holland in the *Daily News* of Friday 23 April
1999, Vice-President Muzenda had caused offence by remarks he had made,
and Sekai was now calling for politicians to start respecting the dead and
bereaved.

> The Vice President told a shocked crowd of mourners at Byron's funeral
> in Harare and in Mwembe that in 1980 Byron was called by the Vice
> President and today's President and asked by the two if he would like to
> be the country's Attorney General. When Byron agreed to take up that
> post he was instructed by the two to return to Britain to wind up his
> affairs and to bring his family back home.
>
> The Vice President went on to say that when Byron left the two he
> proceeded to tell Judith Todd, a journalist, about his appointment. This
> story, mourners were told, was then published in South African news-
> papers. Byron, we were told, failed to keep that secret. This was all said
> in Shona: '*Akatadza kubata hana*' which is a real put-down of a person's
> integrity. Byron's widow was outraged at the funeral at these remarks
> and began to protest the charge. Mourners sitting next to her pleaded
> with her to show restraint which our sister-in-law respectfully did.
>
> Some were going to respond to the Vice President privately after the
> Nyaradzo, memorial service, both for the bereaved widow, immediate
> family and for Judith Todd, who was not present at that gathering to
> defend herself.
>
> In this context whites who contributed to this country's liberation
> are being relentlessly attacked and their contribution to our country's
> liberation is now being ignored and denied. Not that Judith Todd cares.
> She has developed a thick skin like most who have been vilified, margin-
> alised and attacked by our politicians for 19 years. Her work is recorded
> locally and internationally. Only those who attack her stand to lose their
> personal reputations. Yet some felt compelled to respond on her behalf
> as well after the Nyaradzo.

I was touched that Sekai had defended me. Reading her piece was the first I'd heard, ever, that Byron had been offered the post of Attorney-General.

My life quietened down after moving to Bulawayo from Harare and away from its diplomatic and political circles. Leaving the Zimbabwe Project then had cut links with other wide and various constituencies and the donor community. But there were still avenues open now and again, one being writing.

In October 1999, the *Financial Gazette* carried a paean of praise for President Mugabe from Nathan Shamuyarira, who was engaged in writing the long, long and, regrettably, still unfolding history of the life and times of Robert Gabriel Mugabe. I asked the *Financial Gazette* if I could respond, and they swiftly assented. My piece was carried boldly the following week under my byline and with the explicit headline: 'Shamuyarira explodes myth of 1987 Unity Accord'.

I wrote that by stating that the 1980s disturbances had been 'handled the only way possible', Shamuyarira had dashed any hope that those complicit in state violence unleashed since 1980 were repentant. In his words: 'If such a situation were to arise in any part of the country today, the government may be forced to resort to the same measures again as soon as it feels that law and order are being threatened.' Then I noted that this 'handling' by Prime Minister/President Robert Mugabe and his colleagues through bodies such as 5 Brigade, PISI, CIO and, very importantly, the Mass Media Trust, had led to heartbreak throughout Zimbabwe, not only in Matabeleland and the Midlands. Giving examples of the personal tragedies bruising our history, I wrote of the escape of Joshua Nkomo and hundreds of others; the MP Jini Ntuta's attempted flight from his pursuers, when he was shot dead like a rabbit; the detention and torture of people such as Kembo Mohadi; the unanswered letters from Lookout Masuku to Defence Minister Robert Mugabe; the banning of Nitram, and the seizure of its properties and the ZPRA archives.

I quoted Shamuyarira as saying: 'I have had a very open, frank and friendly relationship with the president over the years,' and that he looked forward to writing a biography of the man who, having ousted Nkomo from his cabinet in 1982, warned people prior to the 1985 elections that a vote for Nkomo's party would be interpreted as a vote for dissidents. Many remembered, I wrote, how he urged his people to remove the stumps and how Zanu youth and women then took to the high-density areas in Harare and elsewhere, looting, attacking and killing some Zapu supporters and destroying their properties. I said I wasn't sure if the hotel in Shurugwi had ever been opened again, or whether Joseph Msika ever really recovered from the destruction of his farm.

'It's on record that RG Mugabe speaking on Matabeleland said, after those elections, "we are satisfied ourselves that without Nkomo, without the dissident element, they will fall in line." What RG Mugabe publicly instructed 5 Brigade to do is also on record and will be easy for Shamuyarira to find. Amongst the phrases used then by the man Shamuyarira says "I have supported all along since the time he returned from Ghana in 1960" were words such as ploughing and then sowing again. He didn't leave much to the imagination. Indeed, it seems quite possible that 5 Brigade was planned even before Zimbabwe's independence.'

I concluded by saying that, as Minister Shamuyarira had stated that he had been asked by 'the party' to write Zimbabwe's history from the point of view of Zanu (PF), perhaps we could now assume that ZPRA's stolen archives had eventually landed in his hands.

There was, of course, no response from him, but a number of people approached me after publication to say how glad they were that we still had some independent publications brave enough to carry such information. Without exception, none of them knew the details of Nkomo's escape from Zimbabwe, what had happened to Nitram, Masuku and Dabengwa, the Zapu members of parliament and others. While most had been affected in one way or another by these events and by Gukurahundi, they hadn't had a chance to comprehend the deliberate design and consequent pattern of Zanu (PF)/state repression. So very few Zimbabweans under Zanu (PF) had access to news, and those who were able to read publications such as the *Financial Gazette* were an almost immeasurably tiny percentage of the population.

Up to the beginning of 2000, people knew I was using an office at Edge House, but by the time my old friend Jonathan Moyo's transformation from an apparently independent political analyst to official spokesman, strategist and verbal arsonist for Zanu (PF) was completed in 1999, I was already thinking of retreating completely from public access.

Firstly, I couldn't cope with people who continued to come for assistance even after I had left the Zimbabwe Project. I simply didn't have the resources necessary to be able to help, and so it was difficult to face them. Secondly, I was aware that the all-embracing political atmosphere was becoming ever more treacherous. So, when Omar Hlambelo dropped in, apparently on behalf of Jonathan Moyo, and invited me to take part in the unfolding processes of the state-guided commission of inquiry into a new constitution, I declined, and instead started the process of moving bit by bit and silently from the office to my home.

Omar and I had known each other as children. Her father, JN Hlambelo, had been my father's mature instructor and mentor when the young Todds arrived at Dadaya from New Zealand in 1934. Throughout their many years together, the two had seemed to love, respect and depend upon each other. They both, by the grace of God, survived the war.

Hlambelo and his descendants lived in the house where I was born, at Old Dadaya in the communal lands, to which Hokonui Ranch was adjacent. During the war my father had Hlambelo's car painted a colour the guerrillas would recognise and which the Rhodesians didn't know about, and he was never attacked by any of the warring parties.

When eventually Hlambelo died, my father was so happy about the circumstances. Active to the end of his long life, he one day climbed up into the driver's seat to start his tractor and dropped dead in an instant, apparently without suffering and in full possession of his faculties.

My enduring memory of Hlambelo, whom I loved and profoundly respected, was when I lost my two upper front milk teeth. He cupped my chin in his huge, hard hand and, asking me to smile, said to the surrounding teachers, 'Look at our little Miss Zambezi!'

He went on to tell me that Tonga women in the Zambezi Valley who wished to be beautiful had their two front teeth knocked out. I felt so proud.

Ever since returning home in 1980, I had observed that the more afraid many people became, the more they started behaving like chameleons, making incredibly cautious, wavering moves from one position to the next, their terrified eyes rolling 180 degrees to see who was observing them, their colours changing imperceptibly from one location to another. They believed that they were under threat from their pasts, whatever those were, and so would do almost anything to endorse and safeguard their acceptability by the ruling party, the intimidating Zanu (PF).

But there were others, many others, who resisted fear, and who bravely worked for the salvation of their beloved land. They were an active ingredient in the population that was, according to Zanu (PF), becoming dangerously restive. Pre-eminent among these was the Zimbabwe Congress of Trade Unions, which, at an extraordinary congress in 1988, publicly cut all ties with

Zanu (PF). This newfound independence galvanised the movement under the leadership of Morgan Tsvangirai, who was from a mineworkers' union background, and Gibson Sibanda, from railways. Government started looking askance, and President Mugabe warned: 'We do not want to see a situation where the ZCTU becomes a political party.'

He appointed John Nkomo Minister of Labour. Sibanda and Nkomo had been prominent and influential Zapu men in pre-independence times, and had, for a while, been detainees together under Smith, but the new unity accord displaced any old loyalties. Without wasting time, Nkomo waded in to launch what was going to be an everlasting attack by government on the workers.

Before the 1988 May Day rally, Minister Nkomo asked for an advance copy of the main ZCTU address for the occasion, and underlined sections he said must be deleted. Gibson Sibanda read the speech to the rally, and instead of omitting the underlined sections, read them with special emphasis. The minister, seated behind him, physically kicked him with vigour on each occasion. This incident, which caused some mirth then, presaged distinctly humourless times later.

It was in the same year that the state started intensifying its use of race as a weapon against fellow blacks, and the leaders of the ZCTU were referred to as 'stooges of white imperial interests'.

In May 1997, the extraordinarily tenacious National Constitutional Assembly was formed, an umbrella of civic organisations and individuals working for a new 'home-grown' constitution. Then, from within the ranks of the ZCTU and the NCA, the political party Movement for Democratic Change (MDC) was launched by thousands of enthusiastic people at Harare's Rufaro Stadium on 11 September 1999. There wasn't a white farmer in sight, let alone any representative of Western imperial interests.

Another bold step towards a democratic Zimbabwe was taken with the birth of the *Daily News* in April 1999, another light to shine through the darkness. Over the following months, the brave editor, Geoff Nyarota, management and staff survived arrests, the terrorising of newspaper vendors by agents of Zanu (PF) and bombings, which included the military-style destruction of their printing press. Nyarota was finally run out of the country and, a short while later, in September 2003, the paper was closed down by gun-toting police under the aegis of the Minister for Information, Jonathan Moyo. All equipment was seized, and the police carried off the computers and locked them up in Chikurubi Prison. By 2006, they were still there.

The NCA and MDC vigorously opposed the new draft constitution, published on 25 November 1999. This 'New Democratic Constitution' Mugabe wanted the voters to ratify was really just more of what we were already being force-fed, but dressed up in a different guise. The main enticement promised that presidential tenure would be reduced to a maximum of two five-year terms, but this would not be retroactive. In other words, Mugabe could start all over again for another ten years. A further enticement was the provision that there would be no financial compensation for land seized by the state.

The stormy atmosphere surrounding the workings of the constitutional commission vividly reminded me of the Rhodesian regime's attempt in 1971 and 1972 to compel people to say 'yes' to a deal between them and the British Conservative government, headed by Sir Alec Douglas-Home, which would have led to independence under Ian Smith's Rhodesian Front without majority rule. Despite physical power being in the hands of the Rhodesian authorities, blacks gathered all over the country to shout, 'No!'

Eighteen years later, the majority of the population would not have known of that remarkable triumph of courage over relentless intimidation, and so my contribution to the debate was to write an article that was published in early 2000, just before Zimbabwe's first referendum.

I explained that by 1971 the British government had decided to wash its hands of Rhodesia. They no longer wanted the responsibility. It was agreed with the rebel Smith regime that a British commission under Lord Pearce would canvass all sections of opinion in Rhodesia and report on whether the settlement proposals were acceptable. The proposals were that:

- The principle and intention of unimpeded progress to majority rule, already enshrined in the 1961 constitution (which Mr Smith had torn up in 1965 when he unilaterally declared Rhodesia independent from Britain), would have to be maintained and guaranteed.
- There would also have to be guarantees against retrogressive amendment of the constitution.
- There would have to be immediate improvement in the political status of the African population.
- There would have to be progress towards ending racial discrimination.
- The British government would have to be satisfied that any basis proposed for independence was acceptable to the people of Rhodesia as a whole.

The deal then (*I wrote*) was about the retention of power by Ian Smith and his Rhodesian Front. The deal today is about the retention of power by Robert Mugabe and his Zanu (PF).

On each occasion the deals have been cloaked in fancy words ('vote wisely, vote yes, let's make a change') accompanied by massive bribery (the British had offered up to five million pounds over ten years for the development of African areas – whatever that meant – and President Mugabe was offering land) and identical threats (no possibility of any improvements on this deal).

You have listened to Jonathan Moyo in 1999/2000. Now listen to Ian Smith in 1971/1972:

'Let me reaffirm the government's support for the proposals and, in so doing, commend them to all Rhodesians. Having said that let me make it clear, particularly to our African people, what the consequences would be should the proposals be rejected. I and my party will be perfectly happy for the present Constitution to remain, and if the Africans reject this offer, if their answer to the Pearce Commission is "No" then this is a clear indication of their preference for our present 1969 Constitution.

'If they do this sincerely and honestly, of their own free will, then this will prove to be a most pleasant surprise – indeed, a great day in our history. It is this which would be our "best first prize". But let me reiterate. In order to arrive at this conclusion, the Africans must say "No". In spite of what I have just said, let us hope the answer will be "Yes".

'Let me say to the broad mass of our decent African people, that it would be tragic if history recorded that they were so bemused, so susceptible to intimidation, that they rejected an offer which is obviously so much to their advantage. If the present generation of Africans are so stupid as to reject this offer of advancement for their people, they will bear the curses of their children forever.

'Despite the categorical assurances by both Sir Alec Douglas-Home and myself that there will be no further negotiations, some people are still misleading the Africans, by saying that if they reject these terms, better ones will be offered. Such advice is not only mischievous, but is clearly aimed at deceiving African opinion.'

Today's New Democratic Constitution attempts to defuse the angry desperation of an impoverished population, to derail the work of the NCA and to maintain Zanu (PF) supremacy. Yesterday's Smith (Rhodesian prime minister) Home (British foreign secretary) settlement proposals attempted to get rid of Britain's responsibility for Rhodesia. Both documents were exercises in betrayal, the one leaving power with Ian Smith, the other leaving power with Robert Mugabe.

The agents of betrayal had to be carefully chosen. Britain was lumbered with the commitment that 'any basis proposed for independence' had to be proved to be 'acceptable to the people of Rhodesia as a whole'. It was decided to deal with this principle by appointing a British commission under Lord Pearce to canvass all sections of opinion within Rhodesia and report on whether the proposals were acceptable.

Sir Alec Douglas-Home and the Foreign Office deliberately selected Lord Pearce to head their commission as he had, during his time as the British Lord Justice of Appeal, turned down the appeal to the British courts of Rhodesia's longest incarcerated detainee, Daniel Madzimbamuto. Madzimbamuto had sought relief on grounds that Britain was responsible for her errant colony.

They selected as Lord Pearce's deputy chairman of the commission Sir Frederick Pedler, famously mocked by Mr Samuel Munodawafa at one of the first NO! rallies conducted in 1971 in Masvingo. 'We see that Sir Frederick Pedler has resigned from the commission and is not coming. He was unaware that he had business interests in Rhodesia. He did not know all along that he had interests in Rhodesia. But he has just discovered this.' The crowd of 2 000 laughed. Then they cheered when Munodawafa continued: 'Do not be afraid that Sir Alec says this is the last chance. This is only intimidation from the highest source. We know the truth and the truth will continue.'

Similarly, President Robert Mugabe and his agents carefully selected Mr Justice Chidyausiku to head their constitutional commission as he was regarded as a highly manipulable member of Zanu (PF) who had, as attorney general, overseen the preparation of the state case of treason against people such as Dumiso Dabengwa, Lookout Masuku, Isaac Nyathi and others. The case was thrown out by the courts but the state which Chidyausiku continued and continues to serve, then resorted to detaining these people, found innocent, in Chikurubi Maximum Prison.

Poor Chidyausiku behaved as his masters expected. Lord Pearce did not. Spurning all pressure from the Smith regime, the Foreign Office and Sir Alec Douglas-Home who refused to accept the eventual findings of the Pearce Commission, Lord Pearce found that the proposals were acceptable to most whites, Asians and Coloureds but, as they were unacceptable to the Africans they were not, therefore, acceptable to the people of Rhodesia as a whole. Here is the heart of the Pearce Report which, I believe, still beats in Zimbabwe 28 years on.

'Although statements by British ministers expressly disclaimed all hopes of any improvement in the terms of any future help if this settlement fell through (and we never gave anybody any reason to doubt this), some clearly persisted in the hope that some time, some how, something better would turn up. It may well be that such hopes were fallacious and that it was unwise to abandon some present advancement for the sake of them. But if people genuinely prefer hope to present realities they are entitled to do so. And if they reject on that score one cannot invalidate their rejection or even less turn it into acceptance on the grounds that their hopes were likely to prove vain.'

This article urged repudiation of the Robert Mugabe/Jonathan Moyo/ Godfrey Chidyausiku 'New Democratic Constitution', and stated: 'It cost more in terms of physical suffering to say NO to an outrageous document in 1972 than it will to say NO to another outrageous document today.'

I couldn't have been more mistaken.

When later I received a letter on another matter from Kevin Woods, one of the South African agents held for year after appalling year in Zimbabwe's prisons, saying with such regret: 'It's only in retrospect that we all have 20-20 vision,' he precisely summed up what I was feeling after the referendum in which brave Zimbabweans had rejected the 'New Democratic Constitution'.

I still had not begun to fathom the lengths to which Robert Gabriel Mugabe would go to maintain and consolidate his personal power over the crucified country of Zimbabwe through his organ Zanu (PF). Far from what I said, physical suffering was about to escalate in a way that would have been quite unthinkable in 1972.

The British government and the Rhodesian regime never dreamed, in 1972, that their proposals would or could be rejected, as they were, and reacted with fury. Ian Smith described the Pearce commissioners as 'a group of foreigners stumbling around', and Sir Alec Douglas-Home would not accept the findings and left the rejected proposals 'on the table'.

It seemed that President Mugabe was just as surprised in 2000 as Smith and Douglas-Home had been in 1972.

Once it was announced that well over half of those who voted in the February 2000 referendum had rejected the proposals for a new constitution, I watched the reaction of President Mugabe on television.

This 'no' vote was specifically a rejection of him, personally, and also of what he had thought would be popular with the overwhelmingly (over 99 per cent) black electorate – the ability to seize, by fiat, white-owned commercial farming land without compensation.

'The government accepts the result and accepts the will of the people,' he said, coiled tight as a spring. I wondered then what form his vengeance would take.

While my parents and I personally had no contact with what was happening to the victims of President Mugabe's purge of perceived opponents after his failed February constitutional referendum and his near loss to the opposition MDC in the following June election, we knew that most white farmers, as well as some black farmers, their families and their workers and dependants were being violently driven off commercial farming land by purported war veterans. More than two million people were directly affected, and the economy of Zimbabwe was pulverised.

President Mugabe had never forgotten the retired former Chief Justice Dumbutshena's involvement in the short-lived opposition Forum Party. What was now visited as punishment on Dumbutshena swept away the totally false assertion and smokescreen of 'landless blacks' spontaneously taking over 'white' land.

Dumbutshena's business, a flourishing but still indebted horticultural export concern outside Harare, was one of the farms completely destroyed by Zanu (PF) thugs, or 'war veterans', in 2000. This dignified, honourable and graceful prince of Zimbabwe, Enoch Dumbutshena, was reduced to penury and ill health in his old age by the agents of destruction who always, apparently, are unleashed with such glee and satisfaction against those perceived to be opponents of Robert Mugabe.

My parents' telephone number in Bulawayo was listed under *Hokonui Ranching*. Mine was under *Todd*, so sometimes I received calls intended for them.

One afternoon in 2000 I answered a call and was greeted by a lively male voice that was peculiarly colourless; the lack of any accent was striking. It was slightly reminiscent of the voice of Father Dieter Scholz, who, although originally German, spoke such faultless English that he appeared to have absolutely no accent of any kind. But the caller wasn't Dieter. It was a gentleman who wanted to know if this was the Todd residence. I said it was. He asked to speak to Garfield Todd. I said he wasn't available but I could take a message for him.

'Is that Judy?'

'Yes.'

'We are the war vets from Bindura,' he announced.

I remained silent.

'We are coming to Bulawayo.'

I remained silent.

'We are coming to stay with you.'

'There is not enough room,' I said.

'We can sleep on the stoep.'

'No, you can't,' I said and, to be quite specific, added, 'You are not welcome.'

There was a long and total silence. Then I said 'goodbye' politely, replaced the receiver and noticed I was trembling.

Over and above all the mayhem already covering Zimbabwe, there was talk that urban businesses and properties would be seized too, and my immediate reaction was that this would be the purpose of 'the war vets from Bindura' visiting Bulawayo. I rang a tenant at Edge House, Charles Nyathi, who was close to Dumiso Dabengwa, and told him about the telephone call. He was appalled, rang Dumiso and said we couldn't have war vets toyi-toying round Bulawayo.

Dumiso was no longer Minister of Home Affairs, having been trounced in the June election by Gibson Sibanda of the MDC. But he still had his contacts in and his bodyguards from the police, and he rang the senior assistant commissioner commanding Bulawayo province, Albert Mandizha, who, in turn, dispatched three senior police officers to see me.

They were accompanied by a large woman, who was introduced as being in charge of CIO for the area, and to whom the accompanying three men were extremely deferential. No war vets from Bindura ever materialised, but this event marked the beginning of my mother's spiritual and mental retreat from Zimbabwe.

My parents had an uncanny, almost extrasensory perception about each other and their respective circumstances. Once, in the late 1940s, for example, my father at parliament and my mother teaching at Dadaya many hours away, he woke in the night fearing how she would cope with an asthma attack if her little glass inhaler should break. As soon as the pharmacy opened the next morning, he was there to purchase another inhaler. Getting back to parliament, he found a message to ring her urgently, which he did. Before she could say anything, he said, 'Gracie, I have a new one in my pocket.'

Her inhaler had indeed broken the night before.

We tried to keep as much bad news as possible from my mother, who was increasingly frail and in pain with arthritis. I told my father about the Bindura call, but not my mother. However, she could feel that something was up, and from about that moment she reached the most devastating conclusion possible for both of them.

My mother took me aside at the first possible opportunity and informed me that her husband, my father, Garfield Todd, had been kidnapped by war veterans. The man now looking after her so tenderly and lovingly was an impostor. She couldn't understand his role in her life, but she valued him enormously. However, above all, she mourned the loss of my father and was desperately worried about him. Where was he, and how could we rescue him?

On Thursday 25 October 2001, I was picked up by three members of the fraud squad and driven to Harare. I was not allowed to contact a lawyer or my parents. My mother was seriously ill in bed. But Nyoni, the leader of the group, allowed me to take my car from the centre of Bulawayo under police escort and garage it at my home, where, he said, he would meet us. The police escorting me had no idea where I lived, two blocks from my parents. I had the remote control to their electric gate in my car, and so I drove straight to their place and in, as if it were my home.

I leaped out of the car and sped to my father's study. Thank goodness he was there and not, as he usually was, sitting with my mother in their bedroom. The police were hotfooting just behind me, and didn't know what to do when my father put out his old hand to greet them just as I was saying, 'Oh, Dad, I'm so sorry, I'm under arrest.' I could see him flinch as the only woman police officer led me away, saying I wasn't allowed to talk to anyone. I felt so broken-hearted for my father and I could tell that he felt so broken-hearted for me.

It eventually transpired that the arrest had been masterminded by a local tycoon, Mutumwa Mawere, who, with others, was trying to get control of the *Daily News* through Diamond Insurance, an associate company of Africa Resources Ltd, which he chaired. He seemed to have great influence over some members of the fraud squad. I remembered later that Mawere had telephoned and threatened me previously. But during the long journey in the police Defender to Harare, I had no idea what was up. I was just glad that I had managed to reach my father and that I hadn't simply, as was intended, disappeared without trace. Also, marvellously and fortuitously,

I had been carrying a cellphone, and Derek Smail, an important shareholder in ANZ, had telephoned me from London just as I was being led to my car. I had managed to tell him that I was under arrest.

Derek, one of the most optimistic and comforting individuals I knew, pre-eminent among whom were Washington Sansole and David Coltart, said he would do everything he could for me. Shortly after I was taken to Harare, David Coltart, followed by Washington Sansole, was with my father, comforting him.

We stopped in Gweru for the police to buy takeaways for lunch. They offered me some, and I declined. The youngest of the group, whom I found very disturbing, said, 'Are you on hunger strike?' I didn't answer. Then he said, 'Do you know how someone looks when they haven't been allowed to sleep for three days and nights?' I ignored him, which was difficult to do as he kept staring at me, as if mesmerised. The other two seemed normal. I was silently amused to learn that they came from the serious fraud squad, as this, to me, indicated the possible existence of a frivolous fraud squad.

I was one of four shareholders arrested. We all had to sign warned and cautioned statements, which, in my case, said that I admitted 'having been informed by Detective Chibururu L of the CID Serious Fraud Squad Harare that enquiries are being made ... that I unlawfully and with intent to commit the offence submitted an affidavit statement to the fact that I am a shareholder in ANZ holding a 1.0 % of the issued shares, knowing very well that it was false and that I did not contribute any share capital'.

Of course we all denied the charges, and I thought ruefully of the precious pounds I could ill afford to have moved from a savings account in London to help set up the *Daily News*, which was eventually hounded off the streets by the self-same Jonathan Moyo, now an ally of Mugabe, to whom my father had given shares in Zimpapers to help promote the freedom of the press.

At about 7.30 p.m. we were allowed to leave the serious fraud squad offices and find our own accommodation, so long as we returned first thing in the morning, which we did. We spent hours hanging around, and then, at about two in the afternoon, were told the police would proceed by way of summons and we could go. As they had originally driven all the way to Bulawayo to collect me, I asked to be driven back, and they laughed.

When we walked out of the offices on our way to the *Daily News*, I spotted Mutumwa Mawere walking in.

Eventually the *Daily News* provided a car to take me to Bulawayo via

Masvingo, where Birgit Hoffman-Mohamud lived. She had also been picked up, as her husband, a shareholder, was out of the country. They couldn't get their hands on him, so they took his little German wife instead. I rang my father from Harare to tell him we were safe and free and on our way home. He was pretending to be light-hearted, but I could hear him swallowing hard. My mother didn't know about the arrest. He had told her that I had had to go to Harare suddenly on *Daily News* business, which was true.

The next day, Saturday, the *Daily News* carried a report under the heading, 'Police charge ANZ shareholders with falsifying information'.

> Todd said that on Thursday an officer from Harare took her from her office alleging that she had been involved in a serious case of fraud.
>
> 'It was like a kidnapping. They had no warrant of arrest,' she said. 'They asked me to think hard about anything criminal I had done over the past few months. It dawned on me that Mawere had phoned me, saying he was going to have us arrested.'
>
> Yesterday Mawere said he only called Todd to inform her that he had filed a complaint with the police against her and her fellow directors.
>
> 'As a citizen of Zimbabwe I have a right to complain,' he said. 'I only said to her that she should not be surprised. I have no powers to have anyone arrested.' Mawere said he was at the fraud squad offices because he had been called by the police in connection with the case.

I never heard from the serious fraud squad again. As time passed, Mawere himself fell out with the ruling party and judged it prudent to flee the country. The state then started helping itself to his assets, which, despite his efforts, fortunately did not include Associated Newspapers of Zimbabwe.

CHAPTER 28

Farewell to the Todds

MY MOTHER DIED IN HER OWN HOME, IN HER OWN BED, devotedly attended by her husband in December 2001. He was to follow her ten lonely months later. Each of the funeral services at Dadaya were occasions filled with friends, flowers and feasting for the hundreds of people attending from all over the country and abroad, but especially from the local community among whom the Todds had lived for well over half a century. For each funeral feast John and Christine Mukokwayarira contributed a beast, as did the Vukuzenzele War Disabled Agricultural Cooperative.

The eulogy for my mother was delivered by Dr Aeneas Chigwedere, Zimbabwe's Minister of Education. He recounted what she had done for Zimbabwe in creating the first syllabus for primary education from 1934, thereby laying the foundation for what became arguably the finest education system in sub-Saharan Africa.

A great daughter of Zimbabwe

Eulogy by AS Chigwedere MP
MINISTER

Director of Ceremony, the Midlands Governor, Comrade Cephas Msipa
Sir Garfield and the Todd family
Education Ministry officials present
Ladies and Gentlemen.

I am sorry for the loss of the great lady before us here now. On behalf of the Ministry of Education, Sport and Culture and on behalf of the Government of Zimbabwe I am here to join you in bidding farewell to a great daughter of Zimbabwe and a legend in Education circles. But I must be quick to add that Minister or not, I would have been here all the same for this ceremony, partly as an admirer of the Todd family and partly as an expression of African indebtedness.

When Garfield Todd became Prime Minister of Southern Rhodesia in 1953, I was then in Std 4 in a totally rural setting and he was just a name in current affairs. When he fell from power in February 1958, I had just started on Form III work without access to newspapers or radio or TV set. The political wrangles taking place then were no more than backyard gossip with little relevance to me. I had never heard of Grace Todd although I believed that Sir Garfield was probably married. In March 1962 I registered at the then University College of Rhodesia and Nyasaland with a young girl called Judith Todd. That, indeed, was the nearest I ever got to Grace Todd and Garfield Todd.

But I am an historian and educationist. In 1997, I started working on some aspects of Rhodesian education. It was then that I stumbled on Garfield. I was fascinated by his expansion and development of African education from 1954. Peering deeper into it, I discovered that the African education system he expanded and developed was in fact the Grace Todd system that was then known as the Dadaya Scheme. Gradually I started to appreciate the African indebtedness to the lady lying here now.

The saying goes that some leaders are born but others find leadership imposed on them. Both are true of the lady lying before us here. In 1934, having recently qualified as a primary school teacher, she was dragged to Africa by a breezy young missionary and was dumped at Dadaya, then one of the darkest corners of Southern Rhodesia. Trained for sophisticated New Zealand schools, she found her new environment not only frustrating but frightening. There were probably no more than two or three trained teachers in the whole Mberengwa District. At her own Dadaya she was the only trained teacher and the so-called pupils in Grades I, II and III were men and women some of whom were over the age of 20.

Worse still the Southern Rhodesia Government had not put in place an African Education curriculum i.e. there were no national syllabuses. Each district or each religious denomination or each school fumbled its own way the best it could. What was generally accepted was that the alphabet was important to enable the pupils to read and write. Numbers were also taught to enable the pupils to add, subtract, divide and multiply. Then the Old and New Testaments had to be taught plus some English and Craft.

Thrown into the deep end of a pool like this Mrs Todd accepted the challenge and devised a curriculum for her class. Apart from streamlining the existing subjects she broadened the curriculum and proceeded to make syllabuses for all the classes at Dadaya. The neighbouring schools saw salvation in her and came to borrow her lessons. The neighbouring Districts were not slow to detect the light glowing from Dadaya. Inevitably they pleaded for the Grace Todd Lessons and Dadaya ended up as the Education Service Centre for many districts.

By 1945 the Southern Rhodesia Government had got wind of this development and had asked for the Grace Todd Lessons and adopted them in toto. By 1950 therefore, what had become the African Education System and popularly known as the Dadaya Scheme, was the Grace Todd scheme. When Garfield became Prime Minister in 1953 he, through grants and loans, developed the vast number of schools that ended at Grade III, to Grade V and those that ended at Grade V, to Std VI. But the curriculum was the Grace Todd curriculum. Indeed, Grace Todd's African Primary Education System remained intact with very minor cosmetic changes right up to 1980. I am a product of the Grace Todd scheme, all the Africans here who did primary education before 1980 are children or grandchildren of the Grace Todd Education System.

Ladies and gentlemen, education schemes throughout the world are products of Education Commissions and Education Task Forces. The Southern Rhodesian African Education System was the product of one person, the lady lying before us here. Whoever produces a national system is necessarily a national hero and this explains why I am endeared to her. The Africans of this country are not aware of their indebtedness to this great lady. But in my capacity as historian and educationist I have taken it upon myself to enlighten them on this. Towards that end, I researched into the Todd family and other liberal Europeans. Worried by the great age of both the lady and Sir Garfield I decided, in April 2001, to present my manuscript to them entitled *The White Heroes of Zimbabwe*. My consolation is that I was able to present this to her when she was still alive.

Let me say to Lady Grace Todd, your bones will be buried here but your spirit will live forever. Our situation in the country, political, economic, social and religious will continue to need the intervention of powerful, balanced and just spirits such as yours. Rest in peace in your cherished centre of operations. On behalf of the Ministry of Education, Sport and Culture, on behalf of the Government of Zimbabwe and on behalf of the Africans of this country to whom you devoted your all and sacrificed your all, I salute you!

Among the hundreds who attended my father's funeral at Dadaya in October 2002 was the British ambassador to Zimbabwe, Brian Donnelly, who brought with him three letters. The first was a tribute to my father from the British Foreign Secretary, Jack Straw, whom I had met in 1966, when, as president of the Leeds University Students' Union, he had organised payment for my ticket from Rhodesia to address a teach-in against Ian Smith's UDI at that university.

The second letter was from someone I had never met, and whose address was 10 Downing Street.

Dear Miss Todd

I wanted to write to offer my sincere condolences following the death of your father. He was an exceptional man who made a huge contribution to the country of Zimbabwe.

No words can express what you must be feeling at this time but my thoughts are with you.

With deepest sympathy,

Yours sincerely,
Tony Blair

The third was from Buckingham Palace. I was sitting at the graveside next to Eddison Zvobgo when I opened it, hardly believing my eyes. I showed it to him.

'You must share it with everyone,' he ordered. 'Read it to us! Read it to us all now!' So I did, and the huge crowd, my father's family, murmured and sighed with pleasure.

BUCKINGHAM PALACE
ROYAL COURT TELEGRAM

Ms Judith Todd
Bulawayo
Zimbabwe

I was so sorry to learn of the death of your father. Prince Philip joins me in sending our heartfelt sympathy to you and your family at this difficult time.

ELIZABETH R

Some months later, walking through Bulawayo, I met Teacher Moyo, who was still elated by the circumstances of my father's funeral.

'It was such a wonderful occasion,' he said. 'We saw friends there we hadn't met for years. It was more like a wedding than a funeral. We sang all the way home!'

CHAPTER 29

Mugabe's war on Zimbabwe

I VIVIDLY REMEMBER MY FATHER'S LAST COMMENT ON ROBERT Mugabe.

'*What I cannot forgive is how many people he has corrupted.*'

He was thinking about individuals in Zimbabwe, never anticipating that the corruption would cascade beyond our borders, with many other people affected and harmed by it. Tragically, as Zimbabwean constitutional lawyer Brian Kagoro observed: 'Mugabe has displaced the crisis from the national to the regional level as a pan-African struggle against imperial domination.'

In this way distinguished people were led into the most invidious of positions. They appeared to think that they were supporting the reformist black nation of Zimbabwe against unfair criticism and sanction by white Western imperialists, but were in fact condoning the actions of a relatively small pack of powerful criminals who, like Ian Smith before them, used state resources to hijack their country.

But, unlike Smith, Robert Mugabe and his acolytes also assiduously asset-stripped Zimbabwe and delivered its population into the depths of hellish despair, poverty and illness. In January 2006, a survey conducted by Erasmus University, Rotterdam, found on a world database of happiness that Zimbabwe was the unhappiest country in the world. That April, the World Health Organisation announced that people in Zimbabwe now also had the lowest life expectancy in the world, an average of thirty-seven years for men and, dropping from sixty-one years in 1991, just thirty-four years for women.

Observing the transformation of people once they were absorbed into Zanu (PF), I often thought of President Mugabe as embodying the antithesis of that plea from the Lord's Prayer: 'Lead us not into temptation but deliver us from evil.' Over the years he has perfected the art of leading people into temptation and then, when they fall, delivering them into evil. A dramatic example of this was the offer of irresistibly beautiful stolen farms to judges.

Only the dimmest of his cohorts were not terrified, ripe for blackmail or already being blackmailed. Many had suffered physically at his hands and knew what he was capable of. Augustine Chihuri, a fellow Zezuru and for many years head of Zimbabwe's police, was one of those put into the apparently indescribable horror of the 'pits' in Mozambique before independence. According to Rugare Gumbo in January 1980, Mugabe's 'inordinate lust for power' was demonstrated as far back as 1977, when he ordered the detention of the entire Zimbabwe People's Army command and all field commanders, save for fellow Zezuru Rex Nhongo, now Solomon Mujuru. Rugare Gumbo also experienced the pits.

Just before the 1980 elections, veteran Aaron Mutiti warned: 'What Mugabe himself has done to his fellow Zimbabweans in exile during the last three years deprives his hollow assurances of any credibility. Unless the people of this country are vigilant, they are in for a rude shock. Family life, religious life and economic life as we know it will progressively disappear if Mugabe gets to power. We must not close our eyes to this threat. He rates his communist ideology higher than people.'

SK Moyo, Zimbabwe's ambassador to South Africa, had observed the brutal destruction of Joshua Nkomo and Zapu from up close, as had Kotsho Dube, whom Mugabe appointed representative to Nigeria after 2000. Dumiso Dabengwa and Isaac Nyathi had watched the slow death of Lookout Masuku unfolding in Chikurubi Prison and the demolition of their own proud histories by Mugabe.

Driven by desperation, fear and greed, erstwhile opponents joined the stampede onto the Zanu (PF) gravy train, many reaping rich spoils and keeping their mouths zipped. They knew that if they did not, they would once again be treated abusively, such as Movement for Democratic Change leaders Morgan Tsvangirai and Welshman Ncube, and many others who came close to death at the hands of 'war veterans' or the hangman. All these high-level Zimbabweans undoubtedly loathed Mugabe for his destruction of the country and their integrity, but willy-nilly participated in economic and political crimes against the nation. They thus became complicit, guilty and fearful, bound hand and foot to their corrupter.

The once respected and loved leader, Dumiso Dabengwa, went so far as to meet a group of 'war veterans' arriving in Bulawayo and toyi-toyied with them through the streets as they went on their loudly proclaimed mission to torch the MDC offices. Courage and honour in so many former fighters for freedom was replaced by a desperate will to survive, and so they failed to help targeted victims, such as their former colleague Fletcher Dulini, national treasurer of the MDC, when he faced trumped-up charges and near death in confinement. Dulini was eventually rushed to hospital, where he lay in bed with his limbs shackled and under guard. Wracked with high blood pressure and diabetes, he lost an eye. But Fletcher Dulini was only one in more than half a million cases of violence, abduction, rape, torture and murder recorded against Zimbabweans after 2000.

Then take Zimbabwe's registrar general, Tobaiwa Mudede.

After independence he displayed humility and kindness, helping many people in many different ways. When my father was approached for help by an old white woman in a retirement home, he was able to go to Mudede. The woman wanted to pay a final visit to relatives in South Africa, but had no travel documents. The two men successfully did everything in their power for her, and she had a wonderful last trip.

Yet over the years Mudede became one of the most villainous faces of the Mugabe regime, rigging elections and tearing the skin of citizenship off people. In 2001, my Zimbabwean passport lapsed, as is normal, after ten years. Mudede refused to renew it. Along with his master and fellow Zezuru tribesman, for that was the level to which they had sunk, he and President Mugabe were intent on wiping out the citizenship and voting rights of any Zimbabwean of whatever colour or background thought to be against their ruling clique.

My father was one of the first individuals affected. Stripped of his citizenship before the 2002 presidential elections, his name was put on a special list Mudede had supplied to all polling stations of people who were not allowed to vote, even if their names were actually printed on the current voters' roll, as my father's was.

I was proud of his response. He did not blink at reality and defer action by saying, 'This is an African problem for which there must be an African solution.' No. He went and confronted the evil directly himself. Although almost ninety-four years old and rather shaky, he went to the polls to vote. He got as close to the ballot box as he could before he was turned away by the hapless presiding officer, Noyce Dube, former pupil and then headmaster of Dadaya Secondary School, whose parents had been married to each other decades before by the very man he was now having to deprive of his right to vote.

In May 2002, the late Justice Sandra Mungwira found that I had been stripped of my citizenship illegally, and ordered Mudede to treat me as a citizen by birth and to renew my Zimbabwe passport. Her decision was later endorsed by Justice Benjamin Paradza, now a refugee in New Zealand.

Mudede appealed against the High Court rulings to the Supreme Court, which, like the voters' rolls and citizenship records, was being cleansed and was under the control of fellow Zezuru Godfrey Chidyausiku. By then, practically all high offices in Zimbabwe were held by members of Robert Mugabe's Zezuru clan.

Pending the findings of the Supreme Court, Mudede reluctantly issued a temporary passport of one year's duration in which he pre-empted any judgment by declaring that I was a permanent resident, and not a citizen, of Zimbabwe.

The case was argued before Chief Justice Chidyausiku and others in January 2003. On 27 February, in an agonisingly confused and confusing judgment, the Supreme Court found that I was a citizen of both New Zealand and Zimbabwe, and concluded: 'For the avoidance of doubt the respondent has two days, from the handing down of this judgment, within which to renounce her New Zealand citizenship in accordance with the New Zealand Citizenship Act. In the event of her failure to do so, she will lose her Zimbabwean citizenship by operation of the law.'

I managed to do what was ordered, painfully participating in what I knew was a charade.

The New Zealand authorities responded in July, stating that they had received my application for renunciation of citizenship on 28 February, but that this application could not be processed as I had never laid claim to New Zealand citizenship. They could not help me to renounce what I did not have.

My temporary passport expired on 30 July 2003, and I was stranded in Bulawayo with no citizenship and no travel documents. Washington Sansole took the matter, and New Zealand's response, in writing to Home Affairs Minister Kembo Mohadi, Deputy Minister Rugare Gumbo and the Permanent Secretary of Home Affairs, arguing that obviously the Supreme Court had erred in finding that I was a citizen of New Zealand. There was no response.

In a letter to the minister in September, Sansole wrote:

> Further to my letter to you of the 4th August, 2003, which I faxed to you on even date and my several enquiries by telephone thereafter, I am still awaiting a reply from you.
>
> Miss Todd is very anxious to have a passport. Please have this matter of her citizenship resolved without any further delay. As things stand now, Miss Todd is without a state and citizenship. She was born in this country in 1943 and she has lived in this country believing this was

her one and only country by birth. I trust that it is now time to act honourably towards her.

Again there was no reply.

Sansole eventually reached my old friend Mohadi by telephone and was then given the impression that Registrar General Mudede had been instructed by his superiors in the ministry to recognise my Zimbabwean citizenship and to issue me a passport forthwith. If so, Mudede treated his superiors with contempt, as he routinely did the courts, and ignored their instructions. Instead he turned to his personal lawyer Simplisius Chihambakwe of Chihambakwe, Mutizwa & Partners, to whom Sansole also wrote in December 2003.

> My client was born in Zimbabwe (Southern Rhodesia then) on the 18th March 1943. Thus she is a Zimbabwean Citizen by birth since then till now, notwithstanding any desire to foist upon her a New Zealand Citizenship or any other.
>
> The Supreme Court granted her 'two days, from the handing down of this judgment within which to renounce her New Zealand Citizenship … In the event of her failure to do so, she will lose her Zimbabwean citizenship …'
>
> She complied but as if to confirm her contention all along the New Zealand authorities declined to process her application for renunciation of New Zealand citizenship *because she was never a New Zealand citizen. She does not have dual or multiple citizenship.*
>
> So what does the Registrar General want her to do?
>
> The only honourable and proper thing to do is simply to reinstate her Zimbabwean Citizenship which was mistakenly taken away from her. The most shameful thing about this state of affairs is that she, of all people, should be treated this harshly and unfairly when all along she fought from and in the same trenches with us for the independence of this her and our country. Her history is well known to us all. Justice must be allowed and be seen to prevail in this matter …

A reply to his letter was faxed on 16 December from Simplisius Chihambakwe.

Dear Sirs

Re: CITIZENSHIP OF NEW ZEALAND: JUDITH TODD

We refer to your letter dated the 8th December, 2003 the contents of which have been noted.

Please be advised that the matter went as far as the Supreme Court of Zimbabwe and as far as we are concerned that concluded this matter. Any problems that may have been encountered after the Supreme Court decision are completely beyond our control and we regret to say that we are unable to assist further on this matter.

Yours faithfully,
CHIHAMBAKWE, MUTIZWA & PARTNERS
cc The Registrar General

So, stateless and with no travel documents, I finally turned to New Zealand for help, and applied for citizenship and a passport on the documented basis of my parents having been born and married there, and received a thoughtful and generous response from Gary Basham, acting manager of citizenship, Department of Internal Affairs, New Zealand.

This has obviously been a difficult decision for you to make. We are strongly aware of the importance of citizenship and what it means to those who are faced with surrendering their current citizenship, or indeed for those who are currently stateless. I hope that registering your status as a New Zealand citizen and receiving a New Zealand passport will provide you with the security you are currently lacking, and provide you with a sense of attachment to New Zealand.

My New Zealand passport arrived in Bulawayo by courier on 31 December 2003. I opened it and read the magic words:

The Governor-General in the Realm of New Zealand requests in the Name of Her Majesty The Queen all whom it may concern to allow the holder to pass without delay or hindrance and in case of need to give all lawful assistance and protection.

This was followed by an e-mail from New Zealand Prime Minister Helen Clark: 'Let us hope for a new era in Zimbabwe where it will be proud to recognise as citizens those who have been born there or – as in the case of your father – those who devoted much of their life to the country.

'Meanwhile I am pleased that New Zealand has been able to be helpful at this time of need.'

There were a number of funerals taking place on Sunday 27 March 2005 at Bulawayo's Lady Stanley cemetery, where Lookout Masuku lies, but I found Connie Ndlovu's at the appointed time.

I was approaching the dreaded hole in the ground when someone put her arms around me from behind – Gift Masuku. Her children had moved to the UK and were looking after her from afar.

'God is good,' she said.

She asked what I was doing. I said I was writing a book.

'About Lookout!' she said immediately and decisively. 'And who else?'

Then she opened her handbag and took out a picture of Lookout for the book.

Connie was sixty-five. She hadn't been well, suffering from asthma since the arrest and detention of her husband Johnson in 1985, twenty grim years before. Not long after 'unity', Johnson was killed in a car crash. At his funeral, Tennyson Ndlovu, by then a Zanu (PF) functionary and looking just as unappealing as he had when he'd swaggered around as 'dissident' Tambolenyoka, told me that 'white farmers' had interfered with the brakes of Johnson's car.

'What rubbish!' I replied, but I could tell that Zanu (PF)'s anti-white build-up was accelerating.

A few years later I met Connie in a queue in town, and said, 'I wonder what Johnson would have thought of life in Zimbabwe today,' and she laughed with an echo of her old, sparkling gaiety.

'I'm sure he's so glad that he escaped,' she said.

Her words were more profound than she realised.

That Sunday I also saw Nobel Guduza, whose mother Poppy was buried in Bulawayo in May 1997. Her father Makhatini had finally fled to Johannesburg in 2000 from the injustice and terror of Mugabe's Zimbabwe. After he had gone, Nobel brought me a final, terse, dignified and broken-hearted note from him, telling me he was escaping once more from Zimbabwe.

'I am not wanted.'

He died in exile on 30 November 2004. His much loved elder son, Churchill, transported his body home to Zimbabwe, and the Guduza children buried him with Poppy in her Pelandaba grave.

Churchill was working in South Africa and drove a Mercedes. Dumiso Dabengwa and other Zanu (PF) functionaries attended Guduza's funeral and remarked on Churchill's Mercedes. 'You have a nice car.'

'Yes,' said Churchill, 'and I am paying for it myself.'

Makhatini's old cell mate, Des Bawden, had also died. As with most commercial farmers, his land had also been taken, and he was relatively fortunate to be left with access to the house and yard. Then a friend wrote me, long after the event, that Des had died.

The last 'election' in which I was able to vote, as a 'permanent resident' of Zimbabwe, was on 31 March 2005. After that, permanent residents were also stripped of their right to vote. Five days later, I was buying a Sunday newspaper opposite the town hall and was greeted by Bulawayo's mayor, Japhet Ndabeni-Ncube, a tall, imposing man, once a pupil at Dadaya. A group of dignified ladies carrying bibles passed by, and one of them greeted the mayor.

'Our hearts are breaking,' she said, 'but the sermon helped.'

She moved on, and Ndabeni turned to me in a rage.

'We must expose what is happening!' he said. 'We are told that we are a happy, peaceful people and we have just been enjoying free and fair elections! We are happy because our economy is broken, our people are starving and sick, our election was stolen! Oh, yes, we are happy indeed!'

That night, Zimbabwe television news led with people still celebrating Zanu (PF)'s inevitable victory, portraits of President Mugabe prancing on their bodies. There was a report that 'artificial shortages' of essential items, such as maize-meal, sugar, cooking oil and bread, were now hitting the shops in Harare as unscrupulous traders tried to undermine the election results. There was also a promise from the ministry concerned that rumours of an impending fuel shortage were false.

The election had been found to be free and fair, and here were South African observers Membathisi Mphumzi Shepherd Mdladlana, Minister of Labour, and Phumzile Mlambo-Ngcuka, Minister of Minerals and Energy, to tell us so. The latest in the long line of sleek South Africans to visit Zimbabwe, their conclusion was hardly surprising. Mdladlana had publicly announced, even before voting commenced, that the election was free and fair. But just over a year later, in May 2006, a terrible punishment was exacted from Phumzile Mlambo-Ngcuka, now deputy president of South Africa, for her role in whitewashing Zimbabwe's elections when she was forced to admit that South Africa could do little to shield itself from the consequences of an eventual collapse of Zimbabwe's devastated economy.

In April 2005, I left Bulawayo for a spell in Cape Town, giving thanks that I had a New Zealand passport and a seat on an aircraft, unlike the hundreds who I knew were trudging on foot below, fleeing for their lives from one hostile country to another.

At the beginning of June, Peter Mackay wrote from Marondera about a section of the community that was already under the hammer, although he didn't know this at the time.

⠄ I am evolving a theory that Zimbabwe is a practising democracy, with
the people – the povo – running the country efficiently by means of
informal trading, cross-border trading, the black market, the parallel
market, transporting their maize grown on ad hoc patches to the grinding mills by wheelbarrow and generally making do, while what is called
the government goes its own way, that is in circles ...

This informal sector of the economy Peter was describing was simultaneously being smashed. President Mugabe had started preparing for this
further act of state terror months before by denouncing impoverished urban
dwellers as being totemless, saying this in such a way as to demonstrate
that people with no totems were beings devoid of humanity. Now he was
galvanised into action by the belief everyone shared that the majority of
urban dwellers had voted for the opposition MDC in the March elections.

Operation Murambatsvina, which has been translated in various ways,
but which basically means 'remove the shit', was launched on Tuesday
17 May in the Harare area and spread fast throughout the country. While
most sectors of the economy suffered crippling fuel shortages, bulldozers
and other vehicles moved unimpeded through all parts of Zimbabwe in
their destruction of thousands of concrete houses, informal settlements
and trading centres. Police, army and youth militia used sledgehammers
and fire to destroy homes and businesses, and when they tired, ordered the
victims to destroy their own properties. Even the flower sellers outside
Meikles Hotel in central Harare had their structures destroyed.

On Thursday 30 June, South African radio announced that President
Mugabe had said Operation Murambatsvina had been a campaign planned
well in advance and was 'a long-cherished desire'.

Didymus Mutasa, whom Mugabe had put in charge of both state security
and all matters to do with land, had said as early as August 2002, when it
was estimated that Zimbabwe had a population of thirteen million: 'We
would be better off with only six million people, with our own people who
support the liberation struggle. We don't want all these extra people.' When
Operation Murambatsvina was launched, the people targeted had already
been described by head of police Augustine Chihuri as a 'crawling mass of
maggots' who were destroying the economy.

E-mails poured out of Zimbabwe. One from 'Songbird' in Harare said
his gardener had come to work late in a state of shock, and reported that the
army had threatened to whip anyone who resisted the demolition of their
homes.

'I have seen it now with my own eyes, the destruction and the hate. There is no hope for this country now. It is finished. My own relatives have nowhere to go. If only we had guns.'

Richard Walker wrote from New York on 11 June:

Operation Murambatsvina made the front page of the *New York Times* today – front and centre, with big three-column picture of a disconsolate Gertrude Mbare seated in foreground of a Harare section turned to rubble. Story turns over to fill most of page 6. The headline – 'Zimbabwe's "Cleanup" Takes a Vast Human Toll'. The subhead – 'A crackdown could leave 1.5 million poor people homeless and jobless'. The report by Michael Wines maintained that the campaign to uproot the urban poor and so disperse 'President Robert G Mugabe's most hardened opponents was quickly evolving into a sweeping recasting of society.'

Wines spent four days in and around Harare and Bulawayo and seems to have ventured as far as Brunapeg (on the Botswana border), enabling him to recall how it was epicentre of a 1980s massacre by 'Mr Mugabe's army' of as many as '20 000 ethnic Ndebeles' – slaughter then, starvation now …

By Monday 13 June nothing had been written about Operation Murambatsvina in what I had seen of the South African press, save for a letter from K Rennie in the *Sunday Independent*, re-published the next day in the *Cape Times* under the heading, 'Why the deafening silence on Robert Mugabe's purge of the poor?'

The ANC government, it seems, is so supportive of Mugabe's current 'clean-up' that it kindly supplied spare parts which will enable Mugabe's armed forces to continue their intimidation of would-be protestors by hovering overhead in military helicopters – as they did last week. Perhaps most shocking of all is our media's response. Almost overnight 250 000 people are made homeless and large numbers income-less in a neighbouring country. At best, our newspapers have offered us a story from the wire services, or syndicated from one of the international newspapers … (and) on television, virtual silence.

Once again our neighbours, the workers and the poorest of the poor, have been made homeless, without income, without assistance, in mid-winter. These are real people. Four have already died. Many more will die of cold and hunger alone. But where will it end? It is perhaps timely to recall the tens of thousands of dissenting voices that Mugabe silenced in Matabeleland, who 'disappeared' in the early 1980s.

We must not let these people disappear. We must speak out.

Or by our silence, we are surely complicit.

My sister Cyndie rang from Australia, where they were receiving news of Zimbabwe's grotesque suffering on television. I could find no news in South Africa. On the main TV news bulletin that Sunday night, the only mention of Zimbabwe was a report by John Nyashanu in Harare on role reversals in agriculture, with some whites whose enterprises had been seized now working for the occupying black elite. Such positive developments, Nyashanu said, meant that Zimbabwe's agriculture could now reach only dizzying heights.

At the same time, Mary Ndlovu wrote 'from a devastated Bulawayo'.

When I said that after the election there would be greater repression I could not possibly have imagined what is happening in Zimbabwe now, first in Harare and now coming to us.

The police started yesterday evening and continued today with the result that all the fruit and vegetable stalls on Fifth Avenue, all the stalls of every sort in Lobengula Street mall, the whole of Entumbane informal market, the furniture and mattress makers in Makokoba and all the food and clothing sellers and service-providers at Renkini are history. There are piles of rubble everywhere lying in chaos.

Later this morning the police attacked the sellers along Lobengula Street, dumping their wares into police trucks and burning the stalls. Smoke was wafting everywhere.

There are no words to describe what this means to hundreds of thousands of people who eke out a living selling on the streets, trying to get by when the formal economy has collapsed. If ever any government has behaved like this I don't know where or when it existed. They have not just openly stolen people's goods, but their entire livelihoods. Our brains are evidently not equipped to absorb or give meaning to the destruction that has been perpetrated. We are not, as far as we know, at war, but that is what appears to be happening. Our government is making war on the nation. We cannot attempt to explain it, and everyone is in a state of shock. We cannot 'adjust' any more to our fate, but as a people we are paralysed by fear and desperation. There will be prayer meetings of the faithful, all night vigils, but when the Amen is said, nothing will have changed. Hopelessness in the face of unspeakable evil and violence is our future.

In a speech to the Cape Town Press Club on 30 June, titled 'They Will Not Stop until They Are Stopped', I stressed that what was happening in Zimbabwe was simply another chapter of a saga that had been running since 1980.

> No one must allow themselves to be deluded by what is going on in Zimbabwe. Just as Gukurahundi was designed to kill, so is Operation Murambatsvina. If, in bitter winter, you deprive people and their children of shelter and thus also their food and clothing and warmth; if you deprive them of their tools of trade and their means of survival, you do this for one reason only: you intend them to die.
>
> The longer the life of the Mugabe regime is extended, the more people will die. The regime will not stop with what we know of Operation Murambatsvina. *They will not stop until they are stopped.*

When faced with such appalling tragedies as were being inflicted upon Zimbabwe, it was difficult to comprehend each individual calamity. I tried to give a sense of the human anguish by ending with a quote from John Lloyd from the *Scotsman* (19 June): 'In a tiny scene, captured by a hidden TV camera filming the political cleansing Robert Mugabe has visited on Zimbabweans, one shot expressed a moment of great poignancy. A man reached out and stroked the arm of his daughter as she walked away from him and he gazed down, eyes shaded, at the ground. It was the gesture of a second, hopeless, it seemed, because he could do nothing more to protect or soothe her than this touch, a gesture which only told her he was still a living being, and reassured him that she was too.'

This speech found its way to New Zealand, from where I received a call from John Minto of Global Peace and Justice, and Rod Donald, co-leader of the Green Party, inviting me to join them, along with exiled Zimbabwean cricketer Henry Olonga, in trying to stop the impending Black Caps cricket tour of Zimbabwe. I did. The first and major event for me was an Auckland rally on 16 July, where we were joined by Phil Goff, New Zealand's Minister of Foreign Affairs and Trade, who forthrightly explained New Zealand's principled stand against Mugabe.

> Why Zimbabwe? There are many countries around the world in which there is oppression and abuse of human rights.
>
> Zimbabwe stands out for particular reasons. It stands out because it was a country that had democracy. It was a country that had rule of law. It was a country that had an independent judiciary and media. It was a

wealthy country that could meet the economic and social needs of its people. All of those things have been lost, not because of colonisation or any other excuse that Mugabe might come up with, but because he has run that country down. He has run that country autocratically. He has run that country for the benefit of his cronies and not for the overwhelming majority of his people.

Why Zimbabwe? Because, in Zimbabwe, for the first time since Pol Pot, we have seen a mass of people rendered homeless, as a deliberate policy of government, and sent out in the countryside where they lack shelter and food.

We are approaching the Security Council trying to get Mugabe before the International Criminal Court. We don't know whether we can do it but, by God, that's where he belongs. That's what his fate should be for what he has done to his people.

We have approached the Southern African Development Community. There are many people here who marched in 1981 against the South African rugby tour. We did it because we were begged to do it by the ANC to stand up for the rights of the oppressed, to stand up for the majority of South Africa, and stand up against abuse of human rights.

Now, it is time for the ANC to deliver back. Why should it be wrong only when their rights were stolen from them by the regime of apartheid, yet South Africa has been silent when it comes to condemning the same abuses from the Mugabe regime? New Zealand is one country, one country only, but I'm proud of the fact that we have taken a lead on this in so many fields and internationally.

But to succeed in the true purpose, which is to get rid of Mugabe, get rid of the abuses, we need the support of other countries around the globe. To be effective, we will continue to fight for that.

The International Criminal Court was established in 2002 to investigate and try individuals for transgressing international humanitarian law. There is no statute of limitations, and so the Gukurahundi genocide of the 1980s would fall within its ambit, as would Operation Murambatsvina and all the other crimes against humanity waged by President Mugabe and his accomplices since the birth of Zimbabwe. Action by the ICC could be triggered by the United Nations Security Council referring the situation in Zimbabwe for scrutiny.

When entering South Africa on my New Zealand passport, I get a three-month visa, which can be renewed for a further three months. At the end of that accumulated time, I have to return to my 'place of origin' – Zimbabwe –

for a minimum of ten days. This I did in October 2005, and found Bulawayo in a state of further collapse.

As the urban population tended to support the opposition, the Zanu (PF) government attempted to strangle the city authorities, and council services collapsed. Japhet Ndabeni-Ncube, Bulawayo's mayor, explained that the local authority was 'under the grip of the government and cannot do anything to try and provide solutions to the city's problems', the gravest of which was lack of water.

This, coupled with a lack of fuel, meant the suspension of refuse collection services, and the crippling of attempts to provide water in bowsers to the high-density suburbs, clinics and schools. The misery of hunger and disease was thus underlined by the inability of people to even wash themselves, or their clothes and utensils. There was a terrible joke circulating among the youth: '*I can't take her out any more. She is past the wash-by date.*'

I called on the mayor and found that government had objected to statistics published by the city that revealed the mounting scale of deaths from 'malnutrition'. A delegation from the police, intelligence and the army had visited the mayor to find out where the statistics came from, and were astonished to learn that they were government statistics routinely collected by the council every month over many decades. Since then, council had been deprived of access to the statistics.

I walked through the city and found that some vending had restarted after Operation Murambatsvina and the destruction of the informal business sector. Flower sellers were sheltering inside the railings surrounding the city hall. People were carrying vegetables in bags or on pushcarts, so that they could run if 'police', often Zanu (PF) youth militia in police uniforms, descended. Some old women were sitting where former stalls used to be with little piles of tomatoes or a solitary cabbage. Verging on the residential areas there were people crouched next to trees or bushes with small stacks of goods to sell. I calculated that someone would have to sell fifteen oranges to be able to make the profit necessary to buy one loaf of bread, if it was available.

People in general seemed clueless, eyes cast downwards, about the fate of their fellow citizens who had been abducted and dispersed under Operation Murambatsvina. I found one brave but scared pastor who was able to give me statistics of what was being done to help 1500 people subsisting in Bulawayo and 4000 at Victoria Falls, where, he said, two children had been savagely wounded by police dogs and one man eaten by lion. Those who had not yet been moved to rural villages were trying to exist in the bush with wild animals. These displaced Zimbabweans were in hiding, and only emerged, apparently out of thin air and desperate for help, if they were sure those approaching were friends.

The pastor introduced me to two such people. One, a toothless man so old that the irises of his eyes were white, was no longer able to fend for himself. The other, also old, had been granted a patch of ground by a fellow human and now needed material with which to build a hut. They were thin and hungry, and even the *Financial Gazette*, reputed to have been taken over by CIO, reported while I was there that 'the majority of the country's population of about 12.5 million would not be able to feed themselves until the next harvest', whenever that would be. Seeds, fertiliser and fuel seemed available to so few. Inflation was soaring daily, and in the twelve days I was in Bulawayo the price of the staple, maize-meal, rocketed. Prices and currency valuations were actually meaningless as inflation soared past 1000 per cent per year.

I returned to Cape Town in October 2005 for a further three months, unable to erase three particular memories from my mind.

One was of an old white woman, leaning, arms folded, on her shopping trolley like a self-propelling crutch and reaching the till with only one item, a packet of Pro-Nutro cereal.

Another was of a thin young couple, a baby strapped to the woman's back, standing wide-eyed, silent and apparently transfixed by the realisation that there was absolutely nothing in the entire supermarket that could be purchased with the little sheaf of useless notes the man was holding.

Finally, as I was being driven to the airport by a friend, we passed through the dusty suburb of Paddonhurst. A vehicle carrying maize must have passed earlier, and there were a few kernels scattered on the tarmac. A black skeleton in rags was swaying here and there, collecting them. The kind of rags indicated that this may once have been a woman.

CHAPTER 30

Deliver us from evil

FURTHER HEAVY BLOWS WERE TO DESCEND ON A TRAUMATISED Zimbabwe. In November 2005, the country was left off the agenda at the Commonwealth Heads of Government Meeting in Malta. As my old friend and fellow Zimbabwean Michael Holman, former Africa editor of London's *Financial Times*, wrote in distress:

> For years the Commonwealth has played the role of the international community's canary in the coal pit; or, to change metaphor, a trip wire that warns of distress that lies ahead. You name it, and the Commonwealth has produced a report on it, usually long before the subject became fashionable. From global warming to the global economy, world trade and drug trafficking, micro states and money laundering, from the plight of minorities to the crippling impact of external debt on weak economies, the Commonwealth has produced an informed view. So it is all the more extraordinary that there is not a single reference to Zimbabwe in the Commonwealth secretary general's 50-page report to members, covering the two years since the last summit.
>
> The country has been airbrushed out of Commonwealth history.

Another blow came with the unsurprising fission of Zimbabwe's Movement for Democratic Change (MDC). Over the years since its inception in September 1999, more than 400 of its members had been individually and horribly murdered. At least another half a million citizens, in an overall national population of maybe ten million, were tortured, raped and terrorised, and the MDC hierarchy was under constant pressure with arrests, interrogations and court cases, usually on trumped-up charges of everything from treason to kidnapping to murder.

Like every other organisation in Zimbabwe, including the churches and non-governmental organisations, such as the local committee of the Red Cross, the brave and honourable membership of the MDC was riddled with security agents and *agents provocateurs* intent on destroying the opposition and simultaneously hijacking their resources. Food continued to be denied to rural MDC supporters, maize being sold by government agents only to those with Zanu (PF) membership cards. The pressure had been so intense for so long that it was little wonder people were starting to crack.

No one could have better summed up the plight of the MDC than the renowned former Zanu freedom fighter Wilfred Mhanda, previously known as Dzinashe Machingura, in an interview with Peta Thornycroft, published in October 2005.

'The MDC leadership totally underestimated Mugabe. They believed the struggle for democracy would be hard, but they never understood that he was prepared to destroy everything – them, the economy, the institutions, the infrastructure, the whole country and everything in it – to survive.

'The MDC thought they could win by being right, by appealing to the majority, and they got that support, but that was never enough. Mugabe controls the security forces, the courts, the media, the intelligence services and the assets, and he has perfected the system of patronage, manipulating each and every person in positions of power.

'Mugabe was impossible to defeat in elections because he controls every aspect of them too. The task was too big for the decent MDC, and the party neglected to make inroads in the lower ranks of the army, who are just as poor as everyone else.'

A great tragedy for the southern African region was that Zimbabwe's government was unable to positively assist the new and vulnerable state of South Africa in 1994. Protestations to the contrary, Zanu (PF) did not enjoy the emergence of Nelson Mandela onto the international stage. Consequently, in a strange and unexpected reaction to this implicit hostility, and to the dismay throughout the world of friends and allies from the bad old days of apartheid, prominent members of the ANC started rewriting the history of Zimbabwe's ruling party in their memories, which was then reflected in their actions and statements. In December 2004, the ANC's former deputy secretary general, Henry Makgothi, attended Zanu (PF)'s fourth congress, and, reading from a prepared statement, said: 'Our national executive of the ANC and the people of South Africa are confident that Zanu (PF), as a party of revolution, will continue to play a leading role to assert the political and economic independence of Zimbabwe. As the ANC we take pride in the bilateral relations that we have forged over the years of the struggle. The ANC wishes to reiterate our firm support for the people of Zimbabwe under the leadership of Zanu (PF).'

What was being blinked at here was the fact that the bilateral relations that had been forged during those years of struggle were between the ANC and Zapu under the leadership of Joshua Nkomo, while Zanu, under the leadership of first Ndabaningi Sithole and then Robert Mugabe, had stood with the PAC – not the ANC, lonely and rejected on the fringes of the Organisation of African Unity. This continued to be the position until the ANC won South Africa's 1994 elections, where the PAC, to the consternation of Zanu (PF), received only 1.2 per cent of the vote. Only then did Zanu (PF) switch sides and the rewriting of history begin.

By the skilful deployment as top diplomats of people formerly identified with Zapu and/or Joshua Nkomo, such as SK Moyo to South Africa, Kotsho Dube to Nigeria, Dr Isaac Nyathi to Kuwait and Report Phelekezela Mphoko to Botswana, Zanu (PF) managed to cement and prolong the fiction of being old allies with the ANC and SWAPO from the liberation struggle.

Worse was to follow. South Africa's *Independent Online* carried a report from Gordon Bell on 17 November 2005 under the heading: 'SA and Zimbabwe ink new defence deal'.

CAPE TOWN – South Africa signed a pact with its neighbour Zimbabwe on Thursday to strengthen ties on defence and intelligence, spurning Western government efforts to isolate President Robert Mugabe's government. The agreement will see the two countries share information on security issues. Zimbabwe pilots and instructors will also fly to South Africa for training.

'This week's historic meeting further consolidates a long-standing socio-political and economic relationship between our two countries,' South African intelligence minister Ronnie Kasrils said at the signing in Cape Town.

Zimbabwe's problems were no different to those faced by other countries that had come through a colonial past, he added.

South Africa, roundly criticised for not taking a stronger line against Mugabe, has vowed to continue working with the Zimbabwe government to try to solve that country's difficulties.

'We are not going to do anything based on some of the populism chants that happen on our soil and elsewhere that is going to upset that programme,' South African safety and security minister Charles Nqakula told reporters.

'The greatest threat to the stability of the region and Zimbabwe in particular is the threat of exogenous influences whose aim is to effect regime change especially in regards to my country,' Zimbabwe's minister for state Didymus Mutasa said.

He also criticised non-governmental organisations he claimed were a front for foreign governments.

Zimbabwe defence minister Sydney Sekeremayi said accounts of human rights abuses in Zimbabwe were merely imagined and Mugabe's government would not be swayed by such accusations.

The agreement signed will also see South Africa and Zimbabwe cooperate to better enforce immigration laws, as thousands of Zimbabweans seek refuge in more affluent South Africa.

A further report from Boyd Webb told of Minister Kasrils taking exception to a journalist who asked how South Africa, with its good human rights record, could sign an agreement with Zimbabwe, with its poor human rights record.

Kasrils berated the media.

'I find it rather insulting that you should level such a question here at us with this delegation from Zimbabwe. I apologise to them that they have to sit here on an historic occasion when we have signed two agreements which are so important to the security, stability, the development of both our peoples and countries,' Kasrils said.

He stated that South Africa was committed to working with its neighbours and with Zimbabwe.

'They have very daunting challenges. They are very frank about the kind of problems they have to deal with. We agree with them fully when they situate these problems within a context related to the colonial status of Zimbabwe, which for so many years had the name Rhodesia thrust upon them.'

These reports were followed by a letter to the *Cape Times* from Lorna Daniels of the Ministry for Intelligence Services.

Contrary to the views expressed in *Cape Times* letters the minister for intelligence services, Ronnie Kasrils, supports freedom of expression and the rights of journalists. In this specific instance, the minister had made it very clear to the media present at the signing of the two security agreements with Zimbabwe – one of which he signed as acting minister of defence – that questions should be confined to the occasion.

The journalist concerned contemptuously ignored the request and instead chose to use the event as a platform to reflect his perspective on the current situation in Zimbabwe.

But *Cape Times* readers would not be silenced, and R Spitzner wrote: 'We may see a time ... when the world will hold all South Africans responsible for what happens today in Zimbabwe.

'The accusation will read: all of you knew what was going on – yet you did nothing. On the contrary, you assisted the dictatorial regime. We hold you collectively responsible for all the misery, all the crimes against humanity in Zimbabwe.

'It has happened before.'

January 2006 saw a further symbiosis in relationships between South African state structures and those of Zanu (PF). One evening, as I watched South African television news, I saw South Africa's Minister Membathisi Mphumzi Shepherd Mdladlana and Zimbabwe's feared former Intelligence Minister Nicholas Goche, now Labour Minister, berating Limpopo border farmers. They were accused of employing, and then not properly paying, illegal Zimbabwean immigrants, and even of making holes in their fences so that Zimbabweans could crawl through and gain access to South Africa.

It was also reported that while 97 433 Zimbabweans were deported from South Africa in 2005, in the previous week alone 6 000 had been sent back. In 2004, 72 112 had been deported. The rate of desperate people fleeing Zimbabwe had, since the beginning of 2006, tripled and, undoubtedly, like the rate of inflation in Zimbabwe, would continue to soar.

By 23 July 2006, South Africa's *Sunday Times* was reporting that Ministry of Home Affairs officials were negotiating with Zimbabwe to allow deportation trains to enter that country. 'At the moment Zimbabwean deportees are offloaded at Beitbridge ... quickly finding their way back'. It was stated that South African authorities were considering building a second detention centre in Limpopo to cope with the dramatic increase in illegal immigration from Zimbabwe. Botswana was also considering building a new detention centre, but had yet to switch on the electric fence it had erected against Zimbabwe. No one in authority seemed able to acknowledge that nothing can stop people fleeing from hopelessness, starvation, torture and impending death. No one seemed to be asking: *Why are they fleeing, what is the cause and what is the solution?* No one in the SADC governments was heard expressing any compassion or concern for the people of Zimbabwe.

Minister Kasrils' apparent solidarity with Zimbabwe's Mutasa and Sekeremayi was to a certain extent understandable, as he was intent on procuring the release from torture of Aubrey Welkom, a South African intelligence agent held in Zimbabwe. Thankfully he succeeded. What was beyond comprehension was the trip to Zimbabwe in July 2006 of ANC secretary general Kgalema Motlanthe. It was reported in the *Mail & Guardian* on 14 July that Motlanthe, in televised comments at Harare International Airport, had said his party supported the appointment of former Tanzanian president Benjamin Mkapa as a mediator in the alleged Zimbabwean crisis with Britain, a fiction dreamed up by Mugabe. It was also reported that Motlanthe said that the ANC had taken its cue from Mugabe's ruling Zanu (PF). *That's the view of Zanu (PF), that's what we go along with.*

It was reported that Motlanthe also visited the farm of Zimbabwe's defence force chief, Constantine Chiwenga.

This farm had been seized in 2003 by General Chiwenga's wife Jocelyn from a commercial farmer near Harare, whose horticultural produce, worth millions of dollars, was ready to harvest. Jocelyn Chiwenga gave the farmer a few hours to get off the land, threatening that she had 'not tasted white blood for a long time'. She had also viciously beaten up my tiny friend Gugu Moyo, lawyer for the banned *Daily News*, when Gugu was trying to procure the release from custody of a photographer arrested for taking pictures of Harare residents protesting against the government. The event was recorded by the former editor of the *Daily News*, Geoffrey Nyarota, in his book *Against the Grain*. He wrote that when the police said they did not have the photographer, Philimon Bulawayo, Moyo said, 'But I saw him in the cells.'

Then, Gugu continued, 'An army Range Rover pulled up. A woman came in, talking on a cellphone. My own cellphone rang and I answered it. The woman shouted, "Who is that woman on the phone?"

'I said I worked for Associated Newspapers of Zimbabwe, and she went wild. She shouted at me: "So what if you are a lawyer? Your paper wants to encourage anarchy in this country. You want to represent our enemies." Then she twisted my arm and slapped me in the face. "I am Jocelyn Chiwenga, the wife of the army commander. Your paper says that there is no rule of law in Zimbabwe. Well, I will show you the rule of law!" She said she was powerful and would kill me. She said she would shoot me. She kept hitting me. Policemen folded their arms and watched.'

That's the view of Zanu (PF), that's what we go along with.

South African deputy president Phumzile Mlambo-Ngcuka was quoted in the *Argus* at the end of May 2006 as saying that, should Zimbabwe's devastated economy collapse, 'What South Africa can do is to give Zimbabwe the best support possible to be able to reconstruct.'

She and many of her peers seemed to confuse the country of Zimbabwe with Zanu (PF), the author of Zimbabwe's calamities. They seemed totally unaware that by seeking to contain evil by accommodating it, they were in grave danger of allowing the consequences of that evil to overwhelm their own countries. Maybe unwittingly, they were emboldening all the wrong people in Zimbabwe whose manifold victims went unrecognised and uncomforted, inevitably concluding that South Africa, the apparent ally of Zanu (PF), was also their treacherous enemy.

In August 2006, on the fiftieth anniversary of the march by women on Pretoria's Union Buildings against the pass laws of apartheid South Africa, I listened to the broadcast of President Mbeki's address to the thousands assembled to celebrate courage, followed, eventually, by hard-earned victory. He reminded me of the principles of my mother – be kind to people and comfort those who are hurt.

The president was flanked by members of South Africa's new Progressive Women's Movement, such as Deputy President Mlambo-Ngcuka and the speaker of parliament, Baleka Mbete, who had invited Zimbabwe's vice-president, Joice Mujuru of Zanu (PF), to join them and their august membership on this proud occasion.

No other action could so vividly have highlighted their total incomprehension of the plight of Zimbabwe under Zanu (PF), or their complete indifference. Mrs Mujuru represented a pass system in force in Zimbabwe far worse than anything that had ever existed under South Africa's apartheid rulers. In Zimbabwe, if you didn't have your pass, you couldn't travel by bus in rural areas, you often couldn't have access to a job or medical help, or even food. Sometimes, if you didn't have your pass, you were beaten, hurt and even killed.

In Zimbabwe, the pass was called a Zanu (PF) membership card.

On Wednesday 13 September 2006, Zimbabweans planned to gather peacefully in centres throughout the country and, in Harare, to present a petition to government on unemployment, wages, taxation and HIV/AIDS. Before the action started, Zanu (PF) pounced on the leadership, as described by Jan Raath in *The Times* on 18 September.

'The beating stopped as the sun went down. After two-and-a-half hours, the fourteen men and one woman held at Matapi police station in Mbare township, Harare, had suffered five fractured arms, seven hand fractures, two sets of ruptured eardrums, fifteen cases of severe buttock injuries, deep soft-tissue bruising all over, and open lacerations. The fifteen included

Wellington Chibebe, the leader of the Zimbabwe Congress of Trade Unions, and senior officials of the opposition Movement for Democratic Change. "As a case of police brutality on a group, it is the worst I've ever seen," a doctor who helped attend to them said.

'It was carried out as "a deliberate, premeditated warning, from the highest level, to anyone else who tries mass protest, that this is what will happen to them," a Western diplomatic source said.'

In another report, ZCTU president Lovemore Matombo described how he had heard his colleague Chibebe wailing before the assault on Matombo himself started. Chibebe, critically injured, suffered deep and serious cuts to the head, three broken bones, and severe bruising and swelling all over his body.

I wished in vain that South Africa's Progressive Women's Movement would comment on the thrashing of the MDC's Lucia Matibenga, on her whipped body, her swollen neck, her confusion and her bleeding ears, as well as the fact that she was once again beaten on the arm the police had broken before. However, the South African government did comment on these events through Foreign Affairs spokesman Vincent Hlongwane, quoted by IRIN and other publications on 18 September.

'We are monitoring developments with interest, but we always maintain that Zimbabwe needs to address its own problems and nobody can solve those problems for them, and it would be arrogant for us to pretend we could. We are communicating with them and are in constant contact, but not with the aim of dictating to them ... Zimbabwe can deal with its own problems more effectively.' This seeming indifference inevitably, alas, helped pave the way for the fatal shooting of the MDC's Gift Tandare the following March and the gruesome beatings of Morgan Tsvangirai and others while in police custody.

On Saturday 16 September I was privileged to be among the many in Cape Town honouring the long and lovely life of Hilda Bernstein (1915–2006). A tribute read on behalf of the ANC's secretary general, Kgalema Motlanthe, expressed the mourning of the ANC, democrats and communists 'across the country' at the death of 'a stalwart of our movement and an untiring fighter for the cause of the oppressed and exploited'. Motlanthe lauded the 'profound and selfless contribution she made throughout her long and rich life to the cause of freedom, democracy and equality'.

I wondered why it was that, for the ruling ANC, the cause of the oppressed and exploited now seemed to lie in the past, and why, unlike

Hilda Bernstein to the very end of her life, these 'formerly disadvantaged' but now rich and powerful leaders found it so difficult to lift their eyes over the boundaries of their country to their oppressed and exploited neighbours.

Simple calculations show that allowing the continued existence of a lawless regime in Zimbabwe is too expensive for the region to sustain. The cost of continuously deporting thousands of people, erecting fences, building detention centres, and the strain on all arms of surrounding governments as immigration and crime prevention bodies fail to cope, as health services are overstretched, and foot-and-mouth and other diseases cross the borders from Zimbabwe, are becoming unbearable. A further cost has not even started to be estimated – the damage being done every day to future relations between the cold-hearted region and a resurrected Zimbabwe.

When South Africa and the region eventually take action, as circumstances and the basic instinct of self-preservation will demand, Zimbabwe, not Zanu (PF), will find herself fortunate that among the government and people of South Africa, SADC and bodies such as the Commonwealth, the United Nations and others, there are seasoned and wise people who will be able to devise what best to do.

The goals for which bodies such as the ANC had fought so bravely for so long are precisely the goals yearned for by the oppressed and silenced of Zimbabwe. But while those who continue to oppose the regime in Zimbabwe need all possible support, they cannot be expected to drive change internally because of lack of friends along their borders, and the destruction of the rule of law, the judiciary, the press and the economy; the brutalisation of the population, including both the victims and the perpetrators, and the consequences of attrition. Towards the end of 2006, it was estimated that 70 per cent of the 18 to 65 age group now lived outside the country. Well over 70 per cent of those left inside were sick, poor, hungry, in thousands of cases without shelter, without hope, without stamina and unable to take up cudgels against guns and helicopters and the violence of brutal officials, as seen on 13 September.

Just as the ANC assembled powerful international assistance to successfully plot the destruction of apartheid, so the South African government can single-mindedly and swiftly plan, in concert with what bodies it may choose, the return of its neighbour Zimbabwe to constitutional government and the rule of law. All else will follow, and the survivors of Mugabe will be able to start all over again the rebuilding of Zimbabwe and the healing of the region.

Index

Do you have any comments, suggestions or
feedback about this book or any other Zebra Press titles?
Contact us at **talkback@zebrapress.co.za**